F O R E W O R

This third edition of *Protecting Study Volunteers in Research,* like its predecessors, is intended to help research professionals stay abreast of current issues and address the ethical dimensions of research. The book began as an in-house training mechanism for investigators at the University of Rochester. Since then, it has enjoyed a wide acceptance by investigators, research institutions and research sites as a primer on human research subject protections. Raising awareness and education are important because all members of the research community have a responsibility to ensure that research is scientifically sound and conducted ethically.

The book, in part, draws inspiration from current and past researchers such as Ehrlich, Goffman, Salk and ethicists such as Beauchamp, Childress and Jonsen. It also draws from popular culture and writings about the human spirit. Novelists such as Dan Brown who captures in vivid prose the possibility that good people can become carried away with single focused zeal and fervor to the extent that it clouds their common sense and morality, and Orson Scott Card who so wonderfully describes the flawed, but basically good character of human nature. Those involved in the conduct of research with humans need to understand why we do what we do and how oversight mechanisms support and encourage good science.

There are a few updates in previously published chapters, but the major change in this edition is a chapter devoted to the implementation of the HIPAA Privacy Rule in research. Appropriate protection of privacy and appropriate protection of confidentiality have been considerations in the ethical conduct of research for many years, and are among the original criteria that IRBs have had to find satisfactory before approving research projects. The Privacy Rule adds another layer to the existing regulations and has an impact on all of us in the research community. The length of the chapter is a reflection of both the complexity of the new Privacy Rule as well as how much the public values the protection of privacy.

Rigorous compliance with ethical standards is required by regulation, but it also is the right thing to do. It safeguards the welfare of human subjects, reassures the public, promotes good science and is a direct demonstration of why we chose to become scientists, healthcare providers and professionals in the service of the common good.

—GLC

A C K N O W L E D G M E N T S

Manual Development Coordination

William Kelvie, CCRC
Director, Research Education
Office for Human Subject Protection
University of Rochester

Advisory Review Committee

Peggy Cunningham-Galluzzi,
B.S.N., M.S.
Roche Labs, Inc.

David Forster, J.D., M.A., CIP
Western Institutional Review Board

Paul W. Goebel, Jr., CIP
Chesapeake Research Review

Jeanne Grace, R.N.C., Ph.D.
University of Rochester

Robert Levine, M.D.
Yale University School of Medicine

Louis Lasagna, M.D.
Tufts University

Dale W. McAdam, Ph.D.
University of Rochester

P. Pearl O'Rourke, M.D.
Partners Healthcare Systems

J. Thomas Puglisi, Ph.D.
PriceWaterhouseCoopers

Harold Vanderpool, Ph.D., Th.M.
University of Texas Medical Branch

Karen Woodin, Ph.D.
Independent Consultant

Gary Yingling, J.D.
Kirkpatrick & Lockhart

Protecting Study Volunteers in Research

A Manual for Investigative Sites

Third Edition

Cynthia McGuire Dunn, M.D.
President
CMD Advisor

Gary L. Chadwick, Pharm.D., MPH, CIP
Associate Provost and Director
Office for Human Subject Protection
University of Rochester

THOMSON
CENTERWATCH

22 Thomson Place · Boston, MA 02210
Phone (617) 856-5900 · Fax (617) 856-5901
www.centerwatch.com

THOMSON
TM
CENTERWATCH

Protecting Study Volunteers in Research – Third Edition
by Cynthia McGuire Dunn, M.D. & Gary L. Chadwick, Pharm.D., MPH, CIP

Editor
Sara Gambrill

Design
Paul Gualdoni

ISBN 1-930624-44-1

Acknowledgments

Contributing Authors

Mary Adams, M.T.S., CIP
Director
Research Subjects Review
Board Office
University of Rochester

Christine Burke, J.D.
Interim, General Counsel
University of Rochester
Medical Center

Nora Cavazos, M.D., CIP
Director
Data and Safety Monitoring Services
Western Institutional Review Board

Nancy Chin, Ph.D., MPH
Assistant Professor
Community and Preventive Medicine
Division of Public Health Practice

Ann M. Dozier, R.N., Ph.D.
Assistant Professor
Community and
Preventive Medicine
Division of Public Health Practice

Chin-to Fong, M.D.
Associate Professor
Pediatrics-Genetics
University of Rochester

David Forster, J.D., M.A., CIP
Assistant Vice President
Office of Compliance
Western Institutional Review Board

Timothy Hackett
Manager of Quality Assurance
Office for Human Subject Protection
University of Rochester

Cornelia Kamp, M.B.A., CCRC
Associate
Neurology
University of Rochester

William Kelvie, CCRC
Director, Research Education
Office for Human Subject Protection
University of Rochester

Scott Kim, M.D., Ph.D.
Assistant Professor
Bioethics Program
University of Michigan

Joanne C. Larson, Ph.D.
Associate Professor
Warner Graduate School
of Education and Development

Gunta Liders
Director
Research and Project Administration
University of Rochester

Terry O'Reilly, M.D.
Assistant Vice President
External Affairs
Western Institutional Review Board

Roy M. Poses, M.D.
Associate Professor of Medicine
Brown University
School of Medicine

Carol Pratt, Ph.D., J.D.
Attorney
Davis Wright Tremaine LLP

Aileen Shinaman, J.D.
Director of Administration
Clinical Trials Coordination Center
Neurology
University of Rochester

Rebecca Thom, Ph.D.
Clinical Research Specialist
3M Drug Delivery Systems Division

TABLE OF CONTENTS

Table of Contents

Table of Contents

Instructions for Obtaining Continuing Education Credit

Needs Assessment

This training manual was designed for biomedical and behavioral investigators to ensure they are aware of the fundamental requirements, responsibilities, and ethical and regulatory issues related to the conduct of human subject research. The initial Protecting Study Volunteers in Research training manual was published in 1999 and responded to a need to provide a resource for investigators and their research staff who work with human subjects. The purpose of the third edition is to update the information, to expand on previous topics contained in the first two editions and to add a new chapter to present HIPAA Privacy Rule issues that have developed nationally. The national trend for requiring completion of programs on human subject protection for researcher continues and is now almost a universal requirement. This third edition is intended to add to these training programs.

In an effort to make this manual as relevant to your work as possible, we have focused on topics, regulations and guidelines that are most pertinent to academic research. This manual does not include specific code references to the regulations, nor does it provide sample documents. While some of the regulations are included in the appendix, the regulations, codes and guidance documents are subject to change. Specific resources that can provide additional information are provided in the References, Resources, and Suggested

Reading section of the appendix. Also, remember to contact your Institutional Review Board (IRB) with any questions and for regular updates on relevant regulations and documents.

Certification

For Physicians

The University of Rochester School of Medicine and Dentistry is accredited by the Accreditation Council for Continuing Medical Education to provide continuing medical education for physicians

The University of Rochester School of Medicine and Dentistry designates this educational activity for a maximum 7.5 hours in Category 1 credits toward the AMA Physician's Recognition Award. Each physician should claim only those credits that he/she actually spent in the activity.

Author Declarations

The Accreditation Council for Continuing Medical Education (ACCME) Standards of Commercial Support requires that presentations are free of commercial bias and that any information regarding commercial products/services be based on scientific methods generally accepted by the medical community.

The following authors have disclosed financial interest/arrangements or affiliations with organizations that could be perceived as a real or apparent conflict of interest in the context of the subject of their contribution(s). Only current arrangements/interests are included.

Authors

None of the authors has financial interests or arrangements to be declared.

ACCME Standards of Commercial Support of CME requires that presentations be free of commercial bias and that any information regarding commercial products/services be based on scientific methods generally accepted by the medical community. When discussing therapeutic options, authors are requested to use the generic names. If they use a trade name, then those of several companies should be used. If any information is provided on unlabelled or investigational use of a commercial product, the authors are required to disclose this to the readers.

Category 1 credit valid through May 31, 2007

For Nurses

This activity has also been approved by the New York State Nurses Association's Council on Continuing Education, which is accredited by the American Nurses Credentialing Center's Commission on Accreditation, and is assigned approval code 5WSR4D-04 This has been assigned 9.0 contact hours.

Nursing contact hours valid through March 30, 2006.

To Obtain Credit

1. Read the manual.
2. Answer the exam questions on the answer sheet provided. Questions and answers are based on information in the manual. Participants who answer 85% of the questions correctly will receive up to 7.5 hours of continuing medical education credit or 9.0 nursing contact hours.
3. Complete the evaluation questions on the Protecting Study Volunteers in Research evaluation form. Note! Credit can not be issued if the evaluation form is not received with the answer sheet.
4. Complete the mailing information portion of the answer sheet.
5. Detach and mail the answer sheet and evaluation form by May 31, 2007 for CME credits, and by March 30, 2006 for nursing contact hours.

> University of Rochester School of Medicine and Dentistry
> Office of Continuing Professional Education
> 601 Elmwood Avenue, Box 677
> Rochester, NY 14642-8677

6. You will receive a certificate in the mail within two to four weeks.
7. Call (585) 275-4392 with questions or for further information.

This material is presented as an interpretation of the research process based on the expertise and experiences of the authors. Although designed to be of general application, not all material will be relevant in every situation. Each situation must be individually assessed and appropriate actions chosen based on individual knowledge, and institutional and sponsor requirements.

Sponsored by:

UNIVERSITY OF
ROCHESTER
SCHOOL OF MEDICINE & DENTISTRY
Office of Continuing Professional Education

CHAPTER

Historical Perspectives on Human Subject Research

At the conclusion of this chapter, readers will be able to:
- Describe three events that had significant impact on the federal regulations for the protection of the human research subjects.
- Have a better understanding of why we need federal regulations and how compliance helps protect the rights and welfare of human research subjects.

Introduction

History is not static. Yesterday's events are today's history. The public's perception of research, its benefits and its risks are shaped by the way research is conducted. Recent events have renewed concerns about research ethics. Included are issues regarding informed consent with incapacitated subjects (TD v. New York State) and responsibilities of researchers for subject welfare (after the deaths of volunteers in research studies at Johns Hopkins, Penn and Rochester and the suicide of a schizophrenic subject during a study "washout period" at UCLA). In June of 2001, Ellen Roche, a healthy volunteer, died in an experiment at Johns Hopkins University. Partially in response to this death, the death of Jesse Gelsinger and other similar events, the Maryland Legislature passed a law in 2002 that extends the federal protection requirements to all research involving human subjects conducted in the state, regardless of funding source or FDA jurisdiction. In the United States, concerns such as these often result in government action affecting the conduct and monitoring of research.*

> **The public's perception of research, its benefits and its risks is shaped by the way research is conducted.**

There are three events that have had significant impact on federal regulations for the protection of human research subjects. In chronological order, these are the 1946 Nuremberg Doctors Trial, the 1960s Thalidomide Tragedy and the 1972 Tuskegee Syphilis Study Exposé. While other events such as the Willowbrook Studies, the Wichita Jury Study, the Jewish Chronic Disease Hospital Study and the San Antonio Contraceptive Study also played a role, the cases discussed below had the most direct impact on shaping federal regulations. One additional case, the Milgram Study, will be reviewed. While it did not have the same scope or impact on federal regulations, this study is included because it is often cited in ethics literature as illustrative of potential problems in behavioral research. Also presented is the 1995 report on Human Radiation Experiments that measured how well the regulations are working. Finally, the unfortunate incident at the University of Pennsylvania and the effect it is having on human subject protections, particularly conflict-of-interest standards, is noted.

The Nuremberg Doctors Trial of 1946

Background
At the beginning of World War II, Germany was the most scientifically and technologically advanced country in the world, and it even had a notable code of research ethics. In the field of medicine, the Nazi government supported midwifery, homeopathy and nutrition programs as well as research into ecology, public health, human genetics, cancer, radiation and environmental risk factors such as asbestos. It was the first to ban smoking in public buildings. Women were denied tobacco ration coupons because of concern about the effect of nicotine on the fetus. German physicians stressed the importance of preventive medicine as well as curative medicine. The Nazis, however, exploited people's trust in physicians to disguise discrimination and murder as public health and medical research.

---

* Recent examples are the congressional General Accounting Office (GAO) Report on Human Subject Research (1994); the Department of Health and Human Services (DHHS) Report on Institutional Review Boards (1998); Research Involving Subjects with Disorders that May Affect Decision-making Capacity: a draft report of the President's National Bioethics Advisory Commission (NBAC); Third Report of the [Maryland] Attorney General's Research Working Group; and the 1998 New York State Department of Health (NYS-DH) report on human subjects in research.

Medical Experiments

Legitimate concerns of the Luftwaffe (the German air force) were the survival of pilots at extremely high altitudes and the determination of the maximum safe altitude for bailing out of damaged aircraft. In one series of experiments, researchers placed victims in vacuum chambers that could duplicate the low air pressure and lack of oxygen at altitudes as high as 65,000 feet (about two to three times the maximum altitude that aircraft were flying). Approximately 200 internees at Dachau prison camp were used in these experiments, and about 40% died as a result. Some deaths were caused by extended anoxia; others were attributable to lungs rupturing from the low pressures created in the chamber.

Another Nazi concern was survival time after parachuting into the cold water of the North Atlantic. Some victims of this research were immersed for hours in tubs of ice water; others were fed nothing but salt water for days. Still others were penned outside, unclothed and unsheltered in sub-freezing temperatures for 12 to 14 hours. Some of these "freezing victims" were sprayed with cold water. No attempts were made to relieve the tremendous pain and suffering caused by these experiments. Three hundred Dachau prisoner-subjects suffered a mortality rate of about 30%.

Experiments involving battlefield medicine included treatment of gunshot wounds, burns, traumatic amputations and chemical and biological agent exposures. While these were valid concerns for a country at war, the techniques that were used were inhuman. In these experiments, wounds were first inflicted upon victims (by gunshot, stabbing, amputation or other traumatic method) and then treated by various techniques. For example, in a study of sulfanilamide at the Ravensbrueck camp, Polish women were shot and slashed on the legs. The resulting wounds were stuffed with glass, dirt and various bacteria cultures, and sewn shut. The infected wounds were then treated with experimental anti-infective agents. In another experiment, a mixture of phosphorus and rubber was applied to the skin of victims and ignited. After burning for up to two minutes, the fire was extinguished and the resultant burn treated with various chemicals and ointments. Another series of experiments involved amputation of upper and lower limbs, and attempted treatment with transplanted bones, muscle and nerves. About half of the amputation victims died, the rest were maimed for life.

In the experiments on treating exposure to chemical-warfare agents, prisoners were forced to drink poisoned water and breathe noxious gases. Some were shot with cyanide-tipped bullets or given cyanide capsules. A mortality rate of at least 25% was typical.

The Nuremberg Trial

On August 8, 1945, representatives of the British, French, Soviet and United States governments established the International Military Tribunal in Nuremberg, Germany. After the initial Nuremberg Trial of the Nazi leadership, a series of supplemental trials was held. The trial, officially known as

United States v. Karl Brandt et al., and popularly referred to as "The Nazi Doctors Trial," was held from December 9, 1946, to August 20, 1947. As the title indicates, for this trial, the judges and prosecutors were all from the United States. The 23 defendants (including 20 physicians) were charged with murder, torture and other atrocities committed in the name of medical science.

When the Nazi Doctors Trial was completed on August 20, 1947, 15 of the 23 defendants were found guilty. Seven were sentenced to death. Although, at the time, the trial was called "The Trial of the Century," it would probably have been forgotten except for the fact that the judgment included a set of standards known as the Nuremberg Code. The Code was the "ethical yardstick" by which the defendants had been measured and guilt determined. The "Modern" era of human subject protection is routinely dated from the promulgation of the Nuremberg Code. It set standards that have been accepted and expanded upon by the international research community.

The Code stated that:

- Informed consent of volunteers must be obtained without coercion in any form.
- Human experiments should be based upon prior animal experimentation.
- Anticipated scientific results should justify the experiment.
- Only qualified scientists should conduct medical research.
- Physical and mental suffering and injury should be avoided.
- There should be no expectation of death or disabling injury from the experiment.

> **The "Modern" era of human subject protection is routinely dated from the promulgation of the Nuremberg Code in 1947.**

Post-war Years

In 1953, the World Medical Association (WMA) began drafting a document that would apply the Nuremberg Code principles to the practice of medical research. The WMA code became known as the Declaration of Helsinki. This statement of ethical principles, first issued in 1964, defined rules for "therapeutic" and "non-therapeutic" research. It repeated the Nuremberg Code requirement for consent for non-therapeutic research, but it did allow for enrolling certain patients in therapeutic research without consent. The Declaration of Helsinki also allowed legal guardians to grant permission to enroll subjects in research, both therapeutic and non-therapeutic. Several revisions have been made to the Declaration of Helsinki to keep it aligned with modern ethical theory and current clinical and research practices.

In 1966, following the publication of the Declaration of Helsinki, Dr. Henry K. Beecher reported in the *New England Journal of Medicine* (NEJM) on 22 studies that had serious ethical problems. Beecher cited various problems related to study design and to informed consent. Probably even more than the Nuremberg Trial/Code or the promulgation of the Declaration of Helsinki, this article helped to spur the debate on research ethics in this country.

In addition to the expanding number of numbers of ethical statements and codes, in 1982, the Council for the International Organization of Medical Sciences (CIOMS) published the International Ethics Guidelines for Biomedical Research Involving Human Subjects (CIOMS Guidelines). These were designed to guide researchers from the more technologically advanced countries when conducting research in developing countries. The guidelines sought to correct perceived omissions in the Nuremburg Code and Declaration of Helsinki, especially as applied to cross-cultural research. The CIOMS Guidelines allow for cultural differences in ethical standards. Like the Declaration of Helsinki, the CIOMS Guidelines have been revised to account for current thinking and practices.

The Milgram Study

Background

Stanley Milgram was a researcher in social psychology who, after reading accounts of the Nazi Holocaust, became interested in obedience and humans' response to authority. The defense proposed at Nuremberg of "I was only following orders" and the German citizenry's seeming acceptance of and complacency in regard to the atrocities presented an interesting question. In 1963, Milgram published the results of his study on obedience that raised criticism with implications even today. His 1972 book, *Obedience to Authority* describes the series of studies and addresses some of the concerns the study engendered.

While the Milgram studies come nowhere close to the ethical violations of the Nazi experiments or the other studies often cited, it is a well-known behavioral study that is instructive even today. Importantly, these studies served to remind the drafters of the first federal regulations that even studies that do no physical damage or permanent harm have important ethical considerations that must be addressed.

The Experiment

Adult subjects were recruited by means of newspaper advertisements asking for volunteers for a study of "memory and learning." Participants were paid a modest amount for the one hour experiment. Study participants were part of a triad that consisted of themselves, the investigator and a third person. The investigator explained that the experiment was to study learning and memory, specifically what role punishment played. The subject was to play the role of "teacher" while the third person was to be the "learner." The investigator would monitor the process and record the data.

The learner was placed in a chair with wire leads that ran from a control panel to the chair and were attached to the learner's body. The control panel had switches labeled from 15 volts to 450 volts.

For the experiment, the investigator instructed the subject-teacher to ask the learner a question (word-pair matching) and when the wrong answer was given, to administer "punishment" to the learner in the form of electric shocks in an escalating amount. The learner would display visible evidence of pain from the shocks. After one-third of the shock levels had been given, the learner demanded to stop. At this point, the subject-teacher would usually ask the investigator to stop, but the investigator would state that the procedure should continue. After two-thirds of the shocks had been administered, the learner fell silent and non-responsive. Under the study design, a non-response was treated as a wrong answer and punished. When they continued to seek permission to stop, the highly conflicted subject-teachers were told that the experiment was important to complete for the advancement of science. Fully 60% of subject-teachers were persuaded to administer shocks up to and including the highest level.

The subjects were deceived about a number of things. The third person who played the role of learner was in fact a confederate of the investigator. No shocks were administered. The learner (who deliberately gave wrong answers) only pretended to receive shocks and to be hurt. The real intent of the experiment was to see how far the subject would go under the guise of complying with authority. At the completion of the experiment (either after the maximum shock was ostensibly given or upon firm refusal by the subject to continue), the confederate came out of his room and demonstrated to the subject that he was uninjured. A debriefing with the subject was held that explained the deception and the real purpose of the study. During the debriefing interviews, subjects often justified their actions by saying that they were only trying to follow instructions.

"I observed a mature and initially poised businessman enter the laboratory smiling and confident. Within twenty minutes he was reduced to a twitching, stuttering wreck, who was rapidly approaching a point of nervous collapse."
—Stanley Milgram in *Obedience to Authority*

Impact

Criticism of the Milgram study centered upon the psychological stress experienced by some subjects and on the fact that due to the deception involved, true informed consent had not been obtained. The role of deception in human subject research continues to be debated even today. Common sense and experience tell us that people act differently when they know they are being studied. Ethical codes such as the Nuremberg Code, the Declaration of Helsinki and the Belmont Report point to the importance of obtaining consent that is informed, understood and voluntary. The federal regulations specifically allow for deception in research, but only in limited conditions and only with institutional review board (IRB) approval.

As a result of this study and other problematic behavior, the federal guidelines specifically instruct investigators and IRBs to consider not just physical harms that may be attached to research, but also psychological, social, legal and economic harms.

> **When deception is involved, true informed consent cannot be obtained.**

An additional implication can be drawn from this study that has relevance to today's informed consent process. Milgram demonstrated that the phenomenon of obedience to authority is real. In many research studies, the investigator (or other person obtaining consent) is in a position of authority or power over the potential subject. This response to authority, specially when combined with a general feeling of trust, has led many to question whether consent is truly a voluntarily considered decision. This is of special concern in the medical care setting as well as in student-teacher and in employer-employee situations.

Thalidomide Tragedy

Background

Thalidomide was approved as a sedative in Europe in the late 1950s. Although the U.S. Food and Drug Administration (FDA) had not approved the drug, the manufacturer supplied "samples" to U.S. physicians who were paid to study its safety and efficacy in what was loosely termed "research" by giving the experimental drug to patients. This was a common practice at that time. By 1961, experience in Europe, Canada and, to a lesser extent, the United States, showed that while thalidomide was not harmful to the mother, it was extremely damaging to the fetus if taken in the first trimester of pregnancy. It interfered with the normal development of blood vessels and particularly affected development of arms and legs. Based upon its teratogenicity, use of the drug as a sedative was banned world wide. [Note: Thalidomide has recently received approval for some limited uses that take advantage of its original unforeseen side effect of shrinking blood vessels.]

Thalidomide Hearings and Their Impact

A U.S. Senate Antitrust and Monopoly subcommittee, chaired by Tennessee Senator Estes Kefauver, had been holding hearings (1959–1962) into the business practices of pharmaceutical companies. At his request, two other congressional subcommittees, one chaired by Representative Emanuel Celler and the other chaired by Senator Hubert Humphrey, heard testimony about the thalidomide disaster. In the Celler hearings, Dr. Helen B. Taussig, of Johns Hopkins University, showed slides of the birth defects caused by thalidomide. The pictures of deformed and limbless babies raised questions about the procedures used to test experimental drugs. Dr. Frances O. Kelsey of the FDA testified in the Humphrey hearings about holding up approval for thalidomide because of safety concerns and questions on the drug's testing. In the hearings, it was learned that many people who were taking unapproved drugs were neither informed that they were being given an experimental substance, nor had they been asked to give their consent. The public concern over research practices addressed in these three committees led to the passage of the Drug Amendments of 1962 to the Food, Drug and Cosmetic Act (sometimes referred to as the Kefauver-Harris Amendments). New York Senator Jacob Javits added language to the bill that required informed consent of subjects receiving experimental drugs. This was the first U.S. statute that required researchers to inform subjects of a drug's experimental nature and to receive their consent before starting the research. In 1964, Representative Richard Harris wrote a book on the Amendment's passage process. It was in homage to Kefauver's tenacity, courage and public spirit entitled *The Real Voice,* which referred to the voice of the people being heard in national legislation.

In February 1963, the FDA issued regulations with consent requirements, but it allowed widespread exemptions. Responding to concerns that consent was still not being appropriately obtained, the regulations were rewritten in 1966 to clarify that consent was required except in cases of emergency or experimental therapeutic treatments with children and similar situations. The 1966 rewrite also contained the requirement for documenting consent in writing and informing subjects that they might receive a placebo.

The Study of Untreated Syphilis in the Negro Male

Background

The treatment for syphilis at the turn of the twentieth century was, at best, crude and involved the use of "heavy metal" (mercury and arsenic) compounds. These were poisons, highly toxic to humans, and had to be administered for a year or more. Severe reactions, even death, were not uncommon from the treatment and some evidence suggested that treated patients lived shorter lives than the untreated.

An agency of the U.S. Public Health Service (PHS), which was to become the Centers for Disease Control and Prevention (CDC), designed a study to demonstrate the need for establishing syphilis treatment programs by investigating the effects of untreated disease. This evolved from a genuine concern about minority health problems. The PHS was a key force in promoting

---

* The Tuskegee Study of Untreated Syphilis in the Negro Male has been most commonly called the Tuskegee Study. Due to concern for the negative connotations for the Tuskegee Institute, some are calling for a change in the shorthand name. Therefore, this manual will use the term "The Syphilis Study."

rural medical care. Macon County, Alabama, was selected as the site for the project because previous epidemiological studies had shown an extremely high rate of disease. Thus began the Tuskegee Study of Untreated Syphilis in the Negro Male.* To secure the cooperation of the black subjects, the participation of black physicians was seen as essential. The Tuskegee Institute and its John A. Andrew Hospital were used because of their position of trust in the local community. A local nurse who had trained at the Tuskegee Institute was hired to be the on-site representative. The project was scheduled to end after assessing what health effects had occurred.

In the beginning, there was no intent to deny anyone treatment on a long-term basis. The study called for 200 to 300 syphilitic black males, aged 25 and older, to be enrolled. They were to be given complete physical examinations, a thorough medical history and then followed for six to eight months. During that time, they would not be treated. This study demonstrates that competent and well-intentioned researchers may run into problems if they do not identify and examine the ethical assumptions and consequences of their actions.

The Experiment

In October 1932, subjects were sought and encouraged to participate in the study with offers of free examinations and medical care. The men were not informed about their disease or the fact that the research would not benefit them. Non-therapeutic spinal taps, which were conducted in May 1933, were supposed to end the experiment; but a second phase, or follow-on study started in late 1933. This phase introduced new procedures to strengthen scientific validity and to gain more information. A control group of 200 black men and autopsies of deceased subjects were added to the study. Like the original subjects and according to the conventions of the day, the members of the control group were not informed about the purpose of the study, but were told that "government doctors" were examining people for "bad blood."

Each year, new physicians were sent on special assignment to Alabama to conduct the "roundups" and medical examinations. The study procedures became so routine that the study continued without any exploration or understanding of the potential ramifications of the project. Many of the itinerant physicians later filled positions of authority in the PHS and/ or CDC.

In 1943, penicillin was accepted as the curative treatment for syphilis. However, during World War II, to keep the syphilis study subjects from receiving treatment, it was arranged with the local draft board to exempt them from the military. By 1951, penicillin was widely available as the treatment for syphilis, but it continued to be withheld from the study subjects.

Actually, the availability of penicillin was used by the study investigators as justification for continuing the study because it made the protocol a "never-again" scientific opportunity. Neither the ethical issues nor the fact that the supposedly untreated subjects had received some minimal treatment was addressed. Announcement of the Nuremberg Code and its requirement for informed consent and avoidence of harm had no impact on the study. Publication of the Declaration of Helsinki in 1964, with its extensive set of ethical requirements, had no effect on the study.

Exposé

After obtaining copies of letters and other study-related documents in 1972, the Associated Press assigned an investigative reporter, Jean Heller, to uncover the story. Her best source of information was the CDC itself. The study had never been hidden. Several articles had been published and CDC officials discussed it candidly. Her story was published in the *New York Times* and the *Washington Star* on July 25, 1972.

The public reaction to the Syphilis Study was strong. James B. Allen, a U.S. Senator from Alabama, denounced the study as appalling, "a disgrace to the American concept of justice and humanity." The fact that the PHS had conducted the study was particularly distressing because instead of protecting citizens, it had used them for research. Some people thought that the study was racist. Others believed that social class was the critical issue, i.e., that poor people, regardless of race, were the ones at risk because, at that time, they made up a disproportionate share of subjects in most medical experiments.

An article that appeared in the *Atlanta Constitution* on July 27, 1972, stated, "Sometimes, with the best of intentions, scientists and public officials and others involved in working for the benefit of us all, forget that people are people. They concentrate so totally on plans and programs, experiments, statistics—on abstractions—that people become objects, symbols on paper, figures in a mathematical formula or impersonal "subjects" in a scientific study." Many saw a need to protect people from experiments and scientists who ignored human values.

In reaction to the revelations about the Syphilis Study and other research "scandals," several bills to regulate research were introduced in Congress. During February and March 1973, Senator Edward Kennedy held hearings on experimentation with human subjects. In March 1973, the Syphilis Study was stopped, and treatment was given as needed. In April 1973, the CDC informed the survivors that the government would pay all of their medical expenses for the rest of their lives. In 1975, the government extended treatment to the wives who had contracted syphilis and to their children who had been born with congenital syphilis. This money continues to be paid to these citizens today. In a formal White House ceremony in 1997, President Clinton apologized to study subjects and their families and called for renewed emphasis on research ethics.

In 1974, Congress passed the National Research Act. The Act required regulations for the protection of human subjects that included requirements for informed consent and review of research by institutional review boards (IRBs). This Act also created the National Commission for the Protection of Human Subjects of Biomedical and Behavioral Research. In 1979, the

National Commission published the "Belmont Report," which is the cornerstone statement of ethical principles upon which the federal regulations for the protection of subjects are based.

In 1981, the DHHS and the FDA published convergent regulations that were based on the Belmont Principles. These mandated a role on the IRB for persons with broad backgrounds and members who could represent community attitudes. Informed consent was required for participants, and specific elements of information were required. After 10 years of negotiation and coordination, 17 federal departments and agencies agreed to adopt the basic human subject protections. These were published in 1991 and are referred to as the "Common Rule." Thus, essentially all federally sponsored research is now covered by a common set of regulations that has its origins in the National Research Act and the Syphilis Study.

Human Radiation Experiments

Background

In November 1993, the *Albuquerque Tribune* published a series of articles by Eileen Welsome that revealed that, under government sponsorship, researchers at several major universities had injected plutonium into unknowing subjects to study the effects of the atomic bomb. That same month, a congressional report described 13 cases in which nuclear facilities had intentionally released radiation into the environment for government experiments.

These revelations raised concern about the adequacy of protection provided by federal laws and regulations. In January 1994, President Clinton created the Advisory Committee on Human Radiation Experiments (ACHRE) to explore human radiation experiments and to determine what the ethical and scientific standards were for evaluating these events. When he accepted the Committee's Final Report in 1995, Clinton ordered the creation of the National Bioethics Advisory Commission (NBAC), which reviewed human experimentation and made recommendations on a variety of research topics and regulations.

Experiments

The Advisory Committee discovered that several thousand government-sponsored human radiation experiments and hundreds of intentional releases of radiation from nuclear facilities were conducted from 1944 to 1974. Many well-known and well-respected researchers and research institutions conducted these experiments either without thinking of the ethical implications, or subordinating the interests of their human subjects to scientific pursuit or national interest. Other experiments were not so benign.

The "Manhattan Project" plutonium injection experiments were conducted for national security and to gather safety data to protect the health and safety of nuclear weapons workers. The results are still used in the nuclear industry today. In one series of experiments, over 100 prisoners submitted to non-therapeutic testicular irradiation. Up to 3,000 military personnel served as subjects of research, sometimes unknowingly, in connection with atomic bomb tests. About 2,000 cancer patients were subjected to total body irradiation strictly to find answers to problems in the development and use of atomic weapons. A review conducted by the Atomic Energy Commission (AEC) in 1974 found that while 18 subjects were given plutonium injections between the years 1945 and 1947, the records documented only one subject's consent.

Eighty-one examples of pediatric radiation research projects were identified by the ACHRE. Fortunately, although children are more susceptible than adults to harm from low levels of radiation, the exposures to radiation were very low and probably did not pose a risk of physical harm to these children.

Response

In addition to exploring the case studies summarized above, the ACHRE Report discussed the historical development of research ethics and examined issues related to implementing and interpreting current federal regulations. Clearly, the Nuremberg Code and later the Declaration of Helsinki seemed to be disregarded in the Cold War radiation experiments. Some contemporary consent documents were found to be difficult to read, uninformative, and even misleading. Informed consent was particularly troubling to the Advisory Committee members in research involving patient-subjects with poor prognoses because these patients are so vulnerable, and are often confused about the relationship of research to treatment, often called the "therapeutic misconception." There also was concern about the inappropriate use of the word "treatment" in consent forms, especially in phase 1 trials of new drugs, designed to find toxicities and maximal doses.

The ACHRE found that, when compared to the information in the grant proposal and/or protocol, consent forms often overstated the benefits and therapeutic potential of the research. Such overstatements may inappropriately induce enrollment by playing on the hopes of patients or on the altruism of volunteers. The review also showed that consent forms did not always discuss the risks that subjects faced when removed from standard treatment in order to be placed on experimental interventions. They found that often there was little mention of how participation would affect the subject's daily life or the quality of life. Psychosocial risks were often inadequately addressed in proposal documents, as were potential financial costs that could be incurred by subjects.

The final portion of the report included recommendations to better ensure that those who conduct research involving human subjects act in a manner consistent with the interests and rights of subjects, and with the highest standards of medical and scientific ethics. The recommendations stated that it is essential that the research community come to value the ethics of research as central to the scientific process. Because the future of science depends to a great extent upon public support and public trust, scientists must have a clear understanding of their duties to human subjects and scientific leaders must value good ethics as much as they do good science. The ACHRE's call for making ethics the centerpiece of the research enterprise and recommending increased training in research ethics represents an important step in the continuing evolution of human subject protections.

> **"It is essential that the research community come to value the ethics of research as central to the scientific process"**
>
> **—National Bioethics Advisory Commission**

When the NBAC charter expired in 2001, President George W. Bush appointed the President's Commission on Bioethics (PCB). This group, like its predecessors, serves to focus national debate and to advance ethical thinking in the area of human experimentation.

The University of Pennsylvania Gene Transfer Experiment

In 1999, an eighteen-year-old volunteer in a gene transfer experiment died. The experiment was conducted at the Institute for Human Gene Therapy at the University of Pennsylvania (Penn). The principal investigator and the university owned shares in the private startup company that owned the technology used in the experiment. The young volunteer's name was Jesse Gelsinger.

At first, Jesse's father, Paul Gelsinger, defended Penn and the investigator. As more information about the study surfaced, however, Mr. Gelsinger's initial defense turned into anger at trust abused. The study raises issues and contains lessons to be learned about informed consent, about study design and safeguards for the welfare of subjects, about protocol adherence and about the motivations and influences acting upon institutions and investigators. This last issue—conflict of interest—has been the major focus of response in the research community.

In reaction to the negative publicity surrounding this event and the *Seattle Times* exposé of oncology studies at the Fred Hutchinson Cancer Center (in which the Center and the investigators had financial interests), several groups have published guidelines and statements on conflict of interest. The American Association of Medical Colleges (AAMC) and the Association of American Universities (AAU) both formed national task forces and published guidance documents addressing steps that should be taken by institutions to avoid or mitigate the effects of conflict of interest on investigators. The Office for Human Research Protection (OHRP) also has published a set of "interim" guidelines proposing procedures to limit the impact of conflict of interest on research. The federal Office of Research Integrity (ORI) is also reviewing standards and may publish guidance, based upon the Institute of Medicine (IOM) report on the issue. The concern is that even the perception that investigators may be influenced by interests, such as fame and money, to ignore the welfare of human subjects, will weaken the public's trust in researchers and in research institutions.

These guidance documents focus on the potential for negative consequences of conflict of interest, especially financial conflict of interest, upon investigators. In this case, there was significant "institutional conflict of interest" too. Both the AAMC and the AAU are continuing efforts to explore institutional conflict of interest and find ways to address conflicts from an institutional perspective.

Recognizing that these guidances and voluntary corrections may not be sufficient, Senator Edward Kennedy, who chaired the 1973 Syphilis Study Hearings, which led to the 1974 National Research Act, and Senator Bill Frist (a physician) held hearings in the spring of 2002 re-examining human subject protection issues. Coupled with a detailed report by the NBAC on ways to strengthen and change subject research protection, this interest and parallel legislation proposed in the House by Congresswoman Diana DeGette will most likely lead to new and/or revised federal human subject protection laws and regulations. Among the proposals being discussed as this book goes to press are expanding the federal protections to all research conducted in the United States, requiring accreditation of institutional programs to protect human subjects, requiring more stringent reporting of adverse events, requiring annual reports of research activity and expansion of protections to other classes of vulnerable populations (such as those with mental incapacities).

Conclusion

Investigators bear the ultimate ethical responsibility for their work with human subjects. Society entrusts them with the privilege of using other humans to advance scientific knowledge. In return, society expects that investigators will show respect for research subjects. Unfortunately, as events have shown, some scientists still continue to value the quest for knowledge and the potential for personal fame and financial gain more highly than respect for basic human rights. The research community as a whole suffers when even a few investigators ignore basic principles of ethics. Compliance with human subject protection regulations should not be seen as something that must be done just because it is required by the regulations. Compliance should be seen as the "right thing to do" because it helps protect the rights and welfare of the subjects of human research and maintains public trust in research.

Research Ethics Milestones		Trigger Events
Presidents Council on Bioethics		
	2000	
National Bioethics Advisory Commission		Gene Transfer Subject Death
Advisory Committee on Human Radiation Experiments		
	1990	
Common Rule		
CIOMS Guidelines		
HHS/FDA Human Subject Regulations	1980	
Belmont Report		
		The Syphilis Study (Exposé)
	1970	
		The Beecher Article (NEJM)
Declaration of Helsinki		Milgram Study
Kefauver-Harris Amendments	1960	The Thalidomide Tragedy
	1950	
Nuremberg Code		Human Radiation Experiments (Begin)
		The Nazi Experiments
	1940	
		The Syphilis Study (Begins)
	1930	

C H A P T E R

Ethics and Federal Regulations

At the conclusion of this chapter, readers will be able to:
- Describe the relevance of the Belmont Report on federal human subjects protection regulations.
- Identify what populations are considered vulnerable, and develop an awareness of circumstances requiring sensitivity.
- Define informed consent and describe the three components of valid informed consent.
- Describe the purpose and function of the Institutional Review Board (IRB).
- Define scientific misconduct and describe how it is reported.

Introduction

The ethics of human subject research and the federal regulations have evolved over the past 50 years. Professional associations and international organizations have developed codes of ethics that cover research with human subjects. This chapter (and in fact, the whole book) emphasizes federal regulations because they are seen as a standard for the conduct of research. Compliance with the requirements of the federal regulations, even for non-federally sponsored/regulated research, protects the rights and welfare of subjects. Most research institutions require compliance with federal regulations for all studies regardless of source of support.

Belmont Report

In 1974, Congress passed the National Research Act. The Act created the National Commission for the Protection of Human Subjects of Biomedical and Behavioral Research. The National Commission wrote the Ethical Principles and Guidelines for the Protection of Human Subjects of Research (commonly called the Belmont Report), which was published in the Federal Register in 1979. This document is the cornerstone statement of ethical principles upon which the federal regulations for the protection of subjects are based. A copy of the Belmont Report is included in the appendix and should be considered mandatory reading for anyone involved in the research enterprise.

> **The Belmont Report contains the ethical principles upon which the federal regulations for protection of human subjects are based.**

The Belmont Report begins by stating, "Scientific research has produced substantial social benefits. It has also posed some troubling ethical questions. Public attention was drawn to these questions by reported abuses of human subjects in biomedical experiments...." As a result, national and state laws and regulations, as well as international and professional codes, have been developed to guide investigators. Such rules are based upon broader ethical principles that provide an analytical framework to evaluate human actions. The Belmont Report described three basic principles relevant to the ethics of human subject research: respect for persons, beneficence and justice.

Basic Principles of the Belmont Report

> **Basic Principles of the Belmont Report**
> 1. **Respect for Persons**
> 2. **Beneficence**
> 3. **Justice**

1. Respect for Persons
The Belmont Report says, "Respect for persons incorporates at least two ethical convictions: first, that individuals should be treated as autonomous agents; and second, that persons with diminished autonomy are entitled to protection. The principle of respect for persons thus divides into two separate moral requirements: the requirement to acknowledge autonomy and the requirement to protect those with diminished autonomy."

> **The principle of respect for persons is applied in the consent process.**

Vulnerable Subjects

By definition, "vulnerable populations" are those groups that may contain some individuals who have limited autonomy (i.e., they cannot fully appreciate or participate freely in the consent process). Such groups include children, some mentally incapacitated, individuals with dementia and other cognitive disorders and prisoners. Special considerations apply when conducting research with these populations. Pregnant women are also recognized by the regulations as a vulnerable population because of the additional health concerns during pregnancy and because of the need to avoid unnecessary risk to the fetus. Many institutions have also included the elderly, terminally ill and hospitalized patients, students and employees in the definition of vulnerable populations deserving special consideration by investigators and IRBs.

> **Vulnerable populations include some individuals who have limited autonomy such that they cannot fully participate in the consent process.**

Prisoners—The regulations for human subject protection make special provisions pertaining to research with prison populations. The incarcerated may be at greater risk for true coercion (threat of force) as well as undue influence. Special considerations for prison studies include ensuring that:

- Any potential advantages to the prisoner for participating do not interfere with the ability to make a voluntary choice by outweighing the risks (e.g., parole decisions will not be affected by study participation).
- The risks of participating would be acceptable to non-prisoner volunteers
- Selection of subjects within the prison system is fair.
- Adequate follow-up care is provided, if necessary.

Children—Legally, children have not attained the age where they can grant consent for research or treatment. Additional regulatory protections are established for research with children. Under these regulations, some of the exempt categories are deemed not to apply to research with children. Research that qualifies for exemption with adult subjects, but not for children, includes the use of survey, questionnaire or interview procedures and participatory observation. This is because a child's responses are less guarded than an adult's and, therefore, information may be divulged inappropriately.

Consent cannot be given by another person. Only an individual can provide consent for oneself. Parents or guardians, however, may provide "permission" for their child to participate in a research study. Furthermore, to the extent that they are able, children should be asked about their willingness or "assent" to participate. Information about the research study must be presented to children at their developmental level, so they can understand what is being requested of them. The combination of "assent" (agreement) of the minor subject and "permission" of the parent or legal guardian is recognized by the federal regulations as an adequate substitute for consent.

Adequate provision must be made for soliciting the assent of those children capable of providing a meaningful agreement. The process must be appropriate to the study as well as to the age, maturity and psychological state of the child. An exception to the assent requirement is made for children with life-threatening illnesses who are entered into "open-label treatment protocols" with the expectation of direct benefit. In these cases, the permission of the parent is sufficient, but the understanding of the minor subject is still desirable.

Documentation of the minor-subject's assent and the parents' permission also depends upon the nature of the research and the maturity of the child. For research with very young children (pre-school and under), only the parent's permission is typically needed. For teenagers, a single form that both the minor and the parent(s) sign may be adequate. For children in between (i.e., ages 7 to 12), two forms are generally advisable. One written at a basic level for the child (as a "script" for oral presentation or for reading), and a more detailed form for the parent's understanding and signature.

Research in schools—In addition to the federal children's regulations, investigators who conduct research in schools should be aware of laws governing these studies and disclosure of information. Two laws, Family Educational Rights and Privacy Act (FERPA) and Protection of Pupil Rights Amendment (PPRA) apply to research in schools.

FERPA defines the rights of students and parents concerning reviewing, amending and disclosing education records. Except under certain circumstances involving treatment, subpoena, educational or financial aid, FERPA requires that written permission must be obtained to disclose personally identifiable information from a student's educational records. Researchers who wish to inspect student records must obtain parental permission if identifiers are linked to the data.

Survey research in schools is regulated under PPRA. This law states that surveys, questionnaires and instructional materials can be inspected by parents or guardians; and parental permission must be obtained to allow minors to participate in a survey revealing information concerning the following:

- Political affiliations.
- Mental and psychological problems.
- Income.
- Sexual behavior and attitudes.
- Illegal, anti-social, self-incriminating and demeaning behavior.
- Critical appraisals of other individuals with close family relationships.
- Legally recognized privileged relationships (e.g., lawyers, physicians, ministers).

Subordinate Individuals—College students, employees and other persons in subordinate positions or positions of lesser power/status provide an easily accessible group with the potential for undue influence to impede free choice in the consent process. IRBs and investigators should carefully consider how to protect the autonomy and confidentiality of employees and students. Employees must not be pressured to participate in research due to fear of job loss, delayed promotion or other influence of a superior.

For student subjects, investigators need to consider the following:

- If course credit is given for participation, alternatives should be available for receiving equal credit that are no more burdensome than the participation in research.
- Policies regarding course-related research participation must be clearly understood.
- Incentives for participation should not present undue influence.
- Student subjects must have the ability to decline participation.
- Confidentiality must be maintained for self-disclosures of a personal nature.

Decisionally Impaired—The regulations for human subject protection do not yet make special provisions for persons whose mental status is impaired. This vulnerable population may include persons with psychiatric illness, neurological conditions, substance use and various metabolic disorders. Even persons suffering from acute emotional or physical stress may have impaired decisional capacity. The level of impairment may range from poor judgment to frank coma. The National Bioethics Advisory Commission (NBAC) and several states have examined the issue and have published recommendations and suggested rules.

Until there are federal regulations, most investigators and IRBs use a combination of special protections gathered from the DHHS regulations for children and prisoners. As with children, some individuals in this group may not be able to give informed consent. A combination of "permission" from legally authorized representatives and the "assent" of subjects to participate are substituted for consent. Witnesses to the consent process, periodic reconsent and formal checks of comprehension may be included as additional protections. Special considerations for studies in this population include ensuring that:

- The risks of participating would be acceptable to volunteers in the general public.
- Selection of subjects is fair.
- The consent information is understandable given the expected level of function.
- Adequate follow-up is provided.

Informed Consent

The Belmont Report tells us that, "Respect for persons requires that subjects, to the degree that they are capable, be given the opportunity to choose what shall or shall not happen to them." Informed consent is not just a form or a signature, but a process of information exchange that includes subject recruitment materials, verbal instructions, written materials, question/ answer sessions and agreement documented by signature. The Belmont Report states that "the consent process can be analyzed as containing three components: information, comprehension and voluntariness." The Report regards these components as ethically required.

> **Informed consent process:**
> - **Information**
> - **Comprehension**
> - **Voluntariness**

> **Informed consent is a process of information exchange that takes place between the prospective subject and the investigator, before, during and sometimes after the study.**

Information

Most research codes and regulations establish specific items for disclosure intended to ensure that subjects are given sufficient information. These items generally include: the research procedure, its purpose, risks and antic-ipated benefits, alternative procedures (where therapy is involved), and a statement offering the opportunity to ask questions and to withdraw at any time from the research. Investigators should consider these items necessary, but often not sufficient, for fully informed consent.

> **Freely given informed consent should be obtained from each volunteer before research procedures are begun.**

For judging how much and what sort of information should be pro-vided, a standard of "the reasonable subject" should be used. This implies that the extent and nature of information provided should be such that a reasonable person has enough information to decide whether or not to par-ticipate in the research. "Even when some direct benefit to them is antici-pated, the subjects should understand clearly the range of risk and the voluntary nature of their participation," declares the Belmont Report.

Regarding deception or incomplete disclosure, Belmont states, "In all cases of research involving incomplete disclosure, such research is justified only if it is clear that (1) incomplete disclosure is truly necessary to accom-plish the goals of the research, (2) there are no undisclosed risks to subjects that are more than minimal, and (3) there is an adequate plan for debriefing subjects, when appropriate, and for dissemination of research results to them. Information about risks should never be withheld for the purpose of elicit-ing the cooperation of subjects, and truthful answers should always be given to direct questions about the research. Care should be taken to distinguish cases in which disclosure would destroy or invalidate the research from cases in which disclosure would simply inconvenience the investigator."

Comprehension

"The manner and context in which information is conveyed are as important as the information itself. For example, presenting information in a disorganized and rapid fashion, allowing too little time for consideration, or curtailing opportunities for questioning all may adversely affect a study subject's ability to make an informed choice" explains the Belmont Report.

"Because the subject's ability to understand is a function of intelligence, rationality, maturity and language, it is necessary to adapt the presentation of the information to the subject's capabilities. Investigators are responsible for ascertaining that the subject has comprehended the information." The investigator should encourage the person to ask questions. Investigators should make every attempt to ensure that the person understands the information, which may involve probing for unresolved questions and not just accepting immediate agreement. Investigators must give an opportunity for subjects to resolve any concerns before agreeing to participate in the study. Subjects should feel free to ask questions at any time before, during and even after the experiment.

Belmont tells us, "Special provision may need to be made when comprehension is severely limited—for example, by conditions of immaturity or mental disability. Even for these persons, however, respect requires giving them the opportunity to choose, to the extent they are able, whether or not to participate in research." In addition to this "assent" process, "respect for persons also requires seeking the permission of other parties in order to protect the subjects from harm."

Voluntariness

An agreement to participate in research constitutes valid consent only if voluntarily given. This component of informed consent requires conditions free of coercion and undue influence. Coercion occurs when an overt threat of harm is intentionally presented by one person to another in order to obtain compliance. Undue influence, by contrast, occurs through an offer of an excessive, unwarranted, inappropriate or improper reward (benefit) or other overture to obtain compliance. Investigators should assure that the circumstances (context) in which consent is obtained are free from undue influence. Subjects must understand that they are free to decline participation and to withdraw from the study at any time after it has begun.

2. Beneficence

According to Belmont, "Persons are treated in an ethical manner not only by respecting their decisions and protecting them from harm, but also by making efforts to secure their well-being...Two general rules have been formulated as complementary expressions of beneficent actions: (1) do not harm and (2) maximize possible benefits and minimize possible harms."

"The obligations of beneficence affect both individual investigators and society... Effective ways of treating childhood diseases and fostering healthy development are benefits that serve to justify research involving children— even when individual research subjects are not direct beneficiaries." The principle of beneficence is reflected in regulations as a requirement to perform risk/benefit assessments.

Assessment of Risks and Benefits

"The assessment of risks and benefits... presents both an opportunity and a responsibility to gather systematic and comprehensive information about proposed research. For the investigator, it is a means to examine whether the proposed research is properly designed. For a review committee, it is a method for determining whether the risks that will be presented to subjects are justified. For prospective subjects, the assessment will assist their determination whether or not to participate," instructs the Belmont Report.

Belmont tells us further that, "The term "risk" refers to a possibility that harm may occur... both in the chance (probability) of experiencing a harm and the severity (magnitude) of the envisioned harm. The term "benefit" is used in the research context to refer to something of positive value related to health or welfare... Accordingly, so-called risk/benefit assessments are concerned with the probabilities and magnitudes of possible harm and anticipated benefits... While the most likely harms to research subjects are those of psychological or physical pain or injury, other possible harms should not be overlooked." Except for a narrow segment of research, the potential benefits accrue to society, and there are no benefits to individual study subjects. Often, determining the balance between personal risk borne by the study subject and potential societal benefit constitutes a key ethical dilemma in research ethics.

According to Belmont, "Risks and benefits of research may affect the individual subjects, the families of the individual subjects, and society at large (or special groups within society)... Beneficence... requires that we protect against risk of harm to subjects and also that we be concerned about the loss of the substantial benefits that might be gained from research."

> **The principle of beneficence is applied in risk/benefit assessments.**

3. Justice

The principle of justice requires fairness in distribution. The Belmont Report says that, "An injustice occurs when some benefit to which a person is entitled is denied without good reason or when some burden is imposed unduly... For example, the selection of research subjects needs to be scrutinized in order to determine whether some classes of subjects (e.g., welfare patients, particular racial and ethnic minorities, or persons confined to institutions) are being systematically selected simply because of their easy availability or their compromised position ..." Belmont also says that, "justice demands ... that such research should not unduly involve persons from groups unlikely to be among the beneficiaries of subsequent applications of the research." This principle also requires inclusion of diverse populations/groups so that they may benefit from the findings of research. In the regulations, the principle of justice requires review of procedures for the selection of subjects and the outcome of those procedures.

Selection of Subjects

Justice is relevant to the selection of subjects of research at two levels: the social and the individual. Individual justice in the selection of subjects would require that researchers exhibit fairness. Justice requires fairness in the exclusion and inclusion criteria. Investigators and IRBs must consider subject selection issues including the encouragement by federal agencies for increasing enrollment of women, children and minorities. "Social justice requires that distinction be drawn between classes of subjects that ought and ought not to participate in any particular kind of research, based on the ability ... to bear burdens and on the appropriateness of placing further burdens on already burdened persons ... Certain groups, such as racial minorities, the economically disadvantaged, the very sick, and the institutionalized, ... given their dependent status and their frequently compromised capacity for free consent, ... should be protected against the danger of being involved in research solely for administrative convenience, or because they are easy to manipulate as a result of their illness and/or socioeconomic condition." Research should not use underprivileged persons to benefit the privileged.

> **The principle of justice is applied in the selection of research subjects.**

Federal Regulations

Human Subject Protection Regulations

The federal regulations were directly derived from the ethical principles discussed above. In 1991, 17 federal departments and agencies adopted a common set of regulations, called "the Common Rule," governing human subject research sponsored by the federal government. The Common Rule was derived from the first of four subparts of the Department of Health and Human Services (DHHS) regulations for the protection of human subjects. These regulations date from 1981, when they were published together with Food and Drug Administration (FDA) human subject protection regulations as a response to the National Research Act of 1974 and the 1979 Belmont Report on research ethics. The Common Rule governs research that is conducted or supported by these federal agencies. The equivalent FDA human subject protection regulations govern research with drugs, biologics and devices regardless of study sponsorship. The Common Rule has established three main protective mechanisms: review of research by an institutional review board (IRB), required informed consent of subjects and institutional assurances of compliance.

Protective Mechanisms Established by the Common Rule
1. **Review of research by an IRB.**
2. **Informed consent of subjects.**
3. **Institutional assurances of compliance.**

---

1. Review of Research by an Institutional Review Board (IRB)

Peer scientific review and independent ethical review are key components of the research monitoring system. Scientific merit and methods are reviewed under a system of peer review at major research institutions. The purpose of the IRB is to review research and determine if the rights and welfare of human subjects involved in research are adequately protected. Institutions establish policies that ensure peer review and IRB review are properly conducted. By institutional policy, even studies that may otherwise be exempt from federal regulations may require review and/or verification of exempt status. Documents provided to peer review committees and IRBs by investigators must contain enough information to allow valid judgments about the science and ethics of the research.

The IRB has the authority to approve, require modification in (to approve) or disapprove all research activities, including proposed changes in previously approved human subject research. Based on factors including risk to subjects, IRBs determine which activities require continuing review more frequently than once a year and which need verification that no changes have occurred since previous review and approval.

- Before human subjects are involved in research, the IRB must consider:
  - The risks to the subjects.
  - The anticipated benefits to the subjects and others.
  - The importance of the knowledge that may reasonably result.
  - The informed consent process to be employed.
- The IRB must report promptly to the appropriate institutional officials, OHRP, FDA and any sponsoring agency of the federal government:
  - Injuries to human subjects or other unanticipated problems involving risks to subjects or others.
  - Serious or continuing noncompliance with regulations or requirements of the IRB.
  - Suspension or termination of IRB approval for research.
- Initial and continuing review and approvals must be in compliance with federal regulations. Continuing reviews must be preceded by IRB

receipt of appropriate progress reports from the investigator, including available study-wide findings.

■ Research investigators must request proposed changes in previously approved human subject research activities to the IRB. Proposed changes to the protocol may not be initiated without IRB review and approval, except where necessary to eliminate apparent immediate hazards to the subjects.

2. Informed Consent of Subjects

As described in the Belmont Report, consent must be informed, understood and voluntary. These are the essential ethical and conceptual hallmarks of consent and provide respect for persons by honoring their autonomy. The requirements to ensure "legally effective" consent are intended to maximize the likelihood that consent is an informed autonomous decision.

Consent forms should reflect, in language that is understandable to volunteers, relevant information about the study. Consent, whether written or oral, may not include waivers or the appearance of waivers of any of the subject's legal rights. The same is true for releases (or appearance of releases) from liability for negligence of responsible parties. Technical language should be eliminated or explained in lay terms. Overly optimistic language should be avoided (e.g., "this product has been extensively and safely used elsewhere"). The form serves as a baseline of information for initial presentation and a reference source during the study as well as documentation of voluntary participation. Especially for long and/or complicated studies, investigators should stress to subjects the importance of keeping their copy of the consent form for reference. The original consent form, which is kept in the investigator's records, needs to be signed and dated by the subject.

3. Institutional Assurances of Compliance

Before a federal grant or contract can be awarded, the institution must file an "Assurance of Compliance" with the government. This assurance is called a Federal-Wide Assurance (FWA). In the Assurance, the institution agrees to apply the federal regulations, and to be guided by the ethical principles of the Belmont Report.

The Office for Human Research Protection (OHRP) is the office within the federal government that negotiates Assurances for DHHS and oversees institutions' compliance with their Assurances. Research institutions must periodically reapply for and negotiate the terms of their Assurances as one mechanism by which the OHRP can address any concerns that may have come to its attention regarding the conduct of human subject research at a particular institution.

> **An Assurance imposes requirements on the institution and its researchers with respect to the conduct of human subject research.**

A Federal-Wide Assurance (FWA) is only required for federally sponsored research; however, most institutions voluntarily choose to extend the procedures and protections to all research conducted at the institution. Institutions must maintain certain conditions and requirements in connection with the conduct and review of research projects. One fundamental condition of an Assurance is that the institution must name an institutional review board (IRB) that oversees the conduct of research.

> **The IRB review system is a requirement set forth in the Assurance.**

Assurance Violations: In the past few years, OHRP has enforced sanctions at some major research institutions. These sanctions ranged from the withdrawal of the institution's Assurance to placing limitations on the institutional Assurance and to temporary suspension of federal research at institutions. In some cases, the suspension lasted for a few days, but in others, all human subject research across the entire institution was stopped for months.

Given the potential ramifications of violating an Assurance, it is important for researchers to be compliant with the procedures established by the institution's Assurance for the review and approval of research and to be compliant with applicable laws governing the conduct of human subject research.

If OHRP determines that the obligations set forth in an Assurance have been violated, it has the authority to terminate or suspend the Assurance. This means no federally funded research can be conducted until the Assurance is reinstated. Typically the termination or suspension of an institution's Assurance arises in situations where there have been repeated and systematic violations of human subject research requirements by an institutional review board or by researchers, and as a result, the safety and welfare of research subjects is believed to be at risk.

Another significant sanction available to OHRP is to temporarily suspend new enrollments in existing research protocols. OHRP may also place certain restrictions on the institution's ability to conduct human subject research and/or require that the institution develop corrective actions. OHRP monitors the implementation of these corrective actions by requiring the submission of periodic progress reports and by conducting site visits. If the institution fails to adequately apply the corrective actions, more severe sanctions are imposed.

OHRP also has the authority to impose sanctions on individual researchers. Included among the sanctions that may be imposed on an individual researcher are:

- Recommending to the DHHS that the researcher be barred from receiving federal funds for conducting research.
- Requiring OHRP approval for each study conducted by the researcher.
- Requiring the researcher to undergo remedial training or education.

- Placing certain restrictions on the researcher's ability to conduct research (e.g., requiring supervision of the researcher).

Concerns regarding a particular researcher can come to the attention of OHRP through a number of mechanisms, including complaints by subjects. One mechanism is through a mandated IRB report to OHRP. Federal regulations require the IRB to report to the OHRP (and FDA as appropriate):

- Any serious or continuing noncompliance with regulations or requirements of the IRB.
- Any injuries or unanticipated problems involving risk to research subjects.
- Any suspension or termination of IRB approval for research.

> **Violation of the obligations of Assurance can result in:**
> - **Termination or suspension of the institution's Assurance.**
> - **Suspension or restrictions to ongoing studies.**
> - **Departmental restrictions.**
> - **Individual restrictions.**

Additional FDA Regulations and Sanctions: As stated previously, the FDA has regulations for the protection of human research subjects that are also based on the Belmont Report ethical principles (21 CFR Parts 50 and 56). In addition, the FDA has specific regulations governing the way FDA-regulated products (primarily drugs, biologic products and medical devices) may be used in clinical research settings. These regulations are also intended to protect subjects as well as to ensure sound data upon which to base product approvals. Therefore, it is important that investigators who use FDA-regulated products be familiar with these regulations so that research is conducted in compliance. Like the other FDA regulations, these rules are contained in the Code of Federal Regulations (CFR) and are available in IRB and legal offices as well as on the Internet. The specific references for drugs and devices are 21 CFR Parts 312, 314, 600, 812 and 814, some of which are included in the appendix.

The FDA has an inspection program, the Bioresearch Monitoring Program (BIMO, that conducts routine and "for cause" audits of FDA-regulated research. Investigators, research sites, sponsors and IRBs are inspected under this program.

The FDA works with individuals, companies and institutions to help promote compliance with the laws and regulations that govern clinical research. Most cases of noncompliance are due to misunderstanding the regulations or the responsibilities that individuals have in conducting clinical research. Institutions and individuals who work to resolve areas of noncompliance are generally met with the cooperation of the Agency. Disregard for the regulations and/or their intent, especially after initial goodwill efforts by the FDA, may lead to various levels of sanctions. Often correlated with the level to which research subjects are placed at risk, these include:

- Longer review of applications. Once a level of trust is broken with the FDA, additional safeguards, including more detailed review cycles, are often required.

- Warning Letters for specific documented concerns. These letters require immediate action, usually to cease all noncompliant activity until compliance is assured. Warning Letters are made public and posted on the FDA Website and can be searched by individual, institution, company, date or compliance type. Frequently, although the Warning Letter may be specific to an individual investigator, it is directed to the institution and may result in action against the institution.

- Disqualification/debarment of individuals from conducting clinical research (this can be temporary or permanent). Both the list of disqualified investigators and the list of debarred persons are posted on the FDA Website. Once a name is placed on the list, it stays on the list even if the sanction is removed. It should be noted, that this list is reviewed by companies as they choose investigators and sites for their clinical studies. It is also available to future employers, fellow investigators and researchers.

- Disqualification of institutions and/or IRBs from conducting or approving clinical research. Again, once an institution becomes known for noncompliance, it will take time and effort to re-establish trust with the agency.

- Other sanctions including seizures, injunctions, criminal charges and monetary penalties. These types of penalties are applied when there is evidence of willful serious disregard for the regulations and human subject safety. For individual researchers, these are often last resort efforts to halt criminal activity.

Scientific Misconduct: In addition to enacting regulations that implement the principles of the Belmont Report, the federal government has also enacted regulations governing misconduct in scientific research.

As a condition of accepting federal funding for research, institutions are required to adhere to the Public Health Service (PHS) regulations that apply to scientific misconduct. The regulations require that research institutions have written policies and procedures for investigating scientific misconduct. The current PHS definition of scientific misconduct is as follows:

Misconduct in science means fabrication, falsification, plagiarism or other practices that seriously deviate from those that are commonly accepted within the scientific community for proposing, conducting and reporting research. It does not include honest error or honest differences in interpretations or judgments of data.

The Public Health Service defines falsification to mean changing or falsifying existing data. It defines fabrication as the creation of data out of "thin air." It is important to note that honest errors or differences in interpretation are not considered misconduct. Although they are serious charges, incompetence and negligence are also not considered misconduct. Within the definition of scientific misconduct, however, there is a significant gray area, particularly with respect to "other practices that seriously deviate from those that are commonly accepted." In light of this, if there is a concern that an individual may have engaged in practices that seriously deviate from acceptable research standards, the matter should be brought to the attention of the individual's immediate supervisor who can then further confer with the institutional officials regarding the appropriate action to be taken. If an individual has a concern with respect to his/her immediate supervisor, most institutions' policies designate other institutional officials who can be contacted.

> **The definition of scientific misconduct does not include "honest errors" or "differences in interpretation of the data."**

When an allegation regarding scientific misconduct is made, the regulations require that the institution investigate the allegation in two phases: the inquiry phase and the investigative phase. During the inquiry phase, the accused researcher, the complainant and anyone with knowledge that is relevant to the inquiry must be interviewed. The purpose of this phase is not to determine conclusively whether or not there was misconduct. Instead, the purpose of the inquiry phase is to determine whether or not there may be a basis to believe that misconduct could have occurred. PHS regulations require that the inquiry phase generally be completed within 60 days of receipt of the allegation. At the conclusion of the inquiry phase, the institution is required to write a report summarizing the results of the inquiry.

If, after the inquiry, institutional officials believe that misconduct may have occurred, the institution is required to conduct a more in-depth investigation. The institution is required to report its intention to conduct an investigation to the Office of Research Integrity (ORI). ORI is a division of the PHS which oversees investigations of allegations of scientific misconduct.

> **Institutions are required to report to the Office of Research Integrity when the institution decides to commence an in-depth investigation into an allegation of scientific misconduct.**

When a further investigation is conducted into the allegation of misconduct (the investigative phase), the institution is required to interview the accused researcher, the complainant and others with knowledge relevant to the investigation. Relevant documents are also reviewed. At the conclusion of its investigation, the institution is required to write a report of its findings and its determination as to whether or not the accused individual did com-mit scientific misconduct. The report is submitted to institutional officials, who determine the final action to be taken. The report is also submitted to ORI, which has the authority to either accept or reject the findings. In general, the investigative phase takes no more than 120 days. The PHS regulations require that inquiries and investigations into allegations of misconduct be conducted in as confidential a manner as possible without compromising the ability to conduct an effective investigation.

Individuals who have, in good faith, made an allegation of misconduct ("whistle-blowers") should not be the object of retaliation. Indeed, retaliation against a whistle-blower who made an allegation of misconduct in good faith may itself be construed as an act of misconduct.

> **Retaliation against a "whistle-blower" may be construed as an act of misconduct.**

If an individual is found guilty of scientific misconduct, there is a range of penalties that the institution and ORI may utilize. With respect to the institution, penalties may range from requiring further training for the individual or supervision to terminating his or her appointment. The ORI may impose penalties that range from researcher supervision to the maximal penalty of researcher debarment from conducting federally funded research. Additionally, in some instances, the institution or ORI may require that any publication related to the research in question be retracted or corrected.

CHAPTER 3

Roles and Responsibilities of Institutions in Human Subject Research

At the conclusion of this chapter, readers will be able to:
- Describe the responsibilities of research institutions and federal regulatory agencies in conducting clinical research.
- Discuss the legal basis and the intent of the regulations governing clinical research.
- Describe the term "Good Clinical Practice" and how it applies to clinical research.

Introduction

The roles and responsibilities of the federal agencies, institutions, IRBs and investigators in conducting human subject research are defined in federal and state laws and regulations. This chapter provides a general review of the institutions', IRBs' and federal agencies' roles and responsibilities.

Research Institution

The research institution bears responsibility for compliance with the Department of Health and Human Services (DHHS) and Food and Drug Administration (FDA) regulations for the performance of all research activities that involve human subjects. Institutions are required to use additional safeguards for research in vulnerable populations. This is true for research conducted at sites that are under the direction of any employee or agent of the institution. The institution has responsibility for educating researchers on issues of research ethics and scientific integrity. It also has a mandated responsibility to investigate alleged cases of scientific misconduct. In addition, the institution has a responsibility to have and enforce a policy on conflict of interest.

Issues That Require Institutional Review
- **Ethical (i.e., IRB) Review (of the protocol and informed consent).**
- **Administrative Review of Proposals, Contracts and Grants.**
- **Scientific Peer Review.**

---

1. Ethical Review

Institutions protect the rights, safety and welfare of their research subjects by assuring that an IRB operating in compliance with federal regulations is in place. By regulation, when approving research, the IRB must determine that the following requirements are satisfied:

- Risks to subjects are minimized:
  - by using procedures that are consistent with sound research design and that do not unnecessarily expose subjects to risk, and
  - whenever appropriate, by using procedures already being performed on the subjects for diagnostic or treatment purposes.
- Risks are reasonable in relation to anticipated benefits to subjects, if any, and to the importance of the expected knowledge. In evaluating risks and benefits, the IRB considers only those risks and benefits that may result directly from the research (as distinguished from risks and benefits that people would have even if not participating in the research).
- Selection of subjects is equitable. In making this assessment, the IRB takes into account the purpose(s) of the research and the setting in which the research will be conducted.
- Informed consent will be sought from each prospective subject, or the subject's legally authorized representative unless waived in accordance with regulations.
- Informed consent will be appropriately documented, usually with a signed written consent form.
- Where appropriate, the research plan makes provisions for monitoring the data collected to ensure the safety of subjects.
- Where appropriate, there are provisions to protect the privacy of participants and to maintain the confidentiality of data.
- Additional safeguards are included in the study to protect the rights and welfare of subjects when some or all of them are likely to be vulnerable to coercion or undue influence (children, prisoners, pregnant women, handicapped, mentally disabled persons or economically or educationally disadvantaged persons).

The IRB reviews the investigator's study design/protocol and the information from the IRB review application to make the above determinations. IRB approval is based upon the information provided, and the board expects the researcher to abide by the protocol as written. Any changes in the study must receive prior approval by the IRB before being instituted. Sponsors may require that any changes made by the IRB be relayed to them for concurrence.

Some funding/sponsoring organizations require IRB review of projects before they can be considered for funding/sponsoring. Often, the funding/sponsoring organization's review results in changes to the study design. It is essential that the investigator know that, if the study is to be funded and conducted, all changes must be reviewed and approved by the IRB before the study may begin.

> **To ensure an effective review by the IRB, the board must be provided with certain critical information, including: the protocol/study design, consent form(s) and subject recruitment materials.**

This is also true for changes required by a regulatory agency. For example, in the Investigational New Drug Application (IND) or the Investigational Device Exemption (IDE) review process, if the FDA requires changes to the study, these changes must be submitted to the IRB for approval.

After the initial approval, studies must undergo continuing review by the IRB to ensure that: (1) the risk-benefit relationship of the research remains acceptable, (2) the informed consent process and documents are still appropriate, and (3) the enrollment of subjects has been equitable. By federal regulation, the maximum period between these IRB reviews is one year. As part of the continuing review, the IRB will assess appropriate information such as enrollment figures and demographics; adverse events and unanticipated problems; subject withdrawals; preliminary study results and publications; and the consent process. The investigator is responsible for applying for continuing review in a timely manner to ensure IRB approval is continuous. If a study is not re-approved before the study's expiration date, it is automatically suspended until formal notice of re-approval from the IRB is received. Sponsors require notification of IRB approvals (initial and continuing).

2. Administrative Review of Proposals, Contracts and Grants

Most research institutions establish a sponsored programs office that reviews and authorizes proposals to external sponsors, accepts grants and reviews or approves contracts for all associated researchers.

This office generally ensures that proposals and associated budgets are in compliance with institution and sponsor policies (including IRB review where appropriate) and that investigator assurances are current. These assurances include a determination that a financial interest does not have a significant effect upon the design, conduct or reporting of the proposed study. Generally, if the investigator has a financial interest in the sponsor funding the clinical study, the institution will need to make a determination if the conflict can be managed. Some institutions will not accept funding if this situation exists.

By authorizing a proposal to an external sponsor, the institution is:

- Stating that in the institution's best estimation, the statement of work or protocol can be performed at the proposed funding level.
- Any unique policies of the institution have been considered.
- The proposal meets the requirements of the potential sponsor.
- The institution will comply with all federal and state laws and regulations, as well as institutional policies.

The sponsored programs office addresses contractual issues inherent in clinical research contracts, such as ownership of data, appropriate sharing of liability, responsibility for subject injury and the protection of publication rights for researchers. This office is also responsible for negotiating terms on which sponsor confidential information will be accepted.

Institutions that receive Public Health Service (PHS) funds are mandated to have a conflict-of-interest (COI) policy and a mechanism for reviewing potential conflicts. Usually, institutions have followed the model PHS policy and have established a COI committee that sets institutional policy, reviews reports of potential conflicts and then recommends procedures to eliminate, manage and/or minimize the conflict. These policies have focused upon individual financial COI. However, with greater involvement with industry partners and fostering technological transfer through institutionally sponsored start-up companies, institutional COI is becoming an issue that must be dealt with.

3. Scientific Peer Review

Peer review ensures that sound research design and methods are employed. Institutional peer review committees focus on the scientific concerns of studies. The composition and qualifications of the research team are generally examined and they may also consider resource issues.

Scientific review for both biomedical and behavioral/social science research considers the soundness and worth of hypothesis, the procedures used to test the hypothesis and the adequacy of the analysis to be employed. For clinical trials, sample size justifications are based upon statistical significance and predicted results. For both behavioral and biomedical research, it is important that scientific rigor be maintained because, as the Belmont Report indicates, exposing subjects to any risk is unethical if valid scientific results are not possible.

Institutions have set up various methods to perform scientific review. At most universities and larger research institutions, peer review is conducted by a committee of scientists within the investigator's department. Smaller facilities have assigned this to department heads, or even to the IRB. When the IRB is responsible for scientific review, in addition to its mandated role as reviewer of subject rights and welfare, additional information must be reviewed, and, usually, scientifically qualified people must be added to the IRB. Some IRBs playing this dual role have established a subcommittee to accomplish the scientific review. The major concern is that it may detract from the IRB's ability to comply with the federal human subject protection regulations and institutional responsibilities. It is important for continued public trust and support that research institutions be seen as dedicated to the development of unbiased scientific knowledge for the betterment of humankind.

Federal Agencies

While several federal agencies, such as the Department of Education, the Department of Defense and the National Science Foundation, fund and regulate research, they generally follow the lead of the Department of Health and Human Services (DHHs).

Department of Health and Human Services (DHHS)
Besides the FDA (discussed separately below), the DHHS houses several other agencies that regulate or fund research. The National Institutes of Health's (NIH) mission is to uncover new knowledge that leads to better public health. The NIH's role in research is primarily to conduct studies with its own investigators and to provide funding for research projects at other institutions, especially multi-site national studies. To a lesser extent, other DHHS agencies also function in the role of research conductor/sponsor. Examples include the Centers for Disease Control and Prevention (CDC) and the Agency for Healthcare Research and Quality (AHRQ).

Agencies within the DHHS promulgate regulations applicable to Public Health Service (PHS)-funded research. An example is the conflict-of-interest rule that establishes standards and procedures to be followed by institutions to ensure that the design, conduct or reporting of research funded under PHS grants, cooperative agreements or contracts will not be biased by any conflicting financial interest of its investigators.

The Office for Human Research Protection (OHRP) regulates, in a manner similar to FDA, research involving human subjects for studies conducted with DHHS funds in order to protect the rights and safety of subjects. This includes regulations for the institutional review of studies and informed consent documents.

The Office of Research Integrity (ORI) conducts investigations regarding misconduct in research. As a condition of accepting federal funding for research, institutions are required to adhere to the PHS regulations that apply to scientific misconduct. If an individual is found to have committed scientific misconduct, there is a range of penalties that the institution and the ORI may impose.

Food and Drug Administration (FDA)

The Food and Drug Administration (FDA) is the federal consumer protection agency within the Department of Health and Human Services (DHHS) that enforces the Food, Drug and Cosmetic Act (the FD&C Act) and related federal public health laws. According to these laws, only drugs, biologics and medical devices that have been proven safe and effective can be marketed.

To allow for research with human subjects to determine the safety and effectiveness of new (i.e., investigational) drugs, biologics or device products, the FDA has established regulations that govern study sponsors, investigators and IRBs.

Prior to the initiation of a human research study with an investigational product, an application to the FDA is usually required.

> **Although FDA oversight may not be necessary, the protocol and informed consent still needs to undergo review by the IRB.**

The FDA monitors research through review of required reports from investigators, sponsors, institutions and IRBs as well as through a program of on-site inspections and audits. The Biomedical Monitoring Program (BIMO) inspects all the players in the research enterprise.

Good Clinical Practice

In the United States, Good Clinical Practice (GCP) has been based primarily upon FDA policy and regulation. In the last few years, however, a movement toward international GCP standards has occurred. The International Conference on Harmonization (ICH) is composed of expert working groups from industry and regulatory bodies in the European Union, Japan and the United States. ICH published guidelines for GCP. This worldwide GCP document offers standardization for clinical trials of drugs.

GCP is an ethical and scientific quality standard for designing, conducting, monitoring, recording, auditing, analyzing and reporting drug trials that involve participation of human subjects. GCPs are consistent with ethical principles put forth in the Declaration of Helsinki. The main purposes of GCP are:

1. To protect human subjects during clinical studies, and
2. To protect patients who might receive approved products in the future.

In this country, FDA regulations are the basis for practices that govern clinical research. Compliance with this standard provides public assurance that the rights, safety and well-being of trial subjects are protected, and that the clinical trial data are valid and accurate. When it is anticipated that the study data will be submitted to the EU or to Japan for marketing approval, the studies should conform to the ICH E-6 GCP guidelines as well.

> **GCPs offer protection for human subjects in clinical trials.**

There is no one source of guidance for GCPs. They are embodied within laws, regulations and guidelines such as:
- Ethical codes.
- IRB and consent regulations.
- Guidelines on the obligations of investigators, sponsors and monitors.
- Code of Federal Regulations pertaining to drugs and devices.
- ICH Guidelines.
- Official guidance documents.

> **Following GCPs ensures the accuracy and reliability of data generated in the course of a clinical trial.**

Compliance with GCPs during clinical trials will ensure that:
- The rights and safety of human subjects are not compromised.
- Appropriately and adequately trained staff manage the study.
- The study is carefully documented.
- Protocol is strictly adhered to.

GCPs, therefore, encompass all aspects of a clinical trial including (but not limited to):
- Obtaining informed consent.
- Documenting accurate case histories.
- Maintaining complete "paper trails" for all study documents.
- Reporting adverse events.
- Proper record retention.

Roles and Responsibilities of the Investigator and the Study Process

At the conclusion of this chapter, readers will be able to:
- Describe the roles and responsibilities of the investigator and research team.
- List the items that should be included in a protocol (study design).
- List the required elements of a consent form.
- Describe the issues to consider in subject recruitment for a study.

Introduction

The complex responsibilities of conducting research can make the investigator's role difficult and challenging. On the other hand, once the investigator understands the responsibilities involved, research can be rewarding for both the investigator and for the subjects who participate. The study process begins before the first subject is entered, and continues after the last subject has completed the study. This chapter provides an overview of the roles of the research team members, the responsibilities of investigators, and the steps involved in the process of conducting a successful research study.

Investigator's Roles and Responsibilities

Investigators share with research institutions and sponsors the responsibility for ensuring that study subjects are adequately protected. They are required to assure that the IRB reviewing the study is in compliance with federal regulations. Studies must be properly designed so that they are scientifically sound and likely to yield valid results. Investigators must be appropriately qualified to conduct the research. The investigator is responsible for ensuring that the research is conducted according to the research design as approved by the IRB. Respect for study subjects' rights and dignity requires that informed consent be obtained before a person participates in a study.

> **The safety and welfare of research subjects ultimately rests with the investigator.**

Professional Judgment

The ultimate responsibility for the acceptable conduct of research with human subjects rests with the investigator. Only sound professional judgment can ensure the protection of study subjects. It is up to the investigator to see that:

- The personal dignity and autonomy of the research volunteer are respected.
- Subjects are protected from harm by maximizing anticipated benefits and minimizing possible risks.
- The benefits and burdens of research are shared fairly.

The challenge arises in deciding how to protect the study subjects while also achieving progress in science. Although the two objectives are not mutually exclusive, they also are not without conflict. Understanding the distinction between research and practice is fundamental to resolving any conflict that may arise. It is also essential to recognize the potential for confusion on the part of the subject (e.g., patient, client, student) about his/her relationship to the investigator, who may also be his/her physician, social worker, mentor or teacher.

The purpose of medical or behavioral practice is to provide diagnosis, preventative treatment or therapy. "Practice" involves interventions designed solely to enhance the well-being of the patient or client. These interventions are undertaken because there is a reasonable expectation of a successful outcome. "Research" constitutes activities designed to contribute to generalizable knowledge. Typically, in research, a set of activities is consistently applied to groups of individuals in order to test a hypothesis and draw conclusions. The activities do not necessarily provide direct benefit.

The line between practice and research is often blurred. Novel procedures do not necessarily constitute research and often, research and practice occur simultaneously. The investigator's professional judgment is essential to maintain the integrity of the research process and to keep the study volunteer informed of his/her role in the process and relationship with the investigator(s). People who are used as research subjects without their consent may be wronged, even if they are not harmed.

Good judgment is required throughout the research process to provide the necessary checks and balances. No balance of research/therapy is acceptable if it is likely to result in less than adequate care for the subject. It can be tempting to value knowledge more highly than basic human rights when excited by the prospect of a new scientific method or new understanding of behavioral processes. To avoid this, consider the following questions before undertaking a new study.

- What types of people will be enrolled? Address this from an ethical perspective as well as on the basis of entry criteria.
  - What alternatives are available?
  - Would some potential subjects incur more risks than others? Accrue more benefits?
  - Are all subjects capable of understanding the consent process?
- What is your relationship to the subject?
  - Are you also his or her care-giver, teacher, employer or in any other position of authority?
  - Do the subject delegate his or her decisions for participating in research to you?
  - Is the subject comfortable asking you questions? Are you comfortable asking probing questions to ensure he or she understand sthe study?
- How do you treat someone with an intervention that has not been proven to be safe or effective?
- Are you so involved with the "science," publishing, presenting or grant review, that there is significant potential for conflict?

Good judgment is required throughout the research process to provide the necessary checks and balances.

These are among the many questions that investigators must ask themselves regularly.

There is no standard operating procedure to address the potential issues that can arise when human subjects are involved in research. Because the future of science depends on the goodwill and trust of the public, investigators must understand and meet their duty to human subjects.

Study Conduct

The investigator is personally responsible for the conduct of the research project and for the actions of personnel under his/her supervision. Many studies are conducted by one investigator, commonly referred to as the principal investigator (PI) or, to use the FDA term, clinical investigator (CI).

The investigator of a study is required to conduct the study according to the:

- Investigational plan (including the protocol and IRB stipulations).
- Institutional policies.
- All applicable regulations.

Additional responsibilities for FDA-regulated studies are to:

- Comply with the signed investigators' statement (Form FDA 1572).
- Supervise use of the test article(s).
- Maintain accurate study records.
- Maintain control of all test articles, ensuring that no people other than those identified to the FDA are given access to the test article.

The investigator is responsible for the study conduct.

The term "co-principal-investigator" (co-PI) is used when a study is conducted by more than one investigator, each of whom assumes equal responsibility for the conduct of the study and adherence to the regulations. The reasons for a study being conducted by co-principal-investigators are varied. For example, co-PIs are often used in drug studies when an investigator has multiple sites where different investigators are responsible at each location.

Principal investigators must be qualified by education, training and experience to assume responsibility for the proper conduct of the research project. They should meet all the qualifications specified by the applicable regulatory requirements and provide evidence of such qualifications through an up-to-date curriculum vitae and relevant documentation as requested by the sponsor, the IRB and/or regulatory authorities.

Administration of the Study

Because investigators are required to conduct the study in accordance with institutional policies and all applicable regulations, their responsibilities go beyond the scientific conduct of the study itself.

Other responsibilities of investigators include:

- Compliance with federal/state laws and regulations, including a conflict of interest disclosure.
- Assuming fiscal management.
- Supervising and training of students, postdocs and residents.
- Complying with the terms and conditions of the sponsor's award, for example, non-disclosure of sponsor confidential information.
- Submission of all technical, progress, invention and financial reports on a timely basis.

By accepting the study, the investigator must remain cognizant of these responsibilities. Violations or delinquencies may result in loss of funding or even debarment in certain instances.

Research Team Roles and Responsibilities

The composition of the research team may vary according to the scope and complexity of the research project and the number of investigational sites involved. In some instances the study may be conducted by one individual. Most biomedical studies involve a team of individuals.

When the investigator delegates responsibility to various members of the research team (e.g., survey instruments, follow-up tests, exams or laboratory procedures), the investigator must maintain an effective working relationship with all team members to ensure they perform these procedures as the protocol requires. Normally, the research team meets periodically to discuss study progress and problems as they arise. It is usually helpful to keep notes or minutes, thereby documenting that the investigator is effectively managing the study.

Subinvestigator

A subinvestigator is any team member (e.g., junior faculty, graduate student, resident, lab staff) other than an investigator who may help in the design and conduct of the investigation, but does not actually direct its conduct. A subinvestigator can be any member of a research team designated and supervised by the investigator to perform study-related procedures and/or to make important study-related decisions. The investigator often delegates responsibility to others within their sphere of control.

Subinvestigators designated and supervised by the investigator should be qualified by education, professional qualifications and experience to perform the procedures delegated by the principal investigator. Typically, the competency of a subinvestigator can usually be documented with a curriculum vitae.

> **The subinvestigator may help conduct the study, but does not direct it.**

Clinical Research Coordinator (CRC) or Study Coordinator

The Clinical Research Coordinator (CRC) is a specialized research professional working for and under the direction of a clinical investigator. The CRC is responsible for screening and recruiting subjects, collecting and recording clinical data and maintaining clinical supplies where applicable.

Other Team Members

The principal investigator can delegate study-specific tasks, but the level of responsibility must coincide with the experience and/or capabilities of the team member. Other team members may include a variety of professionals, trainees, statisticians, laboratory technicians and administrative staff.

The investigator should always document in writing the responsibilities delegated to all members of the research team. The time period that each team member participated should also be documented. This is important in the event team members change during the course of the study.

Study Process

The study process includes protocol development, departmental scientific review, funding applications, administrative review of contracts/grants and the application to the IRB. When an investigator is developing a study design, it may be useful to consult with the IRB regarding human subject protections. Other institution officials and administrators should be advised and consulted as necessary. When an award is made, most institutional and sponsor policies require that the protocol and associated contract be formally accepted by the investigator and an official of the institution.

Protocol (Study Design) Development

The protocol is a formal document that establishes the conditions under which the research is to be conducted. When writing the protocol, the investigator should include applicable sections—example items are listed below:

- The specific scientific objectives (aims of the research).
- Budget, personnel and facility considerations.
- The research method(s) and all procedures.
- The statistical/analytical methods to be used, including justification for the number of subjects expected to participate.
- If a data monitoring committee is used, describe its operation (e.g., membership, stopping rules and frequency of review and reports).
- Security measures to protect the research data.
- Human subject issues such as:
  - The inclusion criteria.
  - The exclusion criteria.
  - Justification for inclusion of vulnerable subjects (e.g., those with limited autonomy or those in subordinate positions).
  - The intended sex distribution of the subjects.
  - The age range of the subjects. [Note: Special considerations apply to NIH-funded research, which must address the inclusion of children.]
  - The intended racial and ethnic distribution of the subjects.
  - The potential risks associated with the study.
  - Any potential benefit(s).
  - Alternatives that are available should the subject select not to participate in the study.
  - The recruitment methods.
  - Who will obtain consent and how the process of informed consent will be structured.
  - If all subjects will not be capable of giving consent, include additional protections.
  - Assessment of understanding of the information presented.
  - Justification of any non-disclosure and description of post-study debriefing.

- Justification of any costs that the subjects will incur.
- Description of any reimbursements or incentives such as cash payments.

Informed Consent Requirements

The regulations, codes and institutional policies state items that must be disclosed to satisfy the informed consent requirement. Although each research study involving human subjects is unique, federal regulations require that all consent forms contain the following information elements:

- Introduction (with statement that this activity is research).
- Purpose of study.
- Description of study procedures (identifying any that are experimental).
- Duration of subject involvement.
- Potential risks or discomforts of participation.
- Potential benefits of participation.
- Alternatives (medical treatments or other courses of action, if any).
- Confidentiality of records description.
- Compensation for injury statement (for greater than minimal risk studies).
- Contact persons.
- Statement of voluntary participation.

It is important to include several other elements of information if they apply to the study and are important for subjects to know. These include:

- Unforeseen risks statement (if applicable).
- Reasons for involuntary termination of participation (if applicable).
- Additional costs to participate (if any).
- Consequences for withdrawal (e.g., adverse health/welfare effects if any).
- New findings statement (to be provided if relevant).
- Number of subjects (if it may have an impact on the decision to participate).
- Payments (incentives and/or expense reimbursements if any).

Informed consent is not just a form or a signature, but a process of information exchange that includes:

- **Subject recruitment materials.**
- **Verbal instructions.**
- **Written materials.**
- **Question/answer sessions.**
- **Agreement documented by signature.**

Recruitment Issues

Recruiting subjects is one of the most important, and sometimes difficult and time-consuming, aspects of conducting research. Recruiting is an aspect of a study that must be considered before the study and must continue throughout the duration of the trial.

> **The investigator should determine feasibility of recruiting subjects prior to accepting a study.**

Recruitment issues to consider before conducting a study:
- Competing studies.
  - Other studies being conducted that require same population, and may decrease availability of potential subjects.
- Time frames.
  - The anticipated start/stop dates of the study period may change, which may affect subject availability, investigator workload, etc.
- Subject availability.
  - The protocol inclusion/exclusion criteria define the population to be studied. The characteristics of the subject population are a major consideration in recruitment.
  - The feasibility of recruiting this subject population must be determined prior to accepting the study.
- Recruitment strategy.
  - The recruiting methods that will be used will affect the numbers and mix of potential subjects.
- Sex of the subjects.
  - Equitable inclusion of both men and women in research is important to ensure that each receives a fair share of the benefits and neither carries a disproportionate burden. Therefore, both men and women should be included unless there are medical and/or scientific contraindications. [Note: According to FDA guidelines, women of childbearing potential should not be routinely excluded from participating in clinical research.]
- Age range of subjects.
  - Participation of adult subjects in research should not be age-restricted unless there is scientific and/or medical justification.
  - Participation of children should be considered unless there is sound scientific or medical justification for exclusion.
- Racial and ethnic origin.
  - Within the limitations imposed by the population of the study site(s), research should include sufficient enrollment of persons of diverse racial/ethnic backgrounds in order to ensure that the benefits and burdens of research participation are distributed in an equitable manner.

> **Women of childbearing potential may not be routinely excluded from participating in research.**

A variety of recruitment methods and materials are used by researchers, including:

- Formal referrals or informal word-of-mouth.
- Health workshops, screenings and health fairs.
- Internet.
- Direct advertising.
- Community meeting places (barber shops, recreation spots, etc.).
- Computerized database.
- Chart/record review.

It is unacceptable to use confidential/private data to which the investigator would not ordinarily have access to approach subjects for a research study (i.e., cold contacting). The initial contact with potential subjects should be made by those having legitimate access to the information. This person would convey referral or contact information.

Direct advertising is a frequently used recruitment technique. Direct advertising includes flyers, posters, newspaper ads and press releases. Television and radio spots, websites and electronic mailers are also considered direct advertisements. All direct advertising must have IRB approval before being used for recruiting subjects. It is considered part of the informed consent and subject selection process. In this regard, all direct advertising must:

- Be reviewed by the IRB for the information contained and the mode of communication.
- Not state or imply a certainty of favorable outcome or other benefits beyond what is outlined in the consent document and protocol.
- Not be coercive or use undue pressures.
- Not be misleading to subjects.

> **Advertising don'ts:**
> - **No misleading text.**
> - **No claims of safety, efficacy, equivalence or superiority.**
> - **No overemphasis of payment.**
> - **No overstatement of benefits.**

Advertising for recruitment into investigational drug, biologic or device studies should not use terms such as "new treatment," "new medication" or "new drug" because it inappropriately implies that safety and effectiveness have been determined.

Advertising to recruit subjects should generally be limited to:

- The name and address of the investigator and/or research facility.
- The purpose of study or condition under study.
- A brief description of eligibility requirements.
- Time commitment required of participants.
- Whom to contact for more information.

Payment to Subjects for Participation

Payment for participation requires conscientious judgment calls on the part of the researchers and the IRB. It is not uncommon for people to be paid for their participation in research, especially for research with no direct benefit to the subjects, for example, survey research or the early phases of investigational drug, biologic or device development.

The amount of payment must not be an undue inducement to participate in the research. Frequently study subjects are reimbursed an amount to cover transportation, parking, lunch, etc.—costs associated with participation. The amount of payment and payment schedule should be presented to the IRB. Information regarding payments (including amounts and scheduling of payments) should be included in the consent form. A prorated payment system should be used, so that payments are earned/given as the study progresses, and that subjects do not have to complete the entire study to be paid. A reasonable bonus for completion of a study may be paid if it does not unduly influence participants to continue when they would have withdrawn otherwise.

> **The payments to subjects for participation is not considered a benefit, it is a recruitment incentive.**

> **Prorated system of subject payment means:**
> - **Payments are earned as the study progresses.**
> - **Participants do not have to complete the entire study to be paid.**

Protocol Adherence

The investigator must follow the IRB-approved protocol. This is a specific requirement for the investigator's compliance with the regulations. The time to evaluate study procedures and for the inclusion/exclusion criteria is while the protocol is in its draft form. Once deemed "final," it is a violation of the protocol not to comply with the established procedures and inclusion/exclusion criteria. [Note: Some sponsors may provide the investigator with a final protocol. The investigator must decide in advance if he/she can comply with the entire document as written. There may be no opportunity for protocol input.]

All amendments must be approved by the IRB and sponsor (if applicable) prior to their implementation. Any deviations from the protocol should be documented and for sponsored studies, the sponsor should be consulted in advance if a deviation is requested. Most industrial sponsors will call unauthorized deviations protocol violations and will not be willing to pay for these data.

> **EXCEPTION: The investigator may deviate from the protocol to eliminate an immediate hazard to subjects, without prior IRB approval.**

If changes to the research design and/or the consent form are to be made, they must be approved by the IRB before they are implemented. Changes in the consent form, particularly when new risks are added, may require re-consent of currently enrolled subjects if the IRB deems it necessary. Re-consent is documented in study records through the use of a consent addendum or new consent form.

> **The investigator (or designee) should document and explain all deviations from the protocol.**

Investigators on industry-sponsored studies should also be aware that there also may be special circumstances (e.g., open label therapeutic use) when the sponsor may allow a person into a clinical trial who does not meet the protocol's inclusion/exclusion criteria. This must FIRST be approved by the sponsor and documented in the study records.

Some studies, such as industry-sponsored drug trials and cooperative group studies, include routine auditing or monitoring. The study monitor reviews adherence to the protocol at the monitoring visits. Reviews include, but are not limited to:

- Review of subject eligibility criteria to verify that no inclusion/ exclusion violations occur.
- Scheduling of subject visits and review of subject compliance for visits
- Evaluation procedures.
- Follow-up of study dropouts for safetly issues.
- Records of disposition and use of investigational agent.
- Thoroughness of source documentation.
- Accuracy of case report forms as compared to source documentation.

> **Discovery of major or repeated noncompliance with the protocol can result in termination of the investigator's participation in a trial, or even disqualification as an investigator.**

While most common in drug and medical device studies, adverse events could occur in almost any research study. Investigators have the responsibility to monitor research subjects to detect difficulties, discomfort and other more severe reactions. When these are encountered, the investigator should take appropriate steps to remedy the immediate situation as well as minimize the chance for recurrences. Adverse events must be reported to the IRB. If they were expected and listed in the consent form, they can usually be reported at the time of continuing review. If they are unexpected, especially if severe, adverse events should be reported when they occur to the IRB for review. IRBs have defined time limits for adverse event reporting by investigators. FDA regulations also set timelines for reporting adverse events.

C H A P T E R

FDA-Regulated Research

At the conclusion of this chapter, readers will be able to:
- Describe the Food and Drug Administration (FDA) regulations as they apply to drugs/biologics and medical devices.
- Discuss the responsibilities of the sponsor in FDA-regulated research.
- Describe the study process for industry-sponsored studies.
- Discuss sponsor–investigator–institution interactions.
- Identify the responsibilities of the investigator who assumes the additional role of the sponsor.

Introduction

The FDA regulates drugs, biologics and devices used in the diagnosis, cure, mitigation, treatment or prevention of disease in man and animals. This section addresses FDA-regulated clinical research and the responsibilities of industry sponsors, the additional study processes that industry sponsors may require and the additional responsibilities that investigators take on when they choose to sponsor a study with an FDA-regulated drug, biologic or device.

The FDA conducts a thorough review of drugs, biologics and medical devices for safety and effectiveness for a given indication prior to granting approval for marketing. Before release to the marketplace, the FDA and the sponsor write the package insert (also referred to as the "labeling"). This document summarizes what the FDA has determined to be the safe and effective use of the product. The FDA then exempts further clinical studies that are conducted according to this labeling from the IND/IDE regulations. The FDA does not, however, exempt such studies from the human subjects protection regulations. All research studies with FDA-regulated products that involve human subjects are required to undergo review by an IRB, even if exempt from IND filing.

> **Exemption from IND/IDE regulations is NOT an exemption from IRB review.**

Drugs and Biologics/INDs

If the subject population is different from that indicated in the labeling, it becomes a clinical judgment and/or ethical question as to whether this new population is at greater risk of injury with the product than the indicated population. The use of a placebo for blinding a study does not, by itself, require the filing of an IND. Examples of when an IND is warranted because of greater risk include:

- Increased dose.
- Different route of administration.
- Longer duration.
- If the research population is "vulnerable."
- If there is reason to believe that this population has different pharmacokinetic or pharmacodynamic responses from the indicated population.

> **Exemptions to the IND process apply as long as the product is used according to the product labeling (dose, duration, patient population, etc.).**

Research involving a drug or biologic that has not yet reached the marketplace requires an IND. The FDA carefully and critically reviews these applications and will only allow human exposure if they feel that the risks of the exposure are reasonable. The IND application usually contains:

- Evidence of safety and tolerability in animals.
- A controlled method of manufacture that assures the consistency of the final drug product.
- Specific tests for significant toxins or toxic ingredients.
- A well-developed research plan that minimizes the risks for human subjects.

Form FDA 1572

Each investigator participating in drug or biologic studies, subject to the IND regulations, is required to complete and sign a Form FDA 1572. The 1572 requires the submission of a curriculum vitae or other statement of qualifications. By signing the 1572, also referred to as the "statement of investigator," the investigator agrees to conduct the investigation according to the provisions listed on the Form. The back of the 1572 lists the commitments the investigator is making to the FDA for conduct of the study. These commitments come right from the regulations that govern investigational drugs (i.e., part 312). Among the nine agreement statements are such requirements as protocol adherence, direct supervision of all subinvestigators and compliance with IRB and informed consent regulations.

The Form FDA 1572 is often referred to as the "hanging paper" because it is a criminal offense to sign the document if it contains false information or if commitments made within the signed document are ignored. These investigator commitments should be reviewed prior to signing this form. Investigators have been prosecuted based on this signature in the past.

The FDA Form 1572 requires the names of the individuals involved in the clinical research project.

Investigator

The name and address of the investigator is required. If there are co-principal-investigators involved in the project, the co-PIs' names and addresses can be presented in one of two ways: (1) both co-investigators' names are entered and each signs the one form or (2) each co-investigator completes and signs a separate form. The person/persons signing as the investigator assumes full responsibility for the proper conduct of the study.

Subinvestigator

The form also requests the "Names of the subinvestigators (e.g., other investigators, research fellows, residents, specialists, associates) who will be assisting the investigator in the conduct of the investigation(s)." The issue of who should be listed as a subinvestigator frequently causes confusion for investigators. The regulations are not specific regarding this. Normally, those individuals should be listed who perform significant trial-related procedures and/or make study-related medical decisions regarding the diagnosis and treatment of the condition under investigation.

IRB

The 1572 requires the name and address of the IRB that will be responsible for review and approval of the study. In part, it is from filings of these forms that FDA gets its list of active IRBs and makes assignments for routine audits.

Clinical Laboratory

The form also requires the contact information for any laboratories that will be used in the study to provide results of lab tests, radiographic studies, etc.

It is the research sponsor who submits the completed, signed Form FDA 1572 to the FDA. A sponsor may request that everyone associated with the research project be listed on the form. Different sponsors have different requirements, thus adding to the confusion.

Medical Devices/IDEs

The regulations require that all new devices have an FDA-approved IDE for use in clinical research. A system, unique to devices, to comply with this regulation requires the determination by the reviewing IRB of whether the study presents a significant or non-significant risk to the subject population. A review of the list of typical non-significant risk devices FDA publishes shows that they carry very little risk of harm or potential to have a negative impact on a subject's health status. A non-significant risk device study is considered to have an approved IDE application (i.e., no application need be filed with the FDA). With this non-significant risk determination, the study can be conducted without prior FDA review, as long as the device is properly labeled, has IRB approval, investigators obtain and document informed consent, proper study monitoring is conducted, and compliance is assured for all other IDE regulations. An FDA-approved IDE application is required prior to human subject exposure for all significant-risk device studies. Besides the IDE regulations, significant risk studies must also comply with the IRB, informed consent, monitoring, and compliance regulations.

Although there is no Form FDA 1572 for device studies, documentation of similar commitments by the investigators is required in either the IDE application or in the sponsor's contracts with investigators. All investigators participating in studies with a significant risk device are to be listed in the IDE application.

Sponsor Responsibilities in FDA-Regulated Research

The study sponsor can be an individual, company, institution or other organization that takes responsibility for the initiation, management and financing of a research project or study. Investigators who also take on the role of sponsors must comply with the responsibilities of both roles.

The Responsibilities of the research sponsor can be divided into four main areas:
1. **Qualifying and Informing Investigators.**
2. **Monitoring Study Conduct.**
3. **Completing Regulatory Filings.**
4. **Control of Product (Drug, Biologic or Device) Shipment and Disposition.**

1. Qualifying and Informing Investigators

The sponsor is responsible for selecting and qualifying investigators. This involves reviewing the investigator's training and experience, and obtaining the investigator's commitment to:

- Conduct the study as agreed, including any IRB stipulations.
- Supervise all testing.
- Obtain informed consent.

Once investigators are selected, the study sponsor is responsible for providing investigators with the necessary information to conduct the study, including reports of all prior investigations and the current investigational plan (protocol). For drugs, the sponsor must supply investigators with the most current Investigator's Brochure, which lists results of animal studies, pharmacokinetic and pharmacodynamic information and the like. Any additional significant information learned during the course of the study, including reports of adverse events from other sites, are to be provided to all investigators in timely manner. Information not critical to the conduct of a study may be provided at the time the Investigator Brochure is updated.

2. Monitoring of Study Conduct

Monitoring of studies is viewed as a critical step in securing compliance of all investigators and assuring that adequate subject informed consent is obtained. Any significant new safety information regarding study conduct must be provided to the reviewing IRB(s), the FDA and study investigators. It is the sponsor's responsibility to evaluate and terminate investigations if undue risks to study participants are observed.

For some NIH-funded studies as well as FDA-regulated studies, formal study monitors are appointed. The monitor reviews source documents to determine that reported data are accurate and complete. The monitor also audits the research to assure that the investigator is in compliance with:

- The approved protocol and amendments.
- Good Clinical Practices (GCPs).
- Applicable regulations.

3. Completing Regulatory Filings

It is the sponsor who must determine whether an application for an IDE or IND is necessary for a specific project. Once an application is active, the sponsor is required to keep the FDA informed of any serious, related, unexpected adverse events, withdrawal of IRB approval for any reason, any recalls of test articles, progress reports (usually submitted annually), any emergency use of test articles without informed consent and a final study report.

For significant risk devices, the sponsor must also supply the FDA with a current list of investigators as well as any change in risk category. Sponsors are required to immediately conduct an evaluation of any unanticipated adverse device effect. If the sponsor determines that an unanticipated adverse device effect presents an unreasonable risk to study participants, then the sponsor must terminate all studies (or parts of the studies) that present that risk. This termination is to occur within five working days following sponsor determination, and no later than 15 working days after the sponsor first received notice of the effect. If the device is a significant-risk device, the sponsor may not resume a terminated study without re-approval from both the FDA and the IRB.

4. Control of Product (Drug, Biologic or Device) Shipment and Disposition

It is the sponsor's responsibility to control the distribution and disposition of all investigational test articles. Prior to the initial shipment, there must be documentation indicating that any necessary IDE or IND is filed and active and that the site's IRB has reviewed and approved the study. Test articles may only be shipped to qualified sites. Complete and accurate records are required for the shipment of test articles with an accounting of their final disposition.

> **Prior to the initial shipment of test articles, there must be documentation indicating that the necessary IDE or IND is filed and active, and that the site's IRB has reviewed and approved the study.**

The Study Process for Industry-Sponsored Studies

Clinical studies conducted on the behalf of industry sponsors are generally required to comply with Good Clinical Practices (GCPs), which is an international, ethical and scientific quality standard for designing, conducting, monitoring, recording, auditing, analyzing and reporting trials that involve participation of human subjects. The investigator responsibilities critical to the conduct of industry-sponsored studies include three additional processes.

1. Investigational Materials Handling and Accountability

For the purpose of this section, investigational materials are drugs or medical devices being tested in accordance with an approved protocol or investigational plan. The investigator is responsible for the accurate accountability and use of investigational materials provided to human subjects. By law, the investigator is required to maintain adequate records of the accountability and final disposition of the investigational drugs/devices.

Receipt, Handling and Storage of Investigational Materials

Upon receiving investigational materials, the investigator or appropriate staff member (e.g., investigational drug pharmacist) must adhere to the following:

- Verify the contents and integrity of each shipment against the packing slip and what materials were actually ordered.
- If no discrepancies are found, the investigator must acknowledge in writing to the sponsor the receipt of the materials. This is typically accomplished by signing the shipping document enclosed with the investigational materials. The investigator must notify the sponsor immediately if discrepancies are found.
- A copy of this receipt should be in the investigator's study file (or in pharmacy if the drug is received and dispensed there).
- All investigational materials must be stored in a secure (locked) limited access area.
- Additionally, materials must be stored in accordance with the approved storage conditions (i.e., correct temperature, light and humidity).

Accountability Records

Drug or device accountability records (DARs) are used to provide evidence that, at the conclusion of the investigation, all materials are accounted for and that their final disposition is controlled (i.e., the materials are returned to the sponsor or destroyed). DARs (drug/device accountability records) are customized documents tailored to the individual protocol. The following minimum information should be captured on each form:

- Protocol Identification (protocol # and/or title).
- Principal investigator's name.
- Description of test article(s) received including batch or lot numbers.
- Date and time study drug/device dispensed/used.
- Amount dispensed (for drugs).
- Subject identification.
- Signature and/or initials of person dispensing the drug(s)/device(s).
- Amount returned by the subject, if any.
- Principal investigator's signature and date. [Note: The investigator should review, sign, and date the forms at the conclusion of the subject's participation in the trial.]

DARs may be created to track individual subjects enrolled in a trial or, in the case of small trials with single dose dispensing, may be customized to capture all participating subjects. The main objective of the regulations is to require the investigator to maintain adequate records of the disposition of the drug or device.

Drug/Device Returns (Final Disposition)

At the conclusion, discontinuance or termination of the study for both drugs and devices, the investigator is responsible for returning all unused medical devices and drugs to the trial sponsor. Return shipments should include a list of the contents, which must be reconciled with the amounts originally received and the amounts used by the subjects.

Alternatively, after drug/device accountability records are complete, the sponsor may authorize alternative disposition for these materials (destruction by the investigator). Any directive from the sponsor allowing destruction must be in writing before disposal. The investigator will be responsible for assuring that the destruction is carried out, and the investigator must maintain a written record of destruction.

2. Adverse Events

Drug and Biologic Requirements

All clinical investigators are required to report to the sponsor any adverse events that may be caused by the investigational product (the timeline is defined in the study protocol). The investigator is also required to report to the reviewing IRB any injury (harm caused by involvement in research), deaths and unexpected serious adverse experiences.

Device Requirements

The regulations require that investigators prepare and submit complete, accurate and timely reports of unanticipated adverse device effects to the sponsor and to the reviewing IRB as soon as possible, but no later than 10 business days after the investigator learns of the effect.

3. Documentation

Source Documentation

Investigators are required to prepare and maintain adequate and accurate records of all observations and other data pertinent to the study for each subject. Source documentation is where the information is first recorded. These are the original documents, data, and records (including medical records, lab reports and case report forms).

The investigator must maintain primary source documents supporting significant data for each subject in the case history records. These documents, which are considered "source data," should include documentation of the following:

- Demographic information.
- Evidence supporting the diagnosis/condition for which the subject is being studied (i.e., compliance with inclusion criteria).
- General information or medical history demonstrating that the subject meets the inclusion and exclusion criteria.
- Physical findings.

- Hospital records (if appropriate).
- Each study visit by date.
- Relevant findings/notes by the investigator.
- Occurrence (or lack of) adverse events.
- Changes in test article usage.
- Any relevant telephone conversations with the subject.
- Information regarding the subject's exposure to test or control article.
- Documentation that informed consent was obtained for each subject prior to participation in the study.

The investigator must also retain all printouts/test reports/procedures/forms for each subject. Examples include:
- Original, signed and dated consent forms.
- Diagnostic test results, X-rays and laboratory test results.
- Subject diaries or evaluation checklists.
- Clinical and office charts.
- Consultations.
- Drug and device receipt, accountability and return records (DARs).
- Case report forms (CRFs).
- Test instruments.

Investigators also need to maintain the following:
- Copies of all correspondence sent to or received by the study sponsor and the monitor.
- The protocol.
- Protocol amendments.
- Records of IRB communications and study approval.
- Materials used in recruiting subjects (e.g., flyers and advertisements).
- Materials used in obtaining informed consent.
- Investigator brochure.

> **Source documentation is where the information is first recorded, including medical records and case report forms.**

Case Report Forms

These forms are critical study documents. Study results are a summary of the data reported to the sponsor on case report forms (CRFs). The case report form may or may not duplicate all information in the subject's case history. CRFs may be printed or electronic documents. It is important that:
- The content captures data as required by the protocol.
- The investigator ensures the accuracy of the data recorded.

> **It is the responsibility of the investigator to ensure the accuracy of the data recorded on the case report form.**

The ICH GCP guidelines specify that the protocol should identify any data to be recorded directly on the CRF and classify what is considered to be source data. During monitoring visits, the monitor will validate data recorded on the CRF against source data.

Record Retention

Investigators are required to retain all study records in a secure and safe facility with limited access until one of the following time periods:

- At least two years after notification from the sponsor that the drug/device has been approved for the indication that was investigated.
- Or, if not approved for such indication, at least two years after the investigation is completed or discontinued and the FDA has been notified by the sponsor.

> **Investigators are advised to contact the study sponsor before any study records are destroyed to ensure compliance with the regulatory requirements.**

The investigator should notify the sponsor of any change in the location, disposition or custody of the study files and is advised to contact the study sponsor before any study records are destroyed to ensure compliance with the regulatory requirements.

Sponsor–Investigator–Institution Interaction Issues

The interactions between the sponsor, investigator and institution (including the IRB) may be complex. Generally, sponsors and IRBs do not contact each other directly. Instead, communications flow through the site investigator. This serves to keep the investigator aware of any issues and concerns and maintains the investigator's responsibility for the conduct of the study. This also prevents any appearance of pressure by the sponsor on the IRB to approve a study. The FDA does not prohibit direct IRB–sponsor contact, and there are times when this is the most efficient method for resolving issues, e.g., questions about interpretation of sponsor policies.

An IRB is required to notify the investigator in writing of its decision to approve, disapprove or request modification to a research project. The investigator must provide the sponsor with a copy of this correspondence, because the sponsor is also responsible for ensuring that studies are conducted in compliance with informed consent and IRB regulations. Most sponsors will not ship the investigational product before they have all institutional approvals and other required paperwork.

Responsibilities of the Investigator-Sponsor

When there is no company or other organization acting as sponsor, individuals may become a sponsor of a clinical research study by assuming the role and responsibilities of the study sponsor. For clinical investigators, this means that one individual is assuming all the responsibilities of both study sponsor and investigator. The additional tasks of the sponsor include all of the regulatory reporting (FDA) requirements (see below), responsibility for drug manufacture and control issues (including proper labeling of the investigational product), the assessment of safety, ensuring IRB approval prior to shipping clinical supplies to sites, and informing and monitoring all investigators.

The scope of the regulatory filings vary with the intent of the project. If the data being collected are only for publication, the application is generally short. These projects are usually small studies. The FDA reviews these "noncommercial INDs" mainly for safety concerns.

For commercial development projects, the initial application is generally longer and more detailed. Detailed manufacturing information is required at each step, but especially as the project moves toward the larger efficacy trials (phase 3). All protocols must be submitted for FDA and IRB review prior to study initiation. The FDA reviews these applications for both subject safety and for the ability to satisfy the statutory requirement for efficacy.

Original Application

The investigator-sponsor is responsible for filing adequate information in the initial IND or IDE application to allow the FDA to make a decision on whether the study risks are acceptable. The investigator-sponsor is required to wait 30 days for FDA review prior to enrolling subjects in the study. If insufficient information is filed, the FDA may place a clinical hold on the application. If no notice is received within that 30-day period that indicates that the FDA has no concerns with the application, the IND or IDE is considered to be approved. It is advisable, however, to call the FDA to confirm that they do not have any issues or concerns with the application. Absolutely no subjects are to be enrolled in the study until the FDA has removed all holds on an application. If the FDA denies the application, then the project may not be initiated. It is possible to re-apply to the FDA for the same project, if modified to be acceptable to the FDA.

Amendments to Documentation

Any new clinical study protocol must be submitted under the IND/IDE prior to study initiation. This is true for changes to any other information within an application that has an impact on subject safety. These can be filed at any time, but before any human subjects are exposed. Minor changes that do not impact human subject safety may be submitted in the annual report.

IND Safety Reports

Investigator-sponsors are required to notify the FDA and all participating investigators in writing of any adverse experience that is serious, related (associated) and unexpected. This information may be submitted in a narrative format or on the FDA Form 3500A (the MedWatch form also used to report post-marketing adverse event information). The investigator-sponsor must also determine if any safety reports had previously been filed that are similar to each new reportable event. The significance of the new report must be analyzed with regard to previous, similar reports. The report must be clearly marked "IND Safety Report" and must be filed with the FDA no more than 15 calendar days after the investigator-sponsor initially receives the information. These reports are sent directly to the division of the FDA responsible for reviewing the IND.

The investigator-sponsor is to notify the FDA by telephone of any unexpected, fatal or life-threatening experience associated with the use of a drug in clinical studies conducted under the IND, within seven calendar days after receiving the information. For this purpose only, the FDA defines life-threatening as the subject being at immediate risk of death from the reaction.

> **Serious, related, unexpected adverse experiences must be promptly reported to FDA.**

Note that sponsors of INDs for marketed drugs are NOT required to report adverse events associated with the use of the drug that occur outside of the studies conducted under their INDs (i.e., literature reports and events reported during patient care are not reportable to the IND). However, if such information affects the perceived risks to the subjects in the clinical trials, the information needs to be shared with the investigators and their respective IRBs.

Definitions: The FDA provides the following definitions for reporting adverse events:

- Associated with the use of the drug: There is a reasonable possibility that the experience may have been caused by the drug.
- Disability: A substantial disruption of a person's ability to conduct normal life functions.
- Life-threatening adverse drug experience: Any adverse drug experience that places the subject, in the view of the investigator, at immediate risk of death from the reaction as it occurred, i.e., it does not include a reaction, had it occurred in a more severe form, which might have caused death.
- Unexpected adverse drug experience: Any adverse experience, the specificity or severity of which is not consistent with the current investigator brochure or package insert or not consistent with the risk information described in the general investigational plan or elsewhere in the current application.

- Serious adverse drug experience: Any adverse drug experience occurring at any dose that results in any of the following outcomes:
  - Death.
  - A life-threatening adverse experience.
  - Hospitalization or prolongation of existing hospitalization.
  - A persistent or significant disability/incapacity.
  - Or a congenital anomaly or birth defect.

Important medical events that may not result in death, be life threatening or require hospitalization may be considered serious adverse drug experiences when, based upon medical judgment, they jeopardize the subject and may require medical or surgical intervention to prevent one of the outcomes listed in this definition. [Note: Data from animal studies are also reportable as IND Safety Reports if any serious adverse drug experience is observed that suggests a significant risk for human subjects, including any finding of mutagenicity, teratogenicity or carcinogenicity.]

Unanticipated Adverse Device Effect Reports
The reporting requirements for adverse device effects are different from those for drugs and biologics. The investigator-sponsor must immediately conduct an evaluation of any unanticipated adverse device effect. If this effect presents an unreasonable risk to subjects, the investigator-sponsor is required to terminate all investigations as soon as possible, but no later than five working days after the sponsor makes this determination. This also must occur within 15 working days of when the investigator-sponsor was notified for the adverse effect.

Both the FDA and the IRB must be informed of unanticipated adverse device effects. Any terminated study must NOT be resumed without approval of both the FDA and the reviewing IRB.

Annual Reports
An annual report from the sponsor to the FDA is required for both INDs and IDEs. It is due no later than 60 calendar days after the anniversary date of an application going into effect.

The format for the annual report is provided in regulatory guidance documents. Critical components of these reports include:

- Protocol summaries, for ongoing and completed studies, to document the total human exposure under the application.
- All changes made to protocols or manufacturing information. This is the mechanism to report minor changes that occurred during the year that were not subject to amendments.
- New pre-clinical (animal) and clinical (human) information. Any impact on human subject safety should be addressed.
- Changes to the investigational plan for the coming year.
- Any information that was requested from the FDA but not received should also be documented.

Final Study Reports

The regulations require that a final report be written and submitted for all clinical studies. This report should be submitted within six months of study completion.

Withdrawal of Application

Upon completion of studies, when no additional work is envisioned, the investigator-sponsor should send a letter to the FDA requesting withdrawal of the IND/IDE.

Additional Issues to Consider for Investigator-Sponsors

IRB Approval at Study Sites

A copy of the IRB approval letter should be obtained from each study site prior to the shipment of any investigational materials. For device studies, the determination of significant versus non-significant risk should be documented. Verbal assurance of submission to an IRB should not be considered adequate.

Liability Concerns

For industry-sponsored studies, the company, the institution and the investigator share responsibility for study-related injury to study subjects. For investigator-sponsored studies, the liability for research-related injury lies completely with the investigator and the associated institution.

Conflict of Interest

There may be a conflict of interest for investigator-sponsors, especially where financial or career enhancement benefits exist with a project. Documentation of all financial compensation is required by the FDA prior to approving products for market.

Contracts

Investigator-sponsors must have all contracts related to the conduct of research reviewed and approved by the appropriate institutional office.

Clinical Supplies

Obtaining appropriate clinical supplies for research is the responsibility of the study sponsor. Manufacturing issues are of concern to the FDA when reviewing non-commercial or commercial applications. When pharmaceutical-grade material is not available, documentation of product identity, purity and lack of contamination is generally required. This usually involves testing of each batch of clinical supplies by a qualified laboratory.

CHAPTER

Behavioral Research Issues

At the conclusion of this chapter, readers will be able to:
- Describe the potential risks associated with behavioral research.
- Discuss privacy and confidentiality issues.
- Explain the issues around deception.

Introduction

When people think of research, especially research risk, often they think only of medical research. This is due to the fact that much of the focus on research and research ethics has been on the dangers posed by biomedical research and the harms caused by the transgressions of researchers in that field. However, research with drugs, devices and other medical procedures is only a part of the total research endeavor. Many studies are also conducted in human behavior, social science, education, anthropology, epidemiology and similar areas. For brevity, these will be subsumed here under the broad label "behavioral research." The following issues are also important for bio-medical researchers as many of the concerns may be present to some extent in those studies as well.

Federal Regulations

The federal regulations governing research have included behavioral research from the start. In recognition that these studies often present only slight risks, the regulations allow some activities to be exempt from regulation and others to be given a brief review. This does not imply a lesser ethical standard for these studies, but rather an increased reliance on the investigator to conduct the study within appropriate ethical and scientific bounds. Investigators who believe their research is exempt should check with the IRB to verify that an exemption applies. Exemptions may be granted for some studies in the following categories:

- Activities that use research methods, but are not "research" according to federal definitions (e.g., quality assurance studies and in-house program evaluations).
- Research that does not involve "human subjects."
- Educational research conducted in normal educational settings.
- Survey/interview/observational research with adult subjects.
- Secondary use of de-identified pre-existing data.
- Evaluation of public benefit or service programs.
- Taste and food quality studies.

Psychological/Social Risks

Because there often is no physical intervention, these studies do not generally pose a risk to physical well-being, but they do carry risks of their own. The main points of concern are with other types of potential harms such as psychological, social, economic and legal. These risks may be as harmful as any risk faced by a subject in a medical study. Humans are by nature introspective, and reflecting upon the actions we have or have not taken may cause us emotional pain. While taking a course of action based upon wrong or incomplete information may make it easier to rationalize that action, discovering that we are capable of violating societal and/or our own standards can be psychologically damaging, as in the Milgram study.

Psychological hazards run from temporary anxiety and distress to relapse and precipitation of behavioral disorders. Social harms include both direct personal impact such as embarrassment, ostracism, stigmatization and loss of status as well as similar effects upon the subject's family and community. Risks in the economic area include job loss and decreased employability. Legal risks include arrest, prosecution and civil or criminal liability.

Exposure to risks of biomedical research are typically faced only by the individual. In behavioral research, however, the range of non-physical risks above may have an impact on others including families, social groups, communities, ethnic populations and even entire societies. Prevailing community attitudes are an important consideration in the acceptability of behavioral research. Likewise, the investigator must be responsible in the use and publication of research findings.

Therefore, in assessing the risks presented by a study, investigators, IRBs and subjects must consider a wide range of potential harms. Investigators should anticipate potential problem areas and design the study to provide an adequate level of protection. The traditional risk/benefit balance is also somewhat changed as the benefits rarely accrue to the individual subject, but rather to science and/or society.

Deception

Deception in research is intentionally misleading subjects or withholding full information about the nature of the experiment. Deception may take the form of covert observation or not fully informing the subject when obtaining consent. Intentionally misleading or omitted information might include the purpose of the research, the role of the investigator or what procedures are actually experimental. Deception interferes with the subject's ability to give informed consent. As such, it can be thought of as a wrong in itself, as a limiting influence on the protection afforded by informed consent and a violation of the norms of trust and truthfulness. Ethical concerns are increased whenever the protection of informed consent is compromised in any way because the research subjects are deprived of the opportunity to protect their own interests.

For certain types of behavioral inquiry, deception is arguably necessary because humans act differently depending on circumstances, and the subject's full knowledge would thus bias the results. Federal regulations (Common Rule) permit, but establish limitations on, the use of deception. Use of deception must be scientifically and ethically justified and approved by an IRB. In cases where the study can only be conducted with subjects who are less than fully informed, the missing information should not increase the risks of the study. After the experiment is conducted, subjects should be fully debriefed. This can be a formal process that includes assessment of the subject's reaction to the deception, or an informal discussion. In any event, subjects must have the opportunity to ask questions about the new information and be given the opportunity to withdraw from the study and have their data removed as well. It is not permissible to use deception just to obtain enrollments.

Vulnerable Subjects

People are autonomous when they can deliberate personal goals and then act accordingly. The capacity for self-determination increases with maturity.

Individuals may lose this capacity because of physical illness, mental disability or while under circumstances that severely restrict liberty. The regulations define as "vulnerable populations" those groups that may contain some individuals who have limited autonomy, i.e., they cannot give informed consent. Such groups include children, some mentally incapacitated, individuals with dementia and other cognitive disorders and prisoners. Many institutions have also included the elderly, students and employees in the definition of vulnerable populations deserving special consideration by investigators and IRBs. The regulations require that IRBs treat pregnant women as a vulnerable population because of the need to avoid unnecessary risk to the fetus and because of the additional health concerns during pregnancy. Additional protections when conducting research with these populations may include the use of witnesses, requiring consultants/advocates, formally renewing consent at specified stages and limiting the scope of research projects.

Privacy and Confidentiality

Two areas that generally create more concern for behavioral research than for biomedical studies are confidentiality and privacy. In fact, these concerns are often the central considerations for behavioral research. Privacy is the right of persons not to share information about themselves. Confidentiality is the obligation to keep private information that has been collected from being shared with others.

A major tenet in the protection of human subjects is that persons can be wronged even if they are not harmed. This philosophy focuses upon rights, both individual and societal. We have a right to expect that our private actions will remain private and that information others have about us will be kept confidential and only used for their original purposes (e.g., medical care or college admission). A related concern that will not be addressed here is the public debate about the appropriateness of scientific inquiry into areas considered by society to be private (e.g., sex practices and drug use). These are of concern because the results of social research can impact the core values and the support programs of society at large.

> **A major tenet in the protection of human subjects is that persons can be wronged even if they are not harmed.**

Privacy is itself a form of personal protection. So, a violation of an individual's privacy not only is a harm itself but also may cause the loss of this protective barrier. Risks include public exposure, perceived loss of control of person and a sense of insecurity. Breaches of privacy also erode trust on all levels. Breaches of privacy (e.g., "How did you get my name?") cause some of the angriest responses by subjects and the public to research and researchers.

These are concerns for behavioral studies that observe otherwise private behaviors or obtain private confidential information. Investigators must design studies to maximize data confidentiality to avoid unintentional release or other disclosures. Investigators can avoid violations of privacy, for example, by removing identifiers or using anonymous data. Certificates of Confidentiality may be obtained from DHHS to protect study data from involuntary disclosure through subpoena.

Certificates of Confidentiality

A Certificate of Confidentiality is an important mechanism to protect the privacy of research study participants. Certificates of Confidentiality are issued by the National Institutes of Health (NIH) to protect the privacy of research subjects by protecting investigators and institutions from being compelled to release information (i.e., forced disclosure) that could be used to identify subjects in a research project. They allow the investigator to refuse to disclose identifying information on research participants in any civil, criminal, administrative, legislative or other proceeding, whether at the federal, state, or local level. Researchers are not prevented from the voluntary disclosure of matters such as child abuse, reportable communicable diseases or a subject's threatened violence to self or others; however, the consent form must say if the researcher intends to make any voluntary disclosures.

Certificates of Confidentiality are issued for biomedical, behavioral or other types of research that collect information that, if disclosed, could have adverse consequences for subjects or damage their financial standing, employability, insurability or reputation (i.e., "sensitive" information) or could involve them in criminal or civil litigation. Examples of sensitive information include:

- Genetic information.
- Information on psychological well-being of subjects.
- Information on subjects' sexual attitudes, preferences or practices.
- Data on substance abuse or other illegal behaviors.

Some projects are not eligible for a Certificate of Confidentiality, including activities that are:

- Not research.
- Not collecting personally identifiable information.
- Not reviewed and approved by an IRB.
- Collecting information that if disclosed would not significantly harm or damage the participant.

Further information is available on the NIH web site at:
http://grants1.nih.gov/grants/policy/coc/index.htm.

Study Methods

The diversity in research topics and the research methods appropriate to those studies are unique features in the field of behavioral research. Study methods used include surveys, interviews, questionnaires, record reviews, observation (participatory, overt or covert) and various psychological and social interventions in laboratory and field settings, to mention a few. Each method itself presents ethical and scientific considerations.

> **Every research method presents unique ethical and scientific considerations.**

Laboratory and field experimentation may have no concerns in the areas of privacy and confidentiality but may involve consent issues and the full range of research risks. Survey and interview research may be just the reverse, that is, no concerns regarding consent but possible confidentiality concerns. Record reviews may raise both consent and privacy issues. Thus, investigators must design studies with an eye to minimizing the negative effects of the study's methods themselves.

Quality of Life Issues

Although not a "behavioral" issue in the strict sense, investigators should be aware of the possible effects of studies on the daily life of subjects. The demands of participation in studies can seriously disrupt the flow of normal activities. Side effects and even successful outcome of studies may lead to a decrease in the quality of life (e.g., by prolonging pain and suffering). As indicated above, even surveys can potentially cause psychological stress that may lead to long-term disabilities and a decline in aspects of lifestyle. Investigators need to design studies that take into consideration quality of life issues and they need to ensure that potential subjects understand the potential impacts on their personal lifestyle.

Points to Consider

When designing and conducting behavioral and social science research, investigators should consider the following items:
- Minimize the potential for stress, discomfort and other harms.
- Use deception only when absolutely necessary (i.e., scientifically and ethically justified) and then follow with complete debriefing.
- Search for alternatives to deception.
- Respect subjects' privacy and minimize intrusion.

- Design mechanisms to protect confidentiality of research data.
- Guard against factors leading to undue influence.
- Provide adequate safeguards when studying vulnerable populations.

Publication of Study Results

At the conclusion of this chapter, readers will be able to:
- Explain why investigators, administrators, hospitals, universities and organization sponsors may have different expectations for publishing and presenting data.
- Discuss the implications of publishing study results for the investigator, the sponsor, other researchers, hospitals, universities and the public.
- Identify and minimize potential areas of conflict before starting the study.

Introduction

Surveys show that professionals at the graduate and post-graduate levels receive most of their new knowledge by reading, especially the current peer-reviewed periodicals. Thus, it is important that research be published in a timely manner, in an appropriate venue and that data be presented accurately and clearly. Most of the time, this is the case. However, scientific publication is not immune to fraud and misconduct.

In his book, *Stealing into Print* (1992), Marcel Lafollette defines fraud in scientific communication as "…when an author, editor or referee makes a false representation to obtain some unfair advantage or to injure deliberately the rights or interests of another person or group." This may include any of the following:

- Presenting data that do not exist or have been "made up."
- Misrepresenting or deliberately altering evidence.
- Plagiarism.
- Misrepresentation of authorship.
- Unreasonably delaying review or publication for personal gain.

The underlying reasons for such actions may be personal (i.e., fame, career advancement, institutional pressure to publish) or financial (i.e., monetary gain, investment options, competitive advantage in the market). Another reason is the conflict of interest that may occur between the investigator and the source of funding for the research. This type of conflict directly challenges the accountability and independence of the investigator and can create considerable tension between the investigator, the sponsor and the institution where the research is being done. This chapter reviews some of the key issues for scientific publication related to conflicts of interest between sponsor and investigator.

> **Professionals receive most of their new knowledge by reading, especially the current peer-reviewed periodicals. Research results should be published in a timely manner and in an appropriate venue.**

Examples of fraud in scientific publication can be found in all fields—from archaeology and psychology to engineering and medicine. However, in terms of press coverage, it is misconduct within the biomedical arena that receives the most attention. This probably relates to two factors: (1) there is greater public awareness and interest in matters of health; and (2) more sponsored funding is available from government agencies and from the pharmaceutical and biotechnology industries. Thus, the cases presented in this chapter focus on biomedical research, specifically research sponsored by industry. However, the issues and principles illustrated are not unique to medicine or biology but are applicable to any type of academic research funded by an outside source.

There are no federal regulations governing the dissemination of research results. However, at least one government agency, the Food and Drug Administration (FDA), has published guidelines addressing the dissemination of industry-sponsored research. The FDA does not object to a company providing financial support to an investigator to present data or to publish a manuscript but notes that there may be questions regarding the circumstances that may occur in such an arrangement. For example, there may be questions regarding independence: Will the investigator-author actually write the article or will the sponsor provide assistance in the way of a medical writer? If the latter, how much input will the investigator actually have? There also may be issues around the timing of the publication: Could the sponsor try to delay (or, in extreme cases, even stop) publication of the data if they are not "acceptable" to them? The answers to these questions are not always as straightforward as they might seem. Two cases can serve as illustrations.

> **FDA concerns about publishing industry-sponsored studies most frequently focus on independence and how the sponsor may affect independence.**

Case One: B. Dong v. Boots Pharmaceuticals

In the April 16, 1997, issue of the *Journal of the American Medical Association* (JAMA), Dong et al. (University of California at San Francisco) reported a study of the bioequivalence of generic and branded levothyroxine products in the treatment of hypothyroidism. Two generic products (Geneva Generics, Rugby) were compared with two brand-name medications (Synthroid, Boots Pharmaceuticals [now Knoll Pharmaceuticals]; Levoxine [now Levoxyl], Daniels Pharmaceuticals, Inc. [now Jones Medical Industries]) using current FDA criteria for bioequivalence. The study was funded, in part, by Flint Laboratories (which was taken over by Boots Pharmaceuticals during the course of the study), the manufacturers of Synthroid. As is usual for this type of sponsorship, Dr. Betty Dong signed a contract with Flint Laboratories. Company representatives made regular site visits, and copies of the data were sent to the manufacturer.

Preliminary analysis of the data indicated that all four medications were bioequivalent according to the FDA standards for oral preparations, thereby implying that the products were clinically interchangeable. In reviewing the results, the investigators calculated that if the generics or the other brand-name preparation were substituted for Synthroid, $356 million might be saved annually. These results were obtained in 1990, yet the published report did not appear until 1997. What happened between 1990 and 1997 that delayed publication?

Obviously, the sponsor and the investigators had conflicting views about publication of the results. The investigators believed that the results had important clinical implications and should be shared with the medical and academic community. The sponsor, on the other hand, was concerned that the results would increase market share for the generic products at the expense of the brand-name product. In this case, the sponsor attempted to prevent publication. The company complained to administrators at UCSF that procedures were not carried out as detailed in the protocol, and they suggested that the results were flawed due to problems with patient selection, compliance, assay reliability and statistical analysis. UCSF responded to the complaints with an internal investigation that revealed no major problems with the study. They concluded that the study was rigorously conducted in a way that complied fully with the contract, and they supported publication. Responding to the company after almost four years of review, UCSF noted that all data had been open to the sponsor and that the sponsor had monitored the study closely. Thus, the university concluded that there was no reason to suppress the manuscript, and that to do so would be "an unprecedented intrusion upon academic freedom."

Suppressing publication of study results can be viewed as an intrusion upon academic freedom. However, industry sponsors may have other concerns (e.g. patent infringement, commercial interests, liability issues).

Dr. Dong submitted the manuscript to JAMA in April 1994, along with a letter disclosing the funding of the study and the criticism from the sponsor. Publication was originally intended for early 1995, when Dr. Dong abruptly withdrew the manuscript from the journal due to "impending legal action by Boots Pharmaceutical, Inc. against UCSF and the investigators." The basis for the legal action was the following contract clause: "All information contained in this protocol is confidential and is to be used by the investigator only for the conduct of this study. Data obtained by the investigator while carrying out this study is also considered confidential and is not to be published or otherwise released without written consent from Flint Laboratories, Inc." UCSF did not have this permission, and a University attorney indicated that the authors could not be defended if a suit ensued.

Interestingly, the University of California, like most universities in the United States, prohibits restrictions on publishing rights. In fact, the UCSF contract of employment (signed by Dr. Dong) stated that "...the University will undertake research or studies only if the scientific results can be published or otherwise promptly disseminated." So, how did this happen? The fact is that protocol contracts with pharmaceutical sponsors often contain restrictive clauses, yet rarely have they prevented publication. Dr. Dong and her colleagues believed that these contracts, regardless of content, could not prevent publication.

Protocol contracts with industry sponsors may contain restrictive clauses. Pay attention to confidentiality clauses that prohibit publication without permission from the sponsor.

The issue came to the attention of the public on April 25, 1996, when an article appeared in the *Wall Street Journal*. In the article, Carter Eckert, president, Boots Pharmaceuticals, was quoted as saying, "I stopped a flawed study that would have put millions of patients at risk." Additionally, in 1994, Boots, now Knoll, had received a letter from the FDA stating that a manuscript published by company researchers in 1992 was misleading, and that dissemination of the article by the company should cease. The conclusions of this paper opposed those of Dr. Dong, namely that in normal volunteers studied over 48 hours, the bioavailability of Synthroid was superior to Levoxine. The FDA commented that the study design was not appropriate for comparing bioequivalence, noting specifically that "...a more complex design involving chronic administration in a well-controlled, hypothyroid population with the measurement of several endpoints would be required" (precisely the protocol used by Dong and her colleagues). In their response to the FDA, Knoll referred to the work by Dr. Dong, but dismissed it as "worthless." However, the FDA took exception, writing that the Dong study was appropriate to test bioequivalence and cited Knoll for not previously disclosing the Dong results.

Under pressure from the FDA and scrutiny from the public, Knoll ultimately agreed to publication of the manuscript. JAMA published the paper along with letters from Knoll apologizing for the delay and objecting to the findings. Rebuttals from the investigator/authors were also published. The cost calculations were included in the discussion. The accompanying comments of the journal editors are of particular interest:

We do not claim that we are publishing a perfect study, just one of the best, made as good as expert review can make it. Experience has taught us that there are very few studies in which some reviewers cannot find flaws…it is our belief that this is a good study carried out by highly competent workers following a sensible design that tried to answer an important question. It is hard to believe that the sponsors would have made such extraordinary efforts to delay and block publication of the study for such a very long time and for such an extraordinary number of specious reasons if the results had shown Synthroid to be better.

Case Two: D. Kern v. Microfibres, Inc.

The second case involves a physician/investigator who investigated the outbreak of an occupational disease at an industrial facility. The physician/investigator in this case was Dr. David Kern, an associate professor at Brown University School of Medicine and chief of general internal medicine, director of occupational and environmental health service (OEHS) at the Memorial Hospital of Rhode Island since 1986. In his latter role, Dr. Kern provided consultancy services, as needed, to local industry and agencies regarding occupational and environmental health hazards.

In 1994, a worker at a local textile plant, Microfibres, Inc. (Pawtucket, R.I.) developed worsening shortness of breath, apparently due to interstitial lung disease (ILD). Dr. Kern visited the plant with several medical students in part to fulfill his commitment to the medical school to arrange for industrial site visits for medical students every six weeks. At the door of the plant, company officials asked Dr. Kern and the students to sign an agreement in which they promised not to reveal trade secrets. On this visit, Dr. Kern and the students found nothing at the plant that was clearly responsible for the patient's symptoms.

In early 1996, Dr. Kern learned of another worker at the plant with ILD. At that point, Dr. Kern notified the company and the National Institute for Occupational Health and Safety (NIOSH). Finding that there had been a similar "outbreak" of ILD cases at the company's Canadian facility in 1990, Dr. Kern approached company officials, offering his services as a consultant to study the ILD outbreaks. The company agreed. According to Dr. Kern, at that time the company did not bring up the agreement about trade secrets that he had signed in 1994. Moreover, the company declined to sign a contract covering the new investigation, although it eventually paid the hospital more than $100,000 for Dr. Kern's services. Dr. Kern's ensuing investigation identified another six "work-related" cases of ILD among 150 employees.

Late in 1996, Dr. Kern prepared an abstract of his findings for submission to the 1997 annual meeting of the American Thoracic Society (ATS). Prior to submission, Dr. Kern shared copies of a draft of the abstract with both company and hospital officials. Microfibres asked that the draft not be submitted because it contained information about chemicals it used in manufacturing that it considered proprietary, stating that publication of this information would violate the agreement regarding trade secrets that Kern had signed in 1994. Dr. Kern revised the abstract to make it difficult for readers to identify the company, but the company still forbade publication. Kern notified administrators at both the hospital and the medical school.

> **Sponsors and investigators may have conflicting perspectives on what constitutes a "trade secret." Open communication BEFORE signing agreements is important.**

Lawyers and administrators at Memorial Hospital of Rhode Island, Kern's employer, expressed concern that Microfibres might sue the hospital. One university official suggested that he should not publish, and another suggested that doing so would breach Kern's contract with Microfibres. Nevertheless, Kern submitted his abstract. A week later, hospital officials informed him that his contract would not be renewed, and the occupational medicine program that he directed would be disbanded. In May 1997, Dr. Kern presented the data in a poster session at the ATS meeting.

University administrators defended the hospital's action because Dr. Kern failed to protect himself from pressure from Microfibres and failed to get written assurance that the company would not interfere with his right to publish his results.

Dr. Kern received support from the Rhode Island Medical Society, the Association of Occupational and Environmental Clinics, local physicians, public health advocates and several well-known occupational physicians. In particular, specialists in occupational medicine and environmental science challenged the idea that the trade secret protection agreement that Dr. Kern had signed in 1994, a year before he had begun the investigation of the ILD outbreak at the hospital, had any bearing on his rights to publish the results of this investigation.

Dr. Kern's description of a case series of what is now called flock worker's lung was published in the *Annals of Internal Medicine*. It was accompanied by an editorial that described Dr. Kern's saga as "at best, ... a story of incorrect assumptions and mutual misunderstandings by well-intentioned persons on all sides, starting early in the investigation and leading, over time, to a self-reinforcing downward spiral of further misunderstandings and deepening mistrust. At worst, it is a story of narrow self-interest getting in the way of public disclosure, responsibility to patients, and academic freedom." Since then, more cases of the disease have been reported. Microfibres never filed a lawsuit against any of the involved parties. Dr. Kern left academic medicine and occupational health for a private general internal medicine practice.

Withholding Data

Withholding or delaying the publication or presentation of research results is defined as not publishing or presenting the data for at least six months after completion of the study. It is not only the sponsor who may attempt to delay the dissemination of research data. In fact, when data are withheld, it is most often the investigator who has chosen to do so. This was one of the conclusions of a survey of 3,394 life science faculty in fifty universities in the United States. The universities were identified according to the amount of NIH funding received in 1993: the top fifty were included in the survey.

Approximately 20% of 2,100 researchers who responded to the survey indicated that they had delayed the publication of study results in the past. The majority of the researchers had delayed publication in order to protect the commercial value of the data: 46% cited the time for patent application as a reason; another 33% cited other proprietary and/or financial value of the data; and 26% had delayed publication due to the time needed for licensing. Other common reasons given were to protect their own scientific lead, reported by 46% of the researchers (and often attributed to increased competition for funding), and to delay the publication of "undesirable" results, reported by 28% of the researchers surveyed.

Only 4% of the researchers reported that dissemination of study results had been delayed due to any formal agreement with an industry sponsor. Other reasons included avoiding potential liability issues.

The reasons given by investigators for withholding or delaying the dissemination of data are very similar to the reasons given by companies. However, in addition, a company may delay publication in order to avoid artificial inflation of stock or to wait for FDA approval of a new product or new indication so that claims of efficacy and safety can be made appropriately.

Lessons to Be Learned from These Cases

These two cases provide classic illustrations of the tensions that can develop among industry sponsors, investigators, hospitals and universities about disseminating research results, particulary when those results are in some sense undesirable to one of the parties involved.

> **Tension between investigators and industry may occur due to:**
> ■ **Different interpretations of contractual text.**
> ■ **Different expectations of what will happen to the data.**

The Research Contract

The dispute described in the first case could have been avoided if the investigator/consultant had carefully read the contract and asked for clarification of key points. The dispute described in the second case possibly could have been avoided if the researcher had not commenced the research in the absence of a contract that specifically protected his rights. Some take-away messages that may be important for investigators/consultants are:

■ Before signing any contract, make sure that you have the authority to do so for your institution, and if not, arrange for the appropriate person to deal with the contract.

■ Read the contract! Know exactly what you are signing. Do not sign any contract without expert advice.

■ Obtain the proper institutional reviews/approvals of the grant/contract prior to signing it.

■ Ask the sponsor questions. Do not assume that your interpretation of "trade secret," "proprietary information" or "confidential information" matches that of the sponsor. Ask the sponsor to define these terms explicitly. If your interpretation and the sponsor's interpretation differ, then there should be an open discussion. Most industry sponsors are very open to these types of discussions and negotiations. If the sponsor is not willing to negotiate, get assistance with (or avoid) the agreement.

Even if you and the sponsor are in verbal agreement, do not assume that any agreement that is not written is enforceable. Therefore, make sure any verbal understandings are fully reflected in the written contract.

■ Know your rights. This means knowing your institution's policies. What is the perspective of the institution regarding industry sponsors? How vigorously is the university prepared to defend the academic freedom of its faculty, and/or the hospital prepared to defend the academic freedom of its employee investigators, if at all? If a lawsuit ensues between you and the sponsor, will the institution defend you? Are there any situations in which the institution may not legally be able to defend you?

■ Before signing any agreement, review your employment contract. Specifically, look for any terms that negate points included in the company agreement.

■ Recognize the different concerns of all parties involved—yourself, your colleagues who may be working with you on the project, your institution and the sponsor.

- Remember that if you sign a contract without carefully reviewing it, you may be signing away certain rights.

Three steps to prevent contract conflicts:
- **Read the contract. Know exactly what you are signing.**
- **Ask questions. Clarify all issues and terminology.**
- **Know your rights.**

The Data

It is important to clarify what data are and who controls the data. Different academic institutions have different definitions of what data are, for legal reasons.

All contracts must be approved by the institution before you sign them.

Research data may be created through programs funded by external sponsors (e.g., government agencies, industry, private foundations). However, regardless of the funding, it is the institution that usually holds title to, or "owns," the data produced. The "creator(s)" of the data (i.e., the investigators) and the sponsors of the research retain rights to access and use of the data. To avoid situations such as those faced by Dr. Dong and her colleagues, know how your institution defines data and what the institution's perspective is regarding publication and presentation.

- Read the contract carefully, particularly terms that affect the publication and dissemination of the study results. Do not sign until any issues that you have are addressed by the institution and the sponsor.
- Do not assume that sponsors will encourage (or even permit) publication of unfavorable results, unless agreed to in the contract.
- Do not allow sponsors veto power for publication or presentation of data.
- Know the position of your institution regarding restrictive clauses in relation to the publication and dissemination of data.
- Do not assume that your institution will defend your academic freedom and/or your right to publish in all situations.
- Ask questions about the intentions of the sponsor with regard to publication and dissemination of the results. Consider asking the following questions:
  - Will these data be published? Will they be published if they are equivocal or negative?
  - Who will write the publication?
  - What other studies has the sponsor recently completed? Were the data published? If so, where and how long after the study was conducted?

- When will the data be published?
- Will the publication be limited by any concerns regarding potential claims and fair balance?
- Are there financial or commercial interests at stake in the results? Will publication of the data have potential impact on these interests?
- Be honest about your expectations regarding the presentation and publication of study results.

Sponsors come to researchers at academic institutions in order to establish mutually beneficial and cooperative relationships. They are attracted by an institution's reputation, credibility and prestige. Therefore, it is in the long-term interest of academic institutions to maintain their reputations by being vigorously pro-active in preserving academic freedom.

Most sponsors also should know that academic investigators need to report study results, and that there is a high premium placed on publication. Sponsors should recognize that results may or may not support the initial hypothesis, and that researchers need to present and publish studies in a timely manner.

The investigator/consultant needs to recognize that the sponsor may have legitimate concerns regarding the timing of releasing data to publication: e.g., they may be awaiting FDA approval; there may be potential liability issues; publication might artificially inflate the stock price. Open discussion of the concerns of all parties before an agreement is signed will prevent situations that compromise the credibility of either.

Finally, conflict of interest in the scientific publication of sponsored research is not limited to industry funding. There are published reports of similar cases involving professional societies and government agencies. A well-known example is the restrictions placed by the federal government on publishing data that might impact national security. The conflict arises when the definition of national security and perceptions of "impacting data" are not clearly communicated. Again, open and clear discussion between the sponsor, the researcher and the institution prior to signing an agreement will reduce the likelihood of potential disputes.

Conflicts of Interest in Research

At the conclusion of this chapter, readers will be able to:

- Discuss why various types of conflicts of interest are ethically problematic in human subjects research.
- Recognize the situations that may contribute to conflicts of interest.
- Describe the various strategies for handling conflicts of interest.

Introduction

Since the death of Jesse Gelsinger in 1999, no other issue in research ethics has received such sustained and focused attention from federal, academic and professional institutions as the issue of conflict of interest in clinical research. As of this writing, the Office for Human Research Protection (OHRP), the Association of American Universities (AAU), the Association of American Medical Colleges (AAMC), the National Institutes of Health (NIH), associations of academic journal editors and the General Accounting Office (GAO) have all issued some type of a statement on the issue. While Gelsinger's tragic death may have triggered these reports, it should not be surprising that an enterprise—in this case, our society's clinical research apparatus—that has become a multibillion-dollar activity is in need of further external regulation and/or public scrutiny.

The public's perception of academia (and of academics) as driven by an altruistic societal mission may be lagging behind the current reality. In part, this is because investing great trust in researchers and their institutions has been increasingly questioned. Academia is evolving into an uneasy but willing partnership with profit-conscious, if not profit-driven, companies in the exploration of science and the development of products and technology. This intensifying scrutiny of conflict of interest may lead to an increasingly complex and changing set of rules for investigators to follow. Because mere compliance with the letter of the rules often falls short of meeting the proper ethical standards, this chapter will focus on enduring principles rather than on specific rules that are bound to change.

Financial Conflict of Interest

There are many sources of conflict of interest for an investigator, including conflicts of commitment. A common remark in surveys of study subjects is that they would have liked to have seen the investigator more. Conflicts of commitment are not resolved by disclosure. Instead, avoidance and elimination are the most effective management techniques. Researchers should ensure that they have sufficient time and interest to safely and properly conduct the study.

Money is a potent behavioral incentive, and there is no scientific reason to think that researchers' motivational structures are different from those of most people. Further, the scale of such an incentive present in medical research today is a relatively new phenomenon. Other sources of potential conflict (e.g., personal fame, ambition, even the proverbial "thirst for knowledge") may already be factored into the public's perception of researchers. Of course, there is nothing intrinsically wrong with for-profit science. The question is whether the business of science should be exempted from the usual external regulations that other businesses tend to have. This chapter focuses on financial conflict of interest, recognizing that the discussion and ethical principles should be applicable to other domains of conflict of interest.

> **In addition to financial incentives, personal fame and ambition can be sources of conflict of interest.**

Subject Safety, Scientific Integrity, and Academic Mission are Threatened by Conflict of Interest

Research cannot occur without the generosity and willingness of both healthy and ill human volunteers. Because research, by definition, limits individualized treatment, every volunteer is making some sacrifice by participating in a research protocol. As a society, we allow this to occur because the knowledge to be gained is deemed to outweigh the sacrifice. Conflicts of interest on the part of investigators and institutions cut to the core of this socially sanctioned risk-benefit compromise in two important ways: (1) subjects' safety may be compromised and/or (2) the "knowledge" produced may be biased to serve the interests of the few rather than those of society. This latter problem could have tremendous long-term adverse effects. Conflict of interest may affect the academic mission, such as compromising the career of a student or a fellow investigator who may have difficulty publishing or disseminating scientific work if there are contractual constraints on the project for business reasons.

> **An investigator's motivation for conducting a clinical study can affect subject safety.**

Current Regulatory Framework is Thin and Concerns Only Data Integrity

There is tremendous ferment regarding the need for additional oversight procedures and mechanisms, partly because the current regulatory framework is so slim. There are no federal requirements on managing or disclosing institutional financial conflict of interest. For individual financial conflict of interest, the Public Health Service and the National Science Foundation issued similar guidelines in 1995, entrusting the mechanism of oversight to the local organizations (such as universities). The only concrete guidance offered is the minimum threshold of reporting by individuals to their institutions ($10,000 in income or equity, or 5% ownership in a company) when such interest could affect the investigator's research. In 1998, the FDA issued a rule that required disclosure of greater than $25,000 in financial interest on the part of investigators participating in sponsored clinical trials leading to marketing applications. None of these federal mechanisms is currently coordinated with human subject protections, such as IRB review or informed consent. In fact, the main motivation behind these federal mechanisms is to preserve scientific integrity (and marketing accuracy) rather than protection of human subjects.

Surveys have shown that the rules and policies of local institutions vary widely. Further, scientific journals and societies have issued their own requirements or guidelines on the financial conflict of interest issue. Investigators therefore must learn and adhere to their own institution's requirements as well as pay close attention to the guidelines of other relevant organizations. It is worth repeating that these requirements and guidelines will likely undergo substantial changes in the coming months and years. However, the principles of managing conflicts of interest will remain the same. The first principle in understanding and managing financial conflict of interest is to understand why it is a difficult problem to address.

The Self-Perpetuating Nature of the Conflict of Interest Problem

Conflict of interest problems are difficult to solve because they require that persons under a conflict be able to rise above the limited perspective created by the conflict itself. Because this is the first, the most difficult and the most important ingredient in managing financial conflicts of interest, it is worth examining in some depth.

We care about conflicts of interest when they affect important decisions. Persons who make important decisions are persons with power. Since persons in power also influence policy—including policies regarding conflicts of interest—it is usually the case that persons with conflicts of interest have conflicts of interest about dealing with conflicts of interest. This can take the form of not seeing that there is a problem at all or denying or underestimating one's potential for becoming biased. Another complicating factor in tackling the problem of financial conflict of interest is that it can lead to diverse forms of biased behavior, ranging from outright fraud to subtle and complex bias on the part of well-meaning and honest scientists. Many researchers who would never dream of committing fraud may find it hard to believe the assertion that they are susceptible to acts that fall under the same description (i.e., bias due to financial incentives) and, therefore, resist and even resent the attempts to regulate their behavior. However, the issue is not about their character but rather about situations and the workings of ordinary human nature. For instance, the social psychology principle of reciprocity (the conscious or unconscious returning of favors) is a powerful psychosocial mechanism necessary for sustained, collective coordination and behavior. This principle is routinely exploited by lobbyists in influencing politicians and by pharmaceutical companies in influencing physician behavior. It would be unscientific and unrealistic to think that researchers are exempt from these principles of ordinary human motivation and behavior.

Thus an ethically effective management of conflict of interest requires a genuine willingness on the part of the investigator (or the institution) to accept that he or she, when standing in a conflict situation, is susceptible to biased perception and action. Such internally motivated willingness to address the conflict of interest problem is an ethical imperative.

Types of Financial Conflicts of Interest: A Non-Exhaustive List

A financial interest of any amount that could potentially bias the behavior of an investigator is a morally relevant conflict of interest. While institutions need to create thresholds for practical purposes, such thresholds are arbitrary. For a researcher committed to preserving objectivity and subject safety, it is better to scrutinize all sources of conflict regardless of amount. The table below summarizes the typical situations of financial conflict of interest; other situations may exist.

A non-exhaustive list of types of financial conflicts of interest

Type of Conflict	Institutional Conflicts	Individual Conflicts
Equity ownership, including stocks, stock options, etc.	■	■
Patent rights, licenses and royalties	■	■
Conflict of commitment	■[a]	■
Research funding	■	■
Institutional gifts (endowed chairs, other gifts)	■	■[b]
Gifts to laboratory or research group,	■	■
Per capita fee for contracted clinical trial		■
Consultant or scientific advisory fees		■
Honoraria in CME activities, including speaking at sponsored scientific sessions at professional meetings		■
Informal benefits and gifts (e.g., entertainmententertainment, even if done under the rubric of "scientific consultation")	■[c]	■
Informal (non-documented) compensation arrangements[d]		■
Recruitment incentives		■

a. May differ in nature between institutions and individuals. For institutions, it may mean effects on research focus. For individuals, it may mean a compromise of one's institutionally defined role.
b. If individual investigators play an active role in obtaining such gifts for the institution.
c. If it involves institutional leaders.
d. This is admittedly an elusive category and therefore especially worrisome.

Strategies for Dealing with Financial Conflicts of Interest

Disclosure is the most often discussed strategy for dealing with financial conflicts of interest, and is currently the only mandated federal step. Disclosure alerts others who have a stake in the matter to the potential for bias. Thus there is a prima facie reason to disclose one's financial conflict of interest to a person or an institution who has a direct, substantial stake in the potential bias created by the financial conflict of interest. At minimum, this includes the investigator's IRB, the investigator's institution and those to whom the results are reported (journals, sponsors, FDA, etc.). Increasingly, statements about conflicts of interest are being added to consent forms for research subjects. It is also worth noting that in order for disclosure to serve its intended ethical function, it needs to occur in a system that can make use of the disclosure. Thus, within a university, for example, close coordination between the IRB and the conflict of interest committee (or official) is necessary. In some institutions the conflict of interest (COI) committee may turn selected information over to the IRB, which will then assume the responsibility for deciding what, if anything, should be disclosed to the subject.

> **Establishing a conflict of interest committee is one mechanism for dealing with COI issues.**

Other strategies for addressing financial conflicts of interest go beyond mere disclosure to actually limiting certain behaviors. For example, an investigator with a significant financial conflict of interest might have certain roles in a protocol curbed, e.g., not obtaining direct informed consent from potential subjects. The recent position statement of the American Society for Gene Therapy prohibits certain integral personnel in clinical research from owning equity in the sponsor of the trial, for instance.

The exact application of these strategies will vary, depending on the institution.

Points to Consider for Investigators

1. As a first step, the researcher should remain open to the possibility that his or her perceptions and behaviors are susceptible to external incentives. This is a statement about people in general and not about the researcher's character.
2. At minimum, the researcher must know and comply with his or her institution's conflict of interest standards. Researchers should also be aware of and comply with requirements of sponsors, professional societies, regulatory agencies and scientific journals.
3. Compliance with conflict of interest rules may not be sufficient to eliminate all or even most of the ethical concerns behind financial conflict of interest. For instance, one could comply with all the rules and still be biased due to financial incentives, even intentionally so.
4. Evaluate each sponsor-initiated protocol with a critical eye: What is the primary motivation for agreeing to be part of this project? What would the investigator's comfort level be with one of his or her loved ones being approached to enroll in the research? Are the proposed benefits of the research primarily for marketing advantage? Some researchers feel pressured to maintain their research infrastructure using commercial funding in the hopes of doing "discovery research" with federal or other non-commercial sources of funding.

As a final note, researchers should recognize that being sensitive to and complying with conflict of interest guidelines are not exercises in moral purity. Minimizing or eliminating conflicts of interest is ultimately beneficial to investigators and institutions, because loss of public trust will have a devastating effect on the research enterprise, to the loss of all.

CHAPTER

Informed Consent—
Beyond the Basics

At the conclusion of this chapter, readers will be able to:
- Describe the three qualities of valid consent as presented in the Belmont Report.
- Discuss techniques to decrease undue influences for potential subjects.
- Discuss considerations for obtaining assent of children.
- Address issues pertaining to consent of subjects with limited capacity.
- Frame consent within the context of an ongoing process.

Introduction

The concept of informed consent is easy to understand but can be a challenge to carry out in practice. Informed consent is based upon the principle of respect for persons described in the Belmont Report. This means that subjects are to be granted the right to freely choose what they want to do. As the Report states, the process requires three key components to be ethically valid: information, understanding and voluntary agreement.

The careful, complete application of these three elements sets consent in the context of an integrated, continuous process and helps delineate the difference between clinical practice and research. The Belmont Report discusses distinguishing clinical practice from research.

Much time is spent on the informational component of consent. This reflects the emphasis on the elements of information found in the Code of

Federal Regulations (CFR) that regulates human subject research. (See the chart below.) Investigators labor over consent documents that explain the research. The institutional review board (IRB) spends time reviewing and revising documents to ensure that they meet regulatory requirements for content and reflect local standards for readability and acceptability. Ultimately, subjects are asked to read the final document, which may sometimes exceed 20 pages. Investigators then review the information with subjects, addressing any questions they may have. Sometimes the consent process may even contain a test to ensure subject comprehension as a condition of enrollment.

The federal "Common Rule" regulations for human subject research require that the following information elements—as they apply to the study at hand—be conveyed as part of the consent process:

- Statement that the activity is research.
- Purpose of study.
- Description of study procedures (identifying those that are experimental).
- Duration of subject involvement.
- Potential risks and discomforts of participation.
- Potential benefits of participation (to the subject and others).
- Alternatives, if any.
- Confidentiality of records description.
- Compensation for injury statement (for greater than minimal risk studies).
- Contact persons for questions.
- Statement of voluntary participation.
- Unforeseen risks.
- Reasons for involuntary termination of participation.
- Additional costs to participate (if any).
- Consequences for withdrawal (e.g., adverse health/welfare effects).
- New findings to be provided, if relevant.
- Number of subjects (if it may have an impact on the decision).

Federal regulations require specific information to be conveyed in the consent process; state or local laws and institutional policies may add other standard items. This information represents the "What" of informed consent. To address the other two components of valid consent—understanding and voluntary agreement—we need to consider "Who, Where, When and How"—or the context of the process. These elements, when properly executed, help ensure a consent that is knowledgeably given, voluntary and free of coercion and undue influence.

Context

To ensure that the circumstances in which consent is obtained are free from undue influence, investigators should address the following points in their study design:

Who Will Obtain Consent?

■ While it is usually assumed that the investigator will obtain consent, this is not always the case. Frequently study coordinators or other team members are charged with this responsibility. In some cases, translators, witnesses, advocates and others can help ensure impartiality and enhance the decision-making process.

■ The person or persons obtaining consent must be sufficiently trained and knowledgeable about the study to answer questions posed by subjects. When principal investigators delegate this important task, they need to be sure that those who obtain consent are properly qualified and know when to refer questions that may exceed their expertise.

■ An important issue in deciding who will obtain consent is whether or not the investigator has a pre-existing relationship with the potential subject. If the investigator is in a position of power, e.g., the subject's teacher or personal physician, it may be appropriate to delegate the consent responsibility to someone else. This technique helps avoid undue influence and the possibility—real or perceived—that the subject would feel pressured or obligated to agree to participate.

> **The individual obtaining consent can unintentionally influence a subjects decision to participate in research.**

Where Will Consent Be Obtained?

■ Privacy is of paramount importance to the consent process. The consent process should not be conducted in areas that would permit others to overhear the discussion. The assurance of privacy is of even greater importance when the topic of the research is in sensitive areas of subjects' lives. Typically, a private office or room helps ensure privacy.

■ While consent is often obtained in the investigator's office or laboratory, settings may negatively influence the process. For example, a classroom setting may introduce peer pressure and/or inattention. The pre-operative area of the surgical suite likely adds an unwanted element of stress and anxiety. Also, the prospective subject may feel pressured to make an immediate decision. These situations reduce both comprehension and voluntariness, thus detracting from the decision-making process.

■ A neutral setting, or one in which the potential subject feels comfortable and familiar, may help remove the "intimidation factor" caused by the power and/or knowledge imbalance present between the investigator and the participant.

When Will Consent Be Obtained?

- The timing of the consent process may also have a negative impact on the potential subject's ability to make a considered decision. For example, if the research procedures follow immediately after the consent form is signed, there will be no time for the subject to reflect on potential consequences or to ask questions that might come to mind later on. While this may be acceptable for minimal risk studies, for those posing greater risk or possible negative consequences, lengthening the time between presentation of the consent and the final agreement to participate can help protect subjects.

- Investigators should anticipate circumstances in which it would be difficult to have a satisfactory consent discussion. For example, when evaluating a new drug for the treatment of women during delivery, one should anticipate that once labor begins it will be relatively difficult to have a satisfactory consent discussion; therefore, this discussion should occur during one of the prenatal visits.

- Allowing subjects sufficient time to consult with family, friends and others may also improve the quality of the process.

How Will Consent be Obtained?

- While the traditional model is for the investigator to sit with the potential subject and read/discuss a written consent document, this may not be the best technique for all subjects and for all types of studies. Some subjects may respond better to different modes of presentation. Investigators whose research involves mailed surveys may not actually interact with subjects, so face-to-face consent is not possible. Ethnographic research is another example where alternate methods of seeking consent and providing information are useful.

- For complex studies, additional aids—e.g., videotapes, charts or brochures—may enhance the subject's understanding. Additionally, in long-term studies with many different elements subjects are likely to benefit from a "phased" consent. In this model, an initial explanation of the complete study is supplemented by renewed consent and/or information review prior to each new section.

- Under certain circumstances in research involving minimal risk, the consent process—or its documentation—may be waived. This is often the case for telephone surveys and interviews, where the investigator may note in the study records that the subject gave consent, but a signed document is not obtained.

Although not yet required by regulation, concern about the effect of payments and incentives to both subjects and investigators—and even research institutions—has resulted in consent forms including some reference to:

- Incentive payments and expense reimbursements to subjects (if any).
- Conflict of Interest declaration (as appropriate).
- Institutional/investigator incentives and reimbursements.

The categories noted above provide a foundation on which the consent process is based. Special considerations are described below.

Vulnerable Subjects

The concept of vulnerable subjects is addressed at length in the Belmont Report. The "Common Rule" federal human subject protection regulations [sections 107(a) and 111(a)(3) and (b)] apply specific requirements to help ensure the proper treatment of subjects who have limitations on their capacity or freedom. DHHS has three subparts (B, C and D), which provide additional protections for specific classes of vulnerable subjects. (Note: the FDA and the Department of Education also subscribe to their own versions of the DHHS subpart D protections for children.) Some examples follow:

Children
Because children cannot legally give consent, federal regulations require the permission of their parents and, with the exception of very young children in some treatment protocols, the assent (the affirmative agreement) of the child-subject. In general, the considerations for parental permission are the same as for consent in adult subjects.

Assent has generally been divided into three categories depending upon the age of the child-subject. Very young children have not developed decision-making skills, while older children may function at levels equal to that of adults. The commonly accepted rule of thumb is that children under the age of 7 are too young to assent; children over the age of 12 should be capable of full participation in the consent process (i.e., giving assent and documenting that decision in writing); those children in between—ages 7 to 12—should be capable of assenting, but need not provide written documentation. When assent is to be used in a research study, and a child capable of assenting says, "no" to involvement in research, the child should not be intimidated or enrolled in the research. The investigator's professional judgment and expertise are vital in determining individual variations on this theme to assure an adequate consent process.

> **It is the responsibility of the investigator to decide what is the level of understanding of the child.**

An additional concern is the potential for conflicts of interest when parents enroll their children in research studies. The fact that the enrollment rate for oncology studies with children is an order of magnitude larger than for adult oncology studies raises questions surrounding reasons and influences (due and undue) in parental decision making. Researchers need to be cognizant of parental conflicts when designing the consent process for studies involving children.

Adults With Limited Capacity to Consent

There are no separate federal regulations for this category of human subject research, although state laws may apply. Investigators and IRBs have developed general restrictions and consent techniques when enrolling these subjects:

- *Assent:* As in research involving children, many institutions require the affirmative agreement of the subject. Thus, those subjects who object or who fail to object, but do not affirmatively agree, are not enrolled.
- *Legally Authorized Representative (LAR):* The federal regulations allow for the use of an LAR. The LAR is asked to represent the incompetent subject's previously demonstrated values in enrolling that subject in research, i.e., substituted judgment standard. If they aren't known, then the LAR should use the best interest standard. Again, institutions have established policies to guide investigators when involving subjects who cannot give their own consent for research. Investigators should be sure to comply with these policies, particularly when using family, caregivers and advocates to give permission for enrollment. The ICH guidelines (4.8.12) require assent for all who are entered by a legally authorized representative (LAR). State law determines who qualifies as an LAR for research. Note that this issue is unsettled in most states.
- *Staged consent:* Investigators and IRBs have made use of phased-consent, or staged-consent, when subjects' abilities to retain information may be compromised.
- *Continuing evaluations of capacity and consent understanding:* Depending upon the specific study, formal or informal evaluations of capacity may be helpful to ensure adequate protection is provided by the consent process. There is an inherent conflict of interest/judgment when the investigator determines the capacity of a potential subject to consent or assent to research.

> **Investigators should be aware of any state laws or institutional policies regarding legally authorized representatives.**

Prisoners

Federal regulations note special considerations in both participation in and consent to research studies involving prisoners. Clearly, for research conducted in prison settings, investigators must take extra steps to ensure the voluntary nature of consent is maintained and that subjects understand the research and its effect on them. Consent forms must explain that participation will not affect the prisoner's consideration for parole. Special attention is mandated by the regulations to ensure that the information is presented in language that is understandable to this group of potential subjects.

Additional Consent Considerations

Deception
In order to achieve the objectives of certain studies, particularly those in the behavioral and social sciences, subjects may need to be intentionally misled. The regulations allow deception only in research that presents no greater than minimal risk. When deception is used, obtaining informed consent is problematic, because, by definition, not all the information is provided. To address this concern, some institutions have used a "consent to research procedures" to enroll subjects into the study initially, followed after the subject's participation by a "consent to the use of research data"—a debriefing form that divulges the true nature of the study and offers subjects the opportunity to decline participation.

Non-English Speaking Subjects
Federal regulations require that consent be in language understandable to the subject. This pertains not only to plain English, but also to potential subjects for whom English is not the first language. When subjects who don't speak English are anticipated to be in the study population, a translation of the consent, including all required elements, should be submitted to the IRB for review and approval. Federal regulations also permit a "short-form" document to be used in this instance. The adequacy of non-English consent forms should be checked by having the non-English forms translated back into English. It is particularly important to remember that consent is a process, i.e., once the form is signed, study personnel fluent in the subject's language are needed to ensure ongoing understanding.

Consent Renewal
Subjects need to know about new information that may affect their willingness to continue participating in the research. Such information may include new data concerning efficacy, the need to extend duration of the study, adverse events, previously undocumented toxicities or additional tests or measurements. New information may be conveyed to current/previous subjects through an addendum to the original consent form, or in a new consent form. New subjects enrolled would receive a new consent form (as approved by the IRB) with the additional information listed.

In long and complex studies, renewal of consent may also be desirable to ensure subject understanding and voluntary agreement to participate. This may consist of an informal review of the study and its procedures, or a formal process with forms and signatures ("phased consent"). Again investigator judgment and discussion with the IRB are important to ensure an effective consent process.

> **The consent process does not end after the subject's initial consent to participate, it is an ongoing process.**

Conclusion

Honoring a person's right to make decisions is the basis for obtaining consent in the research context. Because many studies involve benefits that are either nonexistent or unsure, the subject's participation represents a societal good. Investigators need to ensure that the process of consent—the information in the consent form, the setting, the timing and the manner—shows respect for persons and gives subjects the opportunity to choose what is best for themselves. In this way we continue to earn the trust that the public and our subjects have placed in us as researchers.

CHAPTER

Community-Based Qualitative Research

At the conclusion of this chapter, readers will be able to:
- Identify the unique aspects of human subject protection involved in community-based qualitative research.
- Appropriately apply guidelines for the protection of study communities to specific research contexts.
- Recognize the need to actively engage the community during all stages of the research including formulation of the study question and design, data collection and synthesis, and dissemination of the findings.

Introduction

Increasingly at academic medical centers, investigators have begun to use community-based qualitative research to explore public health problems, design programs and policies and evaluate effectiveness. While many of the ethical principles for the protection of human subjects already discussed in this manual also apply to community-based qualitative research (CBQR), there are some issues unique to this approach.

Philosophical Assumptions Unique to CBQR and the Implications for Practice

Assumption #1
The community is the authority on its own situation, strengths, needs and potential solutions.

Practice Implication.—Community engagement at every stage of research through regular meetings with community representatives. This may involve convening a special community advisory board representing all the project's major stakeholders.

Assumption #2
Cultural biases of the research team may unduly skew the formulation of the research questions, the collection of data and the interpretation of the findings.

Practice Implication.—A continual process of critical self-reflection that makes explicit the research team's own cultural values and how they may differ from the cultural values of the study community.

Defining Community-Based Qualitative Research (CBQR)

CBQR is defined as research done at a site away from research centers, engaging people on their own territory. This can include their homes, community centers, work sites, places of worship, schools, chat rooms, list serves and bulletin boards. The data generated are in the form of texts rather than numbers and involve understanding issues from the point of view of the people most affected. The notion of community is flexible. Communities may be bounded by geography (e.g., certain census tracts), or they may be defined socially, culturally, by economic status or by disorder (e.g., Alzheimer's, caregivers or diabetics). Communities may be included in the process of how they would like to be identified. This may take researchers beyond the traditional categories of "white, black, Hispanic" to a more nuanced sense of community and belonging. Some Hispanic communities, for example, may prefer to be identified more specifically as Puerto Rican, Mexican-American or Cuban-American.

> **Researchers need to understand the cultural values of the community under study.**

Maintaining Confidentiality

Responsibility for maintaining confidentiality rests with the researcher; however, study participants may want to be identified. If the participant so desires, and with his/her permission, the participant's real name can be used. This is sometimes the case in a specific type of CBQR known as Participatory Action Research (PAR). PAR partners researchers with communities for the explicit purpose of social change. Community partners in PAR, such as community leaders and grass-roots activists may prefer that their real names be used in the publication of study findings to make themselves available for advancing the process of social change. Identification may be done by attribution of direct quotes, citing ideas, in the description of activities and/or in explanations of the research collaboration.

Alternatively, in protecting community and/or individual identities, the researcher and the participants may elect to avoid gathering or reporting identifying information. Masking identities with pseudonyms and gathering only general information such as gender and age group allow for composite descriptions when reporting while maintaining anonymity. Community identities may also be masked, giving the location a fictional name and locating it in broad geographic terms like "mid-sized, northeastern city." Masking may be undone if acknowledgments specify a cooperating agency in the community.

> **As in other types of research with human subjects, maintaining the confidentiality of the community is important.**

Stigmatizing topics (e.g., HIV status or drug use) or sensitive social identities (gay/lesbian) usually do involve masking names and accurate data might be difficult to collect unless assurances of confidentiality can be made. In such cases, written informed consent may threaten participants' desire to remain anonymous. For these situations, the researcher may request a waiver of documentation of consent from the IRB so that participants may provide verbal rather than written consent, indicating their understanding of the purposes of the research, how their information will be stored and used, and their rights as research subjects. Also, Certificates of Confidentiality may be obtained from the Department of Health and Human Services to protect study data from involuntary disclosure through subpoena.

Study Methods

CBQR may make use of a variety of data collection tools within a single project including participant-observations, in-depth interviews (both structured and unstructured), focus groups and examination of public documents. Data collected using these tools may be captured by videotape, audiotape, field notes (handwritten or on a laptop) or any combination of these. All these approaches require approval from the institution's review board, but are often considered eligible for expedited review as they are generally of minimal risk.

Particular Points to Be Considered

Audio- and Videotaping

In research situations in which audio- or videotapes are necessary, there are some special ethical and regulatory requirements.

In the case of individual interviews, the participant is informed in advance that the researcher wishes to tape the interview. The interviewee's consent can be taped to provide confirmation of his or her willingness to be taped. A participant being taped ought to be told that the tape can be stopped at any time during the interview at his or her request. For groups being taped, all participants should agree to be taped. Similarly, any participant has the prerogative to stop the tape at any time.

How the information on the tapes will be used and the protections provided to the taped information (e.g., secured for researcher use, transcribed and then destroyed; access limited to researcher only or research staff, etc.) need to be specified.

The decision about how taped material will be handled is made at the outset of the research and along with the procedure for obtaining consent (usually a script) must be specified in the application to the institution's review board.

Written Notes

Although the above stipulations apply to the researcher's written notes as well, there are a few other points to consider when taking notes. Investigators might want to consider using only pseudonyms in the notes themselves. If the notes are to be entered into a computer, a decision needs to be made whether to destroy the handwritten notes or to store them in a secure place.

Focus Group Participants

Focus groups are group interviews conducted and facilitated by a moderator. The goal is to generate discussion among focus group members, record their comments and observe their interactions. Because topics may generate heated debate, special steps must be taken in order to protect focus group members from the potential ire of others. Explicating ground rules for participation at the beginning of the group provides a method to clarify how members are expected to conduct themselves during the group and the expectation of maintaining confidentiality afterward.

Because topics discussed in some focus groups may evoke strong emotional reactions, a referral sheet should be distributed at the conclusion of the group that provides each participant with references and resources should they need to further discuss their feelings or concerns. Moderators may want to suggest that participants can contact their health care provider, therapist or case worker. Participants also may want advice on specific problems they have related to the topic area. While such problems cannot be resolved within the context of a focus group, information sheets can be made available to direct them to other resources. Information that should be provided varies based on the focus group topic but commonly includes community referral numbers, hot line numbers and web sites.

Occasionally, the focus group moderator must confront the behavior of a particular participant. Whether the topic of discussion has raised issues that are upsetting to the individual or whether a conflict arises between group members, the moderator ought to intervene. Most often, the upset or disruptive individual is asked to leave, thanked for participation, given the above-mentioned information and referral sheets, and given the agreed-to incentive or payment.

Disclosure

The investigator may also be faced with ethical dilemmas. Hearing information about illegal activities, such as domestic violence or drug use, for example, cannot be treated simply as research data. The researcher's obligation necessitates further action if certain conditions apply. Sometimes information has already been reported by the participant to the proper authorities. In this case, the researcher need only clarify if the participant has taken this action. Reporting activities to the police or other governmental agency requires a level of detail (date/time, place, activity), not just suspicions or vague references. Again, the researcher must also ensure that the participant is not currently in an unsafe situation. In both cases the written information sheets provided by the researcher to the subject can be useful. Certificates of Confidentiality may be issued to protect sensitive data from release under subpoena, etc. If reports will be made, for example, for child abuse, then the moderator should advise participants of that fact.

In anticipation of possible disclosures that indicate the participant is in some danger, or in distress, it is wise to consult with the study communities ahead of time about what they would like to see happen. The community might prefer notifying clergy, health care providers, a case worker, parents, teachers or guidance counselors.

Payment/Incentives

Study participants provide their time and effort to benefit the research or project. Covering transportation costs (e.g., bus or taxi fare) or providing a meal or child care may reduce the burden of participating and improve recruitment. Acknowledging their time can be accomplished through monetary payment such as cash or a gift card. Consultation with the community can help establish what would be considered fair, legitimate compensation. This could range from cash to food or clothing coupons.

Resources for Participants

It is helpful for researchers to keep a list of community resources that participants can access should the need arise. The list may include hot line numbers, contact information for free clinics, community support groups or community-based centers.

Participant Observation

Less intrusive qualitative research includes observing and/or participating at community gatherings or public events. In the case of small gatherings it is important that the researcher identify him- or herself as being there to collect data with the permission of the organizers. Of course, only individuals themselves can give consent for research participation, and researchers must be prepared if some people decline participation/observation. This may mean that people are free to ignore the researcher or not speak with him or her. It may mean that data on/about certain individuals cannot be collected/recorded. It may even mean that the research must withdraw from the event. When the setting is a large public event, which assures subject anonymity, no special measures usually need to be taken.

Disenfranchised Populations

The information on the protection of vulnerable populations (children, pregnant women, etc.) applies during CBQR. However, some communities under study represent disenfranchised populations such as the economically disadvantaged or the incarcerated. These communities may be suspicious of researchers or projects seeking to use their information without a benefit to them or the community. The researcher must be clear about the intent of the research and potential benefits to the community, if any. It is important not to overstate the potential benefits or promise resources that are not directly under the authority of the researcher. Communities that believe their participation will result in a guaranteed service that is not forthcoming will generally feel exploited. Researchers should clearly describe the contingent nature of any benefits. A good rule is not to promise anything that you cannot guarantee.

Dissemination of Study Findings

Researchers should carefully consider how the findings are written for publication and who the audience will be. One of the goals of dissemination is to render accounts that present an empathetic understanding of the study community's circumstances and the logic that informs decision making and actions. Explaining the "other" to outsiders may be difficult, especially in cases where the values and social conditions of the study community are radically different from that of the outside reading audience. Researchers should avoid promoting stereotypes or stigmatizing individuals/communities. Study communities might want to review written accounts and be allowed to comment on them prior to publication or presentation. Think carefully about any unintended consequences that might result from publication of sensitive, embarrassing or divisive information.

Further Resources

The American Anthropological Association's Code of Ethics (http://www. aaanet.org/) and the American Public Health Association guidelines (http:// www.apha.org/) are helpful in considering how CBQR can be conducted in a way that "preserves the confidentiality and dignity of the study community, while promoting trustful, non-exploitive relationships needed for continued study by other researchers."

11

Ethical Issues in Genetic Research

At the conclusion of this chapter, readers will be able to:

- Define the term "genetic research" and discuss the complexities of the definition.
- Discuss the human subject protection issues related to conducting genetic research.
- Define the term "gene transfer" and discuss the complexities of this concept.
- Address issues pertaining to the human subject protections issues related to conducting research with gene transfer.

Introduction

Over the past two decades, human genetic research has focused mainly on rare genetic diseases attributable to single (mendelian) genes, such as cystic fibrosis or Huntington's disease. With the anticipated sequencing of the human genome and definition of the estimated 30,000 genes it is believed to contain, the research focus in medical genetics is rapidly changing. For mendelian disorders with known genes and mutations, the research is shifting to the examination of efficient diagnostic testing (including genetic screening), the search for "modifier genes" that may determine the course and prognosis of the disease and novel interventions, including gene therapy. In addition, a major effort has been initiated to study the genetic contributions to common disorders that have complex inheritance patterns and significant environmental causes as well. The study of these complex disorders generally requires a combined genetic and epidemiological approach. Consequently, much larger numbers of human subjects are usually needed, and the study data collected often involve extensive personal information over long periods of time, including clinical and demographic data, occupational, dietary and other environmental exposure, socioeconomic data and behavioral characteristics. Because these complex disorders have multi-genetic causation, the nature and number of genes to be tested are often unclear at the outset of the research study, resulting in a realistic potential of unintended or undesired genetic testing results. Furthermore, the high prevalence of these common complex disorders, such as coronary heart disease, hypertension, cancer, psychiatric disorders, addictions, diabetes mellitus, allergy or asthma, also means that research data, tissue samples and overall study results have enormous commercial potential. The eventual ability to identify predisposition to a large number of diseases, while having enormous prevention potentials, is also redefining the boundary of what we consider a "patient" and a "non-patient." Thus, modern genetic research, often accompanied by its many ethical, legal and social issues, is challenging the way we interpret what are considered risks and benefits of research, how we deal with privacy, confidentiality and anonymity, how we define conflict of interests, and the consent process itself.

Federal and State Regulations

Currently, there is no comprehensive federal regulation that addresses all facets of genetic research. Previously existing federal regulations on human subject protection is being used to guide how these research studies are done, subject to interpretation by individual IRBs. New legislation at the federal and state level is mainly concerned with protection of patients against genetic discrimination (in insurance or employment) or loss of privacy where genetic testing is concerned. Some of these regulations are also being applied to the protection of human subjects when research genetic testing is involved, sometimes with rather awkward limitations for research and researchers.

Some Points to Consider

There are many different kinds of genetic research and different contexts under which the term "genetic" is used. Being clear about these concepts is an important key to understand what issues need to be addressed in the protection of human subjects in genetic research.

> **Genetic research is rapidly changing. Investigators need to keep their IRB informed of new developments.**

What Does "Genetic" Mean?

Often "genetic" means that which pertains to DNA and/or RNA ("molecular genetics") in the cells within a tissue, organ or the entire individual (e.g., as in the statement "Genetic changes in a cancer cell result in abnormal cell growth"). In other situations, "genetic" is taken to mean that which passes from one generation to another through DNA, the hereditary material (e.g., as in the statement "There is a genetic condition running through that family"). This latter use of the term "genetic" also carries the connotation of "familial" and "hereditary." All these terms should be distinguished from the term "congenital," which simply refers to that which an individual is born with, regardless of whether it is from environmental, genetic, hereditary or familial factors.

What Are the Different Kinds of Genetic Variations?

Genetic variations include what are commonly called genetic mutations and genetic polymorphisms. Genetic mutations are of two broad categories. Molecular genetic alterations present in all cells of an individual mean that such alterations are present within the first cell (i.e., the fertilized egg) that gave rise to the individual. These genetic mutations are considered "constitutional" (or "germ-line") and are generally inherited from one or both parents. They can likewise be passed on to the next generation. Sometimes genetic mutations are only present in certain cells, tissues or organs of an individual, and not in the majority of the body cells of that individual. These individuals are most often born with a normal "constitution," with the genetic mutation taking place later in life. These more confined genetic mutations are called "somatic" mutations. Somatic genetic mutations are not inherited and are likewise not generally passed on to the next generation.

Of course these two categories of genetic mutations are not always mutually exclusive. For example, an individual may inherit a constitutional mutation that predisposes him to more easily develop a somatic mutation. This is the basis for many familial cancer predisposition syndromes. Alternatively, somatic mutations may take place in the gonads of an individual, such that these mutations may be passed on to the next generation through the eggs or sperm.

Genetic polymorphisms represent naturally occurring variations in the general population of an individual's genetic make-up, as manifested in DNA, RNA or protein sequences. A good example of genetic polymorphism is that of ABO blood group differences among individuals. These polymorphisms are generally not thought to be directly disease-causing. However, much of the current human genetic research on common complex disorders seeks to establish associations between specific genetic polymorphisms and predisposition to disease states. A good example of this is the association of ApoE4 polymorphism with an increased risk of Alzheimer's disease. Other genetic polymorphisms are believed to modify an individual's resistance to known pathogens, highlighting the genetic-environmental interaction of many common diseases. A good example of this is the association of mutations in the chemokine gene CCR5 and resistance to HIV infection. Genetic polymorphisms are part of an individual's genetic constitution, and as such are passed on from parents to their children following the known rules of inheritance. They provide a particular challenge in the determination of risks and benefits of study results to human subjects.

Compounding the difficulty in dealing with genetic research protocols is the fact that knowledge about the implications for specific genetic mutations and polymorphisms is constantly evolving, making constant reassessment of protocol a necessary part of the IRB re-approval process. Consultation with individuals who have some expertise in the area is essential. Researchers should assist their IRB to stay current with the field, for example, by including review articles with progress reports or offering a brief update to the board.

Genetic Research and Genetic Testing

Much of the concern and anxiety surrounding human subject protection in modern genetic studies involve genetic testing. Before discussing what constitutes a "genetic test," it is important to point out that there are many genetic studies that do not involve genetic testing. For example, there was a study published in 1990 in the *Journal of Human Genetics* by McGuffin and Huckle that examined whether attending medical school is a genetic trait. This was a survey-based study that utilized family histories on medical school attendance. The pedigree information was analyzed by statistical genetic methods and a specific mode of inheritance was proposed. This was a genetic study, but did not involve genetic testing at all. There are many more serious investigations of this type, including twin studies, sibling studies and extended family history analysis.

The question of what constitutes a "genetic test" cannot be easily answered. One definition of a "genetic test" is "a test that involves looking at the genes." This definition emphasizes the laboratory technique used in the testing process and includes any DNA testing. However, it does not discriminate between the detection of somatic and constitutional genetic variations, even though somatic mutations are usually not familial or heritable.

Another possible definition of a "genetic test" is a test that "determines the genetic status of an individual with respect to a certain trait." This definition focuses on the intent of why a test is done, as opposed to the actual technique employed. This definition can be overly inclusive in that many commonly used non-DNA-based tests can be used to determine an individual status, such as a sweat chloride determination for cystic fibrosis.

In New York State, the Civil Rights Law (section 79-l) defines a "genetic test" as "any laboratory test of human DNA, chromosomes, genes or gene products to diagnose the presence of a genetic variation linked to a predisposition to a genetic disease or disability in the individual or the individual's offspring; such term shall also include DNA profile analysis." It does provide exclusions in that genetic tests do not include "any test of blood or other medically prescribed test in routine use that has been or may be hereafter found to be associated with a genetic variation, unless conducted purposely to identify such genetic variation." While the exclusion still contains some ambiguity as to what "purposely" means, this definition is a reasonable compromise given the complexity of the issues. The larger question is that as more and more diseases are found to have a genetic contribution, it will become increasingly difficult to define what a "genetic disease or disability" is. This will be a challenge for future human subject protection.

What are Some Common Kinds of Genetic Studies and Things to Watch out for?

There are four main kinds of genetic research in which testing of gene or gene products is included. They will be discussed with respect to whether they are "genetic research involving genetic testing," using the definition of "genetic testing" as stated above.

1. **Studies that deal exclusively with the molecular genetic alterations in DNA or RNA in specific cells, tissues or organs involved in the disease process, without any intent to address whether that change is inherited or that it represents a predisposition to the disease or disability.**

This is common in many oncology studies, where a tumor is being analyzed for specific genetic changes related to the biology or treatment response of the tumor. However, in order to show that these genetic changes in tumor cells are indeed somatic mutations, one often has to establish that similar mutations do not exist in the normal tissues of the patient. This is why a sample from the normal (non-cancerous) tissue, most commonly blood, from the affected subjects is often required as a "control" in most genetic studies on cancer patients. The exceptions are perhaps leukemia or lymphoma because blood is the tissue involved in the disease process. Also, unaffected volunteers may be needed to serve as additional controls, though testing on these volunteers can often be done anonymously. Thus, these kinds of studies technically do not involve genetic testing as defined above. However, if a cancer study does look at the "normal" non-tumor tissues for additional constitutional genetic mutations, it is testing for a predisposition to the disease, and thus involves "genetic testing." The results of these studies would have an entirely different set of implications for the subjects and their families.

The results of genetic testing not only affect the subjects but their families as well.

A sub-category of this kind of genetic research is often seen in anthropologic or population genetic studies. These studies aim to use genetic markers to trace the genetic origin, population behavior (e.g., migration, admixture and mating with other populations) and characteristics (e.g., frequencies of specific genes in different populations). The genetic markers being studied can include genes that are associated with disease states. An example of this is a study to compare the frequency of specific mutations of a certain gene in different ethnic populations in order to understand the history of that population or to provide better ethnic-based genetic counseling. Even though these kinds of studies invoke the concept of genetic heritability in the data analysis, the intent is usually not to identify predisposition to diseases in individual subjects or families, and as such are usually allowed some flexibility in consent form requirements. Investigators for studies like this should be encouraged to perform data collection and genetic testing in an anonymous manner to further protect subjects against unintended harm (see Risk and Benefits section below).

2. **Studies involving the detection of mutations in one or more specified gene(s) known to harbor causative mutations in individuals affected with a certain disease.**

For example, a study that examines the association of disease severity with specific mutations in the gene for cystic fibrosis (CFTR gene) in known CF patients falls into this category. Generally speaking, this kind of study does involve genetic testing. However, prior to genetic testing, the subjects have already been determined to have the genetic disorder based on clinical grounds, such that the incremental "risk" associated with genetic testing in these studies is small. In other words, since the genetic test does not reveal a new genetic predisposition and would only confirm the disease status of the patient, it would change little of the psychosocial make-up of the subject.

3. **Studies involving the detection of mutations or DNA polymorphisms in one or more gene regions in which a gene responsible for the disease is suspected to reside. These studies are generally known as "genetic mapping" studies.**

This kind of study generally focuses on subjects known to have the disease under study, as well as their affected or unaffected family members. The clinical information (i.e., disease status and family history) is therefore used to establish that a specific gene is indeed the cause for the disease, or that the causative gene(s) resides in a certain gene region. Even though these studies often involve DNA testing, they do not involve "genetic testing" per se. There are two points to keep in mind about studies of this kind. First, to ascertain the disease status of every family member, it is not unusual that individuals formerly thought to be unaffected may become diagnosed with the disease.

This may represent either a "risk" or a "benefit," depending on the subjects' perspective. Second, as the study progresses, new findings may arise that could lead one to conclude that the causative gene(s) has indeed been identified, and from that point on, any testing of a new study subject with respect to that gene would constitute true "genetic testing." This point emphasizes the ongoing assessment of what is known about the disease under study, and the importance of expert consultation over the course of the study.

4. Studies involving known mutations or DNA polymorphisms in one or more gene regions that is either known or suspected to predispose to a disease. These kinds of studies are often referred to as "genetic association studies."

An important distinction is made here between genetic variations that cause disease and those that predispose to a disease or disability. For example, mutations in the CFTR gene cause cystic fibrosis, whereas having two copies of the ApoE4 gene greatly increases the likelihood for an individual to develop Alzheimer's disease. There is some confusion about this kind of study because, to some, it seems that as long as the testing is not diagnostic of the disease state, it should not be considered "genetic testing." However, it should be clear that testing for a genetic predisposition to a disease does constitute genetic testing.

Association studies are the most common approach to identify genetic contributions to common complex disorders. Depending on the status of knowledge about these various genetic contributions, and whether subjects with known, suspected or unknown disease status are involved, considerations similar to those discussed in categories two and three above may be relevant.

An Example

The above categorizations of genetic studies are not mutually exclusive. The following is a slightly more complicated example that illustrates the complexity of the issues. A disease is caused by mutations in one of at least two genes, one of which is already identified (Gene A), but the remaining one (Gene B) is yet to be discovered. A study is designed to find (or "map") Gene B. To do this, one would have to collect blood samples from individuals affected with the disease, as well from their affected and unaffected family members. In order to show that the affected individual has a mutation in Gene B, you would have to show that the disease is not caused by a mutation in Gene A. Therefore, genetic testing of Gene A is necessary. This testing of Gene A is considered genetic testing, although the risk associated with the testing is low because the subject is already known to have the disease.

When an affected subject tests negative for mutation in Gene A, then the subject and his or her family will be used to map Gene B. This part of the study does not constitute genetic testing because the location of Gene B is still hypothetical. A study like this, which is not uncommon, involves genetic studies of both categories two and three above. If the study is completed and Gene B has been found, then any testing of subsequent subjects for Gene B also constitutes true "genetic testing" (Category two).

Suppose that after the gene mapping study is completed, it is found that a significant number of patients with the disease do not have severe and deleterious mutations in either Gene A or Gene B. Instead, these patients have mild variants of Genes A and/or B, which by themselves would not cause the disease, but when coupled with variants of an additional number of genes, say C, D and E, the disease will be manifested under the right environmental input (e.g., poor diet or lack of exercise). In this case, testing patients with the disease for Genes A and B falls in Categories two and three as described above, and in Category four as well, depending on what is currently known about the gene's relation to the disease. This example highlights how the evolving nature of new information may change how a genetic study needs to be assessed.

Behavioral Genetic Studies

A special kind of genetic study concerns an individual's behavioral characteristics. The behaviors being studied may range from those traditionally considered to be medical problems (such as schizophrenia or manic-depressive illness) to those more recently accepted as partly organic in nature (such as drug addiction or alcoholism) and those that may be considered "normal" variations in the general population (such as personality traits, sexual orientation or intelligence). Many of these behavioral characteristics carry a social stigma and therefore deserve special attention with respect to confidentiality and many other consent issues. The sensitivity of behavioral issues is particularly heightened when a "genetic" component is also being examined. For example, a study that tries to determine the genetic predisposition to drug addiction in an "unaffected" individual may have significant impact on an individual's self-image, social status, employability and insurability. Therefore, behavioral genetics studies deserve a high degree of alertness when being designed and reviewed. A Certificate of Confidentiality should always be considered to further protect subjects against forced disclosure of study data concerning individual subjects (see Chapter 6).

Special Considerations in Protocols and Consent Forms

The basic principles of human subject protection embodied in the Belmont Report apply to genetic research. As a result, the usual protocol and consent form elements required for genetic research are similar to those for other human research. However, because genetic information is inherently different than other personal information in many ways, special considerations are needed for some protocol and consent form items.

Risks and Benefits

For most genetic studies, the physical risk to individuals is minimal, often involving no more than a blood draw, cheek scraping or use of biological tissues obtained in the course of clinical care. However, far more insidious are the risks that are psychosocial or financial in nature. For gene mapping or association studies, clarification of disease status through clinical evaluation or genetic testing as part of the research may result in some individuals being diagnosed with the disease or found to be at a significantly increased risk of developing the disease. To some, this information constitutes a risk in that it is unexpected and undesired, and may have an impact on their self-image, insurability and employability. To other individuals, however, this may represent a benefit because it may lead to early treatment, preventive care and knowledge about future genetic risk to the subjects and their families. In this case, the study protocol should include some provision for referral to genetic counseling and clinical management services should a subject receive a previously unknown diagnosis. The possibility of false-positive and false-negative results in making the diagnosis may also need to be addressed.

For some multi-site research studies, the genetic testing is performed at a site different from the one where the subject is recruited. Some of these studies would not provide genetic testing results to individual subjects despite providing such information to the principal investigator at the recruitment site. Occasionally, this results in an ethical dilemma for the principal investigators at the recruitment site because they may feel a professional obligation to inform the subjects of a potential risk to their health. This is particularly true in studies where the principal investigators are physicians and the subjects are their patients. In fact, the American Society of Human Genetics has issued clear guidelines specifying the duty to inform patients they have previously seen of potential risks to their health due to newly available information. This may compel some investigators to regret the pledge not to provide genetic testing results to their subjects. Because of this, in the initial design of a genetic research study, investigators should consider this possibility carefully, and not just decide against providing genetic testing results out of expediency.

Identifiers, Anonymity and Confidentiality

Genetic research adds complexity to the definition of what is generally considered "identifying" information. As a result, the protection of confidentiality may require one to address a number of questions in addition to those asked for in non-genetic studies.

In general, information such as names, addresses, medical record numbers, social security numbers, telephone numbers, fingerprints, photographs and video recordings are considered complete or partial identifiers. As illustrated by the extensive use of DNA testing in forensic medicine, one might argue that DNA embodies the ultimate identifier of an individual, as suggested by such a term as the "DNA fingerprint" of an individual. As yet, however, most individuals cannot be readily identified through DNA testing results, because there is not an extensive bank of DNA data on individuals to make it a truly good "identifier." In other words, the DNA "code" on any given individual may not exist or is not easily accessible. This may be different for some subjects who, due to their profession or legal status, may have information concerning their DNA stored in an electronic database. Some examples of subjects in this category are criminals and armed services personnel. Therefore, genetic research involving genetic testing needs to be carefully evaluated with respect to this issue.

For rare genetic diseases, a positive disease status is often by itself a powerful identifier. For example, a subject who is the only patient ever to be diagnosed with a certain disease at a medical center will usually be known by virtue of his or her diagnosis. Thus even "anonymous" study records on a subject with this rare diagnosis may actually be identifying information. In family studies, the specific pattern of different kinds of relatives in a pedigree drawing may betray the identity of an individual, especially when linked to the disease being studied. This is common in genetic mapping studies involving large pedigrees. For example, a subject with myotonic dystrophy, who has two affected sisters and one affected brother out of a total of ten siblings, can sometimes be readily identified within a support group community. Thus, when genetic research studies are published in medical journals, there may be a significant likelihood that family and friends reading the articles may be able to identify the subjects who have been studied, even though no names or other obvious identifiers have been given at all. This could be a particularly difficult problem if the published report contains sensitive information not previously known to friends and family, such as non-paternity, previous abortions or history of drug addiction.

In general, it is very difficult to maintain confidentiality of genetic testing results among family members participating in a genetic study as a group. Sometimes, the genetic testing results of one individual may lead one to draw certain conclusions about the results for another individual. There can be significant coercion concerning participation in a study and sharing of testing results in an extended family. Investigators and reviewers of study protocols need to be sensitive to these issues. In addition, the complex and sometimes unpredictable relationship among family members makes it important to protect against disclosure of genetic testing information through legal proceedings. One is encouraged to seriously consider obtaining a Certificate of Confidentiality to protect against such disclosure (See Chapter 6).

Data and Tissue Storage

Any genetic testing protocol should prompt a list of questions concerning tissue and data storage for future research. It is important to have explicit mention in the consent form of the duration of tissue and data storage, how such tissue and data will be used in the future and whether such uses will be limited to studying diseases for which the tissue was obtained to begin with. The issues of whether and how future genetic testing results will be conveyed to study subjects will also need to be addressed. Often, tissue samples and data may be distributed to investigators outside of the study during future research. It is important that the specific points discussed in the last section about confidentiality be addressed.

The Consent Process and Genetic Counseling

The complexity of the issues concerning genetic research outlined above can make consent forms extremely difficult to comprehend. For this reason, some have suggested that genetic counseling should be offered to subjects before or during the consent process. While some states like New York, have made this an explicit requirement for research involving genetic testing, in other more permissive settings, this should be an issue for IRBs to consider. There is no generally agreed upon definition of who is qualified to give genetic research counseling, other than the fact that such genetic counseling should be provided by a "professional," which can be interpreted to include the investigators or support personnel for the study. How such genetic counseling needs to be documented is also unclear and as such is left to local investigators and IRBs.

Points to Consider

It is impossible to have a single protocol or consent form template that can cover all kinds of genetic research. In general, however, a list of questions needs to be considered when designing and reviewing genetic research protocols, in addition to those usually considered for any human subject studies:

- Does the genetic research protocol involve genetic testing? If so, does the genetic testing establish a cause or predisposition to a disease?
- Is the disease status of the subjects undergoing genetic testing established, unclear or unknown?
- Will the results of genetic testing be available to the principal investigator at the site of the study?
- Will the results of genetic testing be available to the subjects?
- If the results of genetic testing will not be available to the subjects, but are available to the principal investigator at the site of the study, will the non-communication of results to the subject infringe on the ethical duty of the investigator to inform subjects of potentially serious harm, particularly if the investigator is a physician and the subject is his or her patient?
- If the results of genetic testing are available to the subjects, will they constitute a risk (e.g., unintended result, false-positive diagnosis, loss of insurability and employment potential) or a benefit (e.g., early diagnosis resulting in early treatment or prevention, determination of future risk to the individual or family)?

- If a subject receives a previously unknown or unsuspected diagnosis as a result of participating in the study, are there any provisions for referral for genetic counseling or to a clinical management service?
- Who else will have access to the genetic testing results?
- Will other partially identifying information, such as information concerning an individual's genetic variation, disease status and family history be disclosed during publications of research data?
- Will a Certificate of Confidentiality be needed to increase the assurance that the subjects' privacy will be protected against disclosure?
- How long will tissue and/or data be retained? Where will tissue and data be stored? Will tissue and data be discarded at the conclusion of the present study? Or will tissue and data be retained for future research, including genetic testing?
- Will there be secondary distribution of tissue and/or data and how will subjects' confidentiality be protected?
- How will the results of future genetic testing be handled with respect to issues listed above?
- Will genetic counseling be necessary prior to a subjects signing the consent document? Who will provide such genetic counseling and what are their qualifications for doing so?
- When withdrawing from participation in a study, can subjects request that samples be destroyed or anonymized or require that the data not be used?

Gene Transfer Research

Clinical gene transfer research has grown significantly since the first human recombinant DNA experiment in 1980, particularly in the area of cancer clinical trials. To date, the vast majority of human gene transfer protocols registered with NIH involve the use of gene transfer in an oncology-related diagnosis and have primarily been phase 1 trials.

Interest in human gene transfer (HGT) research, by both the scientific community and the public, has grown with both an increase in knowledge and misunderstandings about disease-related genes and associated treatment strategies. This research has raised uniquely complex scientific, medical, ethical and social issues that warrant special monitoring.

This section focuses on the regulatory and informed consent issues specific to gene transfer. The roles of the NIH, Recombinant DNA Advisory Committee (also known as RAC) and the FDA in the oversight of HGT studies are briefly discussed. The role of the Institutional Biosafety Committee (IBC) and some special consent considerations associated with gene transfer are summarized.

Background

Since the advent of genetic engineering over 25 years ago, recombinant DNA technology has made possible the manufacture of therapeutic proteins, such as human insulin and human growth hormone, the sequencing of the human genome, and the ability to discern the genetic basis for many diseases. Gene transfer, however, is a relatively recent and still experimental clinical application of recombinant DNA technology that has captured the public's attention—partly because of its promise, but also because of the ethical and social implications of this research.

Gene transfer is a technique to substitute absent or faulty genes causing diseases with working genes, so that cells make the correct enzyme or protein. The transfer is accomplished by carrying the gene fragment to the cells by use of "vectors" (usually of viral or bacterial origin). Gene transfer has been limited to somatic cells in contrast to germline cells which would have the potential to affect not only the individual being treated, but also future offspring. The ethical concern (changing the genetic pool of the entire human species) and certain technical considerations make it unlikely that germline experiments will be tried on humans in the near future.

Human gene transfer research, as with clinical research in general, is not without risk. Efforts to minimize and manage risks both known and unforeseen are paramount. The unexpected death of Jesse Gelsinger, a young man enrolled in a University of Pennsylvania gene transfer study, underscored the need for constant vigilance by researchers, federal agencies, IRBs and institutional biosafety committees (IBCs) in the oversight and conduct of clinical gene transfer research. While IRBs exist to protect the rights and well-being of the human subjects, IBCs have evolved a role to protect the public from potentially broader consequences of gene transfer.

All clinical gene transfer trials, regardless of funding source or research site, are subject to FDA regulations (21 CFR 312) as biological products. The FDA has statutory authority to allow a gene transfer clinical study to proceed after review, or, if necessary, to place a study on clinical hold in order to ensure the safety of human subjects. FDA has issued a "Points to Consider" document (available on the FDA web site) that is directed primarily at the aspects of good manufacturing practices. FDA requirements for clinical trials involving gene transfer are essentially no different than for other biologics with the focus primarily on sponsor requirements.

> **All gene transfer trials are subject to FDA regulations as biological products.**

Additionally, researchers conducting basic or applied gene transfer research, either funded by the NIH or carried out at an institution that receives NIH support for recombinant DNA research of any type, are also expected to comply with the NIH Guidelines. Appendix M of the NIH Guidelines, also known as the "Points to Consider in the Design and Submissions of Protocols for the Transfer of rDNA Molecules Into

One or More Human Subjects" is the section that specifically addresses requirements for human gene transfer. It is intended to assist the principal investigator, the institution, the IBC, the biological safety officer, and the IRB in determining safeguards that should be implemented for these studies. Failure to comply with the requirements set forth in the NIH Guidelines can result in the limitation, suspension or withdrawal of all NIH support to the institution. NIH can also impose a requirement for prior NIH approval of any or all recombinant DNA projects at an institution.

Privately funded gene transfer research conducted at a site that does not receive federal funds for recombinant DNA research is not mandated to follow the NIH Guidelines, but many sponsors and investigative sites choose to voluntarily comply because of the enhanced human subject protections outlined by the Guidelines.

Each institution, through the Institutional Biosafety Committee (IBC), is responsible for ensuring that all recombinant DNA research conducted at, or sponsored by, that institution is conducted in accord with the NIH Guidelines. The questions asked of the investigator by the IBC include scientific issues such as how the vector construct was prepared and how the agent will be contained. Additionally, the IBC is also concerned with how the consent process will be conducted. In other words, the IBC must address not only protection issues for the public at large, but also address protections of the individual research subject.

> **The IBC is responsible for ensuring that recombinant DNA research is conducted according to the NIH Guidelines.**

The roles of the IBC and IRB overlap when considering human subject protections. While many IBCs have minimal experience with clinical settings, many IRBs have little knowledge of the technical issues associated with the gene transfer. Therefore, it is essential that communication exists between these committees.

There are some general concepts that investigators, IBCs and IRBs should keep in mind for consent forms associated with a gene transfer trials:

- What measures have been taken to minimize the risks of transmission?
- If transmission were to occur, what would be the consequences?
- The use of the terms "therapy/treatment/drug" should be avoided; "agent" is preferred.
- The use of recombinant DNA should be clearly stated.
- The potential for recombinant DNA remaining in the body should be addressed.
- What are the risks for the vector to activate an oncogene or inactivate a tumor suppressor gene leading to vector-related malignancy?
- Are there any special issues related to this gene transfer trial, such as uncertainty associated with short- and long-term risks and benefits or the possibility of media attention?

- The possibility that subjects may be contacted for lifelong follow-up should be clear (Appendix M, III, B, 2, b).
- Use of contraception should be explicitly stated for both males and females.
- Potential need for confinement be should be outlined.
- Potential exposure for family members should be noted.
- Risk of media exposure should be explained.
- Subjects should be informed that an autopsy will be requested.

Gene transfer, if successful, will constitute a revolution in medical science. However, gene transfer research has raised uniquely complex scientific, medical, ethical and social issues that warrant special monitoring. Striking the balance between protections of subjects and communities while advancing promising research will continue to be a challenging task.

CHAPTER

Special Ethical Concerns in Clinical Research

At the conclusion of this chapter, readers will be able to:
- Discuss the ethical issues with the use of placebos in clinical research.
- Describe guidelines for using placebos in clinical trials.
- Describe the use, roles and responsibilities of DMCs and how the DMC interacts with IRBs, investigators, sponsors and external regulatory bodies.
- Describe the process by which DMCs make recommendations to modify the conduct of ongoing clinical trials.

The Use of Placebo

The fifth revision of the Declaration of Helsinki included a principle that stated, "The benefits, risks, burdens and effectiveness of a new method should be tested against the best current prophylactic, diagnostic and therapeutic method." This seemed to preclude the use of placebo in clinical research whenever standard treatment is available. Although this statement was subsequently clarified to not preclude all uses of placebo, it intensified the long-standing discussion of and concern about placebo use and the ethical review of clinical research.

A central ethical question with the use of placebo is whether the subjects in placebo control groups of a research study are being unfairly denied a medical benefit. The concern becomes even more important when the use of placebo might imply the risk of irreversible harm or major discomfort. On the other hand, the degree of placebo response in certain conditions and the effectiveness of comparator treatments raise questions about the validity of the use of standard treatments as comparators.

Internationally sponsored research using placebo in developing countries has recently raised concerns regarding justice and the relationship between the welfare of individual subjects and the benefit to society. Some of these studies would have been considered to be unethical in most developed countries, but were justified on the basis of a different local standard of care. This raises the question of whether ehics requires that the practices in all parts of the world be identical.

> **Use of placebo dilemma: potential subject harm and the scientific validity of the study.**

The range of opinions regarding the use of placebo in clinical research varies between two extreme positions:

1. The insistence on placebo-controlled trials, which considers that placebo is the preferred comparator unless it exposes the subject to death or irreversible, severe damage, and provided that the subject consents to participate and tolerate the risks and discomforts of the investigation.
2. The categorical objection to the use of placebo, which maintains that whenever standard treatment exists, the use of placebo is unethical, and in such situations, research treatments should be compared with standard treatments.

All parties agree that the use of placebo is unacceptable in life-threatening diseases or in case of potential irreversible damage when there is effective treatment, but the dilemma persists as to whether it is ethical to deprive subjects of standard treatment and expose them to a lesser degree to risks and discomforts. Some bioethicists agree that if placebo is required for scientific validity in a research study, this constitutes one ethical argument in favor, though not the full justification, of the use of placebo. An appeal to the subjects' autonomy is another justification for the use of placebo. This argument relies heavily upon the disclosure of the risks of placebo in the process of informed consent; however, some believe that this just transfers the ethical burden to the research subject. The ethical acceptability of disclosure as a justification for the use of placebo depends on the subjects' capacity to understand the implications of participating in a research study.

Federal regulations and international guidelines rely on independent ethical review to help ensure that research subjects are not exposed to unnecessary risks including those presented by the use of placebo. Also, they recommend that additional safeguards be taken in research involving vulnerable populations, so studies that have been judged ethical for autonomous adult subjects may not be acceptable for children or people with mental incapacities. Strictly speaking, because placebo is inactive, it does not exert any physiological effect. Subjects' expectations of the encounter with the healing setting (doctor or drug), however, have been shown to produce objective signs of improvement in several medical conditions that, in the absence of a placebo arm, could be inaccurately attributed to the research treatment. The placebo arm is also used to measure the side-effect profile of the treatment under study. The magnitude of placebo response can only be measured by comparing the experimental group with a placebo-controlled group.

On the other hand, the validity of the use of an active comparator depends heavily on the efficacy of the treatment for a certain condition. Unless the efficacy of a standard treatment has been consistently and unequivocally proven, the omission of a placebo arm in the evaluation of a research treatment may be disadvantageous. For scientific validity, the choice of the active comparator would eventually have to be supported by previous studies against placebo; however, limitations to comparability will persist, since placebo response for the same condition may vary geographically and historically depending on the population under study, the medical care environment and the assessment methods. Also, the definition of standard treatment may not be universal, and research outcomes using different local practice comparators would be difficult to interpret and compare.

The use of placebo in clinical research has several purposes:

1. To measure subjective response to the research treatment caused by the subjects' expectations of improvement as opposed to therapeutic effect.
2. To differentiate the improvement attributable to the study treatment from the improvement due to other factors, such as spontaneous remission, diet, local care and supplements.
3. To determine the baseline (no treatment) improvement.
4. To distinguish the adverse events related to the investigational treatment from those caused by chance or concomitant treatments, and from the complications of the disease.
5. To make the subjects of the control group indistinguishable from the subjects who receive the experimental treatment and thus, to blind the assessment of the therapeutic effects and the adverse events.
6. To help pursue the possibility that while a new drug might be less effective on average than the standard, the new drug is at least better than nothing and some individuals might find the new drug better than the standard.

The complexity and variety of ethical and scientific concerns regarding the use of placebo requires that its ethical acceptability be determined on a case-to-case basis. The assessment of the risks and benefits of the use of placebo versus the use of standard treatment is a required step for investigators and IRBs. Although ethical principles are deemed to be universal, potential risks and benefits apply to a concrete time and population, and the ethical acceptability of study designs, including those that use placebo, do differ depending on the particular circumstances of each research study.

Points to Consider

To facilitate and systematize the ethical review of the use of placebo, algorithms and guidelines have been published. In general, they include the following aspects:

The Scientific Justification for the Use of Placebo

References to the expected spontaneous remission in diseases such as viral respiratory tract infections or bacterial conjunctivitis and the magnitude of the "placebo effect" in conditions such as depression and anxiety are valuable to evaluate the scientific need for the use of placebo. The "state of the art" in the use of active comparators, the effectiveness and consistency of the standard treatment and the existence of "gold standards" of efficacy should also be addressed. Additionally, the therapeutic role of concurrent interventions that constitute "standard of care" ought to be considered.

The Evaluation of the Potential Risks of the Use of Placebo as Compared to the Risks and Benefits of Standard Treatment

The risks of irreversible harm or severe discomfort due to the use of placebo are unacceptable if proven therapeutic methods exist. Less severe risks should be evaluated relative to the potential benefits. The risks and benefits of the active treatment should be stated.

Risk Management in the Research Protocol

Per federal regulations and ethical standards, the inherent risks of the use of placebo and other research procedures should be minimized in the research protocol. For instance, high-risk subjects, such as diabetic subjects with a history of ketoacidosis, should not be enrolled in placebo-controlled trials of oral hypoglycemia. The use of placebo should be restricted to the minimum time required to show the medical benefit, and adequate risk monitoring and stopping rules should be in place to identify and manage deterioration in early stages. Should there be a risk of an acute crisis, as in asthma, or the possibility of severe pain, rescue medication should be available.

Whether the Use of Placebo and Its Potential Risks Have Been Adequately Addressed in the Consent Form

Once the risk/benefit assessment has determined that the research study does not expose subjects to excessive, unnecessary risks, the investigator should ensure that the use of placebo and the risks and burdens that it implies are appropriately described in the consent form. Any change in the standard of care that may occur during the conduct of the study and might affect the willingness of the subject to remain in the study should be promptly communicated to the subject. The inclusion of overly reassuring language should be avoided.

> **The subject must be adequately informed of the risks involved in participating in a placebo controlled study.**

Cases

Case #1

Newly depressed subjects were recruited for an eight-week, double-blind study of an investigational antidepressant versus placebo. Treatment-resistant, suicidal and severely depressed subjects were excluded. Assessment visits were planned at weeks one, two, four, six and eight and follow-up visits at weeks ten and twelve. The IRB requested that discontinuation criteria for relapse or deterioration be clearly defined and that emergency treatment be available. The protocol was approved once amended.

Case #2

A double-blind, twelve-week study of an investigational inhaled antiasthmatic steroid versus placebo in mild-to-moderate persistent asthma in teenagers. The parents' permission and the subject's assent would be obtained, and the personal physician would be informed of the subject's participation in the study. After washout, spirometric parameters would be evaluated and high-risk subjects excluded. A personal peak flow meter would be provided for daily monitoring of the expiratory flow. Rescue medication (a $beta_2$-adrenergic bronchodilator) would be available and discontinuation criteria for clinical deterioration were clearly defined. The IRB approved the protocol.

Case #3

Subjects undergoing chemotherapy with the potential to develop mucositis would be enrolled in a double-blind, placebo-controlled study. If they developed mucositis grade ≥ 3, they would be randomized to receive, in addition to standard mucositis care, the investigational drug or placebo. The IRB approved the study.

In conclusion, the use of placebo in clinical research is ethically acceptable if: (1) placebo is necessary for scientific reasons, (2) the use of placebo does not expose the subject to excessive or unnecessary risks, and (3) the subject is adequately informed of the risks and burdens of the use of placebo, and freely consents to participate. Placebo use with vulnerable subjects may also be ethically acceptable if they receive additional appropriate protection and the corresponding permission and assent signatures, as applicable, are obtained.

Data Monitoring Committees

Introduction

When researchers think of the responsibility for human subject protection in clinical trials they often think of the Institutional Review Board (IRB). The fact is that human subject protection in clinical trials is shared among the IRB, principal investigator, clinical trial sponsors and oversight boards/committees. One such committee is the Data Monitoring Committee (DMC). The role of the DMC has recently come to the forefront of research subject protections as a result of some research-related tragedies over the past few years. This chapter provides an overview of the federal guidelines relating to DMCs, when and how they should be formed, and the responsibilities of the DMC, investigator, IRB, trial sponsor and regulatory bodies charged with oversight of clinical research.

DMCs Defined

A DMC is a group of individuals with clinical expertise in the areas pertinent to the disease state and treatments being studied in controlled clinical trials. DMCs typically also include a biostatistician who possesses a background and knowledge relevant to the conduct of clinical trials and analysis of clinical trial data and may also include an ethicist. As a group, the DMC acts as an independent review/advisory board whose primary mission is to measure and report on the continuing safety of current research subjects as well as subjects who have not yet enrolled. The DMC accomplishes this through meeting on a regular basis and reviewing the accumulating data in an ongoing clinical trial. Through this process, the DMC is also assessing the continuing validity and scientific merit of the trial.

Background and History of DMCs

National Institutes of Health (NIH) Sponsored Studies

The use of DMCs was first established in the early 1960s. They were used primarily in large, multi-center trials where the study end points were to assess improved survival or risk of major morbidity. NIH established these committees to conduct in-process monitoring of the studies in order to ensure the safety of the trial subjects. Until the year 2001, DMCs were largely referred to as Data Safety Monitoring Boards (DSMBs). The name was changed to coincide with the proposed wording from the International Conference on Harmonization. This section outlines the history and evolution of significant regulations that form the basis for both the current and future use of DMCs.

- In 1979, the NIH Clinical Trials Committee issued recommendations that "every clinical trial should have provision for data and safety monitoring." The NIH acknowledged that in some cases, the principal investigator (PI) might be expected to perform the monitoring function.

■ In June 1998, the NIH issued a policy for data and safety monitoring. The policy was a result of the Office of Extramural Research's Committee on Clinical Trial Monitoring recommendation that "all trials, even those that pose little likelihood of harm, should consider an external monitoring body." The 1998 policy stated that all clinical trials require monitoring, and that the method and degree of monitoring required should be related to the degree of risk involved.

■ Additional guidance was issued in June 1999. This guidance directed that all multi-site trials with data monitoring boards must forward summary reports of adverse events to IRBs. The guidance specifically addressed the need for communication between the DMC and the IRB.

■ The most recent guidance on data and safety monitoring was issued in June 2000. The purpose of this guidance was twofold: (1) requiring investigators to submit a monitoring plan for phase 1 and 2 clinical trials to the NIH funding Institute and Center (IC) before the trial begins and; (2) to provide further guidance/clarification to the June 1998 policy for monitoring phase 1 and 2 trials.

FDA-Regulated Studies

In November 2001, the FDA issued the Draft Guideline for Clinical Trial Sponsors on the Establishment and Operation of Clinical Trial Data Monitoring Committees. The guidance document was intended to assist sponsors in determining when a DMC may be necessary and how the agency believes such committees should operate. Prior to this guidance, FDA guidelines did not require the use of DMCs except for those studies that allowed the informed consent requirement to be waived, i.e., studies that are conducted in emergency situations. Further, it should be noted that the references in this guidance confer DMC responsibility on any individual or group to which the sponsor has delegated relevant management responsibility (contract research organizations, for example). This was the first FDA document to thoroughly explore DMCs and to provide the public with the agency's current thinking on this topic.

It is important to remember that the following information is based upon the November 2001 guidelines, which are in the draft stage at the time of publication.

When a DMC Is Needed

All clinical trials require safety monitoring, but not all trials require a DMC. The FDA draft guidance specifically states that DMCs should be established for controlled trials where mortality and major morbidity serve as the primary or secondary end points. Other major factors to consider regarding the establishment of a DMC are outlined below. Certainly, research subject safety is of the utmost importance. The following bulleted points are presented in a "points-to-consider" format to allow investigators and sponsors to deliberate the necessity of establishing a DMC:

Subject Safety
- Is mortality or major morbidity an end point?
- Would positive or negative results during the study require termination for ethical reasons?
- Is there little knowledge regarding the safety of the intervention (drug/device) or is there knowledge of safety concerns (potential toxicity)?
- Is the targeted study population fragile, e.g., elderly, children, pregnant women, where there may be an increased risk?
- Is the study a large, multi-center trial, with a long duration, where subjects would have greater exposure possibly resulting in adverse events that would not be as easily identified in single-center studies with shorter durations?

The FDA guidance suggests that if the answer to any or all of the above is yes, then the use of a DMC may be warranted.

> **A DMC should be established in trials where mortality and morbidity serve as end points.**

Practicality
- Is the study a short-term trial where a DMC would not have adequate time to respond?
- If the study is a short-term trial where subject safety is a concern, are there mechanisms in place where a DMC would be notified quickly of unexpected events/results?

The guidance recognizes that many clinical trials evaluate interventions to relieve symptoms. These studies are usually of short duration and smaller than major outcome studies. DMCs usually have not been established to monitor these types of trials.

Scientific Validity
- Is the study of long duration in which changes in the understanding of the disease process, the target population or new treatment discoveries would warrant changes to the trial as it progresses?

The Draft Guideline recognizes that a DMC may be useful in that it is correctly positioned to monitor changes to a trial, over time, in an unbiased and subject-protective manner. Major implications could arise, however, if this process is not carefully managed, i.e., sponsor exposure to un-blinded, interim data. This issue is also addressed in the Draft Guideline.

Composition and Administration of DMCs

Committee Composition

There is a tremendous amount of responsibility placed on the DMC in terms of its power to make recommendations based upon the data it receives from the trial itself as well as from external sources. It is usually the trial sponsor or trial steering committee that appoints the DMC members. The FDA guidance suggests that the following factors be used to consider the selection of DMC members:

- Relevant expertise (clinical specialty, biostatistician, pharmacologist, toxicologist, bioethicist).
- Previous DMC experience.
- Clinical trial experience.
- In all cases, DMC members should be free of conflicts of interest or any perceived conflicts that can be financial, scientific or intellectual in nature.

Administration

Each DMC should establish procedures up front on how it will operate. Factors to consider are:

- Meeting schedule/frequency (based on expected rates of accrual/risks to subjects).
- Meeting structure—open session to allow investigator and sponsor attendance versus closed session where blinded and confidential information is discussed.
- Format of the interim reports that the sponsor provides to the DMC.
- Statistical methods to be used for the interim analyses.

DMC Responsibilities

The main responsibility of a DMC is to review accumulating data from an ongoing clinical trial on a regular basis. After thorough analysis of the accumulated data, the DMC may advise the sponsor and/or IRB regarding the continuing safety of subjects in the trial and of those yet to be recruited, as well as the continuing validity and scientific safety of the trial.

> **The DMC is responsible for recommending trial termination when subject safety is jeopardized.**

The DMC accomplishes this by:

- Safety Monitoring
  - Interim review of adverse events in each arm of the study.
  - Making judgments on early termination of a trial when based on the types and extent of adverse events if the risks outweigh the benefits.

- Monitoring for Effectiveness
  - It is important in studies with serious outcomes that any treatment advance is made available as soon as possible but only when based on the predetermined statistical monitoring plan.
  - It is just as important to terminate a study when the predetermined benefit has no chance of being achieved.

- Monitoring Study Conduct
  - Reviewing and assuring that rates of recruitment are adequate.
  - Assessing whether eligibility requirements are being met.
  - Reviewing any excessive protocol violations.
  - Verifying completeness and timeliness of the data accumulated.
  - Evaluating excessive dropout rates (could affect interpretation of study results).

- Monitoring External Data
  - Reviewing results of related studies, which may affect the design of the ongoing study or its continuation.

- Making Recommendations
  - The primary responsibility of a DMC is to make recommendations to the sponsor and/or IRB regarding the continuation of the study. These recommendations could include continuation with modification, temporary suspension of enrollment or intervention.
  - Recommendations, supported by a rationale, should be documented in a clear, concise manner for review by the sponsor, IRB or regulatory agency.

- Maintenance of Records
  - Keep minutes of all meetings and issue the sponsor a report based on the minutes.
  - Minutes should contain two parts, depending on confidential information (unblinded comparative data) being discussed, i.e., the open and closed parts of the meetings are kept separate.

Regulatory Safety Reporting Requirements

Studies conducted under an Investigational New Drug application (IND) or Investigational Device Exemption (IDE) are subject to safety reporting requirements. These requirements include the reporting of serious unexpected events to the FDA by the sponsor. There may be instances where a DMC may detect a greater frequency of serious adverse events in one arm of a controlled study. This finding, reported to the sponsor as part of a recommendation to modify the study, would be considered serious and unexpected, and the sponsor would be required to report this to the FDA as well as to all other study investigators.

Investigator Responsibilities

In studies where DMCs are involved, the investigator is still responsible for identifying potential adverse events experienced by the study subjects and reporting them to the sponsor.

When the investigator is the sponsor of the clinical research study, the investigator assumes all the roles of a sponsor in addition to that of the investigator. Refer to "Sponsor Responsibilities" below for the sponsor-investigator responsibilities when a DMC is involved.

IRB Responsibilities

After its initial approval of studies, the IRB is responsible for reviewing all available information both from the study site and external sources to ensure the continued acceptability of the trial. The IRB may take actions based on the recommendations of the DMC to the sponsor.

Sponsor Responsibilities

The trial sponsor is responsible for thoroughly reviewing the recommendations of the DMC and taking appropriate actions regarding modifications or termination of the study. In addition to determining when a DMC is needed and the appointment of individuals to serve on the DMC, the following are usually the procedures undertaken by the sponsor:

- Appointing the committee chair.
- Establishing procedures to assess potential conflicts of interests of potential members.
- Ensuring the confidentiality of the interim data analyses.
- Establishing or approving DMC Standard Operating Procedures (SOPs), i.e., meeting schedules, format of reports, statistical methods.
- Submission to FDA of all DMC meeting records and interim reports.
- Notifying FDA and responsible IRBs of any recommendations or requests made by the DMC regarding the safety of the participants.
- Consulting with FDA before accessing interim data, terminating the study or modifying the protocol (could affect the validity of the study).

Other Oversight Groups

There may be additional individuals or groups that assume or share the responsibility of clinical trial monitoring or oversight.

Clinical Trial Steering Committees

A sponsor may appoint a steering committee to design the study, ensure the quality of the study conduct and write the final study report. The committee is usually comprised of investigators, sponsor representatives and experts not directly involved in the study. If a steering committee is in place, the sponsor may have the DMC communicating directly with the committee.

Site Monitoring

The staff of the sponsor, e.g., industry clinical research associates, NIH Institute Centers, or groups under contract to the sponsor, usually perform site monitoring. They monitor for site adherence to Good Clinical Practices (GCPs), which includes adherence to protocol, informed consent compliance, reporting of all adverse events, source documents (case histories) and data accuracy (case report form entries).

13

Participant Recruitment and Retention in Clinical Trials

At the conclusion of this chapter, readers will be able to:

- Identify special populations for inclusion in clinical trials.
- Describe a variety of recruitment methods and the potential benefits and disadvantages of each.
- Define the IRB role in the review of advertising materials.
- Understand the need to set realistic recruitment and retention goals for clinical trials.

Introduction

The process of evaluating new drugs is labor intensive and expensive. It requires a great deal of pre-clinical testing, followed by a range of clinical safety and efficacy studies. It is critical that the findings of a particular clinical efficacy study are generalizable to the projected treatment populations. Therefore, finding appropriate research participants is of paramount importance and probably the most difficult and challenging aspect of a clinical trial. Recruitment is almost inevitably time consuming, expensive, requiring great ingenuity, resourcefulness and flexibility. It has been reported that 25% of all delays in drug development are due to slower than expected subject recruitment. The investigator should be realistic when determining the feasibility of recruiting participants prior to conducting a study.

Recruiting is an issue that must be considered before the study and continuing through the duration of the trial. In a 1999 survey, CenterWatch found that only one out of every 16 people that are eligible actually volunteers or participates in clinical trials. Recruitment efforts fail for a number of reasons including conflicting clinical trials for similar treatments; new and competing products becoming available on the market; poor protocol design; workload of the study investigator and study staff; and negative public perception of and lack of trust in clinical research. Conflicts with potential subjects' schedules are also often cited as a reason for non-participation in clinical trials.

> **The investigator should be realistic when determining the feasibility of recruiting participants prior to conducting a study.**

Education of Potential Participants

One of the key components of successful recruitment stems from educated patients who understand clinical trials, their role in the clinical trial and how they may or may not personally benefit from participation in the trial. Educating potential participants takes time, resources and patience.

In recent years, there has been a rash of negative reports about clinical trials, highlighting deaths and injuries that have occurred. These tragedies have undermined public confidence in research, thus making it more difficult for investigators to recruit participants. Ultimately it is the investigator's responsibility to address any safety concerns that a potential participant may have. This is best done by ensuring the study design does everything possible to protect the safety and welfare of research participants.

Why Patients Join Clinical Trials

Patients join clinical trials for a myriad of reasons, including wanting to help advance the science of their disease, a lack of available therapies, a desire to obtain improved medical care, lack of health insurance, advice from a primary care physician or financial or other reasons. The decision whether or not to participate is a very complex process that involves not only what is known about a drug, but also the patient's reaction to their disease, their relationship with their doctor and their cultural roots. Understanding why a patient chooses to participate is helpful and will aid with recruitment as well as assisting in the retention of participants for the full duration of the trial.

The well-discussed phenomenon of "therapeutic misconception" must be considered among the reasons patients volunteer for trials. Simply put, despite cautions about lack of direct benefit in the consent forms and verbal statements from investigators confirming the questionable nature of benefits, many patients still believe that clinical trials are "treatment." This is particularly evident when patients have serious diseases, such as cancer and AIDS. Investigators must guard against overstating the benefits of research and should ensure that patients make a realistic assessment of benefits and risks before volunteering to become subjects.

The most frequently mentioned concern about why people do not participate in clinical trials is the fear of receiving placebo instead of active drug. Another concern is the fear that study drugs may cause risky side effects. With increased effort focused on education regarding clinical trials, individuals who agree to participate in clinical trials should have a better understanding of the risks and benefits of participation.

Recruitment of Special Populations

It is important to include a representative population in most clinical trials. A representative population generally means that the study should include men, women, minorities and age-appropriate participants, in keeping with the proportion of individuals afflicted with the disease or condition being studied. In many cases, including a representative population is not only important but also mandatory. For example, the National Institutes of Health (NIH) has made the inclusion of appropriate numbers of women and minorities an explicit criterion to be considered when reviewing grant applications. Similarly, the Food and Drug Administration (FDA) now requires that data being submitted in support of a new drug application (NDA) include an appropriate number of female and minority participants, and that the data be analyzed to determine differing effects on these populations.

Specific considerations for recruitment of various populations are:

Minorities
Much has been written about the lack of participation by minorities in clinical trials in the United States. Medical research in general is viewed by African Americans with suspicion, in part due to the legacy of the Syphilis Study. Other barriers include economic factors and lack of awareness about clinical research. However, as many authors have noted, these barriers can be surmounted with careful planning. Specifically, efforts to address minority participant concerns prior to participation via educational materials, the availability of transportation, meals and child care services as needed, the use of home visits or study centers with convenient locations, participation by minority researchers and research staff, the use of study materials in other languages, investigator or other study staff of the same ethnicity, and efforts to educate and develop trust with potential participants can lead to greater minority participation.

> **Barriers to recruiting minorities can be surmounted with careful planning, time and effort upfront to better understand the needs and concerns of the targeted populations.**

Women

Today, in many studies, women make up 50% or more of the study cohort. This has not always been the case. As recently as the early 1990s, it was the FDA's stated guideline that women of childbearing potential were to be excluded from phase 1 and early phase 2 studies. Unfortunately, this policy, which was enacted in the early 1970s due to concerns over possible pregnancy and potential toxicity of experimental medications on the developing fetus, had the unintended effect of restricting participation by women in not only early trials, but later trials as well. In 1993, the FDA reversed that rule by publishing their "Guideline for the Study and Evaluation of Gender Differences in the Clinical Evaluation of Drugs." As noted above, the NIH has also published guidelines about the inclusion of women in NIH-sponsored clinical trials (Outreach Notebook for the NIH Guidelines on Inclusion of Women and Minorities as Subjects in Clinical Research).

The overarching rationales behind the NIH and FDA guidance and regulations apply to most clinical studies; i.e., to ensure that populations at risk for particular disease or receiving treatment are represented in relevant clinical trials, and to assess possible differences in the effects of treatment between women and men, based upon factors such as variations in body size and composition and the effects of hormones. For these reasons, it is important that every recruitment plan include mechanisms to ensure appropriate representation among both women and men.

Children

In 1998 the FDA issued a new rule designed to encourage and in some cases mandate the testing of new products in children. In the preamble to this rule, the FDA pointed out that a number of medications were very commonly prescribed for children, despite the absence of pediatric clinical trial data. The FDA concluded that the absence of pediatric labeling information posed significant risks for children.

Recruitment of children for clinical trials poses a variety of challenges, including the fact that children are legally not able to consent to the treatments or procedures being conducted during the clinical trial. Successful recruitment initiatives have included the use of brightly colored, easy-to-read recruitment materials and the availability of recruitment staff after hours, when parents are more likely to call.

Elderly

Participation of the elderly in clinical trials, as with other special populations, presents unique challenges; however, inclusion of adult participants in research should not be age restricted unless there is valid scientific and/or medical justification. Without recruitment methods directed specifically to the elderly, enrollment of seniors in certain clinical trials may be significantly less than expected. The reasons for this may include misconceptions about the benefits of enrollment in clinical trials, stringent eligibility criteria, coexisting medical conditions and logistical barriers.

To overcome some of these barriers, recruitment initiatives directed to encourage participation by the elderly have included conducting study visits at locations easily accessible by the study population (e.g., senior centers); providing transportation; targeting advertising to newspapers, periodicals and other media more typically read or seen by seniors; recruitment via physician offices; and community-based initiatives that target locations frequented by seniors.

Recruiting Study Participants

Once the appropriate study population has been identified, and recruitment methods have been designed to reach special populations, there are a number of recruitment mechanisms available to study investigators. Regardless of the method used (print, radio, television, Internet, etc.), the IRB should review the methods and the content of the message. IRB review is necessary to ensure that the information is not misleading or coercive to potential participants, does not state a certainty of favorable outcome and does not imply benefit beyond what is outlined in the consent document and the protocol.

Recruitment methods include public relations and direct advertising. Paid advertising may be more expensive and less effective than trying to raise general public awareness via a public relations campaign. Critical to the success of direct advertisement or any of the other alternatives is ensuring that a correct factual message is delivered to get the targeted population interested in making the initial contact with the site. The following venues are commonly used: TV, radio, newspaper, magazines, posters, flyers, brochures, Internet, mass mailings, advocacy group newsletters, support group meetings, formal referrals or informal word-of-mouth, health workshops, screenings, health fairs, chart/record review etc. A few of the most popular recruitment tools are described in further detail below.

Advertising

Direct advertising (e.g., TV, radio or newspaper ads) is seen as part of the informed consent and participant selection process. Making claims either explicitly or implicitly that the test article is safe or effective for the purpose under investigation, or that it is known to be equivalent or superior to any other treatments, is misleading to participants and it is also a violation of FDA regulations [21 CFR 312.7(a) and 21 CFR 812.7(d)]. In general, the FDA believes that advertisements should be limited to the information the prospective participants need to determine their eligibility and interest.

Advertising material for clinical trials should not use terms such as "new treatment," "new medication" or "new drug" without explaining that the test article is investigational. The FDA believes that such characterizations may lead study participants to believe they will be receiving newly improved products of proven worth. Additionally, advertisements should not promise "free medical treatment," when the intent is to say participants will not be charged for taking part in the investigation. Also, the promise of treatment without charge may be coercive to financially constrained participants. Advertisements may state that participants will be paid, but should not emphasize the payment or the amount to be paid.

When setting up a recruitment campaign, the best approach is to utilize several recruitment tactics concurrently and to measure the success rate of each. The investigator should be prepared to change the recruitment campaign mid-stream if some or all of the components are not successful.

Advertising pointers:
- **Avoid acronyms. They may not be understood by the target audience.**
- **Place the ad carefully to reach the appropriate audience.**
- **Advertise frequently in the right places.**
- **Measure the effectiveness of the advertising technique.**
- **Modify tactics as needed.**

Recruitment from Practice and Databases

In some studies, the majority of participants recruited come from the investigator's own practice or through recruitment initiatives that utilize hospital medical record or other databases. The advantage to this recruitment method is that it allows the study staff to review records to pre-select potentially eligible subjects. An important factor to consider when utilizing practice or hospital medical record databases, however, is the Health Insurance Portability and Accountability Act (HIPAA) Privacy Rule, which imposes strict privacy requirements for medical record information. (See Chapter 15 to learn more about HIPAA's impact on recruitment from practice records and databases).

Call Centers

Recent trends in the pharmaceutical industry utilize call centers in order to improve subject identification, study participant management, compliance assistance and study follow-up. These call centers help minimize the burden at the site by referring only pre-screened patients to investigative sites. Services offered include inbound patient screening, outbound calling to recruit patients, scheduling of participant visits, advertising and medical placement assistance and feedback during the trial. (See Chapter 15 to learn more about the impact of the HIPAA Privacy Rule on utilization of call centers.)

Participant Recruitment/ Retention Incentives

Payments to Subjects for Participation

Financial incentives are often used to help recruitment efforts when health benefits to participants are remote or non-existent, e.g., with healthy volunteers in early phases of clinical research. Payments should not present an undue influence to potential subjects. The payment to the participant should not be contingent upon the participant's completing the entire study. When using payments, proposed payment information and the text of any advertising materials must be reviewed by the IRB.

> **Payments to participants are not considered a benefit but a recruitment incentive.**

Retention Incentives

While recruiting the participant into a clinical trial is the most difficult component of conducting clinical trials, maintaining a participant in the study for the full study period may also prove to be challenging. Participants prematurely withdraw from studies for various reasons (e.g., perceived lack of efficacy, interference with work or family schedule, travel becomes burdensome, family members or the primary care physician advises against continued participation, adverse experience, etc.). Too many premature withdrawals have the potential to negatively impact study results. The investigator and the study staff should make a concerted effort to maintain participants in a study for the full study period, while not compromising the rights, safety and welfare of the research participants. Retention of participants requires both selective screening and a good relationship between the subject, investigator, and coordinator. Contacting the participant via phone between in-person visits, sending newsletters to participants about study progress or updating them with new information about their disease are methods that have been successfully used to keep participants vested in the study.

Recruitment Strategies by Sponsors

In an effort to enhance recruitment, sponsors may offer financial and other incentives to sites that meet or exceed enrollment goals. Certain financial incentives, however, may compromise the integrity of studies or may give an appearance of affecting the judgment of the investigator/research team. In some cases, such payments may violate professional ethics codes, federal regulations and/or institutional policies. Examples of commonly prohibited incentives are:

- *Finder's Fees*—payment for referring potential participants to investigators.
- *Bonus Payments*—additional payments to the investigator, study coordinator, enrollers or the institution for enhanced enrollment, when the payments are not related to increased trial costs.

Other types of payments, such as increased payment for additional expenses incurred by the site, and supplemental payments based upon costs of enrollment not originally anticipated are usually permissible. For example, added visits, additional procedures at each visit (e.g., added ECG, diary, blood draw, efficacy evaluation, etc.) are permissible. In all cases where additional payments are made, such payments should be incorporated into the contract with the study sponsor.

Setting the Proper Tone in Recruiting Subjects

In designing recruitment strategies, investigators and sponsors must balance their enthusiasm for the research with the need to maintain an atmosphere that minimizes the possibility of coercion or undue influence (21 CFR 50.20 and 45 CFR 46.116). The FDA Information Sheet (http://www.fda.gov/oc/ohrt/irbs/recruiting) offers additional guidance on recruitment practices.

Communicating an excessive or unrealistic enthusiasm about the possible benefits of the research to potential subjects, either consciously or unconsciously, may unduly influence subjects' enrollment decisions. Both the atmosphere of the consent conference and the language of the consent document must enhance the prospective subject's ability to make a truly informed and objective decision about whether or not to participate.

All recruitment programs must be free of advertising strategies or incentive arrangements that unduly influence subjects' enrollment decisions. IRBs must review the methods and materials that investigators propose to use in recruiting subjects to ensure that they do not present subjects with coercive or other undue influences that could compromise their right to exercise free, autonomous and informed consent.

Conclusion

In general, a successful recruitment strategy requires early planning, with multiple strategies for recruitment and tracking success or lack of success, of each strategy used, reviewing the progress, revising the plan as necessary and treating the participants well. For successful subject recruitment, the research site should have the ability to draw from a broad population, a cohesive staff that can respond to a large number of calls generated by media campaigns, continuous meetings with site staff to ensure everyone understands the goals of the study and the ability to shift rapidly from unsuccessful recruitment strategies. Addressing barriers to enrollment is also important and considerations include appropriate and payment for time and effort. The object of recruitment strategies is to enroll interested, eligible and informed subjects in a manner that respects their privacy and autonomy.

Research with Secondary Subjects, Tissue Studies and Records Reviews

---

At the conclusion of this chapter, readers will be able to:

- Understand the concept of "secondary subjects" and the regulatory basis for this concept.
- Discuss the human subject protection issues related to conducting research with human tissues.
- Address issues pertaining to the human subject protection issues related to conducting research with collections of data.

Introduction

While the greater part of this book addresses research involving direct intervention with subjects, there are also several categories of research that involve the collection of information about individuals from sources other than through direct intervention. The examples discussed in this chapter are the collection of information about the family members of an individual subject with whom the investigator has direct contact ("secondary" or "third party" subjects), the study of human tissue samples, and the study of collected "data sets" such as medical records. The principal risks involved in these types of research are a breach of confidentiality and a violation of privacy. Confidentiality and privacy are supported by two of the three principles identified in the Belmont Report, respect for persons and beneficence. Respect for persons requires that subjects be allowed to exercise their autonomy, including the autonomy to maintain their privacy and to have private information that identifies them kept confidential. Beneficence requires that risks to subjects are minimized, benefits are maximized and that risks to subjects do not outweigh the benefits to subjects and to others. The maintenance of confidentiality and privacy helps to protect subjects from a variety of potential harms, including psychological distress, loss of insurance, loss of employment and damage to social standing.

> **Secondary subjects' confidentiality and privacy must be protected.**

Secondary Subjects

The concept of "secondary" or "third party" subjects has come to light primarily through genetics research, which relies on family history and the creation of pedigrees for critical information and validity. The issue of whether to obtain consent from secondary subjects has a potential impact on genetics research and on other types of research as well.

The definition of a research subject is provided in the DHHS regulations [45 CFR 46.102(f)]and "Common Rule":

- *Human subject* means a living individual about whom an investigator (whether professional or student) conducting research obtains (1) data through intervention or interaction with the individual, or (2) identifiable private information.
- *Intervention* includes both physical procedures by which data are gathered (e.g., venipuncture) and manipulations of the subject or the subject's environment that are performed for research purposes. Interaction includes communication or interpersonal contact between investigator and subject.
- *Private information* includes information about a behavior that occurs in a context in which an individual can reasonably expect that no observation or recording is taking place, and information that has been provided for specific purposes by an individual and that the individual can reasonably expect will not be made public (e.g., a medical record). Private information must be individually identifiable (i.e., the identity of the subject is or may readily be ascertained by the investigator or associated with the information) in order for information to constitute research involving human subjects.

There are four key elements of this definition of a human subject:
- A living individual.
- An individual about whom an investigator obtains data in a research context.
- The investigator obtains the data through intervention or interaction with the individual.

■ The investigator otherwise obtains identifiable private information.

According to the federal definition, "identifiable private information" includes information about an individual:
■ Which occurs in a context with no expectation of observation or recording.
■ That is provided for specific purposes by an individual.
■ Where there is a reasonable expectation it will not be made public.
■ That is individually identifiable or the identity may be readily ascertained.

It is from this definition of a human research subject that the concept of secondary subjects arises. When a detailed family history is obtained from a subject enrolled in a research study, with private information obtained on specific family members, those family members may also need to be considered subjects in the research study. The determination of who is a human subject rests with the IRB.

For instance, in a genetic study of acne, an investigator wishes to track possible genetic inheritance patterns of this disorder and potential co-morbidities. The investigator obtains appropriate informed consent from an individual with acne, and then asks that subject for detailed family medical histories in order to construct a pedigree and identify family members with the same co-morbidities. The investigator and the IRB must consider first whether the information obtained on the family members will be "identifiable private information." If so, those family members are also subjects in the research. Consent from the family members (secondary subjects) must then be obtained prior to soliciting the information from the primary subject, or consent may be waived or altered for these subjects, in accordance with federal regulations.

Obviously, one of the contested issues regarding secondary subjects is what is to be considered "private" information. For example, many researchers argue that information freely shared and known within a family is not "private" information but belongs to each member of that family. Others counter that this is an example of information sharing that an individual "can reasonably expect will not be made public."

This issue becomes more critical and problematic when very sensitive information is being obtained. In research on areas such as mental illness, behavioral disorders, substance abuse and dependence or seizure disorders, obtaining personal identifiable information on third parties can have significant consequences for those individuals. As required by federal regulation, potential harm to subjects resulting from the disclosure of private information, and not just the potential physical risks of research, must be a part of the risk/benefit analysis of the research and its impact on subjects. Prior consent becomes a crucial consideration in such instances.

> **Disclosing personal identifiable information about third parties can potentially cause harm to these subjects.**

The definition of "identifiable information" is also a contested issue. If family member names are not used but reference is made to specific members of the subject's family—such as "mother," "father," "maternal grandfather"—the identity of these un-named family members may still be "readily ascertained by the investigator" in relation to the subject, and therefore is identifiable.

Research Involving Human Tissues

Human tissue samples have long been stored for a variety of purposes, including research, and they can serve as a valuable source of information. There are thousands of collections of stored human tissue samples, which can be referred to generically as tissue banks, maintained in a wide variety of settings. Examples include pathology collections, newborn screening collections, blood banks, umbilical cord blood banks, organ banks, forensic DNA banks, military DNA banks and dedicated tissue storage facilities. They can be located in government, non-profit and for-profit institutions. Many of these tissue banks were not created for research purposes, but they often become a source of research material. Research with human tissues involves several unique considerations regarding subject confidentiality and privacy, regulatory interpretation and IRB oversight.

Research with tissues may require informed consent from subjects, or it may qualify for a waiver of consent, and may even qualify as exempt from IRB review. A key issue in the ethical and regulatory analysis of research with tissues is whether and how easily the person who provided the tissue can be identified. As with secondary subjects, the federal definition of "human subject" determines when IRB review is required for research under Common Rule jurisdiction. If an investigator conducting research with tissue obtains "identifiable private information," then the individuals who provided the tissues are human subjects who must consent to the research use of the tissue unless the IRB finds it acceptable to waive consent.

When consent will be obtained, there are several issues that need to be addressed in the consent process, such as:

- What tissue samples will be collected, and how they will be collected.
- What type(s) of research will, or may, be conducted using the tissue sample, including whether genetic analysis will be performed.
- Potential risks of disclosure of the information, such as negative effects on insurance coverage, employment status, emotional discomfort, familial strife or even harm to a cultural group.
- The potential benefits, including whether any results will be provided to the subject.

- What types of processes are in place to protect confidentiality and privacy. For instance, whether direct identifiers will be kept with the sample, or whether a code will be used. If a code is used, who will maintain the linking information, and how will that information be stored and protected?
- With whom the sample may be shared, if known.
- Whether the sample will eventually be anonymized (i.e., made unidentifiable), and if so, how and when.
- Whether there will be any commercial applications of the research.
- Whether the subject can have the sample destroyed if he or she decides to withdraw from the research.
- How long the samples will be kept.

There can be a great deal of variability in specific circumstances, and the consent process and format will need to be tailored to the specific situation.

Research with tissues may qualify for a waiver of consent for the use of the tissue under 45 CFR 46.116(d), if four conditions are met:

1. The research involves no more than minimal risk to the subjects.
2. The waiver or alteration will not adversely affect the rights and welfare of the subjects.
3. The research could not practicably be carried out without the waiver or alteration.
4. Whenever appropriate, the subjects will be provided with additional pertinent information after participation.

The application of these four criteria is often difficult. While most IRBs have traditionally felt that research with human tissues is minimal risk for the purposes of the first criterion, the recent explosion of genetic research and its possible implications for insurance and employment harms have caused some IRBs to consider at least some tissue research to involve more than minimal risk. For the second criterion, there is often debate whether the use of tissue in research without consent violates the rights and welfare of subjects. This may be a particularly important consideration when the tissues derive from a distinct cultural community such as Native Americans. Finally, the definition of "practicably" in the third criterion is often disputed. For tissue samples that are being collected prospectively, it is often inconvenient but still practicable to get consent from the research subjects.

Research with tissues may also be exempt from IRB review and informed consent requirements if the research involves the collection or study of existing pathological or diagnostic specimens, and if they are publicly available or if the information is recorded by the investigator in such a manner that subjects cannot be identified (45 CFR 46.101(b)(4)). For this exemption, the ability to identify the individual from whom the tissue was taken is a key feature. If all identifiers are severed, so that no one including the investigator can link the identity of the person providing the tissue to the sample, then that specimen is effectively unidentified, and any research using that sample may be exempt from the Common Rule requirements. However, if there is an identifying link kept by, or accessible to, the investigator between the individual donor and the sample, then the subject could be identified and the use of the sample for research falls under the Common Rule requirements. Recently, OHRP has stated that if the link between the individuals and the existing samples is maintained by the repository/bank, and the investigator does not have access to that link and the investigator signs an agreement not to re-identify the specimens, the sample is considered to be unidentified and the research may be exempt.

Furthermore, the research is only exempt under 45 CFR 46.101(b)(4) if the tissue collection is existing, i.e., it has already been collected and stored. If the tissue is going to be collected prospectively, then the exemption does not apply and the research must undergo IRB review. Very often, tissue banks are created for non-research purposes, and therefore are already existing at the time the research is initiated. If new tissues will continue to be added to the tissue bank after the initiation of research, then separate analyses need to be applied to those tissue samples that are already stored and those that will be collected prospectively. It may be possible to waive consent for the existing samples, or even for their use to be exempt, while at the same time obtaining consent for the prospectively collected samples.

Publishing Policies

The publishing policies of medical journals are another factor that may influence an investigator's decision on whether or not to get IRB review for research performed on tissue samples. Approximately half of the medical journals require IRB approval as a prerequisite for the publication of research involving human subjects. Therefore, an investigator conducting research with tissues in a situation in which the Common Rule requirement for IRB review does not apply may still need to have IRB review in order to publish the results.

FDA Regulations

Research with human tissue can also fall under FDA jurisdiction. When human tissues are used to test a device, such as an in vitro diagnostic device, and the sponsor intends to submit the data to the FDA as an application for marketing, then the research involves a clinical investigation and human subjects. When research is conducted under the FDA regulations, the waiver of consent under 45 CFR 46.116(d) is not applicable, and investigators must obtain full consent, including notice that the FDA may review the subject's identifiable research and medical records.

Multiple IRB Reviews

Another difficult matter in tissue research is that multiple IRBs often become involved in the oversight of the research. Often, tissue is collected at one institution, then stored at a tissue bank at a second institution, and finally transferred to a third institution for research purposes. The respective IRB for each of these institutions is responsible for overseeing compliance with federal regulations for the collection, storage and/or use of the tissues at that institution. However, it is often difficult for the IRB at a given institution to determine whether there are identifiers linking the tissue to the individual who provided the tissue, and whether proper consent was obtained for the use of the tissue in research. An investigator who will be using samples stored elsewhere can assist the IRB in its review of tissue research by gathering in advance the relevant documents such as prior IRB approvals, consent forms and privacy policies from the institutions where the tissue has been collected or handled.

Ownership of Tissues and Products Developed from Tissues

Another controversial issue is whether or not subjects have property rights to their tissues or products developed from their tissues. The most prominent legal case addressing this issue is Moore v. Regents of the University of California, in which the California Supreme Court found that the plaintiff, whose tissues were used to create a cell line valuable for producing substances such as immune interferon and macrophage-activating factor, did not have a property right, or any other legal right, to the products developed from his cells. In contrast, at least one state has, by statute, provided individuals a property right in their DNA. In the majority of states there is no legal precedent on the issue. Many sponsors and investigators try to ask subjects to waive their rights to the tissue and the products developed from this tissue as part of the consent process. However, both FDA and the Common Rule regulations state that "no informed consent, whether oral or written, may include any exculpatory language through which the subject or the representative is made to waive or appear to waive any of the subject's legal rights, or releases or appears to release the investigator, the sponsor, the institution or its agents from liability for negligence" (45 CFR 46.116, 21 CFR 50.20). Some have argued that this language is limited by the term "exculpatory" to waivers of blame for injury. However, both the OHRP and the FDA have issued guidance that interprets this regulatory language to apply to all legal rights, including property rights in tissue. This is a complex issue that continues to evolve and involves conflicting legal interpretation issues. However, unless the OHRP and FDA alter their guidance, investigators will be wise to avoid any waivers of legal rights.

Research Involving Record Reviews

Another source of research information that does not involve direct intervention with research subjects is the review of collected information in various media. For the purposes of this book, any type of stored data will be referred to as "data sets," and can include educational records, medical records (including images such as X-rays and photographs), billing records, disease registries, records created for Quality Assurance (QA) purposes, government databases such as prison or driving records and employment records. These data sets may be confidential or public and can be created and maintained by a wide variety of institutions.

Research with data sets may require informed consent from subjects, or may qualify for a waiver of consent or may be exempt from IRB review. A key issue is how easily the person whose information is in the data set can be identified. Another important consideration is whether the person performing the research has access to the data sets as part of their employment duties. For instance, if an investigator does not have access privileges to medical records that he or she wishes to review for research purposes, the issues of a breach of confidentiality and an invasion of privacy are concerns that must be addressed in the protocol and in any consent process.

As with secondary subjects and tissue research, the definition of "human subject" determines whether research with data sets is considered human subject research that requires IRB review. If the investigator is obtaining "identifiable private information" about individuals, then IRB review is required, and subjects must consent to the research use of the data set unless the IRB finds it acceptable to waive consent.

When consent is required, there are several issues to address. However, the consent form can usually be quite short and still include all of the required elements. General issues that need to be addressed on a case-by-case basis include:

- What data sets will be used for research purposes.
- To whom the data set will be released.
- What types of processes are in place to protect confidentiality and privacy. For instance, whether direct identifiers will be kept with the data set, or whether a code will be used. If a code is used, who will maintain the linking information, and how will that information be stored and protected?
- Whether the data set will be made unidentifiable, and if so, how and when.

Research with data sets may also qualify for a waiver of consent under the four criteria listed in 45 CFR 46.116(d).

For research with data sets, the most controversial of these criteria is the third—the definition of "practicably." It is often inconvenient but still practicable to get consent from the research subjects, particularly if they continue to come to the institution for ongoing interventions and/or services.

Like tissue research, some research involving the review of data sets may qualify for exemption from Common Rule requirements if the data sets are already in existence prior to the initiation of the research and the information is recorded/provided in such a way that there is no link between the data set and individuals, or the investigator has no access to such link. If the records or other data sets will be created/reviewed prospectively, then the exemption does not apply.

Also, the publishing policies of journals are particularly troublesome when QA processes provide publishable results. When this occurs, the publication causes the QA activities to become research, which is defined in the Common Rule as "a systematic investigation, including research development, testing and evaluation, designed to develop or contribute to generalizable knowledge." Generally, there is no IRB review and oversight of QA activities, and therefore the investigator must determine as early as possible whether the results may be useful as published research. IRBs cannot retroactively approve research, even the review and analysis of QA results, and therefore many journals will not accept the submission. As soon as QA results begin to look promising for general distribution, the investigator should contact the IRB to get guidance on submitting a research proposal. It may also be acceptable to get IRB approval to conduct a re-analysis of data obtained for non-research purposes.

The federal government and many states have statutes and case law regarding the privacy of data sets such as educational, employment and medical records, and these must be taken into account. Also, the federal Health Insurance Portability and Accountability Act (HIPAA) Privacy Rule affects research involving medical records. (See Chapter 15 to learn about the impact HIPAA has on research databases and repositories.)

Implementing the HIPAA Privacy Rule in Research

At the conclusion of this chapter, readers will be able to:

- Describe the circumstances when the HIPAA Privacy Rule applies to research.
- Distinguish a covered entity from a non-covered entity under the HIPAA Privacy Rule.
- Discuss the general requirements for uses and disclosures of protected health information (PHI) for research.
- Describe the required elements and statements for authorizations.

Introduction

Recognizing the potential cost savings that could be realized by implementing uniform national standards for the electronic transmission of healthcare information, Congress designed the Administrative Simplification provisions of the Health Insurance Portability and Accountability Act of 1996 (HIPAA) to improve efficiencies in the administration of healthcare transactions. HIPAA intends to create these efficiencies by requiring parties involved in the provision, administration and payment of healthcare to move to electronic transmission of health information using standardized formats for transactions and code sets.

At the same time, Congress recognized that facilitating the electronic exchange of health information would pose additional challenges to protection of confidentiality. To address these concerns, the Department of Health and Human Services (HHS) issued standards to protect the security and privacy of identifiable health information. Compliance with the HIPAA Privacy Rule was required as of April 14, 2003. The Privacy Rule protects the use and disclosure by "covered entities" (see page 162) of identifiable health information, referred to as "protected health information" (PHI). The Privacy Rule is not intended to interfere with access to and exchange of PHI for traditional healthcare purposes—treatment, payment for healthcare or healthcare operations ("TPO"). However, the Privacy Rule imposes restrictions on the use or disclosure by covered entities of PHI for non-TPO purposes, including research.

The Privacy Rule has had a substantial impact on medical research involving human subjects, including studies of existing information and/or biological specimens obtained from human subjects. Clinical research typically involves the exchange of information among multiple parties, including research sites, contract research organizations (CROs), site management organizations (SMOs), data safety monitoring boards (DSMBs), institutional review boards (IRBs) and sponsors. All of these parties are affected, even though only some are directly regulated by HIPAA as "covered entities" (defined in detail later in this chapter). Covered entities are the "gatekeepers" of PHI; they must obtain some form of permission under HIPAA to receive, use or disclose PHI for any research purpose.

For research to proceed efficiently under HIPAA, all parties involved in medical research—regardless of whether they are a covered entity—need to understand how the Privacy Rule affects the flow of PHI to and from the gatekeepers of PHI. Covered entities must understand their responsibilities under the Privacy Rule to comply with HIPAA and to minimize legal liability for non-compliance. To meet their compliance requirements, covered entities typically have imposed constraints in research agreements on the use and disclosure of PHI by their non-covered entity research partners. Thus, non-covered entities engaged in medical research need to understand the Privacy Rule's requirements to ensure research contracts are structured to ensure access to necessary PHI. To ensure efficient flow of PHI throughout the research chain, research protocols should include procedures for obtaining the HIPAA permissions or waivers necessary for covered entities to obtain or disclose PHI. Commercial sponsors who draft research protocols will need to determine the Privacy Rule requirements that apply to their study and include procedures in the protocol to meet those requirements.

The scope of research affected by the HIPAA Privacy Rule is different from the Common Rule's (45 CFR 46, Subpart A) or the FDA regulations (21 CFR Parts 50 and 56) governing human subject research. The HIPAA Privacy Rule affects any research use or disclosure of PHI, including: subject screening and recruitment; accessing medical records and other existing health information; collecting, creating or receiving PHI; creating new databases or tissue repositories; secondary uses of existing databases and repositories; site monitoring; management of multi-site studies and publication of results.

The implementation of the Privacy Rule in research is procedurally complex. Different procedures may apply to a particular research activity, such as subject recruitment, depending on who is involved. A comprehensive explanation of the Privacy Rule or its application to research is beyond the scope of this chapter. The goal of this chapter is to provide some practical understanding and basic tools necessary to design and conduct research efficiently and in compliance with the Privacy Rule. While there are some basic rules that researchers can use to resolve questions about the Privacy Rule, many questions will be fact-specific and depend on the types of organizations, individuals and data involved. Readers should seek guidance from their institution's Privacy Officer, research administrator or legal counsel regarding the implementation of the Privacy Rule in their research activities.

Liability for Noncompliance

Failure to comply with HIPAA's Privacy Rule may lead to civil or even criminal penalties. Civil enforcement of the Privacy Rule is the responsibility of HHS' Office of Civil Rights, which may impose civil monetary penalties of up to $100 per violation and up to $25,000 per person/entity per year for each HIPAA standard that is violated. The U.S. Department of Justice is responsible for enforcing criminal penalties against any "person" (not limited to covered entities) who knowingly obtains or discloses PHI in violation of the Privacy Rule. Criminal penalties include up to $250,000 in fines and a maximum of 10 years imprisonment.

Integration with State and Federal Laws

Implementation of the Privacy Rule is, by itself, complex. The fact that the Privacy Rule's requirements must be integrated with related state and federal laws adds another layer of complexity that often will require legal analysis. At the state level, the Privacy Rule preempts (overrides) state privacy laws that are contrary to and provide less protection. Thus, the Privacy Rule provides a federal "floor" of medical privacy protection, but individual state laws may provide more stringent protections. State law protection of medical information related to highly sensitive and potentially damaging information (e.g., HIV/AIDS, drug use, mental illness) often exceeds that of the Privacy Rule and will, therefore, control the use of such information in research. Researchers engaged in such research should seek advice from legal counsel to determine whether state law or the Privacy Rule will control. This state "preemption" analysis can be particularly complicated for multi-site studies.

At the federal level, the Privacy Rule does not preempt either the Common Rule or the FDA's regulations governing use of human subjects in research. Researchers must comply with all applicable laws. There are significant procedural and analytical differences between the Common Rule and the Privacy Rule, especially with regard to research involving existing data or tissue, subject screening and subject recruitment. These differences are discussed in more detail later in this chapter.

Covered Entities in Research

The Privacy Rule regulates the flow of PHI to and from covered entities. The first step in understanding how the Privacy Rule affects research is to determine which parties involved in the research are covered entities. As discussed below, determining who is and is not a covered entity can be very complicated, especially when organizationally and functionally complex institutions (e.g., universities and academic medical centers) are involved.

HIPAA directly regulates the use and disclosure of PHI by three groups of entities involved in treatment, payment for healthcare or healthcare operations (TPO) activities—healthcare providers, healthcare clearinghouses and health plans. HIPAA refers to these parties as "covered entities." Of the three groups that comprise covered entities under HIPAA, healthcare providers are the ones most typically involved in clinical research. However, not all healthcare providers involved in research are a covered entity. Only healthcare providers who transmit health information electronically as part of a HIPAA "transaction" are a covered entity. Essentially, a HIPAA "transaction" involves financial or administrative activities related to healthcare (e.g., processing healthcare claims and administration of healthcare benefits). In general terms, payment to a healthcare provider that involves electronic transmission of health information between two parties makes the provider a covered entity under HIPAA. "Electronic" transmissions include those conducted over the Internet, extranet, leased lines, dial-up lines, private networks and those involving physical relocation by magnetic tape, CD or floppy disk. Payment by third party insurers (health plans) typically involve electronic transmission of health information. Payment by patients using debit cards or flexible savings plans also may involve electronic transmission of health information, thereby making the provider and/or the organization a covered entity. In contrast, merely maintaining billing and payment records on a computer would not be a "transmission" and would not make the provider a covered entity.

A covered entity may be an individual (e.g., a physician) or an institution (e.g., a hospital). In the case of an institution that is a covered entity, all members of the institution's workforce are part of the covered entity. "Workforce" is broadly defined under HIPAA and includes all paid and unpaid persons (employees, volunteers, trainees, etc.) who work under the direct control of the covered entity.

Institutional Covered Entities

There are several types of organizational structures for institutional covered entities under HIPAA. Each structure has significant implications for the implementation of the Privacy Rule in research because whether, and how, research at an institution is subject to the Privacy Rule depends on the functional unit in which the institution has chosen to place research. The implementation of the Privacy Rule in research must be examined through the lens of each institution's organizational structure to determine which requirements, if any, apply. There is no "one size fits all" Privacy Rule for research.

Hybrid Entities

An organization or institution that is a single legal entity that performs both covered and non-covered functions may elect to be a "hybrid entity" under HIPAA. A "covered function" is any function that makes the entity either a health care provider, health plan or healthcare clearinghouse. A hybrid entity may functionally divide itself into one or more health care components and non-health care components. The covered entity must designate all covered functions as part of a health care component. The covered entity may include non-covered functions in either the health care or non-health care component. Designation as a hybrid entity can simplify the implementation of the Privacy Rule at a hybrid entity because the Privacy Rule applies only to the health care component(s). The hybrid entity must erect "firewalls" to functionally segregate the health care and non-health care components to prevent the unauthorized exchange of PHI. Individuals who are a covered entity (e.g., health care providers) may not designate themselves as a hybrid entity because it is not possible for an individual to create internal firewalls.

Many organizationally complex research institutions such as universities, multi-component hospitals and non-profit research organizations have designated themselves as hybrid entities. When engaging in research with hybrid entities, outside researchers need to determine whether research is part of the health care component. If so, the entity's researchers are covered entities.

Affiliated Covered Entities

HIPAA also provides inter-institutional strategies for implementing the Privacy Rule. Legally separate but affiliated institutions may choose to designate themselves or their health care components as a single covered entity under HIPAA if they are under common ownership or control. Organizing as an "Affiliated Covered Entity" (ACE) can create some administrative efficiencies by allowing the institutions that make up the ACE to share solutions (e.g., a common notice of privacy practices). However, each legally distinct covered entity is separately liable for HIPAA noncompliance.

There are advantages and disadvantages associated with designation as an ACE. A research-related benefit of an ACE is that PHI shared among an ACE's health care components is a "use" rather than a "disclosure," thereby avoiding the disclosure tracking requirement (discussed in more detail under the section "Individual Rights"). However, as with hybrid entities, the Privacy Rule still applies to the exchange (disclosure from or receipt by) of PHI between the health care component(s) and non-health care components of the ACE. This creates administrative burdens for researchers who are in the non-health care component but wish to obtain PHI from colleagues in the health care component at their own (or affiliated) institution.

Also, this exchange would be a disclosure that must be tracked by the health care component.

Organized Health Care Arrangements
Organized Health Care Arrangements (OHCA) are another inter-institutional organization under the Privacy Rule. Multiple independent covered entities that hold themselves out to the public as participating in a joint arrangement to provide a clinically integrated care setting may choose to operate as an OHCA. The covered entities in an OHCA must participate in joint activities such as utilization review, quality assessment and improvement or payment. As with affiliated covered entities, members of an OHCA may use one notice of privacy practices.

Classes of Data Under the Privacy Rule

Protected Health Information
The Privacy Rule's regulations apply to PHI, which is (1) "health information" that is (2) "individually identifiable" and (3) created or received by a covered entity. The first step in determining whether research involves PHI is to determine whether the research involves any covered entities as discussed previously. If there are no covered entities involved in the research, either as researchers or as sources of data (e.g., holder of medical records), there is no PHI. If there are covered entities involved, the second question is whether "health information" is involved, and if so, whether it is "individually identifiable."

What Is "Health Information"?
"Health information" is information in any form or medium (paper, electronic, and images such as x-rays or sonograms) that relates to a living or deceased individual's past, present or future physical or mental health or condition, the provision or payment of healthcare to an individual. Note that unlike the Common Rule, the Privacy Rule also applies to deceased persons.

Importantly, biological specimens (e.g., blood and tissues), by themselves, are not PHI. According to HHS, biological specimens are not "information" in and of themselves. In practice, however, biological specimens typically are collected and/or stored with diagnostic information (e.g., breast cancer tissue repository), which is "health information." If the associated health information includes any of the HIPAA identifiers listed in Table 1, the data are "individually identifiable" and, therefore, constitute individually identifiable health information (IIHI). In the hands of a covered entity, the IIHI becomes PHI. Determining when biological material is or is not PHI is a critical part of creating or maintaining repositories and studies of existing material. These issues are discussed in more detail in this chapter under "Research Databases and Repositories."

What Health Information Is "Individually Identifiable"?

Health information is "individually identifiable" under the Privacy Rule if it directly identifies an individual or reasonably could be used to identify an individual. Health information directly identifies an individual if it includes any of eighteen identifiers specified by the Privacy Rule (see "HIPAA Identifiers" in Table 1). Importantly, the identifiers in Table 1 that are part of PHI are subject to all of the protections of the Privacy Rule and may be disclosed for research only in compliance with the Privacy Rule's requirements.

Table 1: HIPAA Identifiers

1. Names;
2. All geographic subdivisions smaller than a State, including ZIP Code (except for the first 3 digits of the ZIP Code if the region contains > 20,000 people, or the last 2 digits if the region contains < 20,00 people);
3. All elements of dates (except year), including birth, death admission and discharge dates; all ages over 89 years (may include age < 89 years);
4. Telephone numbers;
5. Fax numbers;
6. Electronic mail addresses;
7. Social security numbers;
8. Medical record numbers;
9. Health plan beneficiary numbers;
10. Account numbers;
11. Certificate/license numbers;
12. Vehicle identifiers and serial numbers, including license plate numbers;
13. Device identifiers and serial numbers;
14. Web Universal Resource Locators (URLs);
15. Internet Protocol (IP) address numbers;
16. Biometric identifiers, including finger and voice prints;
17. Full face photographic images and any comparable images; and
18. Any other unique identifying number, characteristic or code.

Item 18 is an important "catchall" category that deserves additional explanation for two reasons. First, Item 18 covers any identifier that is not specified in Items 1–17 that could be used to identify an individual. Thus, if a covered entity knew that certain information included with health information could be used to re-identify an individual, even if the information is not a specified HIPAA identifier, it would render the data PHI. Item 18 requires covered entities to make reasonable subjective determinations of what information qualifies as "uniquely identifying."

Coded Data

Item 18 is also important because it includes an "identifying code." Understanding which types of codes would or would not be an identifying code is important and requires some explanation. Part of the confusion in understanding which types of codes would make health information PHI stems from the different nomenclature used in the research community and by federal agencies. Adding to the confusion is the fact that HHS did not provide neat labels for identifying versus non-identifying codes. In this chapter, the term "identifying code" is used to mean a code that could be used in combination with other information to identify the individual who is the subject of the associated health information. Such codes link the health information to an individual's health information and are sometimes referred to as a "code-link." Identifying codes typically are derived from some other identifier. Examples of identifying codes include the last four digits of a person's Social Security number or a clinical trial record number.

In contrast, "non-identifying" code means a code that provides no information about the identity of the individual who is the subject of the associated health information. Under the Privacy Rule, a non-identifying code is one that is not derived from the data or another identifier. An example would be a randomly assigned code or one that uses the sequential number of subjects entered into a study, such as 0001, 0002, 0003, etc. In addition, the covered entity may not use or disclose the code for any other purpose and may not disclose the "key" that can be used to re-link the information to an individual's identity. Thus, without the linking "key," the identity of the individuals in the data set could not be determined. If a covered entity that is holding PHI creates a new data set in which all identifiers that are in the list of HIPAA identifiers are removed and individual records are coded with a non-identifying code, the new data set is not PHI and release by the covered entity to a researcher would not be subject to the Privacy Rule. This is called de-identifying PHI, which is discussed further in the next section, "De-Identified Data."

> **Use this simple formula as a guide to determine if your research involves PHI:**
>
> **IIHI + Covered Entity = PHI**

De-Identified Data

The Privacy Rule does not apply to de-identified data. As described above, PHI may be de-identified by removing all HIPAA identifiers listed in Table 1 and the covered entity must have no actual knowledge that the recipient of the data could identify the individuals on the basis of the de-identified data and any other reasonably available information. De-identified data may contain a non-identifying code, as defined previously.

Because de-identified data are not subject to the Privacy Rule and may be freely shared by covered entities, researchers who do not need identifying information should consider using de-identified data instead of PHI, especially for studies of existing data or biological specimens. Figure 1 illustrates an example in which a researcher obtains de-identified data from a covered entity. The covered entity maintains a database of PHI (Step 1 in Figure 1). The covered entity de-identifies the PHI in the database to create a de-identified database (Step 2). If the covered entity discloses PHI from the PHI Database to a researcher, the disclosure will be subject to the Privacy Rule (Step 3). However, if the covered entity discloses de-identified data from the De-identified Database, the disclosure is not subject to the Privacy Rule (Step 4). In this scenario, the covered entity is responsible for ensuring that the data meet the Privacy Rule's definition of "de-identified." Nonetheless, to facilitate cooperation by the disclosing covered entity, researchers who request de-identified data should carefully review the data fields included in their request to make sure that no HIPAA identifiers are included.

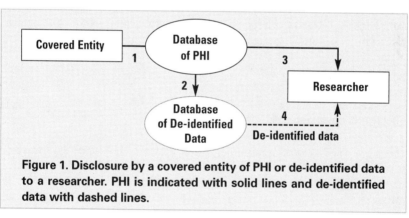

Figure 1. Disclosure by a covered entity of PHI or de-identified data to a researcher. PHI is indicated with solid lines and de-identified data with dashed lines.

Limited Data Sets

There is a third type of data that is recognized under the Privacy Rule that researchers should be familiar with. Recognizing that some research, for example, epidemiological research, requires some, but minimal, identifying information, the HIPAA Privacy Rule provides an alternative to the extremes of de-identified data and PHI. A limited data set is a subset of PHI that excludes all of the HIPAA identifiers in Table 1 except for Items 2 (addresses), 3 (dates) and 18 (indirect identifiers). With regard to the postal address, all information except the street address may be included in a limited data set. With the limited data set, HHS attempted to strike a balance between protecting privacy and facilitating highly valuable epidemiological research. Thus, limited data sets do not have a "free pass" like de-identified data but neither do they require the approval that is necessary for PHI. The requirements that apply to use or disclosure of limited data sets are discussed later in the section "Use or Disclosure of Limited Data Sets."

Case Report Forms

Under the Privacy Rule, case report forms (CRFs) must be carefully screened for HIPAA identifiers that would make the data PHI. If the study is being conducted under an authorization (discussed in detail on page 172) in which subjects have given their permission for their PHI to be disclosed by the researchers to outside parties such as a CRO or a sponsor, the CRF may include PHI. In this situation, the CRF and the authorization must be consistent; any PHI that is included on the CRF must be specified on the authorization. Similarly, if only limited data sets will be disclosed by a covered entity to outside researchers, the CRF needs to be screened to make sure that it complies with the restrictions imposed on limited data sets.

Many commercial sponsors, as a matter of company policy, do not want to receive PHI from research sites. If a study is designed so that outside parties will receive only de-identified data; the CRF must be screened carefully to make sure it does not include any of the HIPAA identifiers included in Table 1. Data fields that have caused problems and may not be included in de-identified CRFs include dates (e.g., birth, treatment, surgical), medical record numbers and five-digit zip codes.

General Requirements for Uses and Disclosures of PHI

There are some general requirements that apply to the use or disclosure of PHI for any non-TPO purpose that also affect research. While these requirements are the responsibility of covered entities, they affect how PHI may be obtained, used or disclosed by any party involved in research. Therefore, all parties involved in research should be familiar with them.

Notice of Privacy Practices

The Privacy Rule requires covered entities to provide notice to individuals of how the covered entity may use or disclose the individual's PHI, the individual's rights afforded by the Privacy Rule and the covered entity's legal duties. This notice is called a "Notice of Privacy Practices (NPP)." There are many detailed requirements regarding the content and provision of the NPP, a full description of which is beyond the scope of this chapter. However, there are some research-related issues that deserve mentioning.

The first issue involves content of the NPP. Among other required content, the NPP must include a description of each purpose for which the covered entity might use or disclosure PHI without the individual's authorization. There are several research-related uses or disclosures that do not require an individual's authorization, including subject screening and recruitment or analysis of existing databases and tissue repositories. These research activities may be conducted under a review preparatory to research or a waiver of authorization (both of which are discussed in detail later in this chapter). To comply with the Privacy Rule's requirements, covered entities that engage in research using PHI should include references to these activities in their NPP.

The second issue involves the provision of the NPP to research subjects. At some research institutions, especially those with a hospital or physician clinics, many of the subjects will be the institution's patients. As patients, they should receive the NPP from the covered entity the first time they receive service after the compliance deadline of April 14, 2003. The NPP must be presented only once. Research subjects who have already received the covered entity's NPP do not need to be presented with it again. However, if an individual's first healthcare interaction with a covered entity is as a research subject, the researcher-provider must present the subject with the covered entity's NPP. Thus, as a practical matter, clinical researchers at a covered entity should query subjects in their first meeting as to whether they previously were presented with the institution's NPP.

Minimum Necessary Rule

An over-arching rule under the Privacy Rule is that a covered entity must use, disclose or request only the minimum PHI that is necessary for the intended purpose. The minimum necessary rule applies to research uses and disclosures of PHI except those made with an authorization. Note that the minimum necessary rule imposes a responsibility on both the requesting and disclosing parties to limit the PHI exchanged to the minimum necessary. The Privacy Rule lessens the compliance burden on covered entities that have asked to disclose PHI to a researcher under a waiver of authorization by allowing the disclosing covered entity to rely on the researcher's request as meeting the minimum necessary requirement if the researcher can document that an IRB or Privacy Board approved the waiver of authorization.

Individual Rights

The Privacy Rule provides individuals with a number of individual rights that include the right to access and amend their PHI and to know to whom the covered entity has disclosed their PHI. These rights create administrative responsibilities for covered entities involved in research.

Individuals have a right to access and copy their PHI that is maintained in a "designated record set." Basically, a designated record set is a medical or billing record maintained by a covered entity. Typically, research data are not entered into a subject's medical record, although this may occur in the case of clinical trials. The Privacy Rule provides an exception to the right of access for clinical trials. A covered entity conducting a clinical trial may suspend a subject's right to access research PHI that is included in a designated record set for the duration of the trial, provided the subject agreed to the suspension of access prior to enrolling in the study. This exception protects the scientific integrity of the data by keeping subjects from breaking blinds associated with various treatment or placebo arms of the study.

Individuals also have a right under the Privacy Rule to amend PHI maintained in a designated record set. Again, this right would affect research PHI only if it were entered into the subject's designated record set. A covered entity may deny this right if the PHI is "accurate and complete."

In contrast to the two provisions above, the rights of individuals to receive an accounting from a covered entity of disclosures of their PHI made in the previous six years (starting from April 14, 2003) will have a substantial impact on research. Fortunately, not all research disclosures of PHI must be tracked by covered entities. Specifically, disclosures of PHI made with a subject's authorization and disclosures of de-identified information and limited data sets do not have to be tracked. However, disclosures of PHI by a covered entity under a waiver of authorization, a "review preparatory to research" (discussed on page 175), or to or by a business associate must be tracked and the tracking information maintained for at least six years so that the covered entity can respond to a request for an accounting of disclosures.

Tracking disclosures poses significant administrative burdens for covered entities that are sources of PHI for research. For each disclosure, the covered entity maintaining the PHI must track: the purpose and date of the disclosure; the name and address of the recipient; and a brief description of the PHI that was disclosed. The Privacy Rule permits an alternative procedure for simplified accounting in cases where there have been multiple disclosures to the same recipient or for large studies in which there are disclosures of PHI from 50 or more subjects, but many institutions have decided against using it because the procedure is not, in fact, very "simple." Because institutions can vary significantly in their policies and procedures for tracking disclosures, researchers need to determine and follow the procedures used at their institution and collaborating sites.

Uses and Disclosures of PHI for Research

What Is "Research"?

The Privacy Rule imposes specific requirements on the use or disclosure of PHI for research. The Privacy Rule uses the same definition of research as does the Common Rule: "a systematic investigation, including research development, testing, and evaluation, designed to develop or contribute to generalizable knowledge." While using the same definition of research, the Privacy Rule actually covers a broader scope of research activities than does the Common Rule. This is because some research that is exempt from the Common Rule's requirements is not exempt from the Privacy Rule. An example is research involving only existing data that are "identifiable" under the Privacy Rule but not under the Common Rule (see 45 CFR § 46.101(b)(4). Another difference is that reviewing existing PHI (e.g., in medical records) for subject screening does not trigger a regulatory requirement under the Common Rule but does under the Privacy Rule (see "Subject Screening"). Therefore, researchers who may be experienced in determining activities that are regulated as research under the Common Rule cannot rely on the same analysis to determine what research activities trigger Privacy Rule requirements.

Different Rules for "Uses" and "Disclosures"

Under the Privacy Rule, different requirements apply to "uses" and "disclosures" of PHI. To determine which Privacy Rule requirements apply, researchers must understand the difference between a "use" and a "disclosure."

A use occurs when a covered entity or members of its workforce utilize (collect, review, analyze, etc.) PHI within the covered entity. A disclosure occurs when a covered entity shares, releases or transfers PHI to a person or entity outside of the covered entity.

As stated previously, an institution's organizational structure can have a significant impact on the procedural implementation of the Privacy Rule in research. As shown in Table 2, what constitutes a use or a disclosure is different in a hybrid entity, an ACE or an OHCA. A hybrid entity is a single legal entity that has been functionally segregated into health care components and non-health care components. If there are multiple health care components, they function as a single covered entity. PHI that is shared within the hybrid entity's health care component is a use; sharing PHI with the non-health care component is a disclosure. In an ACE, multiple institutions function as a single covered entity. Thus, sharing PHI within the ACE is a use even if the PHI is exchanged across institutions. Sharing PHI outside the ACE is a disclosure. Because the members of an OHCA remain separate covered entities, research uses and disclosures of PHI are treated the same as if they were individual covered entities. Sharing PHI with another member of the OHCA for a research purpose is a disclosure that must be tracked and comply with other Privacy Rule requirements.

Table 2: Uses and Disclosures in Different HIPAA Organizational Structures

	Hybrid Entity	Affiliated Covered Entity (ACE)	Organized Health Care Arrangement (OHCA)
Ownership status	A single legal entity	Separate legal entities	Separate legal entities
Covered entity status	Health care component (HCC) and non-health care components (non-HCC)	Single covered entity	Separate covered entities
"Use" of PHI	Within the HCC	Within the ACE	Within each member institution
"Disclosure" of PHI	Outside of the HCC	Outside of the ACE	Outside of each member institution

Authorizations to Use or Disclose PHI for Research

For clinical research, de-identified data or limited data sets are not usually sufficient to accomplish the study. As of April 14, 2003, a covered entity may not use or disclose PHI for research without an authorization signed by the subject unless the research qualifies for a waiver of authorization or one of the exceptions (discussed on page 174). An authorization is a formal permission (either in a separate document or as part of the research consent form) granted by the subject for his or her PHI to be used and disclosed. Subjects in active studies who have already signed IRB-approved consent forms prior to April 14, 2003, do not have to sign a research authorization. Subjects enrolled on or after April 14, 2003, need to sign both the informed consent form and an authorization, or a combined form. One caution, however, is that if a protocol amendment requires that new consent be obtained from already enrolled subjects, those subjects would have to sign both the consent and an authorization.

The required elements in research authorizations go beyond the elements for consent forms required by the Common Rule and FDA regulations (see Table 3). This is because the HIPAA Privacy Rule protects the privacy of information whereas the Common Rule and FDA regulations protect the safety and well-being, including privacy, of people (subjects).

Table 3. Required Elements and Statements in Authorizations

Under the HIPAA Privacy Rule research authorizations must include the following:

- Specific, meaningful description of PHI to be used or disclosed;
- Identification of persons (or classes of persons) authorized to request use or disclosure of PHI;
- Identification of persons (or classes of persons) to whom the covered entity may disclose PHI;
- Description of each purpose of the use/disclosure;
  - Blanket authorizations are not permitted for future unspecified research, e.g., "We will use your PHI for future studies." (This prohibition also affects research databases and repositories, which are discussed in more detail below.)
- Expiration date or event;
  - The "event" may be "the end of research" or equivalent, or
  - "None"
- Subject's signature and date;
  - If signed by a personal representative, include a statement of representative's authority.

- Notice that the subject has the right to revoke the authorization in writing at any time;
- A warning that PHI disclosed under the authorization could be re-disclosed by the recipient and no longer protected by HIPAA;
- A statement that the provision of treatment or benefits will not be conditioned on signing the authorization (except in clinical trials); and
- A statement that the subject will receive a copy of the signed authorization.

Oversight of authorizations to make sure they are valid under the Privacy Rule is a matter of institutional policy, not a regulatory requirement. The Privacy Rule does not require IRB review or approval of research authorizations; but, if the authorization is combined with the informed consent form, IRB review is required under the Common Rule and FDA regulations. To optimize compliance, some institutions have adopted a policy requiring IRB review and approval of all authorizations. Others require the use of an institutionally approved template form that contains all of the required elements. A covered entity may also choose to use an outside party's authorization form. Sponsors and investigators should determine each covered entity's institutional requirements for authorizations. For multi-site studies, sponsors need to plan adequate time to determine the policies and procedures for authorization at each research site.

Revocation of Research Authorizations

Under the Common Rule, subjects may withdraw from a study at any time simply by ceasing to participate; written notice of withdrawal is not required. Under the HIPAA Privacy Rule, subjects may revoke their authorization to use or disclose PHI for research at any time, but this request must be made in writing. The authorization should explain how to revoke the authorization. As a practical matter, subjects may want or need to withdraw from a clinical trial but are willing to have their PHI to remain in the data set. Therefore, investigators conducting clinical trials should use forms that give withdrawing subjects the option of revoking their authorization or allowing researchers to continue to use their PHI.

Under the Privacy Rule, investigators may continue to use or disclose PHI after a revocation only if needed "to protect the integrity of a research study." This standard is open to interpretation, but in general, a covered entity may continue to analyze PHI that was collected prior to a revocation but may disclose PHI only under limited circumstances. Acceptable disclosures would include notifying sponsors of a subject's withdrawal, notifying the IRB, sponsor and FDA of adverse events, and including the PHI in a pre-marketing application to the FDA. Disclosures and uses made prior to a revocation would not be affected.

Waivers of Authorization

Under the HIPAA Privacy Rule, a covered entity may use or disclose PHI for research without an authorization if an IRB or privacy board determines that it is not practicable to obtain a signed authorization and if the research activity poses no more than minimal risk to the privacy of the individuals whose PHI will be used or disclosed. In general, waivers of authorization are used primarily for research limited to the use of existing data (e.g. databases, repositories or medical records) where obtaining authorizations would not be practicable. In contrast, studies that involve direct interaction with subjects typically will not qualify for a waiver of authorization because subjects are available to sign an authorization. Thus, clinical trials or studies in which subjects complete questionnaires or participate in interviews would require authorizations.

An important application for waivers of authorization is in collecting PHI for subject screening and recruitment. Typically, existing PHI is used to identify potential subjects for a clinical trial and to obtain contact information. Investigators may use their covered entity's own PHI to recruit subjects without a waiver of authorization but they may not disclose PHI to a party outside of the covered entity (e.g., CRO or sponsor) without either a waiver or an authorization. Remember that disclosures to persons/entities outside the covered entity under a waiver of authorization must be tracked.

The Privacy Rule contains a provision for "partial waivers" of authorization, which permit an IRB or privacy board to waive authorization for the recruitment portion of a study, while still requiring the authorization for enrollments. Like any waiver, this requires a finding of minimal risk to individual privacy rights. Using PHI only to contact potential subjects is generally found by IRBs or privacy boards to pose no more than minimal risk to the individual's privacy, and obtaining a prior authorization is often not practicable. To demonstrate that a research activity poses no more than minimal risk to privacy researchers must demonstrate to the IRB or privacy board that there is an adequate:

- plan to protect the identifiers from improper use and disclosure,
- plan to destroy the identifiers at the earliest opportunity consistent with the research, unless there is a research justification for retaining the identifiers, and
- written assurance that PHI will not be reused or disclosed except as permitted under the Privacy Rule.

Under the Common Rule, principal investigators must obtain IRB approval of all recruitment procedures and materials. The Privacy Rule requires an additional step. If investigators plan to use PHI to recruit subjects, they must also obtain approval from an IRB or privacy board of a request for a partial waiver of authorization to use or disclose PHI for subject recruitment. Remember that the partial waiver only covers use or disclosure of PHI to contact subjects as part of the recruitment process. When enrolling subjects into the study, investigators need to obtain subjects' authorization for their PHI to be used or disclosed for the stated research purposes.

Reviews Preparatory to Research

For research activities that are "preparatory to research," such as protocol development and screening for subjects, a covered entity may allow researchers to review its PHI on-site under a provision called a "review preparatory to research." The Privacy Rule does not require that reviews preparatory to research be approved by an IRB or privacy board. The researcher must make a "representation" to the covered entity that the PHI:

- will be used to develop a research protocol or for a similar purpose;
- is necessary for the research purpose; and
- will not be removed from the covered entity's site.

For operational reasons, covered entities may require "representations" to access PHI under a review preparatory to research to be in writing even though it is not required by the HIPAA Privacy Rule.

Because the PHI may not be taken off-site, researchers who are not part of the covered entity may use PHI under a review preparatory to research to screen for numbers of potential subjects but may not obtain contact information (or other PHI) that could be used to recruit those subjects. In contrast, researchers within the covered entity may use that covered entity's PHI under a review preparatory to research both to screen and to recruit subjects.

Remember that a "disclosure" of PHI to screen for potential subjects and for recruitment requires covered entities to maintain tracking records even if the covered entity is not otherwise involved in the research. For example, if a CRO wishes to use a hospital's medical records to screen for potential subjects, the hospital must ensure the tracking of the disclosure of each record to the CRO.

PHI For Deceased Persons

The Privacy Rule protects the privacy of PHI from deceased persons. However, procedurally the PHI of decedents is relatively easy to access for research. A covered entity may use or disclose a decedent's PHI for research if the researcher provides a "representation" that the PHI will be used for research only and is necessary for the research. Also, if requested, the researcher must provide documentation of the individual's death. The Privacy Rule does not specify the form of the "representation." Because this is a disclosure that the covered entity must track, the representation will typically be a written form.

Use or Disclosure of Limited Data Sets

The Privacy Rule permits a covered entity to disclose a limited data set with a "data use agreement." Data use agreements must contain certain required elements, including:

- Description of how the limited data set will be used.
- Identification of those who will have access to the limited data set.
- Listing of the recipient's responsibilities, including:
    - to not use the limited data set to contact individuals (for recruitment) or to identify the individuals to others.
    - to report to the covered entity any improper uses/disclosures of the limited data set.
    - to use appropriate safeguards to prevent uses/disclosures outside of the data use agreement.
    - to ensure downstream compliance with those who receive the limited data set.

Disclosures to Business Associates

A business associate is a person or organization that provides a service or function on behalf of a covered entity that involves use of the covered entity's PHI. A covered entity may disclose PHI to a business associate under an agreement that, among other things, defines what the business associate may do with the data. Like data use agreements, the Privacy Rule requires certain provisions in the business associate contract, including:

- Establish the permitted and required uses and disclosures of PHI by the business associate. The business associate may use/disclose PHI only as the covered entity would be allowed to under the Privacy Rule.
- Use appropriate safeguards to protect the privacy and security of the PHI.
- If feasible, destroy or return the PHI to the covered entity at the termination of the contract.
- Ensure downstream compliance with any subcontractors or agents to whom the business associate discloses PHI.

There has been some confusion as to who is a business associate in the context of research. Any party hired by sponsors or their agents (e.g., CROs, SMOs, and recruitment services) are not business associates because they are acting on behalf of the sponsor—not the covered entity. Research collaborators (e.g., researchers at other sites) also are not business associates because sharing PHI for research purposes does not create a business associate relationship.

The Privacy Rule permits a covered entity to hire a third party as a business associate to de-identify the covered entity's PHI. A business associate may de-identify PHI for use by the covered entity or its own use. Once de-identified, the data are no longer subject to HIPAA and may be used or shared by the business associate. However, the business associate may not disclose the original PHI except as permitted or required by the Privacy Rule.

Similarly, a covered entity may disclose its PHI to a business associate to create a limited data set. If the business associate will also use the limited data set, both a business associate contract (to cover the disclosure of PHI) and a data use agreement (to cover the use and disclosure of the limited data set) are required. The elements of both may be combined into one agreement.

Subject Screening

Subject screening typically involves reviewing existing PHI in medical records, a database or a tissue repository to determine the approximate number of potential subjects that might be available from a pool of patients and/or the clinical profile of prospective subjects. As used in this chapter, subject screening does not involve contacting prospective subjects.

There are several HIPAA mechanisms that may be used to obtain or use PHI for subject screening. Depending on institutional policy, researchers may be able to access a covered entity's PHI under either a review preparatory to research or a partial waiver of authorization.

Limited data sets also may be used to screen subjects. A researcher, CRO or sponsor outside the covered entity may obtain a limited data set from a covered entity with a data use agreement and use the information off-site for subject screening. Remember that limited data sets may not be used to contact individuals. Thus, they may be used for subject screening but not subject recruitment.

Subject Recruitment

Recruitment involves contacting prospective subjects. Targeted contacts (e.g., letters, emails or phone calls to pre-screened individuals) require PHI. In contrast, newspaper or radio ads (non-targeted contacts) do not require access to PHI.

Targeted Contacts

Unlike subject screening, different requirements apply to "inside" and "outside" researchers seeking a covered entity's PHI for subject recruitment. A researcher who is a member of the covered entity's workforce may use that covered entity's PHI to screen and recruit subjects under a review preparatory to research. Researchers outside the covered entity may not obtain PHI from a covered entity for subject recruitment under a review preparatory to research because they may not take the PHI off-site. Outside researchers must obtain a "partial" waiver of authorization from an IRB or a privacy board in order for a covered entity to disclose PHI for subject recruitment.

Once prospective subjects have been identified, it is best if they are contacted by a member of their treatment team. This minimizes confidentiality concerns because the communication is between the patient and the person to whom the PHI was initially disclosed. If the healthcare providers are not otherwise involved in the research study, they can be given recruitment letters to send to prospective subjects. The letter should contain a brief description of the study and give contact information for the research team.

There is no restriction under the Privacy Rule on the exchange of PHI between a covered entity and its patients. So, it is acceptable for healthcare providers to discuss participation in a research study with their own patients. This means that investigator-providers may communicate directly to their patients informing them of a study and inviting them to participate.

Non-Targeted Contacts

Non-targeted contacts, such as ads, do not involve PHI in making the initial contact but PHI may be collected as part of follow-up screening process. Covered entity internet sites that are interactive (solicit information from people who visit) may also collect PHI as part of the recruitment process, and, therefore, must comply with the HIPAA Privacy Rule.

Typically, ads announcing a clinical trial provide a telephone number for interested individuals to call to obtain more information. Often screening information (related to the inclusion/exclusion criteria for the clinical trial) is collected from these prospective subjects. If this screening information includes individually identifiable health information (IIHI), it becomes PHI once it is given to a covered entity. If the call-in number is to a covered entity, PHI will be collected as part of subject recruitment. In this situation, the investigator must have obtained approval of a partial waiver of authorization by an IRB or privacy board before collecting the screening PHI. (Remember that subject recruitment is part of the informed consent process under the Common Rule and must be reviewed and approved by an IRB.) If the call-in number is not to a covered entity (e.g., a call center or site management organization), then the IIHI collected over the phone is not PHI. If the screening information is then given to a clinical investigator who is a covered entity, it becomes PHI. As in the previous scenario, the clinical investigator must have obtained approval of a partial waiver of authorization by an IRB or privacy board before collecting the screening PHI as part of the subject recruitment process.

Research Databases and Repositories

The creation and use of databases and repositories of biological specimens are affected by the Privacy Rule. General research issues associated with creating and using research databases and repositories are covered in Chapter 14. In this chapter, we focus on the application of the Privacy Rule to these research activities. The initial collection of data or tissues to create or add to a database or repository and the subsequent analysis of the data or specimens in future research studies are separate research activities under the Privacy Rule.

Creating Databases and Repositories

If the data or specimens include PHI, covered entities must comply with the Privacy Rule to create the database or repository. In the case of data, whether an authorization or a waiver of authorization is required depends in part on whether the collection of data involves direct interaction with subjects. If new PHI will be collected directly from subjects for entry into the database, most likely an authorization will be required. If existing PHI (e.g., medical records or an existing non-research database) will be the source of data for the new database, the collection of data may qualify for a waiver of authorization. An IRB or Privacy Board would need to determine that it poses no more than a minimal risk to the individuals whose PHI will be used or disclosed and meets the other waiver criteria. If the collection of data does not involve interacting with subjects, an IRB or Privacy Board could determine that the research would not be practicable if the researchers had to obtain authorizations.

Often, the collection of biological specimens involves direct interaction with subjects. In this case, an authorization will need be to signed. If a researcher wishes to create a repository using only existing stocks of biological specimens that were collected for clinical purposes only (e.g., residual tissue or pathology specimens), the creation of the research repository may qualify for a waiver of authorization. If the specimens were collected prior to April 14, 2003, and some form of legal permission was obtained to collect and store the tissue, use of the material to create a research repository could be exempt from authorization requirements under the Privacy Rule's transition provisions.

Where an authorization is required to collect data or specimens to create or maintain a research database or repository, a key issue is that the authorization must be drafted to avoid a "blanket" authorization for future unspecified research. This is a very problematic issue for researchers and, unfortunately, there are no clear-cut solutions. As stated in the previous discussion of the required elements of authorizations, they must describe with specificity each purpose for using or disclosing PHI. HHS has repeatedly stated in guidances that this requirement prohibits seeking a subject's authorization to collect and store their PHI (create a database or repository) and to use the PHI in the future for as yet undetermined research (secondary use of the data or tissue for research). According to HHS, referring to "future studies" does not provide subjects with sufficient information regarding the purpose of the use or disclosure.

What this means is that the authorization used by researchers who intend to collect data or tissue to create a research database or repository must be limited to use or disclosure of PHI for analysis in a defined study and/or storing the PHI in a database or repository. The authorization may not seek authorization for future studies unless the authorization describes the specific purpose of those studies. This is why creating databases and repositories must be separated from subsequent use of research databases or repositories under the Privacy Rule. As discussed in the next section, subsequent use of existing PHI in databases or repositories can often be conducted under a waiver of authorization.

Using PHI in Research Databases and Repositories

Researchers who wish to use existing data or tissue in databases or repositories maintained by a covered entity have several alternatives under the Privacy Rule. First, if the researcher does not need identifiable data, the researcher could request the covered entity to provide only de-identified data or tissue. De-identified data is not subject to the Privacy Rule. Second, the researcher could request only a limited data set from the covered entity. The covered entity may provide the limited data set to the researcher, but only with a data use agreement.

Third, if the researcher needs PHI beyond that available in a limited data set, the researcher may request a waiver of authorization from an IRB or Privacy Board. If the use or disclosure of the PHI for the stated research purpose does not pose more than a minimal risk to the subjects' privacy and meets the other waiver criteria, the research most likely would qualify for a waiver of authorization.

Conclusion

Conducting research under HIPAA's Privacy Rule requires more than just new forms and additional compliance concerns for covered entities. Successful and efficient research under the Privacy Rule requires coordinated efforts by all parties involved, including subjects, investigators, IRBs, privacy boards, CROs, SMOs, and sponsors. All parties—not just covered entities—that conduct research that involves PHI need to understand the Privacy Rule requirements that apply to each research activity, including subject screening, recruitment, data collection and exchange, and the creation and use of research databases and repositories.

References, Resources and Suggested Readings

Chapter 1: Historical Perspectives on Human Subject Research

Annas G, Grodin M, eds. *The Nazi Doctors and the Nuremberg Code: Human Rights in Human Experimentation.* New York, NY: Oxford University Press, 1992.

Beecher HK. *Ethics and Clinical Research.* N Engl J Med 1996;274: 1354-60.

Caplan A, ed. *When Medicine Went Mad: Bioethics and the Holocaust.* Totowa, NJ: Humanna Press, 1992.

Ethical and Policy Issues in International Research: Clinical Trials in developing Countries. NBAC. April 2001

Faden R, ed. *Human Radiation Experiments: Final Report of the President's Advisory Committee.* New York, NY: Oxford University Press, 1996.

Faden R, Beauchamp T. *A History and Theory of Informed Consent.* New York, NY: Oxford University Press, 1986.

Jones J. *Bad Blood: The Tuskegee Syphilis Experiment.* New York, NY: Free Press, 1993.

Milgram S. *Obedience to Authority.* New York, NY: Harper & Row Publishers, Inc., 1974.

Research Involving Human Biological Materials: Ethical Issues and Policy Guidance. NBAC January 2000

Research Involving Persons with Mental Disorders That May Affect Decisionmaking Capacity. NBAC. December 1998

Third Report of the Attorney General's Research Working Group. Office of the Maryland Attorney General, Annapolis MD: Office of the Attorney General, August 1997.

Chapter 2: Ethics and Federal Regulations

Belmont Report: Ethical Principles and Guidelines for the Protection of Human Subjects of Research. Federal Register Document 79-12065 (see: www.nih.gov/grants/oprr/humansubjects/guidance/belmont.htm).

Beauchamp TL, Childress JF. *Principles of Biomedical Ethics* (5th ed.). New York, NY: Oxford University Press, 2001.

Food, Drug, & Cosmetic Act (see: www.fda.gov).

Levine RJ. *Ethics and Regulation of Clinical Research* (2nd ed.). New Haven, CT: Yale University Press, 1986.

Office of Research Integrity (see: http://ori.dhhs.gov).

Office for Human Research Protection (see http://ohrp.osophs.dhhs.gov).

Vanderpool, HY. *The Ethics of Research Involving Human Subjects*. Frederick (MD): University Publishing Group, 1996

Chapter 3: Roles and Responsibilities of Institutions in Human Subject Research

21 Code of Federal Regulations (CFR) 312, 314, 600, 812 and 814.

Department of Health and Human Services 45 CFR 46

Amdur, R. & Bankert, E. *Institutional Review Board: Management and Function*. Sudbury, MA: Jones and Bartlett Publishers, 2002

Food and Drug Administration (see: www.fda.gov).

Food, Drug and Cosmetic Act (see: www.fda.gov).

National Institutes of Health (see: www.nih.gov).

Research Subjects Review Board (see:www.urmc.rochester.edu/urmc/rsrb).

Chapter 4: The Roles and Responsibilities of the Investigator and the Study Process

FDA Clinical Investigator and IRB Information Sheets (see: www.fda.gov).

Harwood F. *A Professional's Guide to ACP's Certification Program For Clinical Research Associates and Clinical Research Coordinators*. Washington, DC: Associates of Clinical Research Professionals (ACRP).

ICH Harmonized Tripartite Guideline: Guideline For Good Clinical Practice. (see: http://www.ifpma.org/pdfifpma/e6.pdf.).

Mackintosh DR, Zepp VJ. *GCP Responsibilities of Investigators—Beyond the 1572*. Appl Clin Trials. 1996; 5:32-40.

Sayre JE. *GCP Quality Audit Manual (1st ed.)*. Buffalo Grove, IL: Interpharm Press; 1990.

Stephen L, Papke A. *Certified Clinical Research Coordinators*. Appl Clin Trials 1995; 4:58-63.

Chapter 5: FDA-Regulated Research Issues

21 CFR 312, 314, 600, 812 and 814.

21 CFR 803 (Investigational Devices), 600 (Postmarketing), 310 (Investigational Drugs and Biologics).

Food and Drug Administration (see: www.fda.gov).

Mackintosh DR, Zepp VJ. *GCP Responsibilities of Investigators— Beyond the 1572*. Appl Clin Trials. 1996; 5:32-40.

MEDWATCH: *The FDA Medical Products Reporting Program*

O'Donnell P. *Closer to Harmonized GCP*. Appl Clin Trials 1995; 4:48-53.

Chapter 6: Behavioral Research Issues

Beauchamp, TL, Faden RR, Wallace RJ, et al. *Ethical Issues in Social Science Research*. Baltimore, MD: Johns Hopkins University Press.

OPRR IRB Guidebook: Protecting Human Research Subjects. Washington, DC: Government Printing Office, 1993.

Chapter 7: Publication of Study Results

Berg JA, Mayor GH. *A study in normal human volunteers to compare the rate and extent of levothyroxine absorption from Synthroid and Levoxine*. J Clin Pharmacol 1992; 32:1135-40.

Blumenthal D, Campbell EG, Anderson MS, et al. *Withholding research results by academic life scientists: evidence from a national survey of faculty*. JAMA 1997; 277:1224-1228.

Cohen W, Florida R, Goe WR. *University-industry research centers in the United States*. Pittsburgh, PA: Carnegie Mellon University Press, 1994.

Committee on Science, Engineering, and Public Policy. *On Being A Scientist: Responsible Conduct in Research, (2nd edition)*. Washington, DC: National Academy of Sciences, National Academy of Engineering, Institute of Medicine, National Academy Press, 1995.

Dong BJ, Harck WW, Gambertoglio JG, et al. *Bioequivalence of generic and brand-name levothyroxine products in the treatment of hypothyroidism*. JAMA 1997; 277:1205-1213.

King R. *Bitter pill: how a drug company paid for university study, then undermined it*. Wall Street Journal. April 25, 1996:1.

LaFollette MC. *Stealing into Print*. Los Angeles, CA: University of
  California Press, 1992.
Rennie D. *Thyroid storm*. JAMA 1997; 277:1238-1243.

Chapter 8: Conflicts of Interest in Research

Office for Human Research Protection. *Draft Interim guidelines: Financial
  relationships in clinical research: Issues for institutions, clinical investigators, and IRBs to consider when dealing with issues of financial interests
  and human subject protection*. 1-10-2001(see: http://ohrp.osoph.dhhs.
  gov/nhprac/mtg12-00/finguid.htm).
American Society of Gene Therapy. *Policy of The American Society of Gene
  Therapy on Financial Conflict of Interest in Clinical Research*. American
  Society of Gene Therapy. 4-5-2000
*Task force on research accountability: Report on individual and institutional
  financial conflict of interest*. Association of American Universities, 2001.
*Task Force on Financial Conflicts of Interest in Clinical Research: Protecting
  subjects, preserving trust, promoting progress—policy and guidelines for
  the oversight of individual financial interest in human subjects research*.
  Association of American Medical Colleges, 2001.
21 CFR 54 Financial Disclosure by Clinical Investigators, 63 Federal Register
  5250, Feb. 2, 1998.

Chapter 9: Informed Consent

A History and Theory of Informed Consent; Faden & Beauchamp; Oxford
  University Press; New York; 1986
*Medical Research and the Principle of Respect for Persons in Non-Western
  Cultures*; IJsselmuiden & Faden; in The Ethics of Research Involving
  Human Subjects; Vanderpool; University Publishing Group; Frederick,
  MD

Chapter 10: Community-Based Qualitative Research

The American Anthropological Association's Code of Ethics
  (http://www.aaanet.org/)
American Public Health Association guidelines (http://www.apha.org/)

Chapter 11: Ethical Issues in Genetic Studies

Genetic Testing and Screening in the Age of Genomic Medicine by the New
York State Task Force on Life and the Law, 2001
*NIH Guidelines for Research Involving Recombinant DNA Molecules [NIH
Guidelines]* (see: www4.odinih.gov/oba/)
President's Council on Bioethics (see: http://bioethics.gov)
NBAC Report on Tissue Samples (see: www.georgetown.edu/research/
nrcbl/nbac/pubs.html).

Chapter 12: Special Ethical Concerns in Clinical Research

WMA. *5th Revision of the Declaration of Helsinki*. General Assembly.
Edinburgh, Scotland; October 2000
Temple R, Ellenberg S. *Placebo controlled trials and active-control trials in
the evaluation of new treatments. Part 1: Ethical and scientific issues.* Ann
Intern Med. 2000; 133: 455-63.
Ellenberg S, Temple R. *Placebo controlled trials and active-control trials in
the evaluation of new treatments. Part 2: Practical Issues and Specific
Cases.* Ann Intern Med. 2000; 133: 464-70.
Rothman KJ, Michels KB. *The continuing unethical use of placebo controls.*
N Engl J Med. 1994; 331:394-8.

Chapter 13: Participant Recruitment and Retention in Clinical Trials

*A Word From Study Volunteers, Opinions and Experiences of Clinical Trial
Participants, CenterWatch survey of 1,050 study volunteers 1999/2000,*
p.1-5.
W. M. Vollmer et. al., *Recruiting Children and Their Families for Clinical
Trials: A Case Study.* Controlled Clinical Trials 1992; 13(4): 315-20.
Gorelick, et. al., *The Recruitment Triangle: Reasons Why African Americans
Enroll, Refuse to Enroll, or Voluntarily Withdraw from a Clinical Trial,*
JAMA, 90(3) 141-5, 1998 Mar.
Gorelick, fn.6; El Sadr, et. al, *The Challenges of Minority Recruitment in
Clinical Trials for AIDS,* JAMA 1992; 267 (7): 954-7.
*Guideline for the Study and Evaluation of Gender Differences in the Clinical
Evaluation of Drugs,* 58 FR 139, 39406-39416, July 22, 1993.
National Institutes of Health, *Outreach Notebook for the NIH Guidelines on
Inclusion of Women and Minorities as Subjects in Clinical Research,* 1994.
*21 CFR 312.7(a) (promotion of investigational drugs); 21 CFR 812.7(d) (promo-
tion of investigational devices).*
FDA IRB Information Sheets, *Recruiting Study Subjects,* 9/98.

Silagy, et al, *Comparison of Recruitment Strategies for a Large-Scale Clinical Trial in the Elderly*, J. Clinical Epidemiology, Vol, 33, No 10, 1105-1114, 1991.

Health Insurance Portability and Accountability Act of 1996, Public Law 104-191, August 21, 1996.

Good Clinical Practice Monthly Bulletin, August 2000, p6.

Zisson, S., *Call Centers Dial Up for Patients*, CenterWatch 2001;8(3):1-10.

Nathan, RA, *How Important is Patient Recruitment in Performing Clinical Trials?*, J. of Asthma 1999: 36 (3), 213-216.

A Guide to Patient Recruitment and Retention, edited by Diana Anderson, Ph.D.

Chapter 14: Secondary Subjects, Tissue Studies and Records Reviews

45 CFR Part 46

21 CFR Parts 50 and 56

21 CFR 812

Botkin, *Protecting the Privacy of Family Members in Survey and Pedigree Research,* 285(2) JAMA 207-211 (January 10, 2001).

National Human Research Protections Advisory Committee (NHRPAC), *Clarification of the Status of Third Parties when Referenced by Human Subjects in Research*, January 2002.

National Bioethics Advisory Committee, *Research Involving Human Biological Materials: Ethical Issues and Policy Guidance,* Volumes I and II, August 1999.

Amdur and Biddle, *Institutional Review Board Approval and Publication of Human Research Results,* 277(11) JAMA 909-914 (March 19, 1997).

Moore v. Regents of the University of California, 793 P.2d 479 (Cal. 1990).

Colorado Revised Statute 10-3-1104.7, *Genetic Testing—declaration—limitations of disclosure of information—liability—legislative declaration,"* 1994.

Office for Protection from Research Risks (OPRR), *"Exculpatory Language" in Informed Consents,* November 15, 1996, accessed April 29, 2002 (see: http://ohrp.osophs.dhhs.gov/humansubjects/guidance/exculp.htm).

Food and Drug Administration, *Information Sheets: Guidance for Investigators and IRBs, Frequently Asked Questions,* 14, 1998, accessed April 29, 2002 (see: http://www.fda.gov/oc/ohrt/irbs/faqs.html# Informed Consent Document Content).

Institute of Medicine, *Protecting Data Privacy in Health Services Research,* 2000, accessed online May 1, 2002 (see: http://www.nap.edu/catalog/9952.html).

Chapter 15: Implementing the HIPPA Privacy Rule in Research

45 CFR Parts 160 and 164

Barnes, Mark; Kulynych, Jennifer, *HIPAA and Human Subjects Research: A Question & Answer Reference Guide*, March 2003, Barnett International

Information For Covered Entities And Researchers On Authorizations For Research Uses Or Disclosures Of Protected Health Information (see http://privacyruleandresearch.nih.gov/authorization.asp)

Clinical Research and the HIPAA Privacy Rule (see http://privacyruleand research.nih.gov/clin_research.gov)

Protecting Personal Health Information in Research: Understanding the HIPAA Privacy Rule (see http://privacyruleandresearch.nih.gov/ pr_02.asp)

Institutional Review Boards and the HIPAA Privacy Rule (see http:// privacyruleandresearch.nih.gov/irbandprivacyrule.asp)

Privacy Boards and the HIPAA Privacy Rule (see http://privacyruleand research.nih.gov/privacy_boards_privacy_rule.asp)

Research Repositories, Databases, and the HIPAA Privacy Rule (see http:// privacyruleandresearch.nih.gov/research_repositories.asp).

APPENDIX

The Belmont Report

Ethical Principles & Guidelines for Research Involving Human Subjects

Scientific research has produced substantial social benefits. It has also posed some troubling ethical questions. Public attention was drawn to these questions by reported abuses of human subjects in biomedical experiments, especially during the Second World War. During the Nuremberg War Crime Trials, the Nuremberg code was drafted as a set of standards for judging physicians and scientists who had conducted biomedical experiments on concentration camp prisoners. This code became the prototype of many later codes[1] intended to assure that research involving human subjects would be carried out in an ethical manner.

The codes consist of rules, some general, others specific, that guide the investigators or the reviewers of research in their work. Such rules often are inadequate to cover complex situations; at times they come into conflict, and they are frequently difficult to interpret or apply. Broader ethical principles will provide a basis on which specific rules may be formulated, criticized and interpreted.

Three principles, or general prescriptive judgments, that are relevant to research involving human subjects are identified in this statement. Other principles may also be relevant. These three are comprehensive, however, and are stated at a level of generalization that should assist scientists, subjects, reviewers and interested citizens to understand the ethical issues inherent in research involving human subjects. These principles cannot always be applied so as to resolve beyond dispute particular ethical problems. The objective is to provide an analytical framework that will guide the resolution of ethical problems arising from research involving human subjects.

This statement consists of a distinction between research and practice, a discussion of the three basic ethical principles, and remarks about the application of these principles.

Part A: Boundaries Between Practice & Research

A. Boundaries Between Practice and Research

It is important to distinguish between biomedical and behavioral research, on the one hand, and the practice of accepted therapy on the other, in order to know what activities ought to undergo review for the protection of human subjects of research. The distinction between research and practice is blurred partly because both often occur together (as in research designed to evaluate a therapy) and partly because notable departures from standard practice are often called "experimental" when the terms "experimental" and "research" are not carefully defined.

For the most part, the term "practice" refers to interventions that are designed solely to enhance the well-being of an individual patient or client and that have a reasonable expectation of success. The purpose of medical or behavioral practice is to provide diagnosis, preventive treatment or therapy to particular individuals.[2] By contrast, the term "research" designates an activity designed to test an hypothesis, permit conclusions to be drawn, and thereby to develop or contribute to generalizable knowledge (expressed, for example, in theories, principles, and statements of relationships). Research is usually described in a formal protocol that sets forth an objective and a set of procedures designed to reach that objective.

When a clinician departs in a significant way from standard or accepted practice, the innovation does not, in and of itself, constitute research. The fact that a procedure is "experimental," in the sense of new, untested or different, does not automatically place it in the category of research. Radically new procedures of this description should, however, be made the object of formal research at an early stage in order to determine whether they are safe and effective. Thus, it is the responsibility of medical practice committees, for example, to insist that a major innovation be incorporated into a formal research project.[3]

Research and practice may be carried on together when research is designed to evaluate the safety and efficacy of a therapy. This need not cause any confusion regarding whether or not the activity requires review; the general rule is that if there is any element of research in an activity, that activity should undergo review for the protection of human subjects.

Part B: Basic Ethical Principles

B. Basic Ethical Principles

The expression "basic ethical principles" refers to those general judgments that serve as a basic justification for the many particular ethical prescriptions and evaluations of human actions. Three basic principles, among those generally accepted in our cultural tradition, are particularly relevant to the ethics of research involving human subjects: the principles of respect of persons, beneficence and justice.

1. **Respect for Persons.**—Respect for persons incorporates at least two ethical convictions: first, that individuals should be treated as autonomous agents, and second, that persons with diminished autonomy are entitled to protection. The principle of respect for persons thus divides into two separate moral requirements: the requirement to acknowledge autonomy and the requirement to protect those with diminished autonomy.

An autonomous person is an individual capable of deliberation about personal goals and of acting under the direction of such deliberation. To respect autonomy is to give weight to autonomous persons' considered opinions and choices while refraining from obstructing their actions unless they are clearly detrimental to others. To show lack of respect for an autonomous agent is to repudiate that person's considered judgments, to deny an individual the freedom to act on those considered judgments, or to withhold information necessary to make a considered judgment, when there are no compelling reasons to do so.

However, not every human being is capable of self-determination. The capacity for self-determination matures during an individual's life, and some individuals lose this capacity wholly or in part because of illness, mental disability, or circumstances that severely restrict liberty. Respect for the immature and the incapacitated may require protecting them as they mature or while they are incapacitated.

Some persons are in need of extensive protection, even to the point of excluding them from activities which may harm them; other persons require little protection beyond making sure they undertake activities freely and with awareness of possible adverse consequence. The extent of protection afforded should depend upon the risk of harm and the likelihood of benefit. The judgment that any individual lacks autonomy should be periodically reevaluated and will vary in different situations.

In most cases of research involving human subjects, respect for persons demands that subjects enter into the research voluntarily and with adequate information. In some situations, however, application of the principle is not obvious. The involvement of prisoners as subjects of research provides an instructive example. On the one hand, it would seem that the principle of respect for persons requires that prisoners not be deprived of the opportunity to volunteer for research. On the other hand, under prison conditions they may be subtly coerced or unduly influenced to engage in research activities for which they would not otherwise volunteer. Respect for persons would then dictate that prisoners be protected. Whether to allow prisoners to "volunteer" or to "protect" them presents a dilemma. Respecting persons, in most hard cases, is often a matter of balancing competing claims urged by the principle of respect itself.

2. Beneficence.—Persons are treated in an ethical manner not only by respecting their decisions and protecting them from harm, but also by making efforts to secure their well-being. Such treatment falls under the principle of beneficence. The term "beneficence" is often understood to cover acts of kindness or charity that go beyond strict obligation. In this document, beneficence is understood in a stronger sense, as an obligation. Two general rules have been formulated as complementary expressions of beneficent actions in this sense: (1) do not harm and (2) maximize possible benefits and minimize possible harms.

The Hippocratic maxim "do no harm" has long been a fundamental principle of medical ethics. Claude Bernard extended it to the realm of research, saying that one should not injure one person regardless of the benefits that might come to others. However, even avoiding harm requires learning what is harmful; and, in the process of obtaining this information, persons may be exposed to risk of harm. Further, the Hippocratic Oath requires physicians to benefit their patients "according to their best judgment." Learning what will in fact benefit may require exposing persons to risk. The problem posed by these imperatives is to decide when it is justifiable to seek certain benefits despite the risks involved, and when the benefits should be foregone because of the risks.

The obligations of beneficence affect both individual investigators and society at large, because they extend both to particular research projects and to the entire enterprise of research. In the case of particular projects, investigators and members of their institutions are obliged to give forethought to the maximization of benefits and the reduction of risk that might occur from the research investigation. In the case of scientific research in general, members of the larger society are obliged to recognize the longer term benefits and risks that may result from the improvement of knowledge and from the development of novel medical, psychotherapeutic, and social procedures.

The principle of beneficence often occupies a well-defined justifying role in many areas of research involving human subjects. An example is found in research involving children. Effective ways of treating childhood diseases and fostering healthy development are benefits that serve to justify research involving children—even when individual research subjects are not direct beneficiaries. Research also makes it possible to avoid the harm that may result from the application of previously accepted routine practices that on closer investigation turn out to be dangerous. But the role of the principle of beneficence is not always so unambiguous. A difficult ethical problem remains, for example, about research that presents more than minimal risk without immediate prospect of direct benefit to the children involved. Some have argued that such research is inadmissible, while others have pointed out that this limit would rule out much research promising great benefit to children in the future. Here again, as with all hard cases, the different claims covered by the principle of beneficence may come into conflict and force difficult choices.

3. Justice.—Who ought to receive the benefits of research and bear its burdens? This is a question of justice, in the sense of "fairness in distribution" or "what is deserved." An injustice occurs when some benefit to which a person is entitled is denied without good reason or when some burden is imposed unduly. Another way of conceiving the principle of justice is that equals ought to be treated equally. However, this statement requires explication. Who is equal and who is unequal? What considerations justify departure from equal distribution? Almost all commentators allow that distinctions based on experience, age, deprivation, competence, merit and position do sometimes constitute criteria justifying differential treatment for certain purposes. It is necessary, then, to explain in what respects people should be treated equally. There are several widely accepted formulations of just ways to distribute burdens and benefits. Each formulation mentions some relevant property on the basis of which burdens and benefits should be distributed. These formulations are (1) to each person an equal share, (2) to each person according to individual need, (3) to each person according to individual effort, (4) to each person according to societal contribution, and (5) to each person according to merit.

Questions of justice have long been associated with social practices such as punishment, taxation and political representation. Until recently these questions have not generally been associated with scientific research. However, they are foreshadowed even in the earliest reflections on the ethics of research involving human subjects. For example, during the 19th and early 20th centuries the burdens of serving as research subjects fell largely upon poor ward patients, while the benefits of improved medical care flowed primarily to private patients. Subsequently, the exploitation of unwilling prisoners as research subjects in Nazi concentration camps was condemned as a particularly flagrant injustice. In this country, in the 1940s, the Tuskegee syphilis study used disadvantaged, rural black men to study the untreated course of a disease that is by no means confined to that population. These subjects were deprived of demonstrably effective treatment in order not to interrupt the project, long after such treatment became generally available.

Against this historical background, it can be seen how conceptions of justice are relevant to research involving human subjects. For example, the selection of research subjects needs to be scrutinized in order to determine whether some classes (e.g., welfare patients, particular racial and ethnic minorities, or persons confined to institutions) are being systematically selected simply because of their easy availability, their compromised position, or their manipulability, rather than for reasons directly related to the problem being studied. Finally, whenever research supported by public funds leads to the development of therapeutic devices and procedures, justice demands both that these not provide advantages only to those who can afford them and that such research should not unduly involve persons from groups unlikely to be among the beneficiaries of subsequent applications of the research.

Part C: Applications

C. Applications

Applications of the general principles to the conduct of research leads to consideration of the following requirements: informed consent, risk/benefit assessment, and the selection of subjects of research.

1. **Informed Consent.**—Respect for persons requires that subjects, to the degree that they are capable, be given the opportunity to choose what shall or shall not happen to them. This opportunity is provided when adequate standards for informed consent are satisfied.

While the importance of informed consent is unquestioned, controversy prevails over the nature and possibility of an informed consent. Nonetheless, there is widespread agreement that the consent process can be analyzed as containing three elements: information, comprehension and voluntariness.

Information. Most codes of research establish specific items for disclosure intended to assure that subjects are given sufficient information. These items generally include: the research procedure, their purposes, risks and anticipated benefits, alternative procedures (where therapy is involved), and a statement offering the subject the opportunity to ask questions and to withdraw at any time from the research. Additional items have been proposed, including how subjects are selected, the person responsible for the research, etc.

However, a simple listing of items does not answer the question of what the standard should be for judging how much and what sort of information should be provided. One standard frequently invoked in medical practice, namely the information commonly provided by practitioners in the field or in the locale, is inadequate since research takes place precisely when a common understanding does not exist. Another standard, currently popular in malpractice law, requires the practitioner to reveal the information that reasonable persons would wish to know in order to make a decision regarding their care. This, too, seems insufficient since the research subject, being in essence a volunteer, may wish to know considerably more about risks gratuitously undertaken than do patients who deliver themselves into the hand of a clinician for needed care. It may be that a standard of "the reasonable volunteer" should be proposed: the extent and nature of information should be such that persons, knowing that the procedure is neither necessary for their care nor perhaps fully understood, can decide whether they wish to participate in the furthering of knowledge. Even when some direct benefit to them is anticipated, the subjects should understand clearly the range of risk and the voluntary nature of participation.

A special problem of consent arises where informing subjects of some pertinent aspect of the research is likely to impair the validity of the research. In many cases, it is sufficient to indicate to subjects that they are being invited to participate in research of which some features will not be revealed until the research is concluded. In all cases of research involving incomplete disclosure, such research is justified only if it is clear that (1) incomplete disclosure is truly necessary to accomplish the goals of the research, (2) there are no undisclosed risks to subjects that are more than minimal, and (3) there is an adequate plan for debriefing subjects, when appropriate, and for dissemination of research results to them. Information about risks should never be withheld for the purpose of eliciting the cooperation of subjects, and truthful answers should always be given to direct questions about the research. Care should be taken to distinguish cases in which disclosure would destroy or invalidate the research from cases in which disclosure would simply inconvenience the investigator.

Comprehension. The manner and context in which information is conveyed is as important as the information itself. For example, presenting information in a disorganized and rapid fashion, allowing too little time for consideration or curtailing opportunities for questioning, all may adversely affect a subject's ability to make an informed choice.

Because the subject's ability to understand is a function of intelligence, rationality, maturity and language, it is necessary to adapt the presentation of the information to the subject's capacities. Investigators are responsible for ascertaining that the subject has comprehended the information. While there is always an obligation to ascertain that the information about risk to subjects is complete and adequately comprehended, when the risks are more serious, that obligation increases. On occasion, it may be suitable to give some oral or written tests of comprehension.

Special provision may need to be made when comprehension is severely limited—for example, by conditions of immaturity or mental disability. Each class of subjects that one might consider as incompetent (e.g., infants and young children, mentally disable patients, the terminally ill and the comatose) should be considered on its own terms. Even for these persons, however, respect requires giving them the opportunity to choose to the extent they are able, whether or not to participate in research. The objections of these subjects to involvement should be honored, unless the research entails providing them a therapy unavailable elsewhere. Respect for persons also requires seeking the permission of other parties in order to protect the subjects from harm. Such persons are thus respected both by acknowledging their own wishes and by the use of third parties to protect them from harm.

The third parties chosen should be those who are most likely to understand the incompetent subject's situation and to act in that person's best interest. The person authorized to act on behalf of the subject should be given an opportunity to observe the research as it proceeds in order to be able to withdraw the subject from the research, if such action appears in the subject's best interest.

Voluntariness. An agreement to participate in research constitutes a valid consent only if voluntarily given. This element of informed consent requires conditions free of coercion and undue influence. Coercion occurs when an overt threat of harm is intentionally presented by one person to another in order to obtain compliance. Undue influence, by contrast, occurs through an offer of an excessive, unwarranted, inappropriate or improper reward or other overture in order to obtain compliance. Also, inducements that would ordinarily be acceptable may become undue influences if the subject is especially vulnerable.

Unjustifiable pressures usually occur when persons in positions of authority or commanding influence—especially where possible sanctions are involved—urge a course of action for a subject. A continuum of such influencing factors exists, however, and it is impossible to state precisely where justifiable persuasion ends and undue influence begins. But undue influence would include actions such as manipulating a person's choice through the controlling influence of a close relative and threatening to withdraw health services to which an individual would otherwise be entitle.

2. Assessment of Risks and Benefits.—The assessment of risks and benefits requires a careful arrayal of relevant data, including, in some cases, alternative ways of obtaining the benefits sought in the research. Thus, the assessment presents both an opportunity and a responsibility to gather systematic and comprehensive information about proposed research. For the investigator, it is a means to examine whether the proposed research is properly designed. For a review committee, it is a method for determining whether the risks that will be presented to subjects are justified. For prospective subjects, the assessment will assist the determination whether or not to participate.

The Nature and Scope of Risks and Benefits. The requirement that research be justified on the basis of a favorable risk/benefit assessment bears a close relation to the principle of beneficence, just as the moral requirement that informed consent be obtained is derived primarily from the principle of respect for persons. The term "risk" refers to a possibility that harm may occur. However, when expressions such as "small risk" or "high risk" are used, they usually refer (often ambiguously) both to the chance (probability) of experiencing a harm and the severity (magnitude) of the envisioned harm.

The term "benefit" is used in the research context to refer to something of positive value related to health or welfare. Unlike, "risk," "benefit" is not a term that expresses probabilities. Risk is properly contrasted to probability of benefits, and benefits are properly contrasted with harms rather than risks of harm. Accordingly, so-called risk/benefit assessments are concerned with the probabilities and magnitudes of possible harm and anticipated benefits. Many kinds of possible harms and benefits need to be taken into account. There are, for example, risks of psychological harm, physical harm, legal harm, social harm and economic harm and the corresponding benefits. While the most likely types of harms to research subjects are those of psychological or physical pain or injury, other possible kinds should not be overlooked.

Risks and benefits of research may affect the individual subjects, the families of the individual subjects, and society at large (or special groups of subjects in society). Previous codes and Federal regulations have required that risks to subjects be outweighed by the sum of both the anticipated benefit to the subject, if any, and the anticipated benefit to society in the form of knowledge to be gained from the research. In balancing these different elements, the risks and benefits affecting the immediate research subject will normally carry special weight. On the other hand, interests other than those of the subject may on some occasions be sufficient by themselves to justify the risks involved in the research, so long as the subjects' rights have been protected. Beneficence thus requires that we protect against risk of harm to subjects and also that we be concerned about the loss of the substantial benefits that might be gained from research.

The Systematic Assessment of Risks and Benefits. It is commonly said that benefits and risks must be "balanced" and shown to be "in a favorable ratio." The metaphorical character of these terms draws attention to the difficulty of making precise judgments. Only on rare occasions will quantitative techniques be available for the scrutiny of research protocols. However, the idea of systematic, nonarbitrary analysis of risks and benefits should be emulated insofar as possible. This ideal requires those making decisions about the justifiability of research to be thorough in the accumulation and assessment of information about all aspects of the research, and to consider alternatives systematically. This procedure renders the assessment of research more rigorous and precise, while making communication between review board members and investigators less subject to misinterpretation, misinformation and conflicting judgments. Thus, there should first be a determination of the validity of the presuppositions of the research; then the nature, probability and magnitude of risk should be distinguished with as much clarity as possible. The method of ascertaining risks should be explicit, especially where there is no alternative to the use of such vague categories as small or slight risk. It should also be determined whether an investigator's estimates of the probability of harm or benefits are reasonable, as judged by known facts or other available studies.

Finally, assessment of the justifiability of research should reflect at least the following considerations: (i) Brutal or inhumane treatment of human subjects is never morally justified. (ii) Risks should be reduced to those necessary to achieve the research objective. It should be determined whether it is in fact necessary to use human subjects at all. Risk can perhaps never be entirely eliminated, but it can often be reduced by careful attention to alternative procedures. (iii) When research involves significant risk of serious impairment, review committees should be extraordinarily insistent on the justification of the risk (looking usually to the likelihood of benefit to the subject—or, in some rare cases, to the manifest voluntariness of the participation). (iv) When vulnerable populations are involved in research, the appropriateness of involving them should itself be demonstrated. A number of variables go into such judgments, including the nature and degree of risk, the condition of the particular population involved, and the nature and level of the anticipated benefits. (v) Relevant risks and benefits must be thoroughly arrayed in documents and procedures used in the informed consent process.

3. Selection of Subjects.—Just as the principle of respect for persons finds expression in the requirements for consent, and the principle of beneficence in risk/benefit assessment, the principle of justice gives rise to moral requirements that there be fair procedures and outcomes in the selection of research subjects.

Justice is relevant to the selection of subjects of research at two levels: the social and the individual. Individual justice in the selection of subjects would require that researchers exhibit fairness: thus, they should not offer potentially beneficial research only to some patients who are in their favor or select only "undesirable" persons for risky research. Social justice requires that distinction be drawn between classes of subjects that ought, and ought not, to participate in any particular kind of research, based on the ability of members of that class to bear burdens and on the appropriateness of placing further burdens on already burdened persons. Thus, it can be considered a matter of social justice that there is an order of preference in the selection of classes of subjects (e.g., adults before children) and that some classes of potential subjects (e.g., the institutionalized mentally infirm or prisoners) may be involved as research subjects, if at all, only on certain conditions.

Injustice may appear in the selection of subjects, even if individual subjects are selected fairly by investigators and treated fairly in the course of research. Thus injustice arises from social, racial, sexual and cultural biases institutionalized in society. Thus, even if individual researchers are treating their research subjects fairly, and even if IRBs are taking care to assure that subjects are selected fairly within a particular institution, unjust social patterns may nevertheless appear in the overall distribution of the burdens and benefits of research. Although individual institutions or investigators may not be able to resolve a problem that is pervasive in their social setting, they can consider distributive justice in selecting research subjects.

Some populations, especially institutionalized ones, are already burdened in many ways by their infirmities and environments. When research is proposed that involves risks and does not include a therapeutic component, other less burdened classes of persons should be called upon first to accept these risks of research, except where the research is directly related to the specific conditions of the class involved. Also, even though public funds for research may often flow in the same directions as public funds for health care, it seems unfair that populations dependent on public health care constitute a pool of preferred research subjects if more advantaged populations are likely to be the recipients of the benefits.

One special instance of injustice results from the involvement of vulnerable subjects. Certain groups, such as racial minorities, the economically disadvantaged, the very sick, and the institutionalized may continually be sought as research subjects, owing to their ready availability in settings where research is conducted. Given their dependent status and their frequently compromised capacity for free consent, they should be protected against the danger of being involved in research solely for administrative convenience, or because they are easy to manipulate as a result of their illness or socioeconomic condition.

---

1.   Since 1945, various codes for the proper and responsible conduct of human experimentation in medical research have been adopted by different organizations. The best known of these codes are the Nuremberg Code of 1947, the Helsinki Declaration of 1964 (revised in 1975), and the 1971 Guidelines (codified into Federal Regulations in 1974) issued by the U.S. Department of Health, Education, and Welfare Codes for the conduct of social and behavioral research have also been adopted, the best known being that of the American Psychological Association, published in 1973.

2.   Although practice usually involves interventions designed solely to enhance the well-being of a particular individual, interventions are sometimes applied to one individual for the enhancement of the well-being of another (e.g., blood donation, skin grafts, organ transplants) or an intervention may have the dual purpose of enhancing the well-being of a particular individual, and, at the same time, providing some benefit to others (e.g., vaccination, which protects both the person who is vaccinated and society generally). The fact that some forms of practice have elements other than immediate benefit to the individual receiving an intervention, however, should not confuse the general distinction between research and practice. Even when a procedure applied in practice may benefit some other person, it remains an intervention designed to enhance the well-being of a particular individual or groups of individuals; thus, it is practice and need not be reviewed as research.

3.   Because the problems related to social experimentation may differ substantially from those of biomedical and behavioral research, the Commission specifically declines to make any policy determination regarding such research at this time. Rather, the Commission believes that the problem ought to be addressed by one of its successor bodies.

A P P E N D I X C

Code of Federal Regulations

Code of Federal Regulations

TITLE 21—FOOD AND DRUGS

**Chapter I: Food and Drug Administration,
Department of Health and Human Services
Subchapter A: General**

PART 50

Protection of Human Subjects

Subpart A—General Provisions

Subpart B — Informed Consent of Human Subjects

Subpart C [Reserved]

Subpart D—Additional Safeguards for Children in Clinical Investigations

Authority: 21 U.S.C 321, 343, 346, 346a, 348, 350a, 350b, 352, 353, 355, 360, 360c-360f, 360h-360j, 371, 379e, 381; 42 U.S.C. 216, 241, 262, 263b-263n.

Source: 45 FR 36390, May 30, 1980, unless otherwise noted.

Subpart A—General Provisions

§50.1 Scope.

(a) This part applies to all clinical investigations regulated by the Food and Drug Administration under sections 505(i) and 520(g) of the Federal Food, Drug, and Cosmetic Act, as well as clinical investigations that support applications for research or marketing permits for products regulated by the Food and Drug Administration, including foods, including dietary supplements, that bear a nutrient content claim or a health claim, infant formulas, food and color additives, drugs for human use, medical devices for human use, biological products for human use, and electronic products. Additional specific obligations and commitments of, and standards of conduct for, persons who sponsor or monitor clinical investigations involving particular test articles may also be found in other parts (e.g., parts 312 and 812). Compliance with these parts is intended to protect the rights and safety of subjects involved in investigations filed with the Food and Drug Administration pursuant to sections 403, 406, 409, 412, 413, 502, 503, 505, 510, 513-516, 518-520, 721, and 801 of the Federal Food, Drug, and Cosmetic Act and sections 351 and 354-360F of the Public Health Service Act.

(b) References in this part to regulatory sections of the Code of Federal Regulations are to chapter I of title 21, unless otherwise noted.

[45 FR 36390, May 30, 1980; 46 FR 8979, Jan. 27, 1981, as amended at 63 FR 26697, May 13, 1998; 64 FR 399, Jan. 5, 1999; 66 FR 20597, Apr. 24, 2001]

§50.3 Definitions.

As used in this part:

(a) *Act* means the Federal Food, Drug, and Cosmetic Act, as amended (secs. 201—902, 52 Stat. 1040 et seq. as amended (21 U.S.C. 321—392)).

(b) *Application for research or marketing permit* includes:

(1) A color additive petition, described in part 71.

(2) A food additive petition, described in parts 171 and 571.

(3) Data and information about a substance submitted as part of the procedures for establishing that the substance is generally recognized as safe for use that results or may reasonably be expected to result, directly or indirectly, in its becoming a component or otherwise affecting the characteristics of any food, described in §§170.30 and 570.30.

(4) Data and information about a food additive submitted as part of the procedures for food additives permitted to be used on an interim basis pending additional study, described in §180.1.

(5) Data and information about a substance submitted as part of the procedures for establishing a tolerance for unavoidable contaminants in food and food-packaging materials, described in section 406 of the act.

(6) An investigational new drug application, described in part 312 of this chapter.

(7) A new drug application, described in part 314.

(8) Data and information about the bioavailability or bioequivalence of drugs for human use submitted as part of the procedures for issuing, amending, or repealing a bioequivalence requirement, described in part 320.

(9) Data and information about an over-the-counter drug for human use submitted as part of the procedures for classifying these drugs as generally recognized as safe and effective and not misbranded, described in part 330.

(10) Data and information about a prescription drug for human use submitted as part of the procedures for classifying these drugs as generally recognized as safe and effective and not misbranded, described in this chapter.

(11) [Reserved]

(12) An application for a biologics license, described in part 601 of this chapter.

(13) Data and information about a biological product submitted as part of the procedures for determining that licensed biological products are safe and effective and not misbranded, described in part 601.

(14) Data and information about an in vitro diagnostic product submitted as part of the procedures for establishing, amending, or repealing a standard for these products, described in part 809.

(15) An Application for an Investigational Device Exemption, described in part 812.

(16) Data and information about a medical device submitted as part of the procedures for classifying these devices, described in section 513.

(17) Data and information about a medical device submitted as part of the procedures for establishing, amending, or repealing a standard for these devices, described in section 514.

(18) An application for premarket approval of a medical device, described in section 515.

(19) A product development protocol for a medical device, described in section 515.

(20) Data and information about an electronic product submitted as part of the procedures for establishing, amending, or repealing a standard for these products, described in section 358 of the Public Health Service Act.

(21) Data and information about an electronic product submitted as part of the procedures for obtaining a variance from any electronic product performance standard, as described in §1010.4.

(22) Data and information about an electronic product submitted as part of the procedures for granting, amending, or extending an exemption from a radiation safety performance standard, as described in §1010.5.

(23) Data and information about a clinical study of an infant formula when submitted as part of an infant formula notification under section 412(c) of the Federal Food, Drug, and Cosmetic Act.

(24) Data and information submitted in a petition for a nutrient content claim, described in §101.69 of this chapter, or for a health claim, described in §101.70 of this chapter.

(25) Data and information from investi-

gations involving children submitted in a new dietary ingredient notification, described in §190.6 of this chapter.

(c) Clinical investigation means any experiment that involves a test article and one or more human subjects and that either is subject to requirements for prior submission to the Food and Drug Administration under section 505(i) or 520(g) of the act, or is not subject to requirements for prior submission to the Food and Drug Administration under these sections of the act, but the results of which are intended to be submitted later to, or held for inspection by, the Food and Drug Administration as part of an application for a research or marketing permit. The term does not include experiments that are subject to the provisions of part 58 of this chapter, regarding nonclinical laboratory studies.

(d) Investigator means an individual who actually conducts a clinical investigation, i.e., under whose immediate direction the test article is administered or dispensed to, or used involving, a subject, or, in the event of an investigation conducted by a team of individuals, is the responsible leader of that team.

(e) Sponsor means a person who initiates a clinical investigation, but who does not actually conduct the investigation, i.e., the test article is administered or dispensed to or used involving, a subject under the immediate direction of another individual. A person other than an individual (e.g., corporation or agency) that uses one or more of its own employees to conduct a clinical investigation it has initiated is considered to be a sponsor (not a sponsor-investigator), and the employees are considered to be investigators.

(f) Sponsor-investigator means an individual who both initiates and actually conducts, alone or with others, a clinical investigation, i.e., under whose immediate direction the test article is administered or dispensed to, or used involving, a subject. The term does not include any person other than an individual, e.g., corporation or agency.

(g) Human subject means an individual who is or becomes a participant in research, either as a recipient of the test article or as a control. A subject may be either a healthy human or a patient.

(h) Institution means any public or private entity or agency (including Federal, State, and other agencies). The word facility as used in section 520(g) of the act is deemed to be synonymous with the term institution for purposes of this part.

(i) Institutional review board (IRB) means any board, committee, or other group formally designated by an institution to review biomedical research involving humans as subjects, to approve the initiation of and conduct periodic review of such research. The term has the same meaning as the phrase institutional review committee as used in section 520(g) of the act.

(j) Test article means any drug (including a biological product for human use), medical device for human use, human food additive, color additive, electronic product, or any other article subject to regulation under the act or under sections 351 and 354-360F of the Public Health Service Act (42 U.S.C. 262 and 263b-263n).

(k) Minimal risk means that the probability and magnitude of harm or discomfort anticipated in the research are not greater in and of themselves than those ordinarily encountered in daily life or during the performance of routine physical or psychological examinations or tests.

(l) Legally authorized representative means an individual or judicial or other body authorized under applicable law to consent on behalf of a prospective subject to the subject's particpation in the procedure(s) involved in the research.

(m) Family member means any one of the following legally competent persons: Spouse; parents; children (including adopted children); brothers, sisters, and spouses of brothers and sisters; and any individual related by blood or affinity whose close association with the subject is the equivalent of a family relationship.

(n) Assent means a child's affirmative agreement to participate in a clinical investigation. Mere failure to object may not, absent affirmative agreement, be construed as assent.

(o) Children means persons who have not attained the legal age for consent to treatments or procedures involved in clinical investigations, under the applicable law of the jurisdiction in which the clinical investigation will be conducted.

(p) Parent means a child's biological or adoptive parent.

(q) Ward means a child who is placed in the legal custody of the State or other agency, institution, or entity, consistent with applicable Federal, State, or local law.

(r) Permission means the agreement of parent(s) or guardian to the participation of their child or ward in a clinical investigation. Permission must be obtained in compliance with subpart B of this part and must include the elements of informed consent described in §50.25.

(s) Guardian means an individual who is authorized under applicable State or local law to consent on behalf of a child to general medical care when general medical care includes participation in research. For purposes of subpart D of this part, a guardian also means an individual who is authorized to consent on behalf of a child to participate in research.

[45 FR 36390, May 30, 1980, as amended at 46 FR 8950, Jan. 27, 1981; 54 FR 9038, Mar. 3, 1989; 56 FR 28028, June 18, 1991; 61 FR 51528, Oct. 2, 1996; 62 FR 39440, July 23, 1997; 64 FR 399, Jan. 5, 1999; 64 FR 56448, Oct. 20, 1999; 66 FR 20597, Apr. 24, 2001]

Subpart B—Informed Consent of Human Subjects

Source: 46 FR 8951, Jan. 27, 1981, unless otherwise noted.

§50.20 General requirements for informed consent.

Except as provided in §§50.23 and 50.24, no investigator may involve a human being as a subject in research covered by these regulations unless the investigator has obtained the legally effective informed consent of the subject or the subject's legally authorized representative. An investigator shall seek such consent only under circumstances that provide the prospective subject or the representative sufficient opportunity to consider whether or not to participate and that minimize the possibility of coercion or undue influence. The information that is given to the subject or the representative shall be in language understandable to the subject or the representative. No informed consent, whether oral or written, may include any exculpatory language through which the subject or the representative is made to waive or appear to waive any of the subject's legal rights, or releases or appears to release the investigator, the sponsor, the institution, or its agents from liability for negligence.

[46 FR 8951, Jan. 27, 1981, as amended at 64 FR 10942, Mar. 8, 1999]

§50.23 Exception from general requirements.

(a) The obtaining of informed consent shall be deemed feasible unless, before use of the test article (except as provided in paragraph (b) of this section), both the investigator and a physician who is not otherwise participating in the clinical investigation certify in writing all of the following:

(1) The human subject is confronted by a life-threatening situation necessitating the use of the test article.

(2) Informed consent cannot be obtained from the subject because of an inability to communicate with, or obtain legally effective consent from, the subject.

(3) Time is not sufficient to obtain consent from the subject's legal representative.

(4) There is available no alternative method of approved or generally recog-

nized therapy that provides an equal or greater likelihood of saving the life of the subject.

(b) If immediate use of the test article is, in the investigator's opinion, required to preserve the life of the subject, and time is not sufficient to obtain the independent determination required in paragraph (a) of this section in advance of using the test article, the determinations of the clinical investigator shall be made and, within 5 working days after the use of the article, be reviewed and evaluated in writing by a physician who is not participating in the clinical investigation.

(c) The documentation required in paragraph (a) or (b) of this section shall be submitted to the IRB within 5 working days after the use of the test article.

(d)(1) Under 10 U.S.C. 1107(f) the President may waive the prior consent requirement for the administration of an investigational new drug to a member of the armed forces in connection with the member's participation in a particular military operation. The statute specifies that only the President may waive informed consent in this connection and the President may grant such a waiver only if the President determines in writing that obtaining consent: Is not feasible; is contrary to the best interests of the military member; or is not in the interests of national security. The statute further provides that in making a determination to waive prior informed consent on the ground that it is not feasible or the ground that it is contrary to the best interests of the military members involved, the President shall apply the standards and criteria that are set forth in the relevant FDA regulations for a waiver of the prior informed consent requirements of section

505(i)(4) of the Federal Food, Drug, and Cosmetic Act (21 U.S.C. 355(i)(4)). Before such a determination may be made that obtaining informed consent from military personnel prior to the use of an investigational drug (including an antibiotic or biological product) in a specific protocol under an investigational new drug application (IND) sponsored by the Department of Defense (DOD) and limited to specific military personnel involved in a particular military operation is not feasible or is contrary to the best interests of the military members involved the Secretary of Defense must first request such a determination from the President, and certify and document to the President that the following standards and criteria contained in paragraphs (d)(1) through (d)(4) of this section have been met.

(i) The extent and strength of evidence of the safety and effectiveness of the investigational new drug in relation to the medical risk that could be encountered during the military operation supports the drug's administration under an IND.

(ii) The military operation presents a substantial risk that military personnel may be subject to a chemical, biological, nuclear, or other exposure likely to produce death or serious or life-threatening injury or illness.

(iii) There is no available satisfactory alternative therapeutic or preventive treatment in relation to the intended use of the investigational new drug.

(iv) Conditioning use of the investigational new drug on the voluntary participation of each member could significantly risk the safety and health of any individual member who would decline its use, the safety of other military personnel, and the accomplishment of the military mission.

(v) A duly constituted institutional review board (IRB) established and operated in accordance with the requirements of paragraphs (d)(2) and (d)(3) of this section, responsible for review of the study, has reviewed and approved the investigational new drug protocol and the administration of the investigational new drug without informed consent. DOD's request is to include the documentation required by §56.115(a)(2) of this chapter.

(vi) DOD has explained:

(A) The context in which the investigational drug will be administered, e.g., the setting or whether it will be self-administered or it will be administered by a health professional;

(B) The nature of the disease or condition for which the preventive or therapeutic treatment is intended; and

(C) To the extent there are existing data or information available, information on conditions that could alter the effects of the investigational drug.

(vii) DOD's recordkeeping system is capable of tracking and will be used to track the proposed treatment from supplier to the individual recipient.

(viii) Each member involved in the military operation will be given, prior to the administration of the investigational new drug, a specific written information sheet (including information required by 10 U.S.C. 1107(d)) concerning the investigational new drug, the risks and benefits of its use, potential side effects, and other pertinent information about the appropriate use of the product.

(ix) Medical records of members involved in the military operation will accurately document the receipt by members of the notification required by paragraph (d)(1)(viii) of this section.

(x) Medical records of members involved in the military operation will accurately document the receipt by members of any investigational new drugs in accordance with FDA regulations including part 312 of this chapter.

(xi) DOD will provide adequate followup to assess whether there are beneficial or adverse health consequences that result from the use of the investigational product.

(xii) DOD is pursuing drug development, including a time line, and marketing approval with due diligence.

(xiii) FDA has concluded that the investigational new drug protocol may proceed subject to a decision by the President on the informed consent waiver request.

(xiv) DOD will provide training to the appropriate medical personnel and potential recipients on the specific investigational new drug to be administered prior to its use.

(xv) DOD has stated and justified the time period for which the waiver is needed, not to exceed one year, unless separately renewed under these standards and criteria.

(xvi) DOD shall have a continuing obligation to report to the FDA and to the President any changed circumstances relating to these standards and criteria (including the time period referred to in paragraph (d)(1)(xv) of this section) or

that otherwise might affect the determination to use an investigational new drug without informed consent.

(xvii) DOD is to provide public notice as soon as practicable and consistent with classification requirements through notice in the FEDERAL REGISTER describing each waiver of informed consent determination, a summary of the most updated scientific information on the products used, and other pertinent information.

(xviii) Use of the investigational drug without informed consent otherwise conforms with applicable law.

(2) The duly constituted institutional review board, described in paragraph (d)(1)(v) of this section, must include at least 3 nonaffiliated members who shall not be employees or officers of the Federal Government (other than for purposes of membership on the IRB) and shall be required to obtain any necessary security clearances. This IRB shall review the proposed IND protocol at a convened meeting at which a majority of the members are present including at least one member whose primary concerns are in nonscientific areas and, if feasible, including a majority of the nonaffiliated members. The information required by §56.115(a)(2) of this chapter is to be provided to the Secretary of Defense for further review.

(3) The duly constituted institutional review board, described in paragraph (d)(1)(v) of this section, must review and approve:

(i) The required information sheet;

(ii) The adequacy of the plan to disseminate information, including distribution of the information sheet to potential recipients, on the investigational product (e.g., in forms other than written);

(iii) The adequacy of the information and plans for its dissemination to health care providers, including potential side effects, contraindications, potential interactions, and other pertinent considerations; and

(iv) An informed consent form as required by part 50 of this chapter, in those circumstances in which DOD determines that informed consent may be obtained from some or all personnel involved.

(4) DOD is to submit to FDA summaries of institutional review board meetings at which the proposed protocol has been reviewed.

(5) Nothing in these criteria or standards is intended to preempt or limit FDA's and DOD's authority or obligations under applicable statutes and regulations.

[46 FR 8951, Jan. 27, 1981, as amended at 55 FR 52817, Dec. 21, 1990; 64 FR 399, Jan. 5, 1999; 64 FR 54188, Oct. 5, 1999]

§50.24 Exception from informed consent requirements for emergency research.

(a) The IRB responsible for the review, approval, and continuing review of the clinical investigation described in this section may approve that investigation without requiring that informed consent of all research subjects be obtained if the IRB (with the concurrence of a licensed physician who is a member of or consultant to the IRB and who is not otherwise partici-

pating in the clinical investigation) finds and documents each of the following:

(1) The human subjects are in a life-threatening situation, available treatments are unproven or unsatisfactory, and the collection of valid scientific evidence, which may include evidence obtained through randomized placebo-controlled investigations, is necessary to determine the safety and effectiveness of particular interventions.

(2) Obtaining informed consent is not feasible because:

(i) The subjects will not be able to give their informed consent as a result of their medical condition;

(ii) The intervention under investigation must be administered before consent from the subjects' legally authorized representatives is feasible; and

(iii) There is no reasonable way to identify prospectively the individuals likely to become eligible for participation in the clinical investigation.

(3) Participation in the research holds out the prospect of direct benefit to the subjects because:

(i) Subjects are facing a life-threatening situation that necessitates intervention;

(ii) Appropriate animal and other preclinical studies have been conducted, and the information derived from those studies and related evidence support the potential for the intervention to provide a direct benefit to the individual subjects; and

(iii) Risks associated with the investigation are reasonable in relation to what is known about the medical condition of the potential class of subjects, the risks and benefits of standard therapy, if any, and what is known about the risks and benefits of the proposed intervention or activity.

(4) The clinical investigation could not practicably be carried out without the waiver.

(5) The proposed investigational plan defines the length of the potential therapeutic window based on scientific evidence, and the investigator has committed to attempting to contact a legally authorized representative for each subject within that window of time and, if feasible, to asking the legally authorized representative contacted for consent within that window rather than proceeding without consent. The investigator will summarize efforts made to contact legally authorized representatives and make this information available to the IRB at the time of continuing review.

(6) The IRB has reviewed and approved informed consent procedures and an informed consent document consistent with §50.25. These procedures and the informed consent document are to be used with subjects or their legally authorized representatives in situations where use of such procedures and documents is feasible. The IRB has reviewed and approved procedures and information to be used when providing an opportunity for a family member to object to a subject's participation in the clinical investigation consistent with paragraph (a)(7)(v) of this section.

(7) Additional protections of the rights and welfare of the subjects will be provided, including, at least:

(i) Consultation (including, where appropriate, consultation carried out by the IRB) with representatives of the communities in which the clinical investigation will be conducted and from which the subjects will be drawn;

(ii) Public disclosure to the communities in which the clinical investigation will be conducted and from which the subjects will be drawn, prior to initiation of the clinical investigation, of plans for the investigation and its risks and expected benefits;

(iii) Public disclosure of sufficient information following completion of the clinical investigation to apprise the community and researchers of the study, including the demographic characteristics of the research population, and its results;

(iv) Establishment of an independent data monitoring committee to exercise oversight of the clinical investigation; and

(v) If obtaining informed consent is not feasible and a legally authorized representative is not reasonably available, the investigator has committed, if feasible, to attempting to contact within the therapeutic window the subject's family member who is not a legally authorized representative, and asking whether he or she objects to the subject's participation in the clinical investigation. The investigator will summarize efforts made to contact family members and make this information available to the IRB at the time of continuing review.

(b) The IRB is responsible for ensuring that procedures are in place to inform, at the earliest feasible opportunity, each subject, or if the subject remains incapacitated, a legally authorized representative of the subject, or if such a representative is not reasonably available, a family member, of the subject's inclusion in the clinical investigation, the details of the investigation and other information contained in the informed consent document. The IRB shall also ensure that there is a procedure to inform the subject, or if the subject remains incapacitated, a legally authorized representative of the subject, or if such a representative is not reasonably available, a family member, that he or she may discontinue the subject's participation at any time without penalty or loss of benefits to which the subject is otherwise entitled. If a legally authorized representative or family member is told about the clinical investigation and the subject's condition improves, the subject is also to be informed as soon as feasible. If a subject is entered into a clinical investigation with waived consent and the subject dies before a legally authorized representative or family member can be contacted, information about the clinical investigation is to be provided to the subject's legally authorized representative or family member, if feasible.

(c) The IRB determinations required by paragraph (a) of this section and the documentation required by paragraph (e) of this section are to be retained by the IRB for at least 3 years after completion of the clinical investigation, and the records shall be accessible for inspection and copying by FDA in accordance with §56.115(b) of this chapter.

(d) Protocols involving an exception to the informed consent requirement under this section must be performed under a separate investigational new drug application (IND) or investigational device exemption (IDE) that clearly identifies such protocols as protocols that may include subjects who are unable to consent. The submission of those protocols in a separate IND/IDE is required even if an IND for the same drug product or an IDE for the same device already exists. Applications for investigations under this section may not be submitted as amendments under §§312.30 or 812.35 of this chapter.

(e) If an IRB determines that it cannot approve a clinical investigation because the investigation does not meet the criteria in the exception provided under paragraph (a) of this section or because of other relevant ethical concerns, the IRB must document its findings and provide these findings promptly in writing to the clinical investigator and to the sponsor of the clinical investigation. The sponsor of the clinical investigation must promptly disclose this information to FDA and to the sponsor's clinical investigators who are participating or are asked to participate in this or a substantially equivalent clinical investigation of the sponsor, and to other IRB's that have been, or are, asked to review this or a substantially equivalent investigation by that sponsor.

[61 FR 51528, Oct. 2, 1996]

§50.25 Elements of informed consent.

(a) Basic elements of informed consent. In seeking informed consent, the following information shall be provided to each subject:

(1) A statement that the study involves research, an explanation of the purposes of the research and the expected duration of the subject's participation, a description of the procedures to be followed, and identification of any procedures which are experimental.

(2) A description of any reasonably foreseeable risks or discomforts to the subject.

(3) A description of any benefits to the subject or to others which may reasonably be expected from the research.

(4) A disclosure of appropriate alternative procedures or courses of treatment, if any, that might be advantageous to the subject.

(5) A statement describing the extent, if any, to which confidentiality of records identifying the subject will be maintained and that notes the possibility that the Food and Drug Administration may inspect the records.

(6) For research involving more than minimal risk, an explanation as to whether any compensation and an explanation as to whether any medical treatments are available if injury occurs and, if so, what they consist of, or where further information may be obtained.

(7) An explanation of whom to contact for answers to pertinent questions about the research and research subjects' rights, and whom to contact in the event of a research-related injury to the subject.

(8) A statement that participation is voluntary, that refusal to participate will involve no penalty or loss of benefits to which the subject is otherwise entitled, and that the subject may discontinue participation at any time without penalty or

loss of benefits to which the subject is otherwise entitled.

(b) Additional elements of informed consent. When appropriate, one or more of the following elements of information shall also be provided to each subject:

(1) A statement that the particular treatment or procedure may involve risks to the subject (or to the embryo or fetus, if the subject is or may become pregnant) which are currently unforeseeable.

(2) Anticipated circumstances under which the subject's participation may be terminated by the investigator without regard to the subject's consent.

(3) Any additional costs to the subject that may result from participation in the research.

(4) The consequences of a subject's decision to withdraw from the research and procedures for orderly termination of participation by the subject.

(5) A statement that significant new findings developed during the course of the research which may relate to the subject's willingness to continue participation will be provided to the subject.

(6) The approximate number of subjects involved in the study.

(c) The informed consent requirements in these regulations are not intended to preempt any applicable Federal, State, or local laws which require additional information to be disclosed for informed consent to be legally effective.

(d) Nothing in these regulations is intended to limit the authority of a physician to provide emergency medical care to the extent the physician is permitted to do so under applicable Federal, State, or local law.

§50.27 Documentation of informed consent.

(a) Except as provided in §56.109(c), informed consent shall be documented by the use of a written consent form approved by the IRB and signed and dated by the subject or the subject's legally authorized representative at the time of consent. A copy shall be given to the person signing the form.

(b) Except as provided in §56.109(c), the consent form may be either of the following:

(1) A written consent document that embodies the elements of informed consent required by §50.25. This form may be read to the subject or the subject's legally authorized representative, but, in any event, the investigator shall give either the subject or the representative adequate opportunity to read it before it is signed.

(2) A short form written consent document stating that the elements of informed consent required by §50.25 have been presented orally to the subject or the subject's legally authorized representative. When this method is used, there shall be a witness to the oral presentation. Also, the IRB shall approve a written summary of what is to be said to the subject or the representative. Only the short form itself is to be signed by the subject or the representative. However, the witness shall sign both the short form and a copy of the summary, and the person actually obtaining the consent shall sign a copy of the summary.

A copy of the summary shall be given to the subject or the representative in addition to a copy of the short form.

[46 FR 8951, Jan. 27, 1981, as amended at 61 FR 57280, Nov. 5, 1996]

Subpart C [Reserved]

Subpart D—Additional Safeguards for Children in Clinical Investigations

Source: 66 FR 20598, Apr. 24, 2001, unless otherwise noted.

§50.50 IRB duties.

In addition to other responsibilities assigned to IRBs under this part and part 56 of this chapter, each IRB must review clinical investigations involving children as subjects covered by this subpart D and approve only those clinical investigations that satisfy the criteria described in §50.51, §50.52, or §50.53 and the conditions of all other applicable sections of this subpart D.

§50.51 Clinical investigations not involving greater than minimal risk.

Any clinical investigation within the scope described in §§50.1 and 56.101 of this chapter in which no greater than minimal risk to children is presented may involve children as subjects only if the IRB finds and documents that adequate provisions are made for soliciting the assent of the children and the permission of their parents or guardians as set forth in §50.55.

§50.52 Clinical investigations involving greater than minimal risk but presenting the prospect of direct benefit to individual subjects.

Any clinical investigation within the scope described in §§50.1 and 56.101 of this chapter in which more than minimal risk to children is presented by an intervention or procedure that holds out the prospect of direct benefit for the individual subject, or by a monitoring procedure that is likely to contribute to the subject's well-being, may involve children as subjects only if the IRB finds and documents that:

(a) The risk is justified by the anticipated benefit to the subjects;

(b) The relation of the anticipated benefit to the risk is at least as favorable to the subjects as that presented by available alternative approaches; and

(c) Adequate provisions are made for soliciting the assent of the children and permission of their parents or guardians as set forth in §50.55.

§50.53 Clinical investigations involving greater than minimal risk and no prospect of direct benefit to individual subjects, but likely to yield generalizable knowledge about the subjects' disorder or condition.

Any clinical investigation within the scope described in §§50.1 and 56.101 of this chapter in which more than minimal risk to children is presented by an intervention or procedure that does not hold out the prospect of direct benefit for the individ-

ual subject, or by a monitoring procedure that is not likely to contribute to the well-being of the subject, may involve children as subjects only if the IRB finds and documents that:

(a) The risk represents a minor increase over minimal risk;

(b) The intervention or procedure presents experiences to subjects that are reasonably commensurate with those inherent in their actual or expected medical, dental, psychological, social, or educational situations;

(c) The intervention or procedure is likely to yield generalizable knowledge about the subjects' disorder or condition that is of vital importance for the understanding or amelioration of the subjects' disorder or condition; and

(d) Adequate provisions are made for soliciting the assent of the children and permission of their parents or guardians as set forth in §50.55.

§50.54 Clinical investigations not otherwise approvable that present an opportunity to understand, prevent, or alleviate a serious problem affecting the health or welfare of children.

If an IRB does not believe that a clinical investigation within the scope described in §§50.1 and 56.101 of this chapter and involving children as subjects meets the requirements of §50.51, §50.52, or §50.53, the clinical investigation may proceed only if:

(a) The IRB finds and documents that the clinical investigation presents a reasonable opportunity to further the understanding, prevention, or alleviation of a serious problem affecting the health or welfare of children; and

(b) The Commissioner of Food and Drugs, after consultation with a panel of experts in pertinent disciplines (for example: science, medicine, education, ethics, law) and following opportunity for public review and comment, determines either:

(1) That the clinical investigation in fact satisfies the conditions of §50.51, §50.52, or §50.53, as applicable, or

(2) That the following conditions are met:

(i) The clinical investigation presents a reasonable opportunity to further the understanding, prevention, or alleviation of a serious problem affecting the health or welfare of children;

(ii) The clinical investigation will be conducted in accordance with sound ethical principles; and

(iii) Adequate provisions are made for soliciting the assent of children and the permission of their parents or guardians as set forth in §50.55.

§50.55 Requirements for permission by parents or guardians and for assent by children.

(a) In addition to the determinations required under other applicable sections of this subpart D, the IRB must determine that adequate provisions are made for soliciting the assent of the children when in the judgment of the IRB the children are capable of providing assent.

(b) In determining whether children are capable of providing assent, the IRB must take into account the ages, maturity, and psychological state of the children involved. This judgment may be made for all children to be involved in clinical investigations under a particular protocol, or for each child, as the IRB deems appropriate.

(c) The assent of the children is not a necessary condition for proceeding with the clinical investigation if the IRB determines:

(1) That the capability of some or all of the children is so limited that they cannot reasonably be consulted, or

(2) That the intervention or procedure involved in the clinical investigation holds out a prospect of direct benefit that is important to the health or well-being of the children and is available only in the context of the clinical investigation.

(d) Even where the IRB determines that the subjects are capable of assenting, the IRB may still waive the assent requirement if it finds and documents that:

(1) The clinical investigation involves no more than minimal risk to the subjects;

(2) The waiver will not adversely affect the rights and welfare of the subjects;

(3) The clinical investigation could not practicably be carried out without the waiver; and

(4) Whenever appropriate, the subjects will be provided with additional pertinent information after participation.

(e) In addition to the determinations required under other applicable sections of this subpart D, the IRB must determine that the permission of each child's parents or guardian is granted.

(1) Where parental permission is to be obtained, the IRB may find that the permission of one parent is sufficient, if consistent with State law, for clinical investigations to be conducted under §50.51 or §50.52.

(2) Where clinical investigations are covered by §50.53 or §50.54 and permission is to be obtained from parents, both parents must give their permission unless one parent is deceased, unknown, incompetent, or not reasonably available, or when only one parent has legal responsibility for the care and custody of the child if consistent with State law.

(f) Permission by parents or guardians must be documented in accordance with and to the extent required by §50.27.

(g) When the IRB determines that assent is required, it must also determine whether and how assent must be documented.

§50.56 Wards.

(a) Children who are wards of the State or any other agency, institution, or entity can be included in clinical investigations approved under §50.53 or §50.54 only if such clinical investigations are:

(1) Related to their status as wards; or

(2) Conducted in schools, camps, hospitals, institutions, or similar settings in which the majority of children involved as subjects are not wards.

(b) If the clinical investigation is approved under paragraph (a) of this section, the IRB must require appointment of an advocate for each child who is a ward.

(1) The advocate will serve in addition to any other individual acting on behalf of the child as guardian or in loco parentis.

(2) One individual may serve as advocate for more than one child.

(3) The advocate must be an individual who has the background and experience to act in, and agrees to act in, the best interest of the child for the duration of the child's participation in the clinical investigation.

(4) The advocate must not be associated in any way (except in the role as advocate or member of the IRB) with the clinical investigation, the investigator(s), or the guardian organization.

TITLE 21—FOOD AND DRUGS

Chapter I: Food and Drug Administration,
Department of Health and Human Services
Subchapter A: General

PART 56

Institutional Review Boards

Authority: 21 U.S.C. 321, 343, 346, 346a, 348, 350a, 350b, 351, 352, 353, 355, 360, 360c–360f, 360h–360j, 371, 379e, 381; 42 U.S.C. 216, 241, 262, 263b–263n.
Source: 46 FR 8975, Jan. 27, 1981, unless otherwise noted.

Subpart A—General Provisions

§56.101 Scope.

(a) This part contains the general standards for the composition, operation, and responsibility of an Institutional Review Board (IRB) that reviews clinical investigations regulated by the Food and Drug Administration under sections 505(i) and 520(g) of the act, as well as clinical investigations that support applications for research or marketing permits for products regulated by the Food and Drug Administration, including foods, including dietary supplements, that bear a nutrient content claim or a health claim, infant formulas, food and color additives, drugs for human use, medical devices for human use, biological products for human use, and electronic products. Compliance with this part is intended to protect the rights and welfare of human subjects involved in such investigations.

(b) References in this part to regulatory sections of the Code of Federal Regulations are to chapter I of title 21, unless otherwise noted.

[46 FR 8975, Jan. 27, 1981, as amended at 64 FR 399, Jan. 5, 1999; 66 FR 20599, Apr. 24, 2001]

§56.102 Definitions.

As used in this part:

(a) Act means the Federal Food, Drug, and Cosmetic Act, as amended (secs. 201-902, 52 Stat. 1040 et seq., as amended (21 U.S.C. 321-392)).

(b) Application for research or marketing permit includes:

(1) A color additive petition, described in part 71.

(2) Data and information regarding a substance submitted as part of the procedures for establishing that a substance is generally recognized as safe for a use which results or may reasonably be expected to result, directly or indirectly, in its becoming a component or otherwise affecting the characteristics of any food, described in §170.35.

(3) A food additive petition, described in part 171.

(4) Data and information regarding a food additive submitted as part of the procedures regarding food additives permitted to be used on an interim basis pending additional study, described in §180.1.

(5) Data and information regarding a substance submitted as part of the procedures for establishing a tolerance for unavoidable contaminants in food and food-packaging materials, described in section 406 of the act.

(6) An investigational new drug application, described in part 312 of this chapter.

(7) A new drug application, described in part 314.

(8) Data and information regarding the bioavailability or bioequivalence of drugs for human use submitted as part of the procedures for issuing, amending, or repealing a bioequivalence requirement, described in part 320.

(9) Data and information regarding an over-the-counter drug for human use submitted as part of the procedures for classifying such drugs as generally recognized as safe and effective and not misbranded, described in part 330.

(10) An application for a biologics license, described in part 601 of this chapter.

(11) Data and information regarding a biological product submitted as part of the procedures for determining that licensed biological products are safe and effective and not misbranded, as described in part 601 of this chapter.

(12) An Application for an Investigational Device Exemption, described in parts 812 and 813.

(13) Data and information regarding a medical device for human use submitted as part of the procedures for classifying such devices, described in part 860.

(14) Data and information regarding a medical device for human use submitted as part of the procedures for establishing, amending, or repealing a standard for such device, described in part 861.

(15) An application for premarket approval of a medical device for human use, described in section 515 of the act.

(16) A product development protocol for a medical device for human use, described in section 515 of the act.

(17) Data and information regarding an electronic product submitted as part of the procedures for establishing, amending, or repealing a standard for such products, described in section 358 of the Public Health Service Act.

(18) Data and information regarding an electronic product submitted as part of the procedures for obtaining a variance from any electronic product performance standard, as described in §1010.4.

(19) Data and information regarding an electronic product submitted as part of the procedures for granting, amending, or extending an exemption from a radiation safety performance standard, as described in §1010.5.

(20) Data and information regarding an electronic product submitted as part of the procedures for obtaining an exemption from notification of a radiation safety defect or failure of compliance with a radiation safety performance standard, described in subpart D of part 1003.

(21) Data and information about a clinical study of an infant formula when submitted as part of an infant formula notification under section 412(c) of the Federal Food, Drug, and Cosmetic Act.

(22) Data and information submitted in a petition for a nutrient content claim, described in §101.69 of this chapter, and for a health claim, described in §101.70 of this chapter.

(23) Data and information from investigations involving children submitted in a new dietary ingredient notification, described in §190.6 of this chapter.

(c) Clinical investigation means any experiment that involves a test article and one or more human subjects, and that either must meet the requirements for prior submission to the Food and Drug Administration under section 505(i) or 520(g) of the act, or need not meet the requirements for prior submission to the Food and Drug Administration under these sections of the act, but the results of which are intended to be later submitted to, or held for inspection by, the Food and Drug Administration as part of an application for a research or marketing permit. The term does not include experiments that must meet the provisions of part 58, regarding nonclinical laboratory studies. The terms research, clinical research, clinical study, study, and clinical investigation are deemed to be synonymous for purposes of this part.

(d) Emergency use means the use of a test article on a human subject in a life-threatening situation in which no standard acceptable treatment is available, and in which there is not sufficient time to obtain IRB approval.

(e) Human subject means an individual who is or becomes a participant in research, either as a recipient of the test article or as a control. A subject may be either a healthy individual or a patient.

(f) Institution means any public or private entity or agency (including Federal, State, and other agencies). The term facility as used in section 520(g) of the act is deemed to be synonymous with the term institution for purposes of this part.

(g) Institutional Review Board (IRB) means any board, committee, or other group formally designated by an institution to review, to approve the initiation of, and to conduct periodic review of, biomedical research involving human subjects. The primary purpose of such review is to assure the protection of the rights and welfare of the human subjects. The term has the same meaning as the phrase institutional review committee as used in section 520(g) of the act.

(h) Investigator means an individual who actually conducts a clinical investigation (i.e., under whose immediate direction the test article is administered or dispensed to, or used involving, a subject) or, in the event of an investigation conducted by a team of individuals, is the responsible leader of that team.

(i) Minimal risk means that the probability and magnitude of harm or discomfort anticipated in the research are not greater in and of themselves than those ordinarily encountered in daily life or during the performance of routine physical or psychological examinations or tests.

(j) Sponsor means a person or other entity that initiates a clinical investigation, but that does not actually conduct the investigation, i.e., the test article is administered or dispensed to, or used involving, a subject under the immediate direction of another individual. A person other than an individual (e.g., a corporation or agency) that uses one or more of its own employees to conduct an investigation that it has initiated is considered to be a sponsor (not a sponsor-investigator), and the employees are considered to be investigators.

(k) Sponsor-investigator means an individual who both initiates and actually conducts, alone or with others, a clinical investigation, i.e., under whose immediate direction the test article is administered or dispensed to, or used involving, a subject. The term does not include any person other than an individual, e.g., it does not include a corporation or agency. The obligations of a sponsor-investigator under this part include both those of a sponsor and those of an investigator.

(l) Test article means any drug for human use, biological product for human use, medical device for human use, human food additive, color additive, electronic product, or any other article subject to regulation under the act or under sections 351 or 354-360F of the Public Health Service Act.

(m) IRB approval means the determination of the IRB that the clinical investigation has been reviewed and may be conducted at an institution within the constraints set forth by the IRB and by other institutional and Federal requirements.

[46 FR 8975, Jan. 27, 1981, as amended at 54 FR 9038, Mar. 3, 1989; 56 FR 28028, June 18, 1991; 64 FR 399, Jan. 5, 1999; 64 FR 56448, Oct. 20, 1999; 65 FR 52302, Aug. 29, 2000; 66 FR 20599, Apr. 24, 2001]

§56.103 Circumstances in which IRB review is required.

(a) Except as provided in §§56.104 and 56.105, any clinical investigation which must meet the requirements for prior submission (as required in parts 312, 812, and 813) to the Food and Drug Administration shall not be initiated unless that investigation has been reviewed and approved by, and remains subject to continuing review by, an IRB meeting the requirements of this part.

(b) Except as provided in §§56.104 and 56.105, the Food and Drug Administration may decide not to consider in support of an application for a research or marketing permit any data or information that has been derived from a clinical investigation that has not been approved by, and that was not subject to initial and continuing review by, an IRB meeting the requirements of this part. The determination that a clinical investigation may not be considered in support of an application for a research or marketing permit does not, however, relieve the applicant for such a permit of any obligation under any other applicable regulations to submit the results of the investigation to the Food and Drug Administration.

(c) Compliance with these regulations will in no way render inapplicable pertinent Federal, State, or local laws or regulations.

[46 FR 8975, Jan. 27, 1981; 46 FR 14340, Feb. 27, 1981]

§56.104 Exemptions from IRB requirement.

The following categories of clinical investigations are exempt from the requirements of this part for IRB review:

(a) Any investigation which commenced before July 27, 1981 and was subject to requirements for IRB review under FDA regulations before that date, provided that the investigation remains subject to review of an IRB which meets the FDA requirements in effect before July 27, 1981.

(b) Any investigation commenced before July 27, 1981 and was not otherwise subject to requirements for IRB review under Food and Drug Administration regulations before that date.

(c) Emergency use of a test article, provided that such emergency use is reported to the IRB within 5 working days. Any subsequent use of the test article at the institution is subject to IRB review.

(d) Taste and food quality evaluations and consumer acceptance studies, if wholesome foods without additives are consumed or if a food is consumed that contains a food ingredient at or below the level and for a use found to be safe, or agricultural, chemical, or environmental contaminant at or below the level found to be safe, by the Food and Drug Administration or approved by the Environmental Protection Agency or the

Food Safety and Inspection Service of the U.S. Department of Agriculture.

[46 FR 8975, Jan. 27, 1981, as amended at 56 FR 28028, June 18, 1991]

§56.105 Waiver of IRB requirement.

On the application of a sponsor or sponsor-investigator, the Food and Drug Administration may waive any of the requirements contained in these regulations, including the requirements for IRB review, for specific research activities or for classes of research activities, otherwise covered by these regulations.

Subpart B—Organization and Personnel

§56.107 IRB membership.

(a) Each IRB shall have at least five members, with varying backgrounds to promote complete and adequate review of research activities commonly conducted by the institution. The IRB shall be sufficiently qualified through the experience and expertise of its members, and the diversity of the members, including consideration of race, gender, cultural backgrounds, and sensitivity to such issues as community attitudes, to promote respect for its advice and counsel in safeguarding the rights and welfare of human subjects. In addition to possessing the professional competence necessary to review the specific research activities, the IRB shall be able to ascertain the acceptability of proposed research in terms of institutional commitments and regulations, applicable law, and standards or professional conduct and practice. The IRB shall therefore include

persons knowledgeable in these areas. If an IRB regularly reviews research that involves a vulnerable catgory of subjects, such as children, prisoners, pregnant women, or handicapped or mentally disabled persons, consideration shall be given to the inclusion of one or more individuals who are knowledgeable about and experienced in working with those subjects.

(b) Every nondiscriminatory effort will be made to ensure that no IRB consists entirely of men or entirely of women, including the instituton's consideration of qualified persons of both sexes, so long as no selection is made to the IRB on the basis of gender. No IRB may consist entirely of members of one profession.

(c) Each IRB shall include at least one member whose primary concerns are in the scientific area and at least one member whose primary concerns are in nonscientific areas.

(d) Each IRB shall include at least one member who is not otherwise affiliated with the institution and who is not part of the immediate family of a person who is affiliated with the institution.

(e) No IRB may have a member participate in the IRB's initial or continuing review of any project in which the member has a conflicting interest, except to provide information requested by the IRB.

(f) An IRB may, in its discretion, invite individuals with competence in special areas to assist in the review of complex issues which require expertise beyond or in addition to that available on the IRB. These individuals may not vote with the IRB.

[46 FR 8975, Jan 27, 1981, as amended at 56 FR 28028, June 18, 1991; 56 FR 29756, June 28, 1991]

Subpart C—IRB Functions and Operations

§56.108 IRB functions and operations.

In order to fulfill the requirements of these regulations, each IRB shall:

(a) Follow written procedures: (1) For conducting its initial and continuing review of research and for reporting its findings and actions to the investigator and the institution; (2) for determining which projects require review more often than annually and which projects need verification from sources other than the investigator that no material changes have occurred since previous IRB review; (3) for ensuring prompt reporting to the IRB of changes in research activity; and (4) for ensuring that changes in approved research, during the period for which IRB approval has already been given, may not be initiated without IRB review and approval except where necessary to eliminate apparent immediate hazards to the human subjects.

(b) Follow written procedures for ensuring prompt reporting to the IRB, appropriate institutional officials, and the Food and Drug Administration of: (1) Any unanticipated problems involving risks to human subjects or others; (2) any instance of serious or continuing noncompliance with these regulations or the requirements or determinations of the IRB; or (3) any suspension or termination of IRB approval.

(c) Except when an expedited review procedure is used (see §56.110), review proposed research at convened meetings at which a majority of the members of the IRB are present, including at least one member whose primary concerns are in nonscientific areas. In order for the research to be approved, it shall receive the approval of a majority of those members present at the meeting.

[46 FR 8975, Jan. 27, 1981, as amended at 56 FR 28028, June 18, 1991; 67 FR 9585, Mar. 4, 2002]

§56.109 IRB review of research.

(a) An IRB shall review and have authority to approve, require modifications in (to secure approval), or disapprove all research activities covered by these regulations.

(b) An IRB shall require that information given to subjects as part of informed consent is in accordance with §50.25. The IRB may require that information, in addition to that specifically mentioned in §50.25, be given to the subjects when in the IRB's judgment the information would meaningfully add to the protection of the rights and welfare of subjects.

(c) An IRB shall require documentation of informed consent in accordance with §50.27 of this chapter, except as follows:

(1) The IRB may, for some or all subjects, waive the requirement that the subject, or the subject's legally authorized representative, sign a written consent form if it finds that the research presents no more than minimal risk of harm to subjects and involves no procedures for which written consent is normally required outside the research context; or

(2) The IRB may, for some or all subjects, find that the requirements in §50.24 of this chapter for an exception from informed consent for emergency research are met.

(d) In cases where the documentation requirement is waived under paragraph (c)(1) of this section, the IRB may require the investigator to provide subjects with a written statement regarding the research.

(e) An IRB shall notify investigators and the institution in writing of its decision to approve or disapprove the proposed research activity, or of modifications required to secure IRB approval of the research activity. If the IRB decides to disapprove a research activity, it shall include in its written notification a statement of the reasons for its decision and give the investigator an opportunity to respond in person or in writing. For investigations involving an exception to informed consent under §50.24 of this chapter, an IRB shall promptly notify in writing the investigator and the sponsor of the research when an IRB determines that it cannot approve the research because it does not meet the criteria in the exception provided under §50.24(a) of this chapter or because of other relevant ethical concerns. The written notification shall include a statement of the reasons for the IRB's determination.

(f) An IRB shall conduct continuing review of research covered by these regulations at intervals appropriate to the degree of risk, but not less than once per year, and shall have authority to observe or have a third party observe the consent process and the research.

(g) An IRB shall provide in writing to the sponsor of research involving an exception to informed consent under §50.24 of this chapter a copy of information that has been publicly disclosed under §50.24(a)(7)(ii) and (a)(7)(iii) of this chapter. The IRB shall provide this information to the sponsor promptly so that the sponsor is aware that such disclosure has occurred. Upon receipt, the sponsor shall provide copies of the information disclosed to FDA.

(h) When some or all of the subjects in a study are children, an IRB must determine that the research study is in compliance with part 50, subpart D of this chapter, at the time of its initial review of the research. When some or all of the subjects in a study that is ongoing on April 30, 2001 are children, an IRB must conduct a review of the research to determine compliance with part 50, subpart D of this chapter, either at the time of continuing review or, at the discretion of the IRB, at an earlier date.

[46 FR 8975, Jan. 27, 1981, as amended at 61 FR 51529, Oct. 2, 1996; 66 FR 20599, Apr. 24, 2001]

§56.110 Expedited review procedures for certain kinds of research involving no more than minimal risk, and for minor changes in approved research.

(a) The Food and Drug Administration has established, and published in the FEDERAL REGISTER, a list of categories of research that may be reviewed by the IRB through an expedited review procedure. The list will be amended, as appropriate, through periodic republication in the FEDERAL REGISTER.

(b) An IRB may use the expedited review procedure to review either or both of the following: (1) Some or all of the research appearing on the list and found by the reviewer(s) to involve no more than minimal risk, (2) minor changes in previously approved research during the period (of 1 year or less) for which approval is authorized. Under an expedited review procedure, the review may be carried out by the IRB chairperson or by one or more experienced reviewers designated by the IRB chairperson from among the members of the IRB. In reviewing the research, the reviewers may exercise all of the authorities of the IRB except that the reviewers may not disapprove the research. A research activity may be disapproved only after review in accordance with the nonexpedited review procedure set forth in §56.108(c).

(c) Each IRB which uses an expedited review procedure shall adopt a method for keeping all members advised of research proposals which have been approved under the procedure.

(d) The Food and Drug Administration may restrict, suspend, or terminate an institution's or IRB's use of the expedited review procedure when necessary to protect the rights or welfare of subjects.

[46 FR 8975, Jan. 27, 1981, as amended at 56 FR 28029, June 18, 1991]

§56.111 Criteria for IRB approval of research.

(a) In order to approve research covered by these regulations the IRB shall determine that all of the following requirements are satisfied:

(1) Risks to subjects are minimized: (i) By using procedures which are consistent with sound research design and which do not unnecessarily expose subjects to risk, and (ii) whenever appropriate, by using procedures already being performed on the subjects for diagnostic or treatment purposes.

(2) Risks to subjects are reasonable in relation to anticipated benefits, if any, to subjects, and the importance of the knowledge that may be expected to result. In evaluating

risks and benefits, the IRB should consider only those risks and benefits that may result from the research (as distinguished from risks and benefits of therapies that subjects would receive even if not participating in the research). The IRB should not consider possible long-range effects of applying knowledge gained in the research (for example, the possible effects of the research on public policy) as among those research risks that fall within the purview of its responsibility.

(3) Selection of subjects is equitable. In making this assessment the IRB should take into account the purposes of the research and the setting in which the research will be conducted and should be particularly cognizant of the special problems of research involving vulnerable populations, such as children, prisoners, pregnant women, handicapped, or mentally disabled persons, or economically or educationally disadvantaged persons.

(4) Informed consent will be sought from each prospective subject or the subject's legally authorized representative, in accordance with and to the extent required by part 50.

(5) Informed consent will be appropriately documented, in accordance with and to the extent required by §50.27.

(6) Where appropriate, the research plan makes adequate provision for monitoring the data collected to ensure the safety of subjects.

(7) Where appropriate, there are adequate provisions to protect the privacy of subjects and to maintain the confidentiality of data.

(b) When some or all of the subjects, such as children, prisoners, pregnant women, handicapped, or mentally disabled persons, or economically or educationally disadvantaged persons, are likely to be vulnerable to coercion or undue influence additional safeguards have been included in the study to protect the rights and welfare of these subjects.

(c) In order to approve research in which some or all of the subjects are children, an IRB must determine that all research is in compliance with part 50, subpart D of this chapter.

[46 FR 8975, Jan. 27, 1981, as amended at 56 FR 28029, June 18, 1991; 66 FR 20599, Apr. 24, 2001]

§56.112 Review by institution.

Research covered by these regulations that has been approved by an IRB may be subject to further appropriate review and approval or disapproval by officials of the institution. However, those officials may not approve the research if it has not been approved by an IRB.

§56.113 Suspension or termination of IRB approval of research.

An IRB shall have authority to suspend or terminate approval of research that is not being conducted in accordance with the IRB's requirements or that has been associated with unexpected serious harm to subjects. Any suspension or termination of approval shall include a statement of the reasons for the IRB's action and shall be reported promptly to the investigator, appropriate institutional officials, and the Food and Drug Administration.

§56.114 Cooperative research.

In complying with these regulations, institutions involved in multi-institutional studies may use joint review, reliance upon the review of another qualified IRB, or similar arrangements aimed at avoidance of duplication of effort.

Subpart D—Records and Reports

§56.115 IRB records.

(a) An institution, or where appropriate an IRB, shall prepare and maintain adequate documentation of IRB activities, including the following:

(1) Copies of all research proposals reviewed, scientific evaluations, if any, that accompany the proposals, approved sample consent documents, progress reports submitted by investigators, and reports of injuries to subjects.

(2) Minutes of IRB meetings which shall be in sufficient detail to show attendance at the meetings; actions taken by the IRB; the vote on these actions including the number of members voting for, against, and abstaining; the basis for requiring changes in or disapproving research; and a written summary of the discussion of controverted issues and their resolution.

(3) Records of continuing review activities.

(4) Copies of all correspondence between the IRB and the investigators.

(5) A list of IRB members identified by name; earned degrees; representative capacity; indications of experience such as board

certifications, licenses, etc., sufficient to describe each member's chief anticipated contributions to IRB deliberations; and any employment or other relationship between each member and the institution; for example: full-time employee, part-time employee, a member of governing panel or board, stockholder, paid or unpaid consultant.

(6) Written procedures for the IRB as required by §56.108 (a) and (b).

(7) Statements of significant new findings provided to subjects, as required by §50.25.

(b) The records required by this regulation shall be retained for at least 3 years after completion of the research, and the records shall be accessible for inspection and copying by authorized representatives of the Food and Drug Administration at reasonable times and in a reasonable manner.

(c) The Food and Drug Administration may refuse to consider a clinical investigation in support of an application for a research or marketing permit if the institution or the IRB that reviewed the investigation refuses to allow an inspection under this section.

[46 FR 8975, Jan. 27, 1981, as amended at 56 FR 28029, June 18, 1991; 67 FR 9585, Mar. 4, 2002]

Subpart E—Administrative Actions for Noncompliance

§56.120 Lesser administrative actions.

(a) If apparent noncompliance with these regulations in the operation of an IRB is observed by an FDA investigator during an inspection, the inspector will present an oral

or written summary of observations to an appropriate representative of the IRB. The Food and Drug Administra-tion may subsequently send a letter describing the noncompliance to the IRB and to the parent institution. The agency will require that the IRB or the parent institution respond to this letter within a time period specified by FDA and describe the corrective actions that will be taken by the IRB, the institution, or both to achieve compliance with these regulations.

(b) On the basis of the IRB's or the institution's response, FDA may schedule a reinspection to confirm the adequacy of corrective actions. In addition, until the IRB or the parent institution takes appropriate corrective action, the agency may:

(1) Withhold approval of new studies subject to the requirements of this part that are conducted at the institution or reviewed by the IRB;

(2) Direct that no new subjects be added to ongoing studies subject to this part;

(3) Terminate ongoing studies subject to this part when doing so would not endanger the subjects; or

(4) When the apparent noncompliance creates a significant threat to the rights and welfare of human subjects, notify relevant State and Federal regulatory agencies and other parties with a direct interest in the agency's action of the deficiencies in the operation of the IRB.

(c) The parent institution is presumed to be responsible for the operation of an IRB, and the Food and Drug Administration will ordinarily direct any administrative action under this subpart against the institution. However, depending on the evidence of responsibility for deficiencies, determined during the investigation, the Food and Drug Administration may restrict its administrative actions to the IRB or to a component of the parent institution determined to be responsible for formal designation of the IRB.

§56.121 Disqualification of an IRB or an institution.

(a) Whenever the IRB or the institution has failed to take adequate steps to correct the noncompliance stated in the letter sent by the agency under §56.120(a), and the Commissioner of Food and Drugs determines that this noncompliance may justify the disqualification of the IRB or of the parent institution, the Commissioner will institute proceedings in accordance with the requirements for a regulatory hearing set forth in part 16.

(b) The Commissioner may disqualify an IRB or the parent institution if the Commissioner determines that:

(1) The IRB has refused or repeatedly failed to comply with any of the regulations set forth in this part, and

(2) The noncompliance adversely affects the rights or welfare of the human subjects in a clinical investigation.

(c) If the Commissioner determines that disqualification is appropriate, the Commissioner will issue an order that explains the basis for the determination and that prescribes any actions to be taken with regard to ongoing clinical research conducted under the review of the IRB. The Food and Drug Administration will send notice of the disqualification to the IRB and the parent institution. Other parties with a direct interest, such as sponsors and clinical investigators, may also be sent a notice of the disqualification. In addition, the agency may elect to publish a notice of its action in the FEDERAL REGISTER.

(d) The Food and Drug Administration will not approve an application for a research permit for a clinical investigation that is to be under the review of a disqualified IRB or that is to be conducted at a disqualified institution, and it may refuse to consider in support of a marketing permit the data from a clinical investigation that was reviewed by a disqualified IRB as conducted at a disqualified institution, unless the IRB or the parent institution is reinstated as provided in §56.123.

§56.122 Public disclosure of information regarding revocation.

A determination that the Food and Drug Administration has disqualified an institution and the administrative record regarding that determination are disclosable to the public under part 20.

§56.123 Reinstatement of an IRB or an institution.

An IRB or an institution may be reinstated if the Commissioner determines, upon an evaluation of a written submission from the IRB or institution that explains the corrective action that the institution or IRB plans to take, that the IRB or institution has provided adequate assurance that it will operate in compliance with the standards set forth in this part. Notification of reinstatement shall be provided to all persons notified under §56.121(c).

§56.124 Actions alternative or additional to disqualification.

Disqualification of an IRB or of an institution is independent of, and neither in lieu of nor a precondition to, other proceedings or actions authorized by the act. The Food and Drug Administration may, at any time, through the Department of Justice institute any appropriate judicial proceedings (civil or criminal) and any other appropriate regulatory action, in addition to or in lieu of, and before, at the time of, or after, disqualification. The agency may also refer pertinent matters to another Federal, State, or local government agency for any action that that agency determines to be appropriate.

TITLE 21—FOOD AND DRUGS

Chapter I: Food and Drug Administration,
Department of Health and Human Services
Subchapter D: Drugs for Human Use

PART 312

Investigational New Drug Application

Subpart D—Responsibilities of Sponsors and Investigators

Subpart E—Drugs Intended to Treat Life-threatening and Severely-debilitating Illnesses

Subpart F—Miscellaneous

Subpart G—Drugs for Investigational Use in Laboratory Research Animals or in Vitro Tests

Authority: 21 U.S.C. 321, 331, 351, 352, 353, 355, 371; 42 U.S.C. 262.
Source: 52 FR 8831, Mar. 19, 1987, unless otherwise noted.

Subpart A—General Provisions

§312.1 Scope.

(a) This part contains procedures and requirements governing the use of investigational new drugs, including procedures and requirements for the submission to, and review by, the Food and Drug Administration of investigational new drug applications (IND's). An investigational new drug for which an IND is in effect in accordance with this part is exempt from the pre-marketing approval requirements that are otherwise applicable and may be shipped lawfully for the purpose of conducting clinical investigations of that drug.

(b) References in this part to regulations in the Code of Federal Regulations are to chapter I of title 21, unless otherwise noted.

§312.2 Applicability.

(a) Applicability. Except as provided in this section, this part applies to all clinical investigations of products that are subject to section 505 of the Federal Food, Drug, and Cosmetic Act or to the licensing provisions of the Public Health Service Act (58 Stat. 632, as amended (42 U.S.C. 201 et seq.)).

(b) Exemptions. (1) The clinical investigation of a drug product that is lawfully marketed in the United States is exempt from the requirements of this part if all the following apply:

(i) The investigation is not intended to be reported to FDA as a well-controlled study in support of a new indication for use nor intended to be used to support any other significant change in the labeling for the drug;

(ii) If the drug that is undergoing investigation is lawfully marketed as a prescription drug product, the investigation is not intended to support a significant change in the advertising for the product;

(iii) The investigation does not involve a route of administration or dosage level or use in a patient population or other factor that significantly increases the risks (or decreases the acceptability of the risks) associated with the use of the drug product;

(iv) The investigation is conducted in compliance with the requirements for institutional review set forth in part 56 and with the requirements for informed consent set forth in part 50; and

(v) The investigation is conducted in compliance with the requirements of §312.7.

(2)(i) A clinical investigation involving an in vitro diagnostic biological product listed in paragraph (b)(2)(ii) of this section is exempt from the requirements of this part if (a) it is intended to be used in a diagnostic procedure that confirms the diagnosis made by another, medically established, diagnostic product or procedure and (b) it is shipped in compliance with §312.160.

(ii) In accordance with paragraph (b)(2)(i) of this section, the following products are exempt from the requirements of this part: (a) blood grouping serum; (b) reagent red blood cells; and (c) anti-human globulin.

(3) A drug intended solely for tests in vitro or in laboratory research animals is exempt from the requirements of this part if shipped in accordance with §312.160.

(4) FDA will not accept an application for an investigation that is exempt under the provisions of paragraph (b)(1) of this section.

(5) A clinical investigation involving use of a placebo is exempt from the requirements of this part if the investigation does not otherwise require submission of an IND.

(6) A clinical investigation involving an exception from informed consent under §50.24 of this chapter is not exempt from the requirements of this part.

(c) Bioavailability studies. The applicability of this part to in vivo bioavailability studies in humans is subject to the provisions of §320.31.

(d) Unlabeled indication. This part does not apply to the use in the practice of medicine for an unlabeled indication of a new drug product approved under part 314 or of a licensed biological product.

(e) Guidance. FDA may, on its own initiative, issue guidance on the applicability of this part to particular investigational uses of drugs. On request, FDA will advise on the applicability of this part to a planned clinical investigation.

[52 FR 8831, Mar. 19, 1987, as amended at 61 FR 51529, Oct. 2, 1996; 64 FR 401, Jan. 5, 1999]

§312.3 Definitions and interpretations.

(a) The definitions and interpretations of terms contained in section 201 of the Act apply to those terms when used in this part:

(b) The following definitions of terms also apply to this part:

Act means the Federal Food, Drug, and Cosmetic Act (secs. 201-902, 52 Stat. 1040 et seq., as amended (21 U.S.C. 301-392)).

Clinical investigation means any experiment in which a drug is administered or dispensed to, or used involving, one or more human subjects. For the purposes of this part, an experiment is any use of a drug except for the use of a marketed drug in the course of medical practice.

Contract research organization means a person that assumes, as an independent contractor with the sponsor, one or more of the obligations of a sponsor, e.g., design of a protocol, selection or monitoring of investigations, evaluation of reports, and preparation of materials to be submitted to the Food and Drug Administration.

FDA means the Food and Drug Administration.

IND means an investigational new drug application. For purposes of this part, "IND" is synonymous with "Notice of Claimed Investigational Exemption for a New Drug."

Investigational new drug means a new drug or biological drug that is used in a clinical investigation. The term also includes a biological product that is used in vitro for diagnostic purposes. The terms "investigational drug" and "investigational new drug" are deemed to be synonymous for purposes of this part.

Investigator means an individual who actually conducts a clinical investigation (i.e., under whose immediate direction the drug is administered or dispensed to a subject). In the event an investigation is conducted by a team of individuals, the investigator is the responsible leader of the team. "Subinvestigator" includes any other individual member of that team.

Marketing application means an application for a new drug submitted under section

505(b) of the act or a biologics license application for a biological product submitted under the Public Health Service Act.

Sponsor means a person who takes responsibility for and initiates a clinical investigation. The sponsor may be an individual or pharmaceutical company, governmental agency, academic institution, private organization, or other organization. The sponsor does not actually conduct the investigation unless the sponsor is a sponsor-investigator. A person other than an individual that uses one or more of its own employees to conduct an investigation that it has initiated is a sponsor, not a sponsor-investigator, and the employees are investigators.

Sponsor-Investigator means an individual who both initiates and conducts an investigation, and under whose immediate direction the investigational drug is administered or dispensed. The term does not include any person other than an individual. The requirements applicable to a sponsor-investigator under this part include both those applicable to an investigator and a sponsor.

Subject means a human who participates in an investigation, either as a recipient of the investigational new drug or as a control. A subject may be a healthy human or a patient with a disease.

[52 FR 8831, Mar. 19, 1987, as amended at 64 FR 401, Jan. 5, 1999; 64 FR 56449, Oct. 20, 1999]

§312.6 Labeling of an investigational new drug.

(a) The immediate package of an investigational new drug intended for human use shall bear a label with the statement "Caution: New Drug—Limited by Federal (or United States) law to investigational use."

(b) The label or labeling of an investigational new drug shall not bear any statement that is false or misleading in any particular and shall not represent that the investigational new drug is safe or effective for the purposes for which it is being investigated.

§312.7 Promotion and charging for investigational drugs.

(a) Promotion of an investigational new drug. A sponsor or investigator, or any person acting on behalf of a sponsor or investigator, shall not represent in a promotional context that an investigational new drug is safe or effective for the purposes for which it is under investigation or otherwise promote the drug. This provision is not intended to restrict the full exchange of scientific information concerning the drug, including dissemination of scientific findings in scientific or lay media. Rather, its intent is to restrict promotional claims of safety or effectiveness of the drug for a use for which it is under investigation and to preclude commercialization of the drug before it is approved for commercial distribution.

(b) Commercial distribution of an investigational new drug. A sponsor or investigator shall not commercially distribute or test market an investigational new drug.

(c) Prolonging an investigation. A sponsor shall not unduly prolong an investigation after finding that the results of the investigation appear to establish sufficient data to support a marketing application.

(d) Charging for and commercialization of investigational drugs—(1) Clinical trials under an IND. Charging for an investigational drug in a clinical trial under an IND is not permitted without the prior written approval of FDA. In requesting such approval, the sponsor shall provide a full written explanation of why charging is necessary in order for the sponsor to undertake or continue the clinical trial, e.g., why distribution of the drug to test subjects should not be considered part of the normal cost of doing business.

(2) Treatment protocol or treatment IND. A sponsor or investigator may charge for an investigational drug for a treatment use under a treatment protocol or treatment IND provided: (i) There is adequate enrollment in the ongoing clinical investigations under the authorized IND; (ii) charging does not constitute commercial marketing of a new drug for which a marketing application has not been approved; (iii) the drug is not being commercially promoted or advertised; and (iv) the sponsor of the drug is actively pursuing marketing approval with due diligence. FDA must be notified in writing in advance of commencing any such charges, in an information amendment submitted under §312.31. Authorization for charging goes into effect automatically 30 days after receipt by FDA of the information amendment, unless the sponsor is notified to the contrary.

(3) Noncommercialization of investigational drug. Under this section, the sponsor may not commercialize an investigational drug by charging a price larger than that necessary to recover costs of manufacture, research, development, and handling of the investigational drug.

(4) Withdrawal of authorization. Authorization to charge for an investigational drug under this section may be withdrawn by FDA if the agency finds that the conditions underlying the authorization are no longer satisfied.

[52 FR 8831, Mar. 19, 1987, as amended at 52 FR 19476, May 22, 1987; 67 FR 9585, Mar. 4, 2002]

§312.10 Waivers.

(a) A sponsor may request FDA to waive applicable requirement under this part. A waiver request may be submitted either in an IND or in an information amendment to an IND. In an emergency, a request may be made by telephone or other rapid communication means. A waiver request is required to contain at least one of the following:

(1) An explanation why the sponsor's compliance with the requirement is unnecessary or cannot be achieved;

(2) A description of an alternative submission or course of action that satisfies the purpose of the requirement; or

(3) Other information justifying a waiver.

(b) FDA may grant a waiver if it finds that the sponsor's noncompliance would not pose a significant and unreasonable risk to human subjects of the investigation and that one of the following is met:

(1) The sponsor's compliance with the requirement is unnecessary for the agency to evaluate the application, or compliance cannot be achieved;

(2) The sponsor's proposed alternative satisfies the requirement; or

(3) The applicant's submission otherwise justifies a waiver.

[52 FR 8831, Mar. 19, 1987, as amended at 52 FR 23031, June 17, 1987; 67 FR 9585, Mar. 4, 2002]

Subpart B—Investigational New Drug Application (IND)

§312.20 Requirement for an IND.

(a) A sponsor shall submit an IND to FDA if the sponsor intends to conduct a clinical investigation with an investigational new drug that is subject to §312.2(a).

(b) A sponsor shall not begin a clinical investigation subject to §312.2(a) until the investigation is subject to an IND which is in effect in accordance with §312.40.

(c) A sponsor shall submit a separate IND for any clinical investigation involving an exception from informed consent under §50.24 of this chapter. Such a clinical investigation is not permitted to proceed without the prior written authorization from FDA. FDA shall provide a written determination 30 days after FDA receives the IND or earlier.

[52 FR 8831, Mar. 19, 1987, as amended at 61 FR 51529, Oct. 2, 1996; 62 FR 32479, June 16, 1997]

§312.21 Phases of an investigation.

An IND may be submitted for one or more phases of an investigation. The clinical investigation of a previously untested drug is generally divided into three phases. Although in general the phases are conducted sequentially, they may overlap. These three phases of an investigation are a follows:

(a) Phase 1. (1) Phase 1 includes the initial introduction of an investigational new drug into humans. Phase 1 studies are typically closely monitored and may be conducted in patients or normal volunteer subjects. These studies are designed to determine the metabolism and pharmacologic actions of the drug in humans, the side effects associated with increasing doses, and, if possible, to gain early evidence on effectiveness. During Phase 1, sufficient information about the drug's pharmacokinetics and pharmacological effects should be obtained to permit the design of well-controlled, scientifically valid, Phase 2 studies. The total number of subjects and patients included in Phase 1 studies varies with the drug, but is generally in the range of 20 to 80.

(2) Phase 1 studies also include studies of drug metabolism, structure-activity relationships, and mechanism of action in humans, as well as studies in which investigational drugs are used as research tools to explore biological phenomena or disease processes.

(b) Phase 2. Phase 2 includes the controlled clinical studies conducted to evaluate the effectiveness of the drug for a particular indication or indications in patients with the disease or condition under study and to determine the common short-term side effects and risks associated with the drug. Phase 2 studies are typically well controlled, closely monitored, and conducted in a relatively small number of patients, usually involving no more than several hundred subjects.

(c) Phase 3. Phase 3 studies are expanded controlled and uncontrolled trials. They are performed after preliminary evidence suggesting effectiveness of the drug has been obtained, and are intended to gather the additional information about effectiveness and safety that is needed to evaluate the overall benefit-risk relationship of the drug and to provide an adequate basis for physician labeling. Phase 3 studies usually include from several hundred to several thousand subjects.

§312.22 General principles of the IND submission.

(a) FDA's primary objectives in reviewing an IND are, in all phases of the investigation, to assure the safety and rights of subjects, and, in Phase 2 and 3, to help assure that the quality of the scientific evaluation of drugs is adequate to permit an evaluation of the drug's effectiveness and safety. Therefore, although FDA's review of Phase 1 submissions will focus on assessing the safety of Phase 1 investigations, FDA's review of Phases 2 and 3 submissions will also include an assessment of the scientific quality of the clinical investigations and the likelihood that the investigations will yield data capable of meeting statutory standards for marketing approval.

(b) The amount of information on a particular drug that must be submitted in an IND to assure the accomplishment of the objectives described in paragraph (a) of this section depends upon such factors as the novelty of the drug, the extent to which it has been studied previously, the known or suspected risks, and the developmental phase of the drug.

(c) The central focus of the initial IND submission should be on the general investigational plan and the protocols for specific human studies. Subsequent amendments to the IND that contain new or revised protocols should build logically on previous submissions and should be supported by additional information, including the results of animal toxicology studies or other human studies as appropriate. Annual reports to the IND should serve as the focus for reporting the status of studies being conducted under the IND and should update the general investigational plan for the coming year.

(d) The IND format set forth in §312.23 should be followed routinely by sponsors in the interest of fostering an efficient review of applications. Sponsors are expected to exercise considerable discretion, however, regarding the content of information submitted in each section, depending upon the kind of drug being studied and the nature of the available information. Section 312.23 outlines the information needed for a commercially sponsored IND for a new molecular entity. A sponsor-investigator who uses, as a research tool, an investigational new drug that is already subject to a manufacturer's IND or marketing application should follow the same general format, but ordinarily may, if authorized by the manufacturer, refer to the manufacturer's IND or marketing application in providing the technical information supporting the proposed clinical investigation. A sponsor-investigator who uses an investigational drug not subject to a manufacturer's IND or marketing application is ordinarily required to submit all technical information supporting the IND, unless such information may be referenced from the scientific literature.

§312.23 IND content and format.

(a) A sponsor who intends to conduct a clinical investigation subject to this part shall submit an "Investigational New Drug Application" (IND) including, in the following order:

(1) Cover sheet (Form FDA-1571). A cover sheet for the application containing the following:

(i) The name, address, and telephone number of the sponsor, the date of the application, and the name of the investigational new drug.

(ii) Identification of the phase or phases of the clinical investigation to be conducted.

(iii) A commitment not to begin clinical investigations until an IND covering the investigations is in effect.

(iv) A commitment that an Institutional Review Board (IRB) that complies with the requirements set forth in part 56 will be responsible for the initial and continuing review and approval of each of the studies in the proposed clinical investigation and that the investigator will report to the IRB proposed changes in the research activity in accordance with the requirements of part 56.

(v) A commitment to conduct the investigation in accordance with all other applicable regulatory requirements.

(vi) The name and title of the person responsible for monitoring the conduct and progress of the clinical investigations.

(vii) The name(s) and title(s) of the person(s) responsible under §312.32 for review and evaluation of information relevant to the safety of the drug.

(viii) If a sponsor has transferred any obligations for the conduct of any clinical study to a contract research organization, a statement containing the name and address of the contract research organization, identification of the clinical study, and a listing of the obligations transferred. If all obligations governing the conduct of the study have been transferred, a general statement of this transfer—in lieu of a listing of the specific obligations transferred—may be submitted.

(ix) The signature of the sponsor or the sponsor's authorized representative. If the person signing the application does not reside or have a place of business within the United States, the IND is required to contain the name and address of, and be countersigned by, an attorney, agent, or other authorized official who resides or maintains a place of business within the United States.

(2) A table of contents.

(3) Introductory statement and general investigational plan. (i) A brief introductory statement giving the name of the drug and all active ingredients, the drug's pharmacological class, the structural formula of the drug (if known), the formulation of the dosage form(s) to be used, the route of administration, and the broad objectives and planned duration of the proposed clinical investigation(s).

(ii) A brief summary of previous human experience with the drug, with reference to other IND's if pertinent, and to investigational or marketing experience in other countries that may be relevant to the safety of the proposed clinical investigation(s).

(iii) If the drug has been withdrawn from investigation or marketing in any country for any reason related to safety or effectiveness, identification of the country(ies) where the drug was withdrawn and the reasons for the withdrawal.

(iv) A brief description of the overall plan for investigating the drug product for the following year. The plan should include the following: (a) The rationale for the drug or the research study; (b) the indication(s) to be studied; (c) the general approach to be followed in evaluating the drug; (d) the kinds of clinical trials to be conducted in the first year following the submission (if plans are not developed for the entire year, the sponsor should so indicate); (e) the estimated number of patients to be given the drug in those studies; and (f) any risks of particular severity or seriousness anticipated on the basis of the toxicological data in animals or prior studies in humans with the drug or related drugs.

(4) [Reserved]

(5) Investigator's brochure. If required under §312.55, a copy of the investigator's brochure, containing the following information:

(i) A brief description of the drug substance and the formulation, including the structural formula, if known.

(ii) A summary of the pharmacological and toxicological effects of the drug in animals and, to the extent known, in humans.

(iii) A summary of the pharmacokinetics and biological disposition of the drug in animals and, if known, in humans.

(iv) A summary of information relating to safety and effectiveness in humans obtained from prior clinical studies. (Reprints of published articles on such studies may be appended when useful.)

(v) A description of possible risks and side effects to be anticipated on the basis of prior experience with the drug under investigation or with related drugs, and of precautions or special monitoring to be done as part of the investigational use of the drug.

(6) Protocols. (i) A protocol for each planned study. (Protocols for studies not submitted initially in the IND should be submitted in accordance with §312.30(a).) In general, protocols for Phase 1 studies may be less detailed and more flexible than protocols for Phase 2 and 3 studies. Phase 1 protocols should be directed primarily at pro-

viding an outline of the investigation—an estimate of the number of patients to be involved, a description of safety exclusions, and a description of the dosing plan including duration, dose, or method to be used in determining dose—and should specify in detail only those elements of the study that are critical to safety, such as necessary monitoring of vital signs and blood chemistries. Modifications of the experimental design of Phase 1 studies that do not affect critical safety assessments are required to be reported to FDA only in the annual report.

(ii) In Phases 2 and 3, detailed protocols describing all aspects of the study should be submitted. A protocol for a Phase 2 or 3 investigation should be designed in such a way that, if the sponsor anticipates that some deviation from the study design may become necessary as the investigation progresses, alternatives or contingencies to provide for such deviation are built into the protocols at the outset. For example, a protocol for a controlled short-term study might include a plan for an early crossover of nonresponders to an alternative therapy.

(iii) A protocol is required to contain the following, with the specific elements and detail of the protocol reflecting the above distinctions depending on the phase of study:

(a) A statement of the objectives and purpose of the study.

(b) The name and address and a statement of the qualifications (curriculum vitae or other statement of qualifications) of each investigator, and the name of each subinvestigator (e.g., research fellow, resident) working under the supervision of the investigator; the name and address of the research facilities to be used; and the name and address of each reviewing Institutional Review Board.

(c) The criteria for patient selection and for exclusion of patients and an estimate of the number of patients to be studied.

(d) A description of the design of the study, including the kind of control group to be used, if any, and a description of methods to be used to minimize bias on the part of subjects, investigators, and analysts.

(e) The method for determining the dose(s) to be administered, the planned maximum dosage, and the duration of individual patient exposure to the drug.

(f) A description of the observations and measurements to be made to fulfill the objectives of the study.

(g) A description of clinical procedures, laboratory tests, or other measures to be taken to monitor the effects of the drug in human subjects and to minimize risk.

(7) Chemistry, manufacturing, and control information. (i) As appropriate for the particular investigations covered by the IND, a section describing the composition, manufacture, and control of the drug substance and the drug product. Although in each phase of the investigation sufficient information is required to be submitted to assure the proper identification, quality, purity, and strength of the investigational drug, the amount of information needed to make that assurance will vary with the phase of the investigation, the proposed duration of the investigation, the dosage form, and the amount of information otherwise available. FDA recognizes that modifications to the method of preparation of the new drug substance and dosage form and changes in the dosage form itself are likely as the investigation progresses. Therefore, the emphasis in an initial Phase 1 submission should generally be placed on the identification and control of the raw materials and the new drug substance. Final specifications for the drug substance and drug product are not expected until the end of the investigational process.

(ii) It should be emphasized that the amount of information to be submitted depends upon the scope of the proposed clinical investigation. For example, although stability data are required in all phases of the IND to demonstrate that the new drug substance and drug product are within acceptable chemical and physical limits for the planned duration of the proposed clinical investigation, if very short-term tests are proposed, the supporting stability data can be correspondingly limited.

(iii) As drug development proceeds and as the scale or production is changed from the pilot-scale production appropriate for the limited initial clinical investigations to the larger-scale production needed for expanded clinical trials, the sponsor should submit information amendments to supplement the initial information submitted on the chemistry, manufacturing, and control processes with information appropriate to the expanded scope of the investigation.

(iv) Reflecting the distinctions described in this paragraph (a)(7), and based on the phase(s) to be studied, the submission is required to contain the following:

(a) Drug substance. A description of the drug substance, including its physical, chemical, or biological characteristics; the name and address of its manufacturer; the general method of preparation of the drug substance; the acceptable limits and analytical methods used to assure the identity, strength, quality, and purity of the drug substance; and information sufficient to support stability of the drug substance during the toxicological studies and the planned clinical studies. Reference to the current edition of the United States Pharmacopeia—National Formulary may satisfy relevant requirements in this paragraph.

(b) Drug product. A list of all components, which may include reasonable alternatives for inactive compounds, used in the manufacture of the investigational drug product, including both those components intended to appear in the drug product and those which may not appear but which are used in the manufacturing process, and, where applicable, the quantitative composition of the investigational drug product, including any reasonable variations that may be expected during the investigational stage; the name and address of the drug product manufacturer; a brief general description of the manufacturing and packaging procedure as appropriate for the product; the acceptable limits and analytical methods used to assure the identity, strength, quality, and purity of the drug product; and information sufficient to assure the product's stability during the planned clinical studies. Reference to the current edition of the United States Pharmacopeia—National Formulary may satisfy certain requirements in this paragraph.

(c) A brief general description of the composition, manufacture, and control of any placebo used in a controlled clinical trial.

(d) Labeling. A copy of all labels and labeling to be provided to each investigator.

(e) Environmental analysis requirements. A claim for categorical exclusion under §25.30 or 25.31 or an environmental assessment under §25.40.

(8) Pharmacology and toxicology information. Adequate information about pharma-

cological and toxicological studies of the drug involving laboratory animals or in vitro, on the basis of which the sponsor has concluded that it is reasonably safe to conduct the proposed clinical investigations. The kind, duration, and scope of animal and other tests required varies with the duration and nature of the proposed clinical investigations. Guidance documents are available from FDA that describe ways in which these requirements may be met. Such information is required to include the identification and qualifications of the individuals who evaluated the results of such studies and concluded that it is reasonably safe to begin the proposed investigations and a statement of where the investigations were conducted and where the records are available for inspection. As drug development proceeds, the sponsor is required to submit informational amendments, as appropriate, with additional information pertinent to safety.

(i) Pharmacology and drug disposition. A section describing the pharmacological effects and mechanism(s) of action of the drug in animals, and information on the absorption, distribution, metabolism, and excretion of the drug, if known.

(ii) Toxicology. (a) An integrated summary of the toxicological effects of the drug in animals and in vitro. Depending on the nature of the drug and the phase of the investigation, the description is to include the results of acute, subacute, and chronic toxicity tests; tests of the drug's effects on reproduction and the developing fetus; any special toxicity test related to the drug's particular mode of administration or conditions of use (e.g., inhalation, dermal, or ocular toxicology); and any in vitro studies intended to evaluate drug toxicity.

(b) For each toxicology study that is intended primarily to support the safety of the proposed clinical investigation, a full tabulation of data suitable for detailed review.

(iii) For each nonclinical laboratory study subject to the good laboratory practice regulations under part 58, a statement that the study was conducted in compliance with the good laboratory practice regulations in part 58, or, if the study was not conducted in compliance with those regulations, a brief statement of the reason for the noncompliance.

(9) *Previous human experience with the investigational drug.* A summary of previous human experience known to the applicant, if any, with the investigational drug. The information is required to include the following:

(i) If the investigational drug has been investigated or marketed previously, either in the United States or other countries, detailed information about such experience that is relevant to the safety of the proposed investigation or to the investigation's rationale. If the durg has been the subject of controlled trials, detailed information on such trials that is relevant to an assessment of the drug's effectiveness for the proposed investigational use(s) should also be provided. Any published material that is relevant to the safety of the proposed investigation or to an assessment of the drug's effectiveness for its proposed investigational use should be provided in full. Published material that is less directly relevant may be supplied by a bibliography.

(ii) If the drug is a combination of drugs previously investigated or marketed, the information required under paragraph (a)(9)(i) of this section should be provided for each active drug component. However, if any component in such combination is subject to an approved marketing application or is otherwise lawfully marketed in the United States, the sponsor is not required to submit published material concerning that active drug component unless such material relates directly to the proposed investigational use (including publications relevant to component-component interaction).

(iii) If the drug has been marketed outside the United States, a list of the countries in which the drug has been marketed and a list of the countries in which the drug has been withdrawn from marketing for reasons potentially related to safety or effectiveness.

(10) *Additional information.* In certain applications, as described below, information on special topics may be needed. Such information shall be submitted in this section as follows:

(i) *Drug dependence and abuse potential.* If the drug is a psychotropic substance or otherwise has abuse potential, a section describing relevant clinical studies and experience and studies in test animals.

(ii) *Radioactive drugs.* If the drug is a radioactive drug, sufficient data from animal or human studies to allow a reasonable calculation of radiation-absorbed dose to the whole body and critical organs upon administration to a human subject. Phase 1 studies of radioactive drugs must include studies which will obtain sufficient data for dosimetry calculations.

(iii) *Pediatric studies.* Plans for assessing pediatric safety and effectiveness.

(iv) *Other information.* A brief statement of any other information that would aid evaluation of the proposed clinical investigations with respect to their safety or their design and potential as controlled clinical trials to support marketing of the drug.

(11) Relevant information. If requested by FDA, any other relevant information needed for review of the application.

(b) Information previously submitted. The sponsor ordinarily is not required to resubmit information previously submitted, but may incorporate the information by reference. A reference to information submitted previously must identify the file by name, reference number, volume, and page number where the information can be found. A reference to information submitted to the agency by a person other than the sponsor is required to contain a written statement that authorizes the reference and that is signed by the person who submitted the information.

(c) Material in a foreign language. The sponsor shall submit an accurate and complete English translation of each part of the IND that is not in English. The sponsor shall also submit a copy of each original literature publication for which an English translation is submitted.

(d) Number of copies. The sponsor shall submit an original and two copies of all submissions to the IND file, including the original submission and all amendments and reports.

(e) Numbering of IND submissions. Each submission relating to an IND is required to be numbered serially using a single, three-digit serial number. The initial IND is required to be numbered 000; each subsequent submission (e.g., amendment, report, or correspondence) is required to be numbered chronologically in sequence.

(f) Identification of exception from informed consent. If the investigation involves an exception from informed consent under §50.24 of this chapter, the sponsor shall prominently identify on the cover sheet that the investigation is subject to the requirements in §50.24 of this chapter.

[52 FR 8831, Mar. 19, 1987, as amended at 52 FR 23031, June 17, 1987; 53 FR 1918, Jan. 25, 1988; 61 FR 51529, Oct. 2, 1996; 62 FR 40599, July 29, 1997; 63 FR 66669, Dec. 2, 1998; 65 FR 56479, Sept. 19, 2000; 67 FR 9585, Mar. 4, 2002]

§312.30 Protocol amendments.

Once an IND is in effect, a sponsor shall amend it as needed to ensure that the clinical investigations are conducted according to protocols included in the application. This section sets forth the provisions under which new protocols may be submitted and changes in previously submitted protocols may be made. Whenever a sponsor intends to conduct a clinical investigation with an exception from informed consent for emergency research as set forth in §50.24 of this chapter, the sponsor shall submit a separate IND for such investigation.

(a) New protocol. Whenever a sponsor intends to conduct a study that is not covered by a protocol already contained in the IND, the sponsor shall submit to FDA a protocol amendment containing the protocol for the study. Such study may begin provided two conditions are met: (1) The sponsor has submitted the protocol to FDA for its review; and (2) the protocol has been approved by the Institutional Review Board (IRB) with responsibility for review and approval of the study in accordance with the requirements of part 56. The sponsor may comply with these two conditions in either order.

(b) Changes in a protocol. (1) A sponsor shall submit a protocol amendment describing any change in a Phase 1 protocol that significantly affects the safety of subjects or any change in a Phase 2 or 3 protocol that significantly affects the safety of subjects, the scope of the investigation, or the scientific quality of the study. Examples of changes requiring an amendment under this paragraph include:

(i) Any increase in drug dosage or duration of exposure of individual subjects to the drug beyond that in the current protocol, or any significant increase in the number of subjects under study.

(ii) Any significant change in the design of a protocol (such as the addition or dropping of a control group).

(iii) The addition of a new test or procedure that is intended to improve monitoring for, or reduce the risk of, a side effect or adverse event; or the dropping of a test intended to monitor safety.

(2)(i) A protocol change under paragraph (b)(1) of this section may be made provided two conditions are met:

(a) The sponsor has submitted the change to FDA for its review; and

(b) The change has been approved by the IRB with responsibility for review and approval of the study. The sponsor may comply with these two conditions in either order.

(ii) Notwithstanding paragraph (b)(2)(i) of this section, a protocol change intended to eliminate an apparent immediate hazard to subjects may be implemented immediately provided FDA is subsequently notified by protocol amendment and the reviewing IRB is notified in accordance with §56.104(c).

(c) New investigator. A sponsor shall submit a protocol amendment when a new investigator is added to carry out a previously submitted protocol, except that a protocol amendment is not required when a licensed practitioner is added in the case of a treatment protocol under §312.34. Once the investigator is added to the study, the investigational drug may be shipped to the investigator and the investigator may begin participating in the study. The sponsor shall notify FDA of the new investigator within 30 days of the investigator being added.

(d) Content and format. A protocol amendment is required to be prominently identified as such (i.e., "Protocol Amendment: New Protocol", "Protocol Amendment: Change in Protocol", or "Protocol Amendment: New Investigator"), and to contain the following:

(1)(i) In the case of a new protocol, a copy of the new protocol and a brief description of the most clinically significant differences between it and previous protocols.

(ii) In the case of a change in protocol, a brief description of the change and reference (date and number) to the submission that contained the protocol.

(iii) In the case of a new investigator, the investigator's name, the qualifications to conduct the investigation, reference to the previously submitted protocol, and all additional information about the investigator's study as is required under §312.23(a)(6)(iii)(b).

(2) Reference, if necessary, to specific technical information in the IND or in a concurrently submitted information amendment to the IND that the sponsor relies on to support any clinically significant change in the new or amended protocol. If the reference is

made to supporting information already in the IND, the sponsor shall identify by name, reference number, volume, and page number the location of the information.

(3) If the sponsor desires FDA to comment on the submission, a request for such comment and the specific questions FDA's response should address.

(e) When submitted. A sponsor shall submit a protocol amendment for a new protocol or a change in protocol before its implementation. Protocol amendments to add a new investigator or to provide additional information about investigators may be grouped and submitted at 30-day intervals. When several submissions of new protocols or protocol changes are anticipated during a short period, the sponsor is encouraged, to the extent feasible, to include these all in a single submission.

[52 FR 8831, Mar. 19, 1987, as amended at 52 FR 23031, June 17, 1987; 53 FR 1918, Jan. 25, 1988; 61 FR 51530, Oct. 2, 1996; 67 FR 9585, Mar. 4, 2002]

§312.31 Information amendments.

(a) Requirement for information amendment. A sponsor shall report in an information amendment essential information on the IND that is not within the scope of a protocol amendment, IND safety reports, or annual report. Examples of information requiring an information amendment include:

(1) New toxicology, chemistry, or other technical information; or

(2) A report regarding the discontinuance of a clinical investigation.

(b) Content and format of an information amendment. An information amendment is required to bear prominent identification of its contents (e.g., "Information Amendment: Chemistry, Manufacturing, and Control", "Infor-mation Amendment: Pharmacology-Toxicol-ogy", "Information Amendment: Clinical"), and to contain the following:

(1) A statement of the nature and purpose of the amendment.

(2) An organized submission of the data in a format appropriate for scientific review.

(3) If the sponsor desires FDA to comment on an information amendment, a request for such comment.

(c) When submitted. Information amendments to the IND should be submitted as necessary but, to the extent feasible, not more than every 30 days.

[52 FR 8831, Mar. 19, 1987, as amended at 52 FR 23031, June 17, 1987; 53 FR 1918, Jan. 25, 1988; 67 FR 9585, Mar. 4, 2002]

§312.32 IND safety reports.

(a) Definitions. The following definitions of terms apply to this section:-

Associated with the use of the drug. There is a reasonable possibility that the experience may have been caused by the drug.

Disability. A substantial disruption of a person's ability to conduct normal life functions.

Life-threatening adverse drug experience. Any adverse drug experience that places the patient or subject, in the view of the investigator, at immediate risk of death from the reaction as it occurred, i.e., it does not include a reaction that, had it occurred in a more severe form, might have caused death.

Serious adverse drug experience: Any adverse drug experience occurring at any dose that results in any of the following outcomes: Death, a life-threatening adverse drug experience, inpatient hospitalization or prolongation of existing hospitalization, a persistent or significant disability/incapacity, or a congenital anomaly/birth defect. Important medical events that may not result in death, be life-threatening, or require hospitalization may be considered a serious adverse drug experience when, based upon appropriate medical judgment, they may jeopardize the patient or subject and may require medical or surgical intervention to prevent one of the outcomes listed in this definition. Examples of such medical events include allergic bronchospasm requiring intensive treatment in an emergency room or at home, blood dyscrasias or convulsions that do not result in inpatient hospitalization, or the development of drug dependency or drug abuse.

Unexpected adverse drug experience: Any adverse drug experience, the specificity or severity of which is not consistent with the current investigator brochure; or, if an investigator brochure is not required or available, the specificity or severity of which is not consistent with the risk information described in the general investigational plan or elsewhere in the current application, as amended. For example, under this definition, hepatic necrosis would be unexpected (by virtue of greater severity) if the investigator brochure only referred to elevated hepatic enzymes or hepatitis. Similarly, cerebral thromboembolism and cerebral vasculitis would be unexpected (by virtue of greater specificity) if the investigator

brochure only listed cerebral vascular accidents. "Unexpected," as used in this definition, refers to an adverse drug experience that has not been previously observed (e.g., included in the investigator brochure) rather than from the perspective of such experience not being anticipated from the pharmacological properties of the pharmaceutical product.

(b) Review of safety information. The sponsor shall promptly review all information relevant to the safety of the drug obtained or otherwise received by the sponsor from any source, foreign or domestic, including information derived from any clinical or epidemiological investigations, animal investigations, commercial marketing experience, reports in the scientific literature, and unpublished scientific papers, as well as reports from foreign regulatory authorities that have not already been previously reported to the agency by the sponsor.

(c) IND safety reports. (1) Written reports—
(i) The sponsor shall notify FDA and all participating investigators in a written IND safety report of:

(A) Any adverse experience associated with the use of the drug that is both serious and unexpected; or

(B) Any finding from tests in laboratory animals that suggests a significant risk for human subjects including reports of mutagenicity, teratogenicity, or carcinogenicity. Each notification shall be made as soon as possible and in no event later than 15 calendar days after the sponsor's initial receipt of the information. Each written notification may be submitted on FDA Form 3500A or in a narrative format (foreign events may be submitted either on an FDA Form 3500A or, if preferred, on a CIOMS I form; reports from animal or epidemiological studies shall be submitted in a narrative format) and shall bear prominent identification of its contents, i.e., "IND Safety Report." Each written notification to FDA shall be transmitted to the FDA new drug review division in the Center for Drug Evaluation and Research or the product review division in the Center for Biologics Evaluation and Research that has responsibility for review of the IND. If FDA determines that additional data are needed, the agency may require further data to be submitted.

(ii) In each written IND safety report, the sponsor shall identify all safety reports previously filed with the IND concerning a similar adverse experience, and shall analyze the significance of the adverse experience in light of the previouos, similar reports.

(2) Telephone and facsimile transmission safety reports. The sponsor shall also notify FDA by telephone or by facsimile transmission of any unexpected fatal or life-threatening experience associated with the use of the drug as soon as possible but in no event later than 7 calendar days after the sponsor's initial receipt of the information. Each telephone call or facsimile transmission to FDA shall be transmitted to the FDA new drug review division in the Center for Drug Evaluation and Research or the product review division in the Center for Biologics Evaluation and Research that has responsibility for review of the IND.

(3) Reporting format or frequency. FDA may request a sponsor to submit IND safety reports in a format or at a frequency different than that required under this paragraph. The sponsor may also propose and adopt a different reporting format or frequency if the change is agreed to in advance by the director of the new drug review division in the Center for Drug Evaluation and Research or the director of the products

review division in the Center for Biologics Evaluation and Research which is responsible for review of the IND.

(4) A sponsor of a clinical study of a marketed drug is not required to make a safety report for any adverse experience associated with use of the drug that is not from the clinical study itself.

(d) Followup. (1) The sponsor shall promptly investigate all safety information received by it.

(2) Followup information to a safety report shall be submitted as soon as the relevant information is available.

(3) If the results of a sponsor's investigation show that an adverse drug experience not initially determined to be reportable under paragraph (c) of this section is so reportable, the sponsor shall report such experience in a written safety report as soon as possible, but in no event later than 15 calendar days after the determination is made.

(4) Results of a sponsor's investigation of other safety information shall be submitted, as appropriate, in an information amendment or annual report.

(e) Disclaimer. A safety report or other information submitted by a sponsor under this part (and any release by FDA of that report or information) does not necessarily reflect a conclusion by the sponsor or FDA that the report or information constitutes an admission that the drug caused or contributed to an adverse experience. A sponsor need not admit, and may deny, that the report or information submitted by the sponsor constitutes an admission that the drug caused or contributed to an adverse experience.

[52 FR 8831, Mar. 19, 1987, as amended at 52 FR 23031, June 17, 1987; 55 FR 11579, Mar. 29, 1990; 62 FR 52250, Oct. 7, 1997; 67 FR 9585, Mar. 4, 2002]

§312.33 Annual reports.

A sponsor shall within 60 days of the anniversary date that the IND went into effect, submit a brief report of the progress of the investigation that includes:

(a) Individual study information. A brief summary of the status of each study in progress and each study completed during the previous year. The summary is required to include the following information for each study:

(1) The title of the study (with any appropriate study identifiers such as protocol number), its purpose, a brief statement identifying the patient population, and a statement as to whether the study is completed.

(2) The total number of subjects initially planned for inclusion in the study; the number entered into the study to date, tabulated by age group, gender, and race; the number whose participation in the study was completed as planned; and the number who dropped out of the study for any reason.

(3) If the study has been completed, or if interim results are known, a brief description of any available study results.

(b) Summary information. Information obtained during the previous year's clinical and nonclinical investigations, including:

(1) A narrative or tabular summary showing the most frequent and most serious adverse experiences by body system.

(2) A summary of all IND safety reports submitted during the past year.

(3) A list of subjects who died during participation in the investigation, with the cause of death for each subject.

(4) A list of subjects who dropped out during the course of the investigation in association with any adverse experience, whether or not thought to be drug related.

(5) A brief description of what, if anything, was obtained that is pertinent to an understanding of the drug's actions, including, for example, information about dose response, information from controlled trails, and information about bioavailability.

(6) A list of the preclinical studies (including animal studies) completed or in progress during the past year and a summary of the major preclinical findings.

(7) A summary of any significant manufacturing or microbiological changes made during the past year.

(c) A description of the general investigational plan for the coming year to replace that submitted 1 year earlier. The general investigational plan shall contain the information required under §312.23(a)(3)(iv).

(d) If the investigator brochure has been revised, a description of the revision and a copy of the new brochure.

(e) A description of any significant Phase 1 protocol modifications made during the previous year and not previously reported to the IND in a protocol amendment.

(f) A brief summary of significant foreign marketing developments with the drug during the past year, such as approval of marketing in any country or withdrawal or suspension from marketing in any country.

(g) If desired by the sponsor, a log of any outstanding business with respect to the IND for which the sponsor requests or expects a reply, comment, or meeting.

[52 FR 8831, Mar. 19, 1987, as amended at 52 FR 23031, June 17, 1987; 63 FR 6862, Feb. 11, 1998; 67 FR 9585, Mar. 4, 2002]

§312.34 Treatment use of an investigational new drug.

(a) General. A drug that is not approved for marketing may be under clinical investigation for a serious or immediately life-threatening disease condition in patients for whom no comparable or satisfactory alternative drug or other therapy is available. During the clinical investigation of the drug, it may be appropriate to use the drug in the treatment of patients not in the clinical trials, in accordance with a treatment protocol or treatment IND. The purpose of this section is to facilitate the availability of promising new drugs to desperately ill patients as early in the drug development process as possible, before general marketing begins, and to obtain additional data on the drug's safety and effectiveness. In the case of a serious disease, a drug ordinarily may be made available for treatment use under this section during Phase 3 investigations or after all clinical trials have been completed; however, in appropriate circumstances, a drug may be made available for treatment use during Phase 2. In the case of an immediately life-threatening disease, a drug may be made available for treatment use under this section earlier than Phase 3, but ordinarily not earlier than Phase 2. For purposes of this section, the "treatment use" of a drug includes the use of a drug for diagnostic purposes. If a protocol for an investigational drug meets the criteria of this section, the protocol is to be submitted as a treatment protocol under the provisions of this section.

(b) Criteria. (1) FDA shall permit an investigational drug to be used for a treatment use under a treatment protocol or treatment IND if:

(i) The drug is intended to treat a serious or immediately life-threatening disease;

(ii) There is no comparable or satisfactory alternative drug or other therapy available to treat that stage of the disease in the intended patient population;

(iii) The drug is under investigation in a controlled clinical trial under an IND in effect for the trial, or all clinical trials have been completed; and

(iv) The sponsor of the controlled clinical trial is actively pursuing marketing approval of the investigational drug with due diligence.

(2) Serious disease. For a drug intended to treat a serious disease, the Commissioner may deny a request for treatment use under a treatment protocol or treatment IND if there is insufficient evidence of safety and effectiveness to support such use.

(3) Immediately life-threatening disease. (i) For a drug intended to treat an immediately life-threatening disease, the Commissioner may deny a request for treatment use of an investigational drug under a treatment protocol or treatment IND if the available scientific evidence, taken as a whole, fails to provide a reasonable basis for concluding that the drug:

(A) May be effective for its intended use in its intended patient population; or

(B) Would not expose the patients to whom the drug is to be administered to an unreasonable and significant additional risk of illness or injury.

(ii) For the purpose of this section, an "immediately life-threatening" disease means a stage of a disease in which there is a reasonable likelihood that death will occur within a matter of months or in which premature death is likely without early treatment.

(c) *Safeguards.* Treatment use of an investigational drug is conditioned on the sponsor and investigators complying with the safeguards of the IND process, including the regulations governing informed consent (21 CFR part 50) and institutional review boards (21 CFR part 56) and the applicable provisions of part 312, including distribution of the drug through qualified experts, maintenance of adequate manufacturing facilities, and submission of IND safety reports.

(d) *Clinical hold.* FDA may place on clinical hold a proposed or ongoing treatment protocol or treatment IND in accordance with §312.42.

[52 FR 19476, May 22, 1987, as amended at 57 FR 13248, Apr. 15, 1992]

§312.35 Submissions for treatment use.

(a) *Treatment protocol submitted by IND sponsor.* Any sponsor of a clinical investigation of a drug who intends to sponsor a treatment use for the drug shall submit to FDA a treatment protocol under §312.34 if the sponsor believes the criteria of §312.34

are satisfied. If a protocol is not submitted under §312.34, but FDA believes that the protocol should have been submitted under this section, FDA may deem the protocol to be submitted under §312.34. A treatment use under a treatment protocol may begin 30 days after FDA receives the protocol or on earlier notification by FDA that the treatment use described in the protocol may begin.

(1) A treatment protocol is required to contain the following:

(i) The intended use of the drug.

(ii) An explanation of the rationale for use of the drug, including, as appropriate, either a list of what available regimens ordinarily should be tried before using the investigational drug or an explanation of why the use of the investigational drug is preferable to the use of available marketed treatments.

(iii) A brief description of the criteria for patient selection.

(iv) The method of administration of the drug and the dosages.

(v) A description of clinical procedures, laboratory tests, or other measures to monitor the effects of the drug and to minimize risk.

(2) A treatment protocol is to be supported by the following:

(i) Informational brochure for supplying to each treating physician.

(ii) The technical information that is relevant to safety and effectiveness of the drug for the intended treatment purpose. Information contained in the sponsor's IND may be incorporated by reference.

(iii) A commitment by the sponsor to assure compliance of all participating investigators with the informed consent requirements of 21 CFR part 50.

(3) A licensed practioner who receives an investigational drug for treatment use under a treatment protocol is an "investigator" under the protocol and is responsible for meeting all applicable investigator responsibilities under this part and 21 CFR parts 50 and 56.

(b) Treatment IND submitted by licensed practitioner. (1) If a licensed medical practitioner wants to obtain an investigational drug subject to a controlled clinical trial for a treatment use, the practitioner should first attempt to obtain the drug from the sponsor of the controlled trial under a treatment protocol. If the sponsor of the controlled clinical investigation of the drug will not establish a treatment protocol for the drug under paragraph (a) of this section, the licensed medical practitioner may seek to obtain the drug from the sponsor and submit a treatment IND to FDA requesting authorization to use the investigational drug for treatment use. A treatment use under a treatment IND may begin 30 days after FDA receives the IND or on earlier notification by FDA that the treatment use under the IND may begin. A treatment IND is required to contain the following:

(i) A cover sheet (Form FDA 1571) meeting §312.23(g)(1).

(ii) Information (when not provided by the sponsor) on the drug's chemistry, manufacturing, and controls, and prior clinical and nonclinical experience with the drug submitted in accordance with §312.23. A sponsor of a clinical investigation subject to an IND who supplies an investigational drug to a licensed medical practitioner for purposes of a separate treatment clinical investigation shall be deemed to authorize the incorporation-by-reference of the technical information contained in the sponsor's IND into the medical practitioner's treatment IND.

(iii) A statement of the steps taken by the practitioner to obtain the drug under a treatment protocol from the drug sponsor.

(iv) A treatment protocol containing the same information listed in paragraph (a)(1) of this section.

(v) A statement of the practitioner's qualifications to use the investigational drug for the intended treatment use.

(vi) The practitioner's statement of familiarity with information on the drug's safety and effectiveness derived from previous clinical and nonclinical experience with the drug.

(vii) Agreement to report to FDA safety information in accordance with §312.32.

(2) A licensed practitioner who submits a treatment IND under this section is the sponsor-investigator for such IND and is responsible for meeting all applicable sponsor and investigator responsibilities under this part and 21 CFR parts 50 and 56.

[52 FR 19477, May 22, 1987, as amended at 57 FR 13249, Apr. 15, 1992; 67 FR 9585, Mar. 4, 2002]

§312.36 Emergency use of an investigational new drug.

Need for an investigational drug may arise in an emergency situation that does not allow time for submission of an IND in accordance with §312.23 or §312.34. In such a case, FDA may authorize shipment of the drug for a specified use in advance of submission of an IND. A request for such authorization may be transmitted to FDA by telephone or other rapid communication means. For investigational biological drugs, the request should be directed to the Division of Biological Investigational New Drugs (HFB-230), Center for Biologics Evaluation and Research, 8800 Rockville Pike, Bethesda, MD 20892, 301-443-4864. For all other investigational drugs, the request for authorization should be directed to the Document Management and Reporting Branch (HFD-53), Center for Drug Evaluation and Research, 5600 Fishers Lane, Rockville, MD 20857, 301-443-4320. After normal working hours, eastern standard time, the request should be directed to the FDA Division of Emergency and Epidemiological Operations, 202-857-8400. Except in extraordinary circumstances, such authorization will be conditioned on the sponsor making an appropriate IND submission as soon as practicable after receiving the authorization.

[52 FR 8831, Mar. 19, 1987, as amended at 52 FR 23031, June 17, 1987; 55 FR 11579, Mar. 29, 1990; 67 FR 9585, Mar. 4, 2002]

§312.38 Withdrawal of an IND.

(a) At any time a sponsor may withdraw an effective IND without prejudice.

(b) If an IND is withdrawn, FDA shall be so notified, all clinical investigations conducted under the IND shall be ended, all current investigators notified, and all stocks of the drug returned to the sponsor or otherwise disposed of at the request of the sponsor in accordance with §312.59.

(c) If an IND is withdrawn because of a safety reason, the sponsor shall promptly so inform FDA, all participating investigators, and all reviewing Institutional Review Boards, together with the reasons for such withdrawal.

[52 FR 8831, Mar. 19, 1987, as amended at 52 FR 23031, June 17, 1987; 67 FR 9586, Mar. 4, 2002]

Subpart C—Administrative Actions

§312.40 General requirements for use of an investigational new drug in a clinical investigation.

(a) An investigational new drug may be used in a clinical investigation if the following conditions are met:

(1) The sponsor of the investigation submits an IND for the drug to FDA; the IND is in effect under paragraph (b) of this section; and the sponsor complies with all applicable requirements in this part and parts 50 and 56 with respect to the conduct of the clinical investigations; and

(2) Each participating investigator conducts his or her investigation in compliance with the requirements of this part and parts 50 and 56.

(b) An IND goes into effect:

(1) Thirty days after FDA receives the IND, unless FDA notifies the sponsor that the investigations described in the IND are subject to a clinical hold under §312.42; or

(2) On earlier notification by FDA that the clinical investigations in the IND may begin. FDA will notify the sponsor in writing of the date it receives the IND.

(c) A sponsor may ship an investigational new drug to investigators named in the IND:

(1) Thirty days after FDA receives the IND; or

(2) On earlier FDA authorization to ship the drug.

(d) An investigator may not administer an investigational new drug to human subjects until the IND goes into effect under paragraph (b) of this section.

§312.41 Comment and advice on an IND.

(a) FDA may at any time during the course of the investigation communicate with the sponsor orally or in writing about deficiencies in the IND or about FDA's need for more data or information.

(b) On the sponsor's request, FDA will provide advice on specific matters relating to an IND. Examples of such advice may include advice on the adequacy of technical data to support an investigational plan, on the design of a clinical trial, and on whether proposed investigations are likely to produce the data and information that is needed to meet requirements for a marketing application.

(c) Unless the communication is accompanied by a clinical hold order under §312.42, FDA communications with a sponsor under this section are solely advisory and do not require any modification in the planned or ongoing clinical investigations or response to the agency.

[52 FR 8831, Mar. 19, 1987, as amended at 52 FR 23031, June 17, 1987; 67 FR 9586, Mar. 4, 2002]

§312.42 Clinical holds and requests for modification.

(a) General. A clinical hold is an order issued by FDA to the sponsor to delay a proposed clinical investigation or to suspend an ongoing investigation. The clinical hold order may apply to one or more of the investigations covered by an IND. When a proposed study is placed on clinical hold, subjects may not be given the investigational drug. When an ongoing study is placed on clinical hold, no new subjects may be recruited to the study and placed on the investigational drug; patients already in the study should be taken off therapy involving the investigational drug unless specifically permitted by FDA in the interest of patient safety.

(b) Grounds for imposition of clinical hold—(1) Clinical hold of a Phase 1 study under an IND. FDA may place a proposed or ongoing Phase 1 investigation on clinical hold if it finds that:

(i) Human subjects are or would be exposed to an unreasonable and significant risk of illness or injury;

(ii) The clinical investigators named in the IND are not qualified by reason of their scientific training and experience to conduct the investigation described in the IND;

(iii) The investigator brochure is misleading, erroneous, or materially incomplete; or

(iv) The IND does not contain sufficient information required under §312.23 to assess the risks to subjects of the proposed studies.

(v) The IND is for the study of an investigational drug intended to treat a life-threatening disease or condition that affects both genders, and men or women with reproductive potential who have the disease or condition being studied are excluded from eligibility because of a risk or potential risk from use of the investigational drug of reproductive toxicity (i.e., affecting reproductive organs) or developmental toxicity (i.e., affecting potential offspring). The phrase "women with reproductive potential" does not include pregnant women. For purposes of this paragraph, "life-threatening illnesses or diseases" are defined as "diseases or conditions where the likelihood of death is high unless the course of the disease is interrupted." The clinical hold would not apply under this paragraph to clinical studies conducted:

(A) Under special circumstances, such as studies pertinent only to one gender (e.g., studies evaluating the excretion of a drug in semen or the effects on menstrual function);

(B) Only in men or women, as long as a study that does not exclude members of the other gender with reproductive potential is being conducted concurrently, has been conducted, or will take place within a reasonable time agreed upon by the agency; or

(C) Only in subjects who do not suffer from the disease or condition for which the drug is being studied.

(2) Clinical hold of a Phase 2 or 3 study under an IND. FDA may place a proposed or ongoing Phase 2 or 3 investigation on clinical hold if it finds that:

(i) Any of the conditions in paragraphs (b)(1)(i) through (b)(1)(v) of this section apply; or

(ii) The plan or protocol for the investigation is clearly deficient in design to meet its stated objectives.

(3) Clinical hold of a treatment IND or treatment protocol.

(i) Proposed use. FDA may place a proposed treatment IND or treatment protocol on clinical hold if it is determined that:

(A) The pertinent criteria in §312.34(b) for permitting the treatment use to begin are not satisfied; or

(B) The treatment protocol or treatment IND does not contain the information required under §312.35 (a) or (b) to make the specified determination under §312.34(b).

(ii) Ongoing use. FDA may place an ongoing treatment protocol or treatment IND on clinical hold if it is determined that:

(A) There becomes available a comparable or satisfactory alternative drug or other therapy to treat that stage of the disease in the intended patient population for which the investigational drug is being used;

(B) The investigational drug is not under investigation in a controlled clinical trial under an IND in effect for the trial and not all controlled clinical trials necessary to support a marketing application have been completed, or a clinical study under the IND has been placed on clinical hold:

(C) The sponsor of the controlled clinical trial is not pursuing marketing approval with due diligence;

(D) If the treatment IND or treatment protocol is intended for a serious disease, there is insufficient evidence of safety and effectiveness to support such use; or

(E) If the treatment protocol or treatment IND was based on an immediately life-threatening disease, the available scientific evidence, taken as a whole, fails to provide a reasonable basis for concluding that the drug:

(1) May be effective for its intended use in its intended population; or

(2) Would not expose the patients to whom the drug is to be administered to an unreasonable and significant additional risk of illness or injury.

(iii) FDA may place a proposed or ongoing treatment IND or treatment protocol on clinical hold if it finds that any of the conditions in paragraph (b)(4)(i) through (b)(4)(viii) of this section apply.

(4) Clinical hold of any study that is not designed to be adequate and well-controlled. FDA may place a proposed or ongoing investigation that is not designed to be adequate and well-controlled on clinical hold if it finds that:

(i) Any of the conditions in paragraph (b)(1) or (b)(2) of this section apply; or

(ii) There is reasonable evidence the investigation that is not designed to be adequate and well-controlled is impeding enrollment in, or otherwise interfering with the conduct or completion of, a study that is designed to be an adequate and well-controlled investigation of the same or another investigational drug; or

(iii) Insufficient quantities of the investigational drug exist to adequately conduct both the investigation that is not designed to be adequate and well-controlled and the investigations that are designed to be adequate and well-controlled; or

(iv) The drug has been studied in one or more adequate and well-controlled investigations that strongly suggest lack of effectiveness; or

(v) Another drug under investigation or approved for the same indication and available to the same patient population has demonstrated a better potential benefit/risk balance; or

(vi) The drug has received marketing approval for the same indication in the same patient population; or

(vii) The sponsor of the study that is designed to be an adequate and well-controlled investigation is not actively pursuing marketing approval of the investigational drug with due diligence; or

(viii) The Commissioner determines that it would not be in the public interest for the study to be conducted or continued. FDA ordinarily intends that clinical holds under paragraphs (b)(4)(ii), (b)(4)(iii) and (b)(4)(v) of this section would only apply to additional enrollment in nonconcurrently controlled trials rather than eliminating continued access to individuals already receiving the investigational drug.

(5) Clinical hold of any investigation involving an exception from informed consent under §50.24 of this chapter. FDA may place a proposed or ongoing investigation involving an exception from informed consent under §50.24 of this chapter on clinical hold if it is determined that:

(i) Any of the conditions in paragraphs (b)(1) or (b)(2) of this section apply; or

(ii) The pertinent criteria in §50.24 of this chapter for such an investigation to begin or continue are not submitted or not satisfied.

(6) Clinical hold of any investigation involving an exception from informed consent under §50.23(d) of this chapter. FDA may place a proposed or ongoing investigation involving an exception from informed consent under §50.23(d) of this chapter on clinical hold if it is determined that:

(i) Any of the conditions in paragraphs (b)(1) or (b)(2) of this section apply; or

(ii) A determination by the President to waive the prior consent requirement for the administration of an investigational new drug has not been made.

(c) *Discussion of deficiency.* Whenever FDA concludes that a deficiency exists in a clinical investigation that may be grounds for the imposition of clinical hold FDA will, unless patients are exposed to immediate and serious risk, attempt to discuss and satisfactorily resolve the matter with the sponsor before issuing the clinical hold order.

(d) *Imposition of clinical hold.* The clinical hold order may be made by telephone or other means of rapid communication or in writing. The clinical hold order will identify the studies under the IND to which the hold applies, and will briefly explain the basis for the action. The clinical hold order will be made by or on behalf of the Division Director with responsibility for review of the IND. As soon as possible, and no more than 30 days after imposition of the clinical hold, the Division Director will provide the sponsor a written explanation of the basis for the hold.

(e) *Resumption of clinical investigations.* An investigation may only resume after FDA (usually the Division Director, or the Director's designee, with responsibility for review of the IND) has notified the sponsor that the investigation may proceed.

Resumption of the affected investigation(s) will be authorized when the sponsor corrects the deficiency(ies) previously cited or otherwise satisfies the agency that the investigation(s) can proceed. FDA may notify a sponsor of its determination regarding the clinical hold by telephone or other means of rapid communication. If a sponsor of an IND that has been placed on clinical hold requests in writing that the clinical hold be removed and submits a complete response to the issue(s) identified in the clinical hold order, FDA shall respond in writing to the sponsor within 30-calendar days of receipt of the request and the complete response. FDA's response will either remove or maintain the clinical hold, and will state the reasons for such determination. Notwithstanding the 30-calendar day response time, a sponsor may not proceed with a clinical trial on which a clinical hold has been imposed until the sponsor has been notified by FDA that the hold has been lifted.

(f) *Appeal.* If the sponsor disagrees with the reasons cited for the clinical hold, the sponsor may request reconsideration of the decision in accordance with §312.48.

(g) *Conversion of IND on clinical hold to inactive status.* If all investigations covered by an IND remain on clinical hold for 1 year or more, the IND may be placed on inactive status by FDA under §312.45.

[52 FR 8831, Mar. 19, 1987, as amended at 52 FR 19477, May 22, 1987; 57 FR 13249, Apr. 15, 1992; 61 FR 51530, Oct. 2, 1996; 63 FR 68678, Dec. 14, 1998; 64 FR 54189, Oct. 5, 1999; 65 FR 34971, June 1, 2000]

§312.44 Termination.

(a) *General.* This section describes the procedures under which FDA may terminate an

IND. If an IND is terminated, the sponsor shall end all clinical investigations conducted under the IND and recall or otherwise provide for the disposition of all unused supplies of the drug. A termination action may be based on deficiencies in the IND or in the conduct of an investigation under an IND. Except as provided in paragraph (d) of this section, a termination shall be preceded by a proposal to terminate by FDA and an opportunity for the sponsor to respond. FDA will, in general, only initiate an action under this section after first attempting to resolve differences informally or, when appropriate, through the clinical hold procedures described in §312.42.

(b) Grounds for termination—(1) Phase 1. FDA may propose to terminate an IND during Phase 1 if it finds that:

(i) Human subjects would be exposed to an unreasonable and significant risk of illness or unjury.

(ii) The IND does not contain sufficient information required under §312.23 to assess the safety to subjects of the clinical investigations.

(iii) The methods, facilities, and controls used for the manufacturing, processing, and packing of the investigational drug are inadequate to establish and maintain appropriate standards of identity, strength, quality, and purity as needed for subject safety.

(iv) The clinical investigations are being conducted in a manner substantially different than that described in the protocols submitted in the IND.

(v) The drug is being promoted or distributed for commercial purposes not justified by the requirements of the investigation or permitted by §312.7.

(vi) The IND, or any amendment or report to the IND, contains an untrue statement of a material fact or omits material information required by this part.

(vii) The sponsor fails promptly to investigate and inform the Food and Drug Administration and all investigators of serious and unexpected adverse experiences in accordance with §312.32 or fails to make any other report required under this part.

(viii) The sponsor fails to submit an accurate annual report of the investigations in accordance with §312.33.

(ix) The sponsor fails to comply with any other applicable requirement of this part, part 50, or part 56.

(x) The IND has remained on inactive status for 5 years or more.

(xi) The sponsor fails to delay a proposed investigation under the IND or to suspend an ongoing investigation that has been placed on clinical hold under §312.42(b)(4).

(2) Phase 2 or 3. FDA may propose to terminate an IND during Phase 2 or Phase 3 if FDA finds that:

(i) Any of the conditions in paragraphs (b)(1)(i) through (b)(1)(xi) of this section apply; or

(ii) The investigational plan or protocol(s) is not reasonable as a bona fide scientific plan to determine whether or not the drug is safe and effective for use; or

(iii) There is convincing evidence that the drug is not effective for the purpose for which it is being investigated.

(3) FDA may propose to terminate a treatment IND if it finds that:

(i) Any of the conditions in paragraphs (b)(1)(i) through (x) of this section apply; or

(ii) Any of the conditions in §312.42(b)(3) apply.

(c) Opportunity for sponsor response. (1) If FDA proposes to terminate an IND, FDA will notify the sponsor in writing, and invite correction or explanation within a period of 30 days.

(2) On such notification, the sponsor may provide a written explanation or correction or may request a conference with FDA to provide the requested explanation or correction. If the sponsor does not respond to the notification within the allocated time, the IND shall be terminated.

(3) If the sponsor responds but FDA does not accept the explanation or correction submitted, FDA shall inform the sponsor in writing of the reason for the nonacceptance and provide the sponsor with an opportunity for a regulatory hearing before FDA under part 16 on the question of whether the IND should be terminated. The sponsor's request for a regulatory hearing must be made within 10 days of the sponsor's receipt of FDA's notification of nonacceptance.

(d) Immediate termination of IND. Notwith-standing paragraphs (a) through (c) of this section, if at any time FDA concludes that continuation of the investigation presents an immediate and substantial danger to the health of individuals, the agency shall immediately, by written notice to the sponsor from the Director of the Center for Drug Evaluation and Research or the Director of the Center for Biologics Evaluation and Research, terminate the IND. An IND so terminated is subject to reinstatement by the Director on the basis of additional submissions that eliminate such danger. If an IND is terminated under this paragraph, the agency will afford the sponsor an opportunity for a regulatory hearing under part 16 on the question of whether the IND should be reinstated.

[52 FR 8831, Mar. 19, 1987, as amended at 52 FR 23031, June 17, 1987; 55 FR 11579, Mar. 29, 1990; 57 FR 13249, Apr. 15, 1992; 67 FR 9586, Mar. 4, 2002]

§312.45 Inactive status.

(a) If no subjects are entered into clinical studies for a period of 2 years or more under an IND, or if all investigations under an IND remain on clinical hold for 1 year or more, the IND may be placed by FDA on inactive status. This action may be taken by FDA either on request of the sponsor or on FDA's own initiative. If FDA seeks to act on its own initiative under this section, it shall first notify the sponsor in writing of the proposed inactive status. Upon receipt of such notification, the sponsor shall have 30 days to respond as to why the IND should continue to remain active.

(b) If an IND is placed on inactive status, all investigators shall be so notified and all stocks of the drug shall be returned or otherwise disposed of in accordance with §312.59.

(c) A sponsor is not required to submit annual reports to an IND on inactive status. An inactive IND is, however, still in effect for purposes of the public disclosure of data and information under §312.130.

(d) A sponsor who intends to resume clinical investigation under an IND placed on inactive status shall submit a protocol amendment under §312.30 containing the proposed general investigational plan for the coming year and appropriate protocols. If the protocol amendment relies on information previously submitted, the plan shall reference such information. Additional information supporting the proposed investigation, if any, shall be submitted in an information amendment. Notwithstanding the provisions of §312.30, clinical investigations under an IND on inactive status may only resume (1) 30 days after FDA receives the protocol amendment, unless FDA notifies the sponsor that the investigations described in the amendment are subject to a clinical hold under §312.42, or (2) on earlier notification by FDA that the clinical investigations described in the protocol amendment may begin.

(e) An IND that remains on inactive status for 5 years or more may be terminated under §312.44.

[52 FR 8831, Mar. 19, 1987, as amended at 52 FR 23031, June 17, 1987; 67 FR 9586, Mar. 4, 2002]

§312.47 Meetings.

(a) General. Meetings between a sponsor and the agency are frequently useful in resolving questions and issues raised during the course of a clinical investigation. FDA encourages such meetings to the extent that they aid in the evaluation of the drug and in the solution of scientific problems concerning the drug, to the extent that FDA's resources permit. The general principle underlying the conduct of such meetings is that there should be free, full, and open communication about any scientific or medical question that may arise during the clinical investigation. These meetings shall be conducted and documented in accordance with part 10.

(b) "End-of-Phase 2" meetings and meetings held before submission of a marketing application. At specific times during the drug investigation process, meetings between FDA and a sponsor can be especially helpful in minimizing wasteful expenditures of time and money and thus in speeding the drug development and evaluation process. In particular, FDA has found that meetings at the end of Phase 2 of an investigation (end-of-Phase 2 meetings) are of considerable assistance in planning later studies and that meetings held near completion of Phase 3 and before submission of a marketing application ("pre-NDA" meetings) are helpful in developing methods of presentation and submission of data in the marketing application that facilitate review and allow timely FDA response.

(1) End-of-Phase 2 meetings—(i) Purpose. The purpose of an end-of-phase 2 meeting is to determine the safety of proceeding to Phase 3, to evaluate the Phase 3 plan and protocols and the adequacy of current studies and plans to assess pediatric safety and effectiveness, and to identify any additional information necessary to support a marketing application for the uses under investigation.

(ii) Eligibility for meeting. While the end-of-Phase 2 meeting is designed primarily for IND's involving new molecular entities or major new uses of marketed drugs, a sponsor of any IND may request and obtain an end-of-Phase 2 meeting.

(iii) Timing. To be most useful to the sponsor, end-of-Phase 2 meetings should be held before major commitments of effort and resources to specific Phase 3 tests are made. The scheduling of an end-of-Phase 2 meeting is not, however, intended to delay the transition of an investigation from Phase 2 to Phase 3.

(iv) *Advance information.* At least 1 month in advance of an end-of-Phase 2 meeting, the sponsor should submit background information on the sponsor's plan for Phase 3, including summaries of the Phase 1 and 2 investigations, the specific protocols for Phase 3 clinical studies, plans for any additional nonclinical studies, plans for pediatric studies, including a time line for protocol finalization, enrollment, completion, and data analysis, or information to support any planned request for waiver or deferral of pediatric studies, and, if available, tentative labeling for the drug. The recommended contents of such a submission are described more fully in FDA Staff Manual Guide 4850.7 that is publicly available under FDA's public information regulations in part 20.

(v) *Conduct of meeting.* Arrangements for an end-of-Phase 2 meeting are to be made with the division in FDA's Center for Drug Evaluation and Research or the Center for Biologics Evaluation and Research which is responsible for review of the IND. The meeting will be scheduled by FDA at a time convenient to both FDA and the sponsor. Both the sponsor and FDA may bring consultants to the meeting. The meeting should be directed primarily at establishing agreement between FDA and the sponsor of the overall plan for Phase 3 and the objectives and design of particular studies. The adequacy of the technical information to support Phase 3 studies and/or a marketing application may also be discussed. FDA will also provide its best judgment, at that time, of the pediatric studies that will be required for the drug product and whether their submission will be deferred until after approval.

Agreements reached at the meeting on these matters will be recorded in minutes of the conference that will be taken by FDA in accordance with §10.65 and provided to the sponsor. The minutes along with any other written material provided to the sponsor will serve as a permanent record of any agreements reached. Barring a significant scientific development that requires otherwise, studies conducted in accordance with the agreement shall be presumed to be sufficient in objective and design for the purpose of obtaining marketing approval for the drug.

(2) *"Pre-NDA" and "pre-BLA" meetings.* FDA has found that delays associated with the initial review of a marketing application may be reduced by exchanges of information about a proposed marketing application. The primary purpose of this kind of exchange is to uncover any major unresolved problems, to identify those studies that the sponsor is relying on as adequate and well-controlled to establish the drug's effectiveness, to identify the status of ongoing or needed studies adequate to assess pediatric safety and effectiveness, to acquaint FDA reviewers with the general information to be submitted in the marketing application (including technical information), to discuss appropriate methods for statistical analysis of the data, and to discuss the best approach to the presentation and formatting of data in the marketing application. Arrangements for such a meeting are to be initiated by the sponsor with the division responsible for review of the IND. To permit FDA to provide the sponsor with the most useful advice on preparing a marketing application, the sponsor should submit to FDA's reviewing division at least 1 month in advance of the meeting the following information:

(i) A brief summary of the clinical studies to be submitted in the application.

(ii) A proposed format for organizing the submission, including methods for presenting the data.

(iii) Information on the status of needed or ongoing pediatric studies.

(iv) Any other information for discussion at the meeting.

[52 FR 8831, Mar. 19, 1987, as amended at 52 FR 23031, June 17, 1987; 55 FR 11580, Mar. 29, 1990; 63 FR 66669, Dec. 2, 1998; 67 FR 9586, Mar. 4, 2002]

§312.48 Dispute resolution.

(a) General. The Food and Drug Administration is committed to resolving differences between sponsors and FDA reviewing divisions with respect to requirements for IND's as quickly and amicably as possible through the cooperative exchange of information and views.

(b) Administrative and procedural issues. When administrative or procedural disputes arise, the sponsor should first attempt to resolve the matter with the division in FDA's Center for Drug Evaluation and Research or Center for Biologics Evaluation and Research which is responsible for review of the IND, beginning with the consumer safety officer assigned to the application. If the dispute is not resolved, the sponsor may raise the matter with the person designated as ombudsman, whose function shall be to investigate what has happened and to facilitate a timely and equitable resolution. Appropriate issues to raise with the ombudsman include resolving difficulties in scheduling meetings and obtaining timely replies to inquiries. Further details on this procedure are contained in FDA Staff Manual Guide 4820.7 that is publicly available under FDA's public information regulations in part 20.

(c) Scientific and medical disputes. (1) When scientific or medical disputes arise during the drug investigation process, sponsors should discuss the matter directly with the responsible reviewing officials. If necessary, sponsors may request a meeting with the appropriate reviewing officials and management representatives in order to seek a resolution. Requests for such meetings shall be directed to the director of the division in FDA's Center for Drug Evaluation and Research or Center for Biologics Evaluation and Research which is responsible for review of the IND. FDA will make every attempt to grant requests for meetings that involve important issues and that can be scheduled at mutually convenient times.

(2) The "end-of-Phase 2" and "pre-NDA" meetings described in §312.47(b) will also provide a timely forum for discussing and resolving scientific and medical issues on which the sponsor disagrees with the agency.

(3) In requesting a meeting designed to resolve a scientific or medical dispute, applicants may suggest that FDA seek the advice of outside experts, in which case FDA may, in its discretion, invite to the meeting one or more of its advisory committee members or other consultants, as designated by the agency. Applicants may rely on, and may bring to any meeting, their own consultants. For major scientific and medical policy issues not resolved by informal meetings, FDA may refer the matter to one of its standing advisory committees for its consideration and recommendations.

[52 FR 8831, Mar. 19, 1987, as amended at 55 FR 11580, Mar. 29, 1990]

Subpart D—Responsibilities of Sponsors and Investigators

§312.50 General responsibilities of sponsors.

Sponsors are responsibile for selecting qualified investigators, providing them with the information they need to conduct an investigation properly, ensuring proper monitoring of the investigation(s), ensuring that the investigation(s) is conducted in accordance with the general investigational plan and protocols contained in the IND, maintaining an effective IND with respect to the investigations, and ensuring that FDA and all participating investigators are promptly informed of significant new adverse effects or risks with respect to the drug. Additional specific responsibilities of sponsors are described elsewhere in this part.

§312.52 Transfer of obligations to a contract research organization.

(a) A sponsor may transfer responsibility for any or all of the obligations set forth in this part to a contract research organization. Any such transfer shall be described in writing. If not all obligations are transferred, the writing is required to describe each of the obligations being assumed by the contract research organization. If all obligations are transferred, a general statement that all obligations have been transferred is acceptable. Any obligation not covered by the written description shall be deemed not to have been transferred.

(b) A contract research organization that assumes any obligation of a sponsor shall comply with the specific regulations in this chapter applicable to this obligation and shall be subject to the same regulatory action as a sponsor for failure to comply with any obligation assumed under these regulations. Thus, all references to "sponsor" in this part apply to a contract research organization to the extent that it assumes one or more obligations of the sponsor.

§312.53 Selecting investigators and monitors.

(a) Selecting investigators. A sponsor shall select only investigators qualified by training and experience as appropriate experts to investigate the drug.

(b) Control of drug. A sponsor shall ship investigational new drugs only to investigators participating in the investigation.

(c) Obtaining information from the investigator. Before permitting an investigator to begin participation in an investigation, the sponsor shall obtain the following:

(1) A signed investigator statement (Form FDA-1572) containing:

(i) The name and address of the investigator;

(ii) The name and code number, if any, of the protocol(s) in the IND identifying the study(ies) to be conducted by the investigator;

(iii) The name and address of any medical school, hospital, or other research facility where the clinical investigation(s) will be conducted;

(iv) The name and address of any clinical laboratory facilities to be used in the study;

(v) The name and address of the IRB that is responsible for review and approval of the study(ies);

(vi) A commitment by the investigator that he or she:

(a) Will conduct the study(ies) in accordance with the relevant, current protocol(s) and will only make changes in a protocol after notifying the sponsor, except when necessary to protect the safety, the rights, or welfare of subjects;

(b) Will comply with all requirements regarding the obligations of clinical investigators and all other pertinent requirements in this part;

(c) Will personally conduct or supervise the described investigation(s);

(d) Will inform any potential subjects that the drugs are being used for investigational purposes and will ensure that the requirements relating to obtaining informed consent (21 CFR part 50) and institutional review board review and approval (21 CFR part 56) are met;

(e) Will report to the sponsor adverse experiences that occur in the course of the investigation(s) in accordance with §312.64;

(f) Has read and understands the information in the investigator's brochure, including the potential risks and side effects of the drug; and

(g) Will ensure that all associates, colleagues, and employees assisting in the conduct of the study(ies) are informed about their obligations in meeting the above commitments.

(vii) A commitment by the investigator that, for an investigation subject to an institutional review requirement under part 56, an IRB that complies with the requirements of that part will be responsible for the initial and continuing review and approval of the clinical investigation and that the investigator will promptly report to the IRB all changes in the research activity and all unanticipated problems involving risks to human subjects or others, and will not make any changes in the research without IRB approval, except where necessary to eliminate apparent immediate hazards to the human subjects.

(viii) A list of the names of the subinvestigators (e.g., research fellows, residents) who will be assisting the investigator in the conduct of the investigation(s).

(2) Curriculum vitae. A curriculum vitae or other statement of qualifications of the investigator showing the education, training, and experience that qualifies the investigator as an expert in the clinical investigation of the drug for the use under investigation.

(3) Clinical protocol. (i) For Phase 1 investigations, a general outline of the planned investigation including the estimated duration of the study and the maximum number of subjects that will be involved.

(ii) For Phase 2 or 3 investigations, an outline of the study protocol including an approximation of the number of subjects to be treated with the drug and the number to be employed as controls, if any; the clinical uses to be investigated; characteristics of subjects by age, sex, and condition; the kind of clinical observations and laboratory tests to be conducted; the estimated duration of the study; and copies or a description of case report forms to be used.

(4) Financial disclosure information. Sufficient accurate financial information to allow the sponsor to submit complete and accurate certification or disclosure statements required under part 54 of this chapter. The sponsor shall obtain a commitment from the clinical investigator to promptly update this information if any relevant changes occur during the course of the investigation and for 1 year following the completion of the study.

(d) Selecting monitors. A sponsor shall select a monitor qualified by training and experience to monitor the progress of the investigation.

[52 FR 8831, Mar. 19, 1987, as amended at 52 FR 23031, June 17, 1987; 61 FR 57280, Nov. 5, 1996; 63 FR 5252, Feb. 2, 1998; 67 FR 9586, Mar. 4, 2002]

§312.54 Emergency research under §50.24 of this chapter.

(a) The sponsor shall monitor the progress of all investigations involving an exception from informed consent under §50.24 of this chapter. When the sponsor receives from the IRB information concerning the public disclosures required by §50.24(a)(7)(ii) and (a)(7)(iii) of this chapter, the sponsor promptly shall submit to the IND file and to Docket Number 95S-0158 in the Dockets Management Branch (HFA-305), Food and Drug Administration, 5630 Fishers Lane, rm. 1061, Rockville, MD 20852, copies of the information that was disclosed, identified by the IND number.

(b) The sponsor also shall monitor such investigations to identify when an IRB determines that it cannot approve the research because it does not meet the criteria in the exception in §50.24(a) of this chapter or

because of other relevant ethical concerns. The sponsor promptly shall provide this information in writing to FDA, investigators who are asked to participate in this or a substantially equivalent clinical investigation, and other IRB's that are asked to review this or a substantially equivalent investigation.

[61 FR 51530, Oct. 2, 1996, as amended at 68 FR 24879, May 9, 2003]

§312.55 Informing investigators.

(a) Before the investigation begins, a sponsor (other than a sponsor-investigator) shall give each participating clinical investigator an investigator brochure containing the information described in §312.23(a)(5).

(b) The sponsor shall, as the overall investigation proceeds, keep each participating investigator informed of new observations discovered by or reported to the sponsor on the drug, particularly with respect to adverse effects and safe use. Such information may be distributed to investigators by means of periodically revised investigator brochures, reprints or published studies, reports or letters to clinical investigators, or other appropriate means. Important safety information is required to be relayed to investigators in accordance with §312.32.

[52 FR 8831, Mar. 19, 1987, as amended at 52 FR 23031, June 17, 1987; 67 FR 9586, Mar. 4, 2002]

§312.56 Review of ongoing investigations.

(a) The sponsor shall monitor the progress of all clinical investigations being conducted under its IND.

(b) A sponsor who discovers that an investigator is not complying with the signed agreement (Form FDA-1572), the general investigational plan, or the requirements of this part or other applicable parts shall promptly either secure compliance or discontinue shipments of the investigational new drug to the investigator and end the investigator's participation in the investigation. If the investigator's participation in the investigation is ended, the sponsor shall require that the investigator dispose of or return the investigational drug in accordance with the requirements of §312.59 and shall notify FDA.

(c) The sponsor shall review and evaluate the evidence relating to the safety and effectiveness of the drug as it is obtained from the investigator. The sponsors shall make such reports to FDA regarding information relevant to the safety of the drug as are required under §312.32. The sponsor shall make annual reports on the progress of the investigation in accordance with §312.33.

(d) A sponsor who determines that its investigational drug presents an unreasonable and significant risk to subjects shall discontinue those investigations that present the risk, notify FDA, all institutional review boards, and all investigators who have at any time participated in the investigation of the discontinuance, assure the disposition of all stocks of the drug outstanding as required by §312.59, and furnish FDA with a full report of the sponsor's actions. The sponsor shall discontinue the investigation as soon as possible, and in no event later than 5 working days after making the determination that the investigation should be discontinued. Upon request, FDA will confer with a sponsor on the need to discontinue an investigation.

[52 FR 8831, Mar. 19, 1987, as amended at 52 FR 23031, June 17, 1987; 67 FR 9586, Mar. 4, 2002]

§312.57 Recordkeeping and record retention.

(a) A sponsor shall maintain adequate records showing the receipt, shipment, or other disposition of the investigational drug. These records are required to include, as appropriate, the name of the investigator to whom the drug is shipped, and the date, quantity, and batch or code mark of each such shipment.

(b) A sponsor shall maintain complete and accurate records showing any financial interest in §54.4(a)(3)(i), (a)(3)(ii), (a)(3)(iii), and (a)(3)(iv) of this chapter paid to clinical investigators by the sponsor of the covered study. A sponsor shall also maintain complete and accurate records concerning all other financial interests of investigators subject to part 54 of this chapter.

(c) A sponsor shall retain the records and reports required by this part for 2 years after a marketing application is approved for the drug; or, if an application is not approved for the drug, until 2 years after shipment and delivery of the drug for investigational use is discontinued and FDA has been so notified.

(d) A sponsor shall retain reserve samples of any test article and reference standard identified in, and used in any of the bioequivalence or bioavailability studies described in, §320.38 or §320.63 of this chapter, and release the reserve samples to FDA upon request, in accordance with, and for the period specified in §320.38.

[52 FR 8831, Mar. 19, 1987, as amended at 52 FR 23031, June 17, 1987; 58 FR 25926,

Apr. 28, 1993; 63 FR 5252, Feb. 2, 1998; 67 FR 9586, Mar. 4, 2002]

§312.58 Inspection of sponsor's records and reports.

(a) FDA inspection. A sponsor shall upon request from any properly authorized officer or employee of the Food and Drug Administration, at reasonable times, permit such officer or employee to have access to and copy and verify any records and reports relating to a clinical investigation conducted under this part. Upon written request by FDA, the sponsor shall submit the records or reports (or copies of them) to FDA. The sponsor shall discontinue shipments of the drug to any investigator who has failed to maintain or make available records or reports of the investigation as required by this part.

(b) Controlled substances. If an investigational new drug is a substance listed in any schedule of the Controlled Substances Act (21 U.S.C. 801; 21 CFR part 1308), records concerning shipment, delivery, receipt, and disposition of the drug, which are required to be kept under this part or other applicable parts of this chapter shall, upon the request of a properly authorized employee of the Drug Enforcement Administration of the U.S. Department of Justice, be made available by the investigator or sponsor to whom the request is made, for inspection and copying. In addition, the sponsor shall assure that adequate precautions are taken, including storage of the investigational drug in a securely locked, substantially constructed cabinet, or other securely locked, substantially constructed enclosure, access to which is limited, to prevent theft or diversion of the substance into illegal channels of distribution.

§312.59 Disposition of unused supply of investigational drug.

The sponsor shall assure the return of all unused supplies of the investigational drug from each individual investigator whose participation in the investigation is discontinued or terminated. The sponsor may authorize alternative disposition of unused supplies of the investigational drug provided this alternative disposition does not expose humans to risks from the drug. The sponsor shall maintain written records of any disposition of the drug in accordance with §312.57.

[52 FR 8831, Mar. 19, 1987, as amended at 52 FR 23031, June 17, 1987; 67 FR 9586, Mar. 4, 2002]

§312.60 General responsibilities of investigators.

An investigator is responsible for ensuring that an investigation is conducted according to the signed investigator statement, the investigational plan, and applicable regulations; for protecting the rights, safety, and welfare of subjects under the investigator's care; and for the control of drugs under investigation. An investigator shall, in accordance with the provisions of part 50 of this chapter, obtain the informed consent of each human subject to whom the drug is administered, except as provided in §§50.23 or 50.24 of this chapter. Additional specific responsibilities of clinical investigators are set forth in this part and in parts 50 and 56 of this chapter.

[52 FR 8831, Mar. 19, 1987, as amended at 61 FR 51530, Oct. 2, 1996]

§312.61 Control of the investigational drug.

An investigator shall administer the drug only to subjects under the investigator's personal supervision or under the supervision of a subinvestigator responsible to the investigator. The investigator shall not supply the investigational drug to any person not authorized under this part to receive it.

§312.62 Investigator recordkeeping and record retention.

(a) Disposition of drug. An investigator is required to maintain adequate records of the disposition of the drug, including dates, quantity, and use by subjects. If the investigation is terminated, suspended, discontinued, or completed, the investigator shall return the unused supplies of the drug to the sponsor, or otherwise provide for disposition of the unused supplies of the drug under §312.59.

(b) Case histories. An investigator is required to prepare and maintain adequate and accurate case histories that record all observations and other data pertinent to the investigation on each individual administered the investigational drug or employed as a control in the investigation. Case histories include the case report forms and supporting data including, for example, signed and dated consent forms and medical records including, for example, progress notes of the physician, the individual's hospital chart(s), and the nurses' notes. The case history for each individual shall document that informed consent was obtained prior to participation in the study.

(c) Record retention. An investigator shall retain records required to be maintained under this part for a period of 2 years following the date a marketing application is approved for the drug for the indication for which it is being investigated; or, if no application is to be filed or if the application is not approved for such indication, until 2 years after the investigation is discontinued and FDA is notified.

[52 FR 8831, Mar. 19, 1987, as amended at 52 FR 23031, June 17, 1987; 61 FR 57280, Nov. 5, 1996; 67 FR 9586, Mar. 4, 2002]

§312.64 Investigator reports.

(a) Progress reports. The investigator shall furnish all reports to the sponsor of the drug who is responsible for collecting and evaluating the results obtained. The sponsor is required under §312.33 to submit annual reports to FDA on the progress of the clinical investigations.

(b) Safety reports. An investigator shall promptly report to the sponsor any adverse effect that may reasonably be regarded as caused by, or probably caused by, the drug. If the adverse effect is alarming, the investigator shall report the adverse effect immediately.

(c) Final report. An investigator shall provide the sponsor with an adequate report shortly after completion of the investigator's participation in the investigation.

(d) Financial disclosure reports. The clinical investigator shall provide the sponsor with sufficient accurate financial information to allow an applicant to submit complete and accurate certification or disclosure statements as required under part 54 of this chapter. The clinical investigator shall promptly update this information if any relevant changes occur during the course of the investigation and for 1 year following the completion of the study.

[52 FR 8831, Mar. 19, 1987, as amended at 52 FR 23031, June 17, 1987; 63 FR 5252, Feb. 2, 1998; 67 FR 9586, Mar. 4, 2002]

§312.66 Assurance of IRB review.

An investigator shall assure that an IRB that complies with the requirements set forth in part 56 will be responsible for the initial and continuing review and approval of the proposed clinical study. The investigator shall also assure that he or she will promptly report to the IRB all changes in the research activity and all unanticipated problems involving risk to human subjects or others, and that he or she will not make any changes in the research without IRB approval, except where necessary to eliminate apparent immediate hazards to human subjects.

[52 FR 8831, Mar. 19, 1987, as amended at 52 FR 23031, June 17, 1987; 67 FR 9586, Mar. 4, 2002]

§312.68 Inspection of investigator's records and reports.

An investigator shall upon request from any properly authorized officer or employee of FDA, at reasonable times, permit such officer or employee to have access to, and copy and verify any records or reports made by the investigator pursuant to §312.62. The investigator is not required to divulge subject names unless the records of particular individuals require a more detailed study of the cases, or unless there is reason to believe that the records do not represent actual case studies, or do not represent actual results obtained.

§312.69 Handling of controlled substances.

If the investigational drug is subject to the Controlled Substances Act, the investigator shall take adequate precautions, including storage of the investigational drug in a securely locked, substantially constructed cabinet, or other securely locked, substantially constructed enclosure, access to which is limited, to prevent theft or diversion of the substance into illegal channels of distribution.

§312.70 Disqualification of a clinical investigator.

(a) If FDA has information indicating that an investigator (including a sponsor-investigator) has repeatedly or deliberately failed to comply with the requirements of this part, part 50, or part 56 of this chapter, or has submitted to FDA or to the sponsor false information in any required report, the Center for Drug Evaluation and Research or the Center for Biologics Evaluation and Research will furnish the investigator written notice of the matter complained of and offer the investigator an opportunity to explain the matter in writing, or, at the option of the investigator, in an informal conference. If an explanation is offered but not accepted by the Center for Drug Evaluation and Research or the Center for Biologics Evaluation and Research, the investigator will be given an opportunity for a regulatory hearing under part 16 on the question of whether the investigator is entitled to receive investigational new drugs.

(b) After evaluating all available information, including any explanation presented by the investigator, if the Commissioner determines that the investigator has repeatedly or deliberately failed to comply with the requirements of this part, part 50, or part 56 of this chapter, or has deliberately or repeatedly submitted false information to FDA or to the sponsor in any required report, the Commissioner will notify the investigator and the sponsor of any investigation in which the investigator has been named as a participant that the investigator is not entitled to receive investigational drugs. The notification will provide a statement of basis for such determination.

(c) Each IND and each approved application submitted under part 314 containing data reported by an investigator who has been determined to be ineligible to receive investigational drugs will be examined to determine whether the investigator has submitted unreliable data that are essential to the continuation of the investigation or essential to the approval of any marketing application.

(d) If the Commissioner determines, after the unreliable data submitted by the investigator are eliminated from consideration, that the data remaining are inadequate to support a conclusion that it is reasonably safe to continue the investigation, the Commissioner will notify the sponsor who shall have an opportunity for a regulatory hearing under part 16. If a danger to the public health exists, however, the Commissioner shall terminate the IND immediately and notify the sponsor of the determination. In such case, the sponsor shall have an opportunity for a regulatory hearing before FDA under part 16 on the question of whether the IND should be reinstated.

(e) If the Commissioner determines, after the unreliable data submitted by the investigator are eliminated from consideration, that the continued approval of the drug product for which the data were submitted cannot be justified, the Commissioner will proceed to withdraw approval of the drug product in accordance with the applicable provisions of the act.

(f) An investigator who has been determined to be ineligible to receive investigational drugs may be reinstated as eligible when the Commissioner determines that the investigator has presented adequate assurances that the investigator will employ investigatioal drugs solely in compliance with the provisions of this part and of parts 50 and 56.

[52 FR 8831, Mar. 19, 1987, as amended at 52 FR 23031, June 17, 1987; 55 FR 11580, Mar. 29, 1990; 62 FR 46876, Sept. 5, 1997; 67 FR 9586, Mar. 4, 2002]

Subpart E—Drugs Intended to Treat Life-threatening and Severely-debilitating Illnesses

Authority: 21 U.S.C. 351, 352, 353, 355, 371; 42 U.S.C. 262.

Source: 53 FR 41523, Oct. 21, 1988, unless otherwise noted.

§312.80 Purpose.

The purpose of this section is to establish procedures designed to expedite the development, evaluation, and marketing of new therapies intended to treat persons with life-threatening and severely-debilitating illnesses, especially where no satisfactory alternative therapy exists. As stated §314.105(c) of this chapter, while the statutory standards of safety and effectiveness apply to all drugs, the many kinds of drugs that are subject to them, and the wide range of uses for those drugs, demand flexibility in applying the standards. The Food and Drug Administration (FDA) has determined that it is appropriate to exercise the broadest flexibility in applying the statutory standards, while preserving appropriate guarantees for safety and effectiveness. These procedures reflect the recognition that physicians and patients are generally willing to accept greater risks or side effects from products that treat life-threatening and severely-debilitating illnesses, than they would accept from products that treat less serious illnesses. These procedures also reflect the recognition that the benefits of the drug need to be evaluated in light of the severity of the disease being treated. The procedure outlined in this section should be interpreted consistent with that purpose.

§312.81 Scope.

This section applies to new drug and biological products that are being studied for their safety and effectiveness in treating life-threatening or severely-debilitating diseases.

(a) For purposes of this section, the term "life-threatening" means:

(1) Diseases or conditions where the likelihood of death is high unless the course of the disease is interrupted; and

(2) Diseases or conditions with potentially fatal outcomes, where the end point of clinical trial analysis is survival.

(b) For purposes of this section, the term "severely debilitating" means diseases or conditions that cause major irreversible morbidity.

(c) Sponsors are encouraged to consult with FDA on the applicability of these procedures to specific products.

[53 FR 41523, Oct. 21, 1988, as amended at 64 FR 401, Jan. 5, 1999]

§312.82 Early consultation.

For products intended to treat life-threatening or severely-debilitating illnesses, sponsors may request to meet with FDA-reviewing officials early in the drug development process to review and reach agreement on the design of necessary preclinical and clinical studies. Where appropriate, FDA will invite to such meetings one or more outside expert scientific consultants or advisory committee members. To the extent FDA resources permit, agency reviewing officials will honor requests for such meetings

(a) Pre-investigational new drug (IND) meetings. Prior to the submission of the initial IND, the sponsor may request a meeting with FDA-reviewing officials. The primary purpose of this meeting is to review and reach agreement on the design of animal studies needed to initiate human testing. The meeting may also provide an opportunity for discussing the scope and design of phase 1 testing, plans for studying the drug product in pediatric populations, and the best approach for presentation and formatting of data in the IND.

(b) End-of-phase 1 meetings. When data from phase 1 clinical testing are available, the sponsor may again request a meeting with FDA-reviewing officials. The primary purpose of this meeting is to review and reach agreement on the design of phase 2 controlled clinical trials, with the goal that such testing will be adequate to provide sufficient data on the drug's safety and effectiveness to support a decision on its approvability for marketing, and to discuss the need for, as well as the design and timing of, studies of the drug in pediatric patients. For drugs for life-threatening diseases, FDA will provide its best judgment, at that time, whether pediatric studies will be required and whether their submission will be deferred until after approval. The procedures outlined in §312.47(b)(1) with respect to end-of-phase 2 conferences, including documentation of agreements reached, would also be used for end-of-phase 1 meetings.

[53 FR 41523, Oct. 21, 1988, as amended at 63 FR 66669, Dec. 2, 1998]

§312.83 Treatment protocols.

If the preliminary analysis of phase 2 test results appears promising, FDA may ask the sponsor to submit a treatment protocol to be reviewed under the procedures and criteria listed in §§312.34 and 312.35. Such a treatment protocol, if requested and granted, would normally remain in effect while the complete data necessary for a marketing application are being assembled by the sponsor and reviewed by FDA (unless grounds exist for clinical hold of ongoing protocols, as provided in §312.42(b)(3)(ii)).

§312.84 Risk-benefit analysis in review of marketing applications for drugs to treat life-threatening and severely-debilitating illnesses.

(a) FDA's application of the statutory standards for marketing approval shall recognize the need for a medical risk-benefit judgment in making the final decision on approvability. As part of this evaluation, consistent with the statement of purpose in §312.80, FDA will consider whether the benefits of the drug outweigh the known and potential risks of the drug and the need to answer remaining questions about risks and benefits of the drug, taking into consideration the

severity of the disease and the absence of satisfactory alternative therapy.

(b) In making decisions on whether to grant marketing approval for products that have been the subject of an end-of-phase 1 meeting under §312.82, FDA will usually seek the advice of outside expert scientific consultants or advisory committees. Upon the filing of such a marketing application under §314.101 or part 601 of this chapter, FDA will notify the members of the relevant standing advisory committee of the application's filing and its availability for review.

(c) If FDA concludes that the data presented are not sufficient for marketing approval, FDA will issue (for a drug) a not approvable letter pursuant to §314.120 of this chapter, or (for a biologic) a deficiencies letter consistent with the biological product licensing procedures. Such letter, in describing the deficiencies in the application, will address why the results of the research design agreed to under §312.82, or in subsequent meetings, have not provided sufficient evidence for marketing approval. Such letter will also describe any recommendations made by the advisory committee regarding the application.

(d) Marketing applications submitted under the procedures contained in this section will be subject to the requirements and procedures contained in part 314 or part 600 of this chapter, as well as those in this subpart.

§312.85 Phase 4 studies.

Concurrent with marketing approval, FDA may seek agreement from the sponsor to conduct certain postmarketing (phase 4) studies to delineate additional information about the drug's risks, benefits, and optimal use. These studies could include, but would not be limited to, studying different doses or schedules of administration than were used in phase 2 studies, use of the drug in other patient populations or other stages of the disease, or use of the drug over a longer period of time.

§312.86 Focused FDA regulatory research.

At the discretion of the agency, FDA may undertake focused regulatory research on critical rate-limiting aspects of the preclinical, chemical/manufacturing, and clinical phases of drug development and evaluation. When initiated, FDA will undertake such research efforts as a means for meeting a public health need in facilitating the development of therapies to treat life-threatening or severely debilitating illnesses.

§312.87 Active monitoring of conduct and evaluation of clinical trials.

For drugs covered under this section, the Commissioner and other agency officials will monitor the progress of the conduct and evaluation of clinical trials and be involved in facilitating their appropriate progress.

§312.88 Safeguards for patient safety.

All of the safeguards incorporated within parts 50, 56, 312, 314, and 600 of this chapter designed to ensure the safety of clinical testing and the safety of products following marketing approval apply to drugs covered by this section. This includes the requirements for informed consent (part 50 of this chapter) and institutional review boards (part 56 of this chapter). These safeguards further include the review of animal studies prior to initial human testing (§312.23), and

the monitoring of adverse drug experiences through the requirements of IND safety reports (§312.32), safety update reports during agency review of a marketing application (§314.50 of this chapter), and postmarketing adverse reaction reporting (§314.80 of this chapter).

Subpart F—Miscellaneous

§312.110 Import and export requirements.

(a) Imports. An investigational new drug offered for import into the United States complies with the requirements of this part if it is subject to an IND that is in effect for it under §312.40 and: (1) The consignee in the United States is the sponsor of the IND; (2) the consignee is a qualified investigator named in the IND; or (3) the consignee is the domestic agent of a foreign sponsor, is responsible for the control and distribution of the investigational drug, and the IND identifies the consignee and describes what, if any, actions the consignee will take with respect to the investigational drug.

(b) Exports. An investigational new drug intended for export from the United States complies with the requirements of this part as follows:

(1) If an IND is in effect for the drug under §312.40 and each person who receives the drug is an investigator named in the application; or

(2) If FDA authorizes shipment of the drug for use in a clinical investigation. Authorization may be obtained as follows:

(i) Through submission to the International Affairs Staff (HFY-50), Associate Commissioner for Health Affairs, Food and Drug Administra-tion, 5600 Fishers Lane, Rockville, MD 20857, of a written request from the person that seeks to export the drug. A request must provide adequate information about the drug to satisfy FDA that the drug is appropriate for the proposed investigational use in humans, that the drug will be used for investigational purposes only, and that the drug may be legally used by that consignee in the importing country for the proposed investigational use. The request shall specify the quantity of the drug to be shipped per shipment and the frequency of expected shipments. If FDA authorizes exportation under this paragraph, the agency shall concurrently notify the government of the importing country of such authorization.

(ii) Through submission to the International Affairs Staff (HFY-50), Associate Commissioner for Health Affairs, Food and Drug Administra-tion, 5600 Fishers Lane, Rockville, MD 20857, of a formal request from an authorized official of the government of the country to which the drug is proposed to be shipped. A request must specify that the foreign government has adequate information about the drug and the proposed investigational use, that the drug will be used for investigational purposes only, and that the foreign government is satisfied that the drug may legally be used by the intended consignee in that country. Such a request shall specify the quantity of drug to be shipped per shipment and the frequency of expected shipments.

(iii) Authorization to export an investigational drug under paragraph (b)(2)(i) or (ii) of this section may be revoked by FDA if the agency finds that the conditions underlying its authorization are not longer met.

(3) This paragraph applies only where the drug is to be used for the purpose of clinical investigation.

(4) This paragraph does not apply to the export of new drugs (including biological products, antibiotic drugs, and insulin) approved or authorized for export under section 802 of the act (21 U.S.C. 382) or section 351(h)(1)(A) of the Public Health Service Act (42 U.S.C. 262(h)(1)(A)).

[52 FR 8831, Mar. 19, 1987, as amended at 52 FR 23031, June 17, 1987; 64 FR 401, Jan. 5, 1999; 67 FR 9586, Mar. 4, 2002]

§312.120 Foreign clinical studies not conducted under an IND.

(a) Introduction. This section describes the criteria for acceptance by FDA of foreign clinical studies not conducted under an IND. In general, FDA accepts such studies provided they are well designed, well conducted, performed by qualified investigators, and conducted in accordance with ethical principles acceptable to the world community. Studies meeting these criteria may be utilized to support clinical investigations in the United States and/or marketing approval. Marketing approval of a new drug based solely on foreign clinical data is governed by §314.106.

(b) Data submissions. A sponsor who wishes to rely on a foreign clinical study to support an IND or to support an application for marketing approval shall submit to FDA the following information:

(1) A description of the investigator's qualifications;

(2) A description of the research facilities;

(3) A detailed summary of the protocol and results of the study, and, should FDA request, case records maintained by the investigator or additional background data such as hospital or other institutional records;

(4) A description of the drug substance and drug product used in the study, including a description of components, formulation, specifications, and bioavailability of the specific drug product used in the clinical study, if available; and

(5) If the study is intended to support the effectiveness of a drug product, information showing that the study is adequate and well controlled under §314.126.

(c) Conformance with ethical principles. (1) Foreign clinical research is required to have been conducted in accordance with the ethical principles stated in the "Declaration of Helsinki" (see paragraph (c)(4) of this section) or the laws and regulations of the country in which the research was conducted, whichever represents the greater protection of the individual.

(2) For each foreign clinical study submitted under this section, the sponsor shall explain how the research conformed to the ethical principles contained in the "Declaration of Helsinki" or the foreign country's standards, whichever were used. If the foreign country's standards were used, the sponsor shall explain in detail how those standards differ from the "Declaration of Helsinki" and how they offer greater protection.

(3) When the research has been approved by an independent review committee, the sponsor shall submit to FDA documentation of such review and approval, including the names and qualifications of the members of the committee. In this regard, a "review committee" means a committee composed of scientists and, where practicable, individuals who are otherwise qualified (e.g., other health professionals or laymen). The investigator may not vote on any aspect of the review of his or her protocol by a review committee.

(4) The "Declaration of Helsinki" states as follows:

Recommendations Guiding Physicians in Biomedical Research Involving Human Subjects

Introduction

It is the mission of the physician to safeguard the health of the people. His or her knowledge and conscience are dedicated to the fulfillment of this mission.

The Declaration of Geneva of the World Medical Association binds the physician with the words, "The health of my patient will be my first consideration," and the International Code of Medical Ethics declares that, "A physician shall act only in the patient's interest when providing medical care which might have the effect of weakening the physical and mental condition of the patient."

The purpose of biomedical research involving human subjects must be to improve diagnostic, therapeutic and prophylactic procedures and the understanding of the aetiology and pathogenesis of disease.

In current medical practice most diagnostic, therapeutic or prophylactic procedures involve hazards. This applies especially to biomedical research.

Medical progress is based on research which ultimately must rest in part on experimentation involving human subjects.

273

In the field of biomedical research a fundamental distinction must be recognized between medical research in which the aim is essentially diagnostic or therapeutic for a patient, and medical research, the essential object of which is purely scientific and without implying direct diagnostic or therapeutic value to the person subjected to the research.

Special caution must be exercised in the conduct of research which may affect the environment, and the welfare of animals used for research must be respected.

Because it is essential that the results of laboratory experiments be applied to human beings to further scientific knowledge and to help suffering humanity, the World Medical Association has prepared the following recommendations as a guide to every physician in biomedical research involving human subjects. They should be kept under review in the future. It must be stressed that the standards as drafted are only a guide to physicians all over the world. Physicians are not relieved from criminal, civil and ethical responsibilities under the laws of their own countries.

I. Basic Principles

1. Biomedical research involving human subjects must conform to generally accepted scientific principles and should be based on adequately performed laboratory and animal experimentation and on a thorough knowledge of the scientific literature.

2. The design and performance of each experimental procedure involving human subjects should be clearly formulated in an experimental protocol which should be transmitted for consideration, comment and guidance to a specially appointed committee independent of the investigator and the sponsor provided that this independent committee is in conformity with the laws and regulations of the country in which the research experiment is performed.

3. Biomedical research involving human subjects should be conducted only by scientifically qualified persons and under the supervision of a clinically competent medical person. The responsibility for the human subject must always rest with a medically qualified person and never rest on the subject of the research, even though the subject has given his or her consent.

4. Biomedical research involving human subjects cannot legitimately be carried out unless the importance of the objective is in proportion to the inherent risk to the subject.

5. Every biomedical research project involving human subjects should be preceded by careful assessment of predictable risks in comparison with foreseeable benefits to the subject or to others. Concern for the interests of the subject must always prevail over the interests of science and society.

6. The right of the research subject to safeguard his or her integrity must always be respected. Every precaution should be taken to respect the privacy of the subject and to minimize the impact of the study on the subject's physical and mental integrity and on the personality of the subject.

7. Physicians should abstain from engaging in research projects involving human subjects unless they are satisfied that the hazards involved are believed to be predictable. Physicians should cease any investigation if the hazards are found to outweigh the potential benefits.

8. In publication of the results of his or her research, the physician is obliged to preserve

the accuracy of the results. Reports of experimentation not in accordance with the principles laid down in this Declaration should not be accepted for publication.

9. In any research on human beings, each potential subject must be adequately informed of the aims, methods, anticipated benefits and potential hazards of the study and the discomfort it may entail. He or she should be informed that he or she is at liberty to abstain from participation in the study and that he or she is free to withdraw his or her consent to participation at any time. The physician should then obtain the subject's freely-given informed consent, preferably in writing.

10. When obtaining informed consent for the research project the physician should be particularly cautious if the subject is in a dependent relationship to him or her or may consent under duress. In that case the informed consent should be obtained by a physician who is not engaged in the investigation and who is completely independent of this official relationship.

11. In case of legal incompetence, informed consent should be obtained from the legal guardian in accordance with national legislation. Where physical or mental incapacity makes it impossible to obtain informed consent, or when the subject is a minor, permission from the responsible relative replaces that of the subject in accordance with national legislation.

Whenever the minor child is in fact able to give a consent, the minor's consent must be obtained in addition to the consent of the minor's legal guardian.

12. The research protocol should always contain a statement of the ethical considerations involved and should indicate that the principles enunciated in the present Declaration are complied with.

II. Medical Research Combined with Professional Care (Clinical Research)

1. In the treatment of the sick person, the physician must be free to use a new diagnostic and therapeutic measure, if in his or her judgment it offers hope of saving life, reestablishing health or alleviating suffering.

2. The potential benefits, hazards and discomfort of a new method should be weighed against the advantages of the best current diagnostic and therapeutic methods.

3. In any medical study, every patient—including those of a control group, if any—should be assured of the best proven diagnostic and therapeutic method.

4. The refusal of the patient to participate in a study must never interfere with the physician-patient relationship.

5. If the physician considers it essential not to obtain informed consent, the specific reasons for this proposal should be stated in the experimental protocol for transmission to the independent committee (I, 2).

6. The physician can combine medical research with professional care, the objective being the acquisition of new medical knowledge, only to the extent that medical research is justified by its potential diagnostic or therapeutic value for the patient.

III. Non-Therapeutic Biomedical Research Involving Human Subjects (Non-Clinical Biomedical Research)

1. In the purely scientific application of medical research carried out on a human being, it is the duty of the physician to remain the pro-

tector of the life and health of that person on whom biomedical research is being carried out.

2. The subjects should be volunteers—either healthy persons or patients for whom the experimental design is not related to the patient's illness.

3. The investigator or the investigating team should discontinue the research if in his/her or their judgment it may, if continued, be harmful to the individual.

4. In research on man, the interest of science and society should never take precedence over considerations related to the well-being of the subject.

[52 FR 8831, Mar. 19, 1987, as amended at 52 FR 23031, June 17, 1987; 56 FR 22113, May 14, 1991; 64 FR 401, Jan. 5, 1999; 67 FR 9586, Mar. 4, 2002]

§312.130 Availability for public disclosure of data and information in an IND.

(a) The existence of an investigational new drug application will not be disclosed by FDA unless it has previously been publicly disclosed or acknowledged.

(b) The availability for public disclosure of all data and information in an investigational new drug application for a new drug will be handled in accordance with the provisions established in §314.430 for the confidentiality of data and information in applications submitted in part 314. The availability for public disclosure of all data and information in an investigational new drug application for a biological product will be governed by the provisions of §§601.50 and 601.51.

(c) Notwithstanding the provisions of §314.430, FDA shall disclose upon request to an individual to whom an investigational new drug has been given a copy of any IND safety report relating to the use in the individual.

(d) The availability of information required to be publicly disclosed for investigations involving an exception from informed consent under §50.24 of this chapter will be handled as follows: Persons wishing to request the publicly disclosable information in the IND that was required to be filed in Docket Number 95S-0158 in the Dockets Management Branch (HFA-305), Food and Drug Administration, 5630 Fishers Lane, rm. 1061, Rockville, MD 20852, shall submit a request under the Freedom of Information Act.

[52 FR 8831, Mar. 19, 1987. Redesignated at 53 FR 41523, Oct. 21, 1988, as amended at 61 FR 51530, Oct. 2, 1996; 64 FR 401, Jan. 5, 1999; 68 FR 24879, May 9, 2003]

§312.140 Address for correspondence.

(a) Except as provided in paragraph (b) of this section, a sponsor shall send an initial IND submission to the Central Document Room, Center for Drug Evaluation and Research, Food and Drug Administration, Park Bldg., Rm. 214, 12420 Parklawn Dr., Rockville, MD 20852. On receiving the IND, FDA will inform the sponsor which one of the divisions in the Center for Drug Evaluation and Research or the Center for Biologics Evaluation and Research is responsible for the IND. Amendments, reports, and other correspondence relating to matters covered by the IND should be directed to the appropriate division. The outside wrapper of each submission shall state what is contained in the submission, for example, "IND Application", "Protocol Amendment", etc.

(b) Applications for the products listed below should be submitted to the Division of Biological Investigational New Drugs (HFB-230), Center for Biologics Evaluation and Research, Food and Drug Administration, 8800 Rockville Pike, Bethesda, MD 20892. (1) Products subject to the licensing provisions of the Public Health Service Act of July 1, 1944 (58 Stat. 682, as amended (42 U.S.C. 201 et seq.)) or subject to part 600; (2) ingredients packaged together with containers intended for the collection, processing, or storage of blood or blood components; (3) urokinase products; (4) plasma volume expanders and hydroxyethyl starch for leukapheresis; and (5) coupled antibodies, i.e., products that consist of an antibody component coupled with a drug or radionuclide component in which both components provide a pharmacological effect but the biological component determines the site of action.

(c) All correspondence relating to biological products for human use which are also radioactive drugs shall be submitted to the Division of Oncology and Radiopharmaceutical Drug Products (HFD-150), Center for Drug Evaluation and Research, Food and Drug Administration, 5600 Fishers Lane, Rockville, MD 20857, except that applications for coupled antibodies shall be submitted in accordance with paragraph (b) of this section.

(d) All correspondence relating to export of an investigational drug under §312.110(b)(2) shall be submitted to the International Affairs Staff (HFY-50), Office of Health Affairs, Food and Drug Administration, 5600 Fishers Lane, Rockville, MD 20857.

[52 FR 8831, Mar. 19, 1987, as amended at 52 FR 23031, June 17, 1987; 55 FR 11580, Mar. 29, 1990; 67 FR 9586, Mar. 4, 2002]

§312.145 Guidance documents.

(a) FDA has made available guidance documents under §10.115 of this chapter to help you to comply with certain requirements of this part.

(b) The Center for Drug Evaluation and Research (CDER) and the Center for Biologics Evaluation and Research (CBER) maintain lists of guidance documents that apply to the centers' regulations. The lists are maintained on the Internet and are published annually in the FEDERAL REGISTER. A request for a copy of the CDER list should be directed to the Office of Training and Communications, Division of Communications Management, Drug Information Branch (HFD-210), Center for Drug Evaluation and Research, Food and Drug Administration, 5600 Fishers Lane, Rockville, MD 20857. A request for a copy of the CBER list should be directed to the Office of Communication, Training, and Manufacturers Assistance (HFM-40), Center for Biologics Evaluation and Research, Food and Drug Administration, 1401 Rockville Pike, Rockville, MD 20852-1448.

Subpart G—Drugs for Investigational Use in Laboratory Research Animals or In Vitro Tests

§312.160 Drugs for investigational use in laboratory research animals or in vitro tests.

(a) Authorization to ship. (1)(i) A person may ship a drug intended solely for tests in vitro or in animals used only for laboratory research purposes if it is labeled as follows:

"CAUTION: Contains a new drug for investigational use only in laboratory research animals, or for tests in vitro. Not for use in humans."

(ii) A person may ship a biological product for investigational in vitro diagnostic use that is listed in §312.2(b)(2)(ii) if it is labeled as follows:

"CAUTION: Contains a biological product for investigational in vitro diagnostic tests only."

(2) A person shipping a drug under paragraph (a) of this section shall use due diligence to assure that the consignee is regularly engaged in conducting such tests and that the shipment of the new drug will actually be used for tests in vitro or in animals used only for laboratory research.

(3) A person who ships a drug under paragraph (a) of this section shall maintain adequate records showing the name and post office address of the expert to whom the drug is shipped and the date, quantity, and batch or code mark of each shipment and delivery. Records of shipments under paragraph (a)(1)(i) of this section are to be maintained for a period of 2 years after the shipment. Records and reports of data and shipments under paragraph (a)(1)(ii) of this section are to be maintained in accordance with §312.57(b). The person who ships the drug shall upon request from any properly authorized officer or employee of the Food and Drug Administration, at reasonable times, permit such officer or employee to have access to and copy and verify records required to be maintained under this section.

(b) Termination of authorization to ship. FDA may terminate authorization to ship a drug under this section if it finds that:

(1) The sponsor of the investigation has failed to comply with any of the conditions for shipment established under this section; or

(2) The continuance of the investigation is unsafe or otherwise contrary to the public interest or the drug is used for purposes other than bona fide scientific investigation. FDA will notify the person shipping the drug of its finding and invite immediate correction. If correction is not immediately made, the person shall have an opportunity for a regulatory hearing before FDA pursuant to part 16.

(c) Disposition of unused drug. The person who ships the drug under paragraph (a) of this section shall assure the return of all unused supplies of the drug from individual investigators whenever the investigation discontinues or the investigation is terminated. The person who ships the drug may authorize in writing alternative disposition of unused supplies of the drug provided this alternative disposition does not expose humans to risks from the drug, either directly or indirectly (e.g., through food-producing animals). The shipper shall maintain records of any alternative disposition.

[52 FR 8831, Mar. 19, 1987, as amended at 52 FR 23031, June 17, 1987. Redesignated at 53 FR 41523, Oct. 21, 1988; 67 FR 9586, Mar. 4, 2002]

TITLE 21—FOOD AND DRUGS

**Chapter I: Food and Drug Administration,
Department of Health and Human Services
Subchapter D: Drugs for Human Use**

PART 600

Biological Products: General

Authority: 21 U.S.C. 321, 351, 352, 353, 355, 360, 360i, 371, 374; 42 U.S.C. 216, 262, 263, 263a, 264, 300aa–25. Cross References:

For U.S. Customs Service regulations relating to viruses, serums, and toxins, see 19 CFR 12.21–12.23. For U.S. Postal Service regulations relating to the admissibility to the United States mails see parts 124 and 125 of the Domestic Mail Manual, that is incorporated by reference in 39 CFR part 111.

Subpart A—General Provisions

§600.3 **Definitions.** As used in this subchapter:

(a) Act means the Public Health Service Act (58 Stat. 682), approved July 1, 1944.

(b) Secretary means the Secretary of Health and Human Services and any other officer or employee of the Department of Health and Human Services to whom the authority involved has been delegated.

(c) Commissioner of Food and Drugs means the Commissioner of the Food and Drug Administration.

(d) Center for Biologics Evaluation and Research means Center for Biologics Evaluation and Research of the Food and Drug Administration.

(e) State means a State or the District of Columbia, Puerto Rico, or the Virgin Islands.

(f) Possession includes among other possessions, Puerto Rico and the Virgin Islands.

(g) Products includes biological products and trivalent organic arsenicals.

(h) Biological product means any virus, therapeutic serum, toxin, antitoxin, or analogous product applicable to the prevention, treatment or cure of diseases or injuries of man:

(1) A virus is interpreted to be a product containing the minute living cause of an infectious disease and includes but is not limited to filterable viruses, bacteria, rickettsia, fungi, and protozoa.

(2) A therapeutic serum is a product obtained from blood by removing the clot or clot components and the blood cells.

(3) A toxin is a product containing a soluble substance poisonous to laboratory animals or to man in doses of 1 milliliter or less (or equivalent in weight) of the product, and having the property, following the injection of non-fatal doses into an animal, of causing to be produced therein another soluble substance which specifically neutralizes the poisonous substance and which is demonstrable in the serum of the animal thus immunized.

(4) An antitoxin is a product containing the soluble substance in serum or other body fluid of an immunized animal which specifically neutralizes the toxin against which the animal is immune.

(5) A product is analogous:

(i) To a virus if prepared from or with a virus or agent actually or potentially infectious, without regard to the degree of virulence or toxicogenicity of the specific strain used.

(ii) To a therapeutic serum, if composed of whole blood or plasma or containing some organic constituent or product other than a hormone or an amino acid, derived from whole blood, plasma, or serum.

(iii) To a toxin or antitoxin, if intended, irrespective of its source of origin, to be applicable to the prevention, treatment, or cure of disease or injuries of man through a specific immune process.

(i) Trivalent organic arsenicals means arsphenamine and its derivatives (or any other trivalent organic arsenic compound) applicable to the prevention, treatment, or cure of diseases or injuries of man.

(j) A product is deemed applicable to the prevention, treatment, or cure of diseases or injuries of man irrespective of the mode of administration or application recommended, including use when intended through administration or application to a person as an aid in diagnosis, or in evaluating the degree of susceptibility or immunity possessed by a person, and including also any other use for purposes of diagnosis if the diagnostic substance so used is prepared from or with the aid of a biological product.

(k) Proper name, as applied to a product, means the name designated in the license for use upon each package of the product.

(l) Dating period means the period beyond which the product cannot be expected beyond reasonable doubt to yield its specific results.

(m) Expiration date means the calendar month and year, and where applicable, the day and hour, that the dating period ends.

(n) The word standards means specifications and procedures applicable to an establishment or to the manufacture or release of products, which are prescribed in this subchapter or established in the biologics license application designed to insure the continued safety, purity, and potency of such products.

(o) The word continued as applied to the safety, purity and potency of products is interpreted to apply to the dating period.

(p) The word safety means the relative freedom from harmful effect to persons affected, directly or indirectly, by a product when prudently administered, taking into consideration the character of the product in relation to the condition of the recipient at the time.

(q) The word sterility is interpreted to mean freedom from viable contaminating microorganisms, as determined by the tests prescribed in §610.12 of this chapter.

(r) Purity means relative freedom from extraneous matter in the finished product, whether or not harmful to the recipient or deleterious to the product. Purity includes but is not limited to relative freedom from residual moisture or other volatile substances and pyrogenic substances.

(s) The word potency is interpreted to mean the specific ability or capacity of the product, as indicated by appropriate laboratory tests or by adequately controlled clinical data obtained through the administration of the product in the manner intended, to effect a given result.

(t) Manufacturer means any legal person or entity engaged in the manufacture of a product subject to license under the act; "Manufacturer" also includes any legal person or entity who is an applicant for a license where the applicant assumes responsibility for compliance with the applicable product and establishment standards.

(u) Manufacture means all steps in propagation or manufacture and preparation of products and includes but is not limited to filling, testing, labeling, packaging, and storage by the manufacturer.

(v) Location includes all buildings, appurtenances, equipment and animals used, and personnel engaged by a manufacturer within a particular area designated by an address adequate for identification.

(w) Establishment has the same meaning as "facility" in section 351 of the Public Health Service Act and includes all locations.

(x) Lot means that quantity of uniform material identified by the manufacturer as having been thoroughly mixed in a single vessel.

(y) A filling refers to a group of final containers identical in all respects, which have been filled with the same product from the same bulk lot without any change that will affect the integrity of the filling assembly.

(z) Process refers to a manufacturing step that is performed on the product itself which may affect its safety, purity or potency, in contrast to such manufacturing steps which do not affect intrinsically the safety, purity or potency of the product.

(aa) Selling agent or distributor means any person engaged in the unrestricted distribution, other than by sale at retail, of products subject to license.

(bb) Container (referred to also as "final container") is the immediate unit, bottle, vial, ampule, tube, or other receptacle containing the product as distributed for sale, barter, or exchange.

(cc) Package means the immediate carton, receptacle, or wrapper, including all labeling matter therein and thereon, and the contents of the one or more enclosed containers. If no package, as defined in the preceding sentence, is used, the container shall be deemed to be the package.

(dd) Label means any written, printed, or graphic matter on the container or package or any such matter clearly visible through the immediate carton, receptacle, or wrapper.

(ee) Radioactive biological product means a biological product which is labeled with a radionuclide or intended solely to be labeled with a radionuclide.

(ff) Amendment is the submission of information to a pending license application or supplement, to revise or modify the application as originally submitted.

(gg) Supplement is a request to the Director, Center for Biologics Evaluation and Research, to approve a change in an approved license application.

(hh) Distributed means the biological product has left the control of the licensed manufacturer.

(ii) Control means having responsibility for maintaining the continued safety, purity, and potency of the product and for compliance with applicable product and establishment standards, and for compliance with current good manufacturing practices.

[38 FR 32048, Nov. 20, 1973, as amended at 40 FR 31313, July 25, 1975; 55 FR 11014, Mar. 26, 1990; 61 FR 24232, May 14, 1996; 62 FR 39901, July 24, 1997; 64 FR 56449, Oct. 20, 1999; 65 FR 66634, Nov. 7, 2000]

Subpart B—Establishment Standards

§600.10 Personnel.

(a) [Reserved]

(b) Personnel. Personnel shall have capabilities commensurate with their assigned functions, a thorough understanding of the manufacturing operations which they perform, the necessary training and experience relating to individual products, and adequate information concerning the application of the pertinent provisions of this subchapter to their respective functions.

Personnel shall include such professionally trained persons as are necessary to insure the competent performance of all manufacturing processes.

(c) Restrictions on personnel—(1) Specific duties. Persons whose presence can affect adversely the safety and purity of a product shall be excluded from the room where the manufacture of a product is in progress.

(2) Sterile operations. Personnel performing sterile operations shall wear clean or sterilized protective clothing and devices to the extent necessary to protect the product from contamination.

(3) Pathogenic viruses and spore-bearing organisms. Persons working with viruses pathogenic for man or with spore-bearing microorganisms, and persons engaged in the care of animals or animal quarters, shall be excluded from areas where other products are manufactured, or such persons shall change outer clothing, including shoes, or wear protective covering prior to entering such areas.

(4) Live vaccine work areas. Persons may not enter a live vaccine processing area after having worked with other infectious agents in any other laboratory during the same working day. Only persons actually concerned with propagation of the culture, production of the vaccine, and unit maintenance, shall be allowed in live vaccine processing areas when active work is in progress. Casual visitors shall be excluded from such units at all times and all others having business in such areas shall be admitted only under supervision. Street clothing, including shoes, shall be replaced or covered by suitable laboratory clothing before entering a live vaccine processing unit. Persons caring for animals used in the manufacture of live vaccines shall be excluded from other animal quar-ters and from contact with other animals during the same working day.

[38 FR 32048, Nov. 20, 1973, as amended at 49 FR 23833, June 8, 1984; 55 FR 11014, Mar. 26, 1990; 62 FR 53538, Oct. 15, 1997]

§600.11 Physical establishment, equipment, animals, and care.

(a) Work areas. All rooms and work areas where products are manufactured or stored shall be kept orderly, clean, and free of dirt, dust, vermin and objects not required for manufacturing. Precautions shall be taken to avoid clogging and back-siphonage of drainage systems. Precautions shall be taken to exclude extraneous infectious agents from manufacturing areas. Work rooms shall be well lighted and ventilated. The ventilation system shall be arranged so as to prevent the dissemination of microorganisms from one manufacturing area to another and to avoid other conditions unfavorable to the safety of the product. Filling rooms, and other rooms where open, sterile operations are conducted, shall be adequate to meet manufacturing needs and such rooms shall be constructed and equipped to permit thorough cleaning and to keep air-borne contaminants at a minimum. If such rooms are used for other purposes, they shall be cleaned and prepared prior to use for sterile operations. Refrigerators, incubators and warm rooms shall be maintained at temperatures within applicable ranges and shall be free of extraneous material which might affect the safety of the product.

(b) Equipment. Apparatus for sterilizing equipment and the method of operation shall be such as to insure the destruction of contaminating microorganisms. The effectiveness of the sterilization procedure shall be no less than that achieved by an attained temperature of 121.5° C maintained for 20 minutes by saturated steam or by an attained temperature of 170° C maintained for 2 hours with dry heat. Processing and storage containers, filters, filling apparatus, and other pieces of apparatus and accessory equipment, including pipes and tubing, shall be designed and constructed to permit thorough cleaning and, where possible, inspection for cleanliness. All surfaces that come in contact with products shall be clean and free of surface solids, leachable contaminants, and other materials that will hasten the deterioration of the product or otherwise render it less suitable for the intended use. For products for which sterility is a factor, equipment shall be sterile, unless sterility of the product is assured by subsequent procedures.

(c) Laboratory and bleeding rooms. Rooms used for the processing of products, including bleeding rooms, shall be effectively flyproofed and kept free of flies and vermin. Such rooms shall be so constructed as to insure freedom from dust, smoke and other deleterious substances and to permit thorough cleaning and disinfection. Rooms for animal injection and bleeding, and rooms for smallpox vaccine animals, shall be disinfected and be provided with the necessary water, electrical and other services.

(d) Animal quarters and stables. Animal quarters, stables and food storage areas shall be of appropriate construction, fly-proofed, adequately lighted and ventilated, and maintained in a clean, vermin-free and sanitary condition. No manure or refuse shall be stored as to permit the breeding of flies on the premises, nor shall the establishment be located in close proximity to off-property manure or refuse storage capable of engendering fly breeding.

(e) Restrictions on building and equipment use—(1) Work of a diagnostic nature. Laboratory procedures of a clinical diagnostic nature involving materials that may be contaminated, shall not be performed in space used for the manufacture of products except that manufacturing space which is used only occasionally may be used for diagnostic work provided spore-bearing pathogenic microorganisms are not involved and provided the space is thoroughly cleaned and disinfected before the manufacture of products is resumed.

(2) Spore-bearing organisms for supplemental sterilization procedure control test. Spore-bearing organisms used as an additional control in sterilization procedures may be introduced into areas used for the manufacture of products, only for the purposes of the test and only immediately before use for such purposes: Provided, That (i) the organism is not pathogenic for man or animals and does not produce pyrogens or toxins, (ii) the culture is demonstrated to be pure, (iii) transfer of test cultures to culture media shall be limited to the sterility test area or areas designated for work with spore-bearing organisms, (iv) each culture be labeled with the name of the microorganism and the statement "Caution: microbial spores. See directions for storage, use and disposition.", and (v) the container of each culture is designed to withstand handling without breaking.

(3) Work with spore-bearing organisms. Except as provided in the previous paragraph, all work with spore-bearing microorganisms shall be done in an entirely separate building: Provided, That such work may be done in a portion of a building used in the manufacture of products not containing spore-bearing microorganisms if such portion is completely walled-off and is constructed so as to prevent contamination of

other areas and if entrances to such portion are independent of the remainder of the building. All vessels, apparatus and equipment used for spore-bearing microorganisms shall be permanently identified and reserved exclusively for use with those organisms. Materials destined for further manufacturing may be removed from such an area only under conditions which will prevent the introduction of spores into other manufacturing areas.

(4) Live vaccine processing. Space used for processing a live vaccine shall not be used for any other purpose during the processing period for that vaccine and such space shall be decontaminated prior to initiation of the processing. Live vaccine processing areas shall be isolated from and independent of any space used for any other purpose by being either in a separate building, in a separate wing of a building, or in quarters at the blind end of a corridor and shall include adequate space and equipment for all processing steps up to filling into final containers. Test procedures which potentially involve the presence of microorganisms other than the vaccine strains, or the use of tissue culture cell lines other than primary cultures, shall not be conducted in space used for processing live vaccine.

(5) Equipment and supplies—contamination. Equipment and supplies used in work on or otherwise exposed to any pathogenic or potentially pathogenic agent shall be kept separated from equipment and supplies used in the manufacture of products to the extent necessary to prevent cross-contamination.

(f) Animals used in manufacture—(1) Care of animals used in manufacturing. Caretakers and attendants for animals used for the manufacture of products shall be sufficient in number and have adequate experience to insure adequate care. Animal quar-

ters and cages shall be kept in sanitary condition. Animals on production shall be inspected daily to observe response to production procedures. Animals that become ill for reasons not related to production shall be isolated from other animals and shall not be used for production until recovery is complete. Competent veterinary care shall be provided as needed.

(2) Quarantine of animals—(i) General. No animal shall be used in processing unless kept under competent daily inspection and preliminary quarantine for a period of at least 7 days before use, or as otherwise provided in this subchapter. Only healthy animals free from detectable communicable diseases shall be used. Animals must remain in overt good health throughout the quarantine periods and particular care shall be taken during the quarantine periods to reject animals of the equine genus which may be infected with glanders and animals which may be infected with tuberculosis.

(ii) Quarantine of monkeys. In addition to observing the pertinent general quarantine requirements, monkeys used as a source of tissue in the manufacture of vaccine shall be maintained in quarantine for at least 6 weeks prior to use, except when otherwise provided in this part. Only monkeys that have reacted negatively to tuberculin at the start of the quarantine period and again within 2 weeks prior to use shall be used in the manufacture of vaccine. Due precaution shall be taken to prevent cross-infection from any infected or potentially infected monkeys on the premises. Monkeys to be used in the manufacture of a live vaccine shall be maintained throughout the quarantine period in cages closed on all sides with solid materials except the front which shall be screened, with no more than two monkeys housed in one cage. Cage mates shall not be interchanged.

(3) Immunization against tetanus. Horses and other animals susceptible to tetanus, that are used in the processing steps of the manufacture of biological products, shall be treated adequately to maintain immunity to tetanus.

(4) Immunization and bleeding of animals used as a source of products. Toxins or other nonviable antigens administered in the immunization of animals used in the manufacture of products shall be sterile. Viable antigens, when so used, shall be free of contaminants, as determined by appropriate tests prior to use. Injections shall not be made into horses within 6 inches of bleeding site. Horses shall not be bled for manufacturing purposes while showing persistent general reaction or local reaction near the site of bleeding. Blood shall not be used if it was drawn within 5 days of injecting the animals with viable microorganisms. Animals shall not be bled for manufacturing purposes when they have an intercurrent disease. Blood intended for use as a source of a biological product shall be collected in clean, sterile vessels. When the product is intended for use by injection, such vessels shall also be pyrogen-free.

(5) [Reserved]

(6) Reporting of certain diseases. In cases of actual or suspected infection with foot and mouth disease, glanders, tetanus, anthrax, gas gangrene, equine infectious anemia; equine encephalomyelitis, or any of the pock diseases among animals intended for use or used in the manufacture of products, the manufacturer shall immediately notify the Director, Center for Biologics Evaluation and Research.

(7) Monkeys used previously for experimental or test purposes. Monkeys that have been used previously for experimental or test purposes with live microbiological agents shall not be used as a source of kidney tissue for the manufacture of vaccine. Except as provided otherwise in this subchapter, monkeys that have been used previously for other experimental or test purposes may be used as a source of kidney tissue upon their return to a normal condition, provided all quarantine requirements have been met.

(8) Necropsy examination of monkeys. Each monkey used in the manufacture of vaccine shall be examined at necropsy under the direction of a qualified pathologist, physician, or veterinarian having experience with diseases of monkeys, for evidence of ill health, particularly for (i) evidence of tuberculosis, (ii) presence of herpes-like lesions, including eruptions or plaques on or around the lips, in the buccal cavity or on the gums, and (iii) signs of conjunctivitis. If there are any such signs or other significant gross pathological lesions, the tissue shall not be used in the manufacture of vaccine.

(g) Filling procedures. Filling procedures shall be such as will not affect adversely the safety, purity or potency of the product.

(h) Containers and closures. All final containers and closures shall be made of material that will not hasten the deterioration of the product or otherwise render it less suitable for the intended use. All final containers and closures shall be clean and free of surface solids, leachable contaminants and other materials that will hasten the deterioration of the product or otherwise render it less suitable for the intended use. After filling, sealing shall be performed in a manner that will maintain the integrity of the product during the dating period. In addition, final containers and closures for products intended for use by injection shall be sterile and free from pyrogens. Except as otherwise provided in the regulations of this subchapter, final containers for products intended for use by injection shall be colorless and sufficiently transparent to permit visual examination of the contents under normal light. As soon as possible after filling final containers shall be labeled as prescribed in §610.60 et seq. of this chapter, except that final containers may be stored without such prescribed labeling provided they are stored in a sealed receptacle labeled both inside and outside with at least the name of the product, the lot number, and the filling identification.

[38 FR 32048, Nov. 20, 1973, as amended at 41 FR 10428, Mar. 11, 1976; 49 FR 23833, June 8, 1984; 55 FR 11013, Mar. 26, 1990]

§600.12 Records.

(a) Maintenance of records. Records shall be made, concurrently with the performance, of each step in the manufacture and distribution of products, in such a manner that at any time successive steps in the manufacture and distribution of any lot may be traced by an inspector. Such records shall be legible and indelible, shall identify the person immediately responsible, shall include dates of the various steps, and be as detailed as necessary for clear understanding of each step by one experienced in the manufacture of products.

(b) Records retention—(1) General. Records shall be retained for such interval beyond the expiration date as is necessary for the individual product, to permit the return of any clinical report of unfavorable reactions. The retention period shall be no less than five years after the records of manufacture have been completed or six months after the latest expiration date for the individual product, whichever represents a later date.

(2) Records of recall. Complete records shall be maintained pertaining to the recall from distribution of any product upon notification by the Director, Center for Biologics Evaluation and Research, to recall for failure to conform with the standards prescribed in the regulations of this subchapter, because of deterioration of the product or for any other factor by reason of which the distribution of the product would constitute a danger to health.

(3) Suspension of requirement for retention. The Director, Center for Biologics Evaluation and Research, may authorize the suspension of the requirement to retain records of a specific manufacturing step upon a showing that such records no longer have significance for the purposes for which they were made: Provided, That a summary of such records shall be retained.

(c) Records of sterilization of equipment and supplies. Records relating to the mode of sterilization, date, duration, temperature and other conditions relating to each sterilization of equipment and supplies used in the processing of products shall be made by means of automatic recording devices or by means of a system of recording which gives equivalent assurance of the accuracy and reliability of the record. Such records shall be maintained in a manner that permits an identification of the product with the particular manufacturing process to which the sterilization relates.

(d) Animal necropsy records. A necropsy record shall be kept on each animal from which a biological product has been obtained and which dies or is sacrificed while being so used.

(e) Records in case of divided manufacturing responsibility. If two or more establishments participate in the manufacture of a product, the records of each such establishment must show plainly the degree of its responsibility. In addition, each participating manufacturer shall furnish to the manufacturer who prepares the product in final form for sale, barter or exchange, a copy of all records relating to the manufacturing operations performed by such participating manufacturer insofar as they concern the safety, purity and potency of the lots of the product involved, and the manufacturer who prepares the product in final form shall retain a complete record of all the manufacturing operations relating to the product.

[38 FR 32048, Nov. 20, 1973, as amended at 49 FR 23833, June 8, 1984; 55 FR 11013, Mar. 26, 1990]

§600.13 Retention samples.

Manufacturers shall retain for a period of at least 6 months after the expiration date, unless a different time period is specified in additional standards, a quantity of representative material of each lot of each product, sufficient for examination and testing for safety and potency, except Whole Blood, Cryoprecipitated AHF, Platelets, Red Blood Cells, Plasma, and Source Plasma and Allergenic Products prepared to a physician's prescription. Samples so retained shall be selected at random from either final container material, or from bulk and final containers, provided they include at least one final container as a final package, or package-equivalent of such filling of each lot of the product as intended for distribution. Such sample material shall be stored at temperatures and under conditions which will maintain the identity and integrity of the product. Samples retained as required in this section shall be in addition to samples of specific products

required to be submitted to the Center for Biologics Evaluation and Research. Exceptions may be authorized by the Director, Center for Biologics Evaluation and Research, when the lot yields relatively few final containers and when such lots are prepared by the same method in large number and in close succession.

[41 FR 10428, Mar. 11, 1976, as amended at 49 FR 23833, June 8, 1984; 50 FR 4133, Jan. 29, 1985; 55 FR 11013, Mar. 26, 1990]

§600.14 Reporting of biological product deviations by licensed manufacturers.

(a) Who must report under this section? (1) You, the manufacturer who holds the biological product license and who had control over the product when the deviation occurred, must report under this section. If you arrange for another person to perform a manufacturing, holding, or distribution step, while the product is in your control, that step is performed under your control. You must establish, maintain, and follow a procedure for receiving information from that person on all deviations, complaints, and adverse events concerning the affected product.

(2) Exceptions:

(i) Persons who manufacture only in vitro diagnostic products that are not subject to licensing under section 351 of the Public Health Service Act do not report biological product deviations for those products under this section but must report in accordance with part 803 of this chapter;

(ii) Persons who manufacture blood and blood components, including licensed manufacturers, unlicensed registered blood establishments, and transfusion services, do not report biological product deviations for those products under this section but must report under §606.171 of this chapter;

(iii) Persons who manufacture Source Plasma or any other blood component and use that Source Plasma or any other blood component in the further manufacture of another licensed biological product must report:

(A) Under §606.171 of this chapter, if a biological product deviation occurs during the manufacture of that Source Plasma or any other blood component; or

(B) Under this section, if a biological product deviation occurs after the manufacture of that Source Plasma or any other blood component, and during manufacture of the licensed biological product.

(b) What do I report under this section? You must report any event, and information relevant to the event, associated with the manufacturing, to include testing, processing, packing, labeling, or storage, or with the holding or distribution, of a licensed biological product, if that event meets all the following criteria:

(1) Either:

(i) Represents a deviation from current good manufacturing practice, applicable regulations, applicable standards, or established specifications that may affect the safety, purity, or potency of that product; or

(ii) Represents an unexpected or unforeseeable event that may affect the safety, purity, or potency of that product; and

(2) Occurs in your facility or another facility under contract with you; and

(3) Involves a distributed biological product.

(c) When do I report under this section? You should report a biological product deviation as soon as possible but you must report at a date not to exceed 45-calendar days from the date you, your agent, or another person who performs a manufacturing, holding, or distribution step under your control, acquire information reasonably suggesting that a reportable event has occurred.

(d) How do I report under this section? You must report on Form FDA–3486.

(e) Where do I report under this section? You must send the completed Form FDA–3486 to the Director, Office of Compliance and Biologics Quality (HFM–600), Center for Biologics Evaluation and Research, 1401 Rockville Pike, suite 200N, Rockville, MD 20852–1448, by either a paper or an electronic filing:

(1) If you make a paper filing, you should identify on the envelope that a BPDR (biological product deviation report) is enclosed; or

(2) If you make an electronic filing, you may submit the completed Form FDA–3486 electronically through CBER's website at www.fda.gov/cber.

(f) How does this regulation affect other FDA regulations? This part supplements and does not supersede other provisions of the regulations in this chapter. All biological product deviations, whether or not they are required to be reported under this section, should be investigated in accordance with the applicable provisions of parts 211 and 820 of this chapter.

[65 FR 66634, Nov. 7, 2000]

§600.15 Temperatures during shipment.

The following products shall be maintained during shipment at the specified temperatures:

(a) Products.

Product	Temperature
Cryoprecipitated AHF	-18 °C or colder.
Measles and Rubella Virus Vaccine Live	10 °C or colder.
Measles Live and Smallpox Vaccine	Do.
Measles, Mumps, and Rubella Virus Vaccine Live	Do.
Measles and Mumps Virus Vaccine Live	Do.
Measles Virus Vaccine Live	Do.
Mumps Virus Vaccine Live	Do.
Fresh Frozen Plasma	-18 °C or colder.
Liquid Plasma	1 to 10 °C.
Plasma	-18 °C or colder.
Platelet Rich Plasma	Between 1 and 10 °C if the label indicates storage between 1 and 6 °C, or all reasonable methods to maintain the temperature as close as possible to a range between 20 and 24°C, if the label indicates storage between 20 and 24 °C.
Platelets	Between 1 and 10 °C if the label indicates storage between 1 and 6 °C, or all reasonable methods to maintain the temperature as close as possible to a range between 20 to 24°C, if the label indicates storage between 20 and 24 °C.
Poliovirus Vaccine Live Oral Trivalent	0 °C or colder.
Poliovirus Vaccine Live Oral Type I	Do.
Poliovirus Vaccine Live Oral Type II	Do.
Poliovirus Vaccine Live Oral Type III	Do.
Red Blood Cells (liquid product)	Between 1 and 10 °C.
Red Blood Cells Frozen	-65 °C or colder.
Rubella and Mumps Virus Vaccine Live	10 °C or colder.
Rubella Virus Vaccine Live	Do.
Smallpox Vaccine (Liquid Product)	0 °C or colder.
Source Plasma	-5 °C or colder.

Source Plasma Liquid — 10 °C or colder.

Whole Blood — Blood that is transported from the collecting facility to the processing facility shall be transported in an environment capable of continuously cooling the blood toward a temperature range of 1 to 10 °C, or at a temperature as close as possible to 20 to 24°C for a period not to exceed 6 hours. Blood transported from the storage facility shall be placed in an appropriate environment to maintain a temperature range between 1 to 10 °C during shipment.

Yellow Fever Vaccine — 0 °C or colder.

(b) Exemptions. Exemptions or modifications shall be made only upon written approval, in the form of a supplement to the biologics license application, approved by the Director, Center for Biologics Evaluation and Research.

[39 FR 39872, Nov. 12, 1974, as amended at 49 FR 23833, June 8, 1984; 50 FR 4133, Jan. 29, 1985; 50 FR 9000, Mar. 6, 1985; 55 FR 11013, Mar. 26, 1990; 59 FR 49351, Sept. 28, 1994; 64 FR 56449, Oct. 20, 1999]

Subpart C—Establishment Inspection

§600.20 Inspectors.

Inspections shall be made by an officer of the Food and Drug Administration having special knowledge of the methods used in the manufacture and control of products and designated for such purposes by the Commissioner of Food and Drugs, or by any officer, agent, or employee of the Department of Health and Human Services specifically designated for such purpose by the Secretary.

[38 FR 32048, Nov. 20, 1973]

§600.21 Time of inspection.

The inspection of an establishment for which a biologics license application is pending need not be made until the establishment is in operation and is manufacturing the complete product for which a biologics license is desired. In case the license is denied following inspection for the original license, no reinspection need be made until assurance has been received that the faulty conditions which were the basis of the denial have been corrected. An inspection of each licensed establishment and its additional location(s) shall be made at least once every 2 years. Inspections may be made with or without notice, and shall be made during regular business hours unless otherwise directed.

[38 FR 32048, Nov. 20, 1973, as amended at 48 FR 26314, June 7, 1983; 64 FR 56449, Oct. 20, 1999]

§600.22 Duties of inspector.

The inspector shall:

(a) Call upon the active head of the establishment, stating the object of his visit,

(b) Interrogate the proprietor or other personnel of the establishment as he may deem necessary,

(c) Examine the details of location, construction, equipment and maintenance, including stables, barns, warehouses, manufacturing laboratories, bleeding clinics maintained for the collection of human blood, shipping rooms, record rooms, and any other structure or appliance used in any part of the manufacture of a product,

(d) Investigate as fully as he deems necessary the methods of propagation, processing, testing, storing, dispensing, recording, or other details of manufacture and distribution of each licensed product, or product for which a license has been requested, including observation of these procedures in actual operation,

(e) Obtain and cause to be sent to the Director, Center for Biologics Evaluation and Research, adequate samples for the examination of any product or ingredient used in its manufacture,

(f) Bring to the attention of the manufacturer any fault observed in the course of inspection in location, construction, manufacturing methods, or administration of a licensed establishment which might lead to impairment of a product,

(g) Inspect and copy, as circumstances may require, any records required to be kept pursuant to §600.12,

(h) Certify as to the condition of the establishment and of the manufacturing methods followed and make recommendations as to action deemed appropriate with respect to any application for license or any license previously issued.

[38 FR 32048, Nov. 20, 1973, as amended at 49 FR 23833, June 8, 1984; 55 FR 11013, Mar. 26, 1990]

Subpart D—Reporting of Adverse Experiences

Source: 59 FR 54042, Oct. 27, 1994, unless otherwise noted.

§600.80 Postmarketing reporting of adverse experiences.

(a) Definitions. The following definitions of terms apply to this section:

Adverse experience. Any adverse event associated with the use of a biological product in humans, whether or not considered product related, including the following: An adverse event occurring in the course of the use of a biological product in professional practice; an adverse event occurring from overdose of the product whether accidental or intentional; an adverse event occurring from abuse of the product; an adverse event occurring from withdrawal of the product; and any failure of expected pharmacological action.

Blood Component. As defined in §606.3(c) of this chapter.

Disability. A substantial disruption of a person's ability to conduct normal life functions.

Life-threatening adverse experience. Any adverse experience that places the patient, in the view of the initial reporter, at immediate risk of death from the adverse experience as it occurred, i.e., it does not include an adverse experience that, had it occurred in a more severe form, might have caused death.

Serious adverse experience. Any adverse experience occurring at any dose that results in any of the following outcomes: Death, a life-threatening adverse experience, inpatient hospitalization or prolongation of existing hospitalization, a persistent or significant disability/incapacity, or a congenital anomaly/birth defect. Important medical events that may not result in death, be life-threatening, or require hospitalization may be considered a serious adverse experience when, based upon appropriate medical judgment, they may jeopardize the patient or subject and may require medical or surgical intervention to prevent one of the outcomes listed in this definition. Examples of such medical events include allergic bronchospasm requiring intensive treatment in an emergency room or at home, blood dyscrasias or convulsions that do not result in inpatient hospitalization, or the development of drug dependency or drug abuse.

Unexpected adverse experience: Any adverse experience that is not listed in the current labeling for the biological product. This includes events that may be symptomatically and pathophysiologically related to an event listed in the labeling, but differ from the event because of greater severity or specificity. For example, under this definition, hepatic necrosis would be unexpected (by virtue of greater severity) if the labeling only referred to elevated hepatic enzymes or hepatitis. Similarly, cerebral thromboembolism and cerebral vasculitis would be unexpected (by virtue of greater specificity) if the labeling only listed cerebral vascular accidents. "Unexpected," as used in this definition, refers to an adverse experience that has not been previously observed (i.e., included in the labeling) rather than from the perspective of such experience not being anticipated from the pharmacological properties of the pharmaceutical product.

(b) Review of adverse experiences. Any person having a biologics license under §601.20 of this chapter shall promptly review all adverse experience information pertaining to its product obtained or otherwise received by the licensed manufacturer from any source, foreign or domestic, including information derived from commercial marketing experience, postmarketing clinical investigations, postmarketing epidemiological/surveillance studies, reports in the scientific literature, and unpublished scientific papers. Licensed manufacturers are not required to resubmit to FDA adverse product experience reports forwarded to the licensed manufacturer by FDA; licensed manufacturers, however, must submit all followup information on such reports to FDA. Any person subject to the reporting requirements under paragraph (c) of this section shall also develop written procedures for the surveillance, receipt, evaluation, and reporting of postmarketing adverse experiences to FDA.

(c) Reporting requirements. The licensed manufacturer shall report to FDA adverse experience information, as described in this section. The licensed manufacturer shall submit two copies of each report described in this section for nonvaccine biological products, to the Center for Biologics Evaluation and Research (HFM–210), Food and Drug Administration, 1401 Rockville Pike, suite 200 N., Rockville, MD 20852–1448. Submit all vaccine adverse experience reports to: Vaccine Adverse Event Reporting System (VAERS), P.O. Box 1100,

Rockville, MD 20849–1100. FDA may waive the requirement for the second copy in appropriate instances.

(1)(i) Postmarketing 15-day "Alert reports". The licensed manufacturer shall report each adverse experience that is both serious and unexpected, whether foreign or domestic, as soon as possible but in no case later than 15 calendar days of initial receipt of the information by the licensed manufacturer.

(ii) Postmarketing 15-day "Alert reports"— followup. The licensed manufacturer shall promptly investigate all adverse experiences that are the subject of these postmarketing 15-day Alert reports and shall submit followup reports within 15 calendar days of receipt of new information or as requested by FDA. If additional information is not obtainable, records should be maintained of the unsuccessful steps taken to seek additional information. Postmarketing 15-day Alert reports and followups to them shall be submitted under separate cover.

(iii) Submission of reports. The requirements of paragraphs (c)(1)(i) and (c)(1)(ii) of this section, concerning the submission of postmarketing 15-day Alert reports, shall also apply to any person whose name appears on the label of a licensed biological product as a manufacturer, packer, distributor, shared manufacturer, joint manufacturer, or any other participant involved in divided manufacturing. To avoid unnecessary duplication in the submission to FDA of reports required by paragraphs (c)(1)(i) and (c)(1)(ii) of this section, obligations of persons other than the licensed manufacturer of the final biological product may be met by submission of all reports of serious adverse experiences to the licensed manufacturer of the final product. If a person elects to submit adverse experience reports to the licensed manufacturer of the final

product rather than to FDA, the person shall submit each report to the licensed manufacturer of the final product within 5 calendar days of receipt of the report by the person, and the licensed manufacturer of the final product shall then comply with the requirements of this section. Under this circumstance, a person who elects to submit reports to the licensed manufacturer of the final product shall maintain a record of this action which shall include:

(A) A copy of all adverse biological product experience reports submitted to the licensed manufacturer of the final product;

(B) The date the report was received by the person;

(C) The date the report was submitted to the licensed manufacturer of the final product; and–

(D) The name and address of the licensed manufacturer of the final product.

(iv) Report identification. Each report submitted under this paragraph shall bear prominent identification as to its contents, i.e., "15-day Alert report," or "15-day Alert report-followup."

(2) Periodic adverse experience reports. (i) The licensed manufacturer shall report each adverse experience not reported under paragraph (c)(1)(i) of this section at quarterly intervals, for 3 years from the date of issuance of the biologics license, and then at annual intervals. The licensed manufacturer shall submit each quarterly report within 30 days of the close of the quarter (the first quarter beginning on the date of issuance of the biologics license) and each annual report within 60 days of the anniversary date of the issuance of the biologics license. Upon written notice, FDA may extend or reestablish

the requirement that a licensed manufacturer submit quarterly reports, or require that the licensed manufacturer submit reports under this section at different times than those stated. Followup information to adverse experiences submitted in a periodic report may be submitted in the next periodic report.

(ii) Each periodic report shall contain:

(A) A narrative summary and analysis of the information in the report and an analysis of the 15-day Alert reports submitted during the reporting interval (all 15-day Alert reports being appropriately referenced by the licensed manufacturer's patient identification number, adverse reaction term(s), and date of submission to FDA);

(B) A form designated for Adverse Experience Reporting by FDA for each adverse experience not reported under paragraph (c)(1)(i) of this section (with an index consisting of a line listing of the licensed manufacturer's patient identification number and adverse reaction term(s)); and

(C) A history of actions taken since the last report because of adverse experiences (for example, labeling changes or studies initiated).

(iii) Periodic reporting, except for information regarding 15-day Alert reports, does not apply to adverse experience information obtained from postmarketing studies (whether or not conducted under an investigational new drug application), from reports in the scientific literature, and from foreign marketing experience.

(d) Scientific literature. (1) A 15-day Alert report based on information from the scientific literature shall be accompanied by a copy of the published article. The 15-day

Alert reporting requirements in paragraph (c)(1)(i) of this section (i.e., serious, unexpected adverse experiences) apply only to reports found in scientific and medical journals either as case reports or as the result of a formal clinical trial.

(2) As with all reports submitted under paragraph (c)(1)(i) of this section, reports based on the scientific literature shall be submitted on the reporting form designated by FDA or comparable format as prescribed by paragraph (f) of this section. In cases where the licensed manufacturer believes that preparing the form designated by FDA constitutes an undue hardship, the licensed manufacturer may arrange with the Division of Biostatistics and Epidemiology (HFM–210) for an acceptable alternative reporting format.

(e) Postmarketing studies. (1) Licensed manufacturers are not required to submit a 15-day Alert report under paragraph (c) of this section for an adverse experience obtained from a postmarketing clinical study (whether or not conducted under a biological investigational new drug application) unless the licensed manufacturer concludes that there is a reasonable possibility that the product caused the adverse experience.

(2) The licensed manufacturer shall separate and clearly mark reports of adverse experiences that occur during a postmarketing study as being distinct from those experiences that are being reported spontaneously to the licensed manufacturer.

(f) Reporting forms. (1) Except as provided in paragraph (f)(3) of this section, the licensed manufacturer shall complete the reporting form designated by FDA for each report of an adverse experience (FDA Form 3500A, or, for vaccines, a VAERS form; foreign events including those associated with the use of vaccines, may be submitted either on an FDA Form 3500A or, if preferred, on a CIOMS I form).

(2) Each completed form should refer only to an individual patient or single attached publication.

(3) Instead of using a designated reporting form, a licensed manufacturer may use a computer-generated form or other alternative format (e.g., a computer-generated tape or tabular listing) provided that:

(i) The content of the alternative format is equivalent in all elements of information to those specified in the form designated by FDA; and

(ii) the format is approved in advance by MEDWATCH: The FDA Medical Products Reporting Program; or, for alternatives to the VAERS Form, by the Division of Biostatistics and Epidemiology.

(4) Copies of the reporting form designated by FDA (FDA–3500A) for nonvaccine biological products may be obtained from the Center for Biologics Evaluation and Research (address above). Additional supplies of the form may be obtained from the Consolidated Forms and Publications Distribution Center, 3222 Hubbard Rd., Landover, MD 20785. Supplies of the VAERS form may be obtained from VAERS by calling 1–800–822–7967.

(g) Multiple reports. A licensed manufacturer should not include in reports under this section any adverse experience that occurred in clinical trials if they were previously submitted as part of the biologics license application. If a report refers to more than one biological product marketed by a licensed manufacturer, the licensed manufacturer

should submit the report to the biologics license application for the product listed first in the report.

(h) Patient privacy. For nonvaccine biological products, a licensed manufacturer should not include in reports under this section the names and addresses of individual patients; instead, the licensed manufacturer should assign a unique code number to each report, preferably not more than eight characters in length. The licensed manufacturer should include the name of the reporter from whom the information was received. The names of patients, health care professionals, hospitals, and geographical identifiers in adverse experience reports are not releasable to the public under FDA's public information regulations in part 20 this of chapter. For vaccine adverse experience reports, these data will become part of the CDC Privacy Act System 09–20–0136, "Epidemiologic Studies and Surveillance of Disease Problems." Information identifying the person who received the vaccine or that person's legal representative will not be made available to the public, but may be available to the vaccinee or legal representative.

(i) Recordkeeping. The licensed manufacturer shall maintain for a period of 10 years records of all adverse experiences known to the licensed manufacturer, including raw data and any correspondence relating to the adverse experiences.

(j) Revocation of biologics license. If a licensed manufacturer fails to establish and maintain records and make reports required under this section with respect to a licensed biological product, FDA may revoke the biologics license for such a product in accordance with the procedures of §601.5 of this chapter.

(k) Exemptions. Manufacturers of the following listed products are not required to submit adverse experience reports under this section:

(1) Whole blood or components of whole blood.

(2) In vitro diagnostic products, including assay systems for the detection of antibodies or antigens to retroviruses. These products are subject to the reporting requirements for devices.

(l) Disclaimer. A report or information submitted by a licensed manufacturer under this section (and any release by FDA of that report or information) does not necessarily reflect a conclusion by the licensed manufacturer or FDA that the report or information constitutes an admission that the biological product caused or contributed to an adverse effect. A licensed manufacturer need not admit, and may deny, that the report or information submitted under this section constitutes an admission that the biological product caused or contributed to an adverse effect. For purposes of this provision, this paragraph also includes any person reporting under paragraph (c)(1)(iii) of this section.

[59 FR 54042, Oct. 27, 1994, as amended at 62 FR 34168, June 25, 1997; 62 FR 52252, Oct. 7, 1997; 63 FR 14612, Mar. 26, 1998; 64 FR 56449, Oct. 20, 1999]

§600.81 Distribution reports.

The licensed manufacturer shall submit information about the quantity of the product distributed under the biologics license, including the quantity distributed to distributors. The interval between distribution reports shall be 6 months. Upon written notice, FDA may require that the licensed manufacturer submit distribution reports under this section at times other than every 6 months. The distribution report shall consist of the bulk lot number (from which the final container was filled), the fill lot numbers for the total number of dosage units of each strength or potency distributed (e.g., fifty thousand per 10-milliliter vials), the label lot number (if different from fill lot number), labeled date of expiration, number of doses in fill lot/label lot, date of release of fill lot/label lot for distribution at that time. If any significant amount of a fill lot/label lot is returned, include this information. Disclosure of financial or pricing data is not required. As needed, FDA may require submission of more detailed product distribution information. Upon written notice, FDA may require that the licensed manufacturer submit reports under this section at times other than those stated. Requests by a licensed manufacturer to submit reports at times other than those stated should be made as a request for a waiver under §600.90.

[59 FR 54042, Oct. 27, 1994, as amended at 64 FR 56449, Oct. 20, 1999]

§600.90 Waivers.

(a) A licensed manufacturer may ask the Food and Drug Administration to waive under this section any requirement that applies to the licensed manufacturer under §§600.80 and 600.81. A waiver request under this section is required to be submitted with supporting documentation. The waiver request is required to contain one of the following:

(1) An explanation why the licensed manufacturer's compliance with the requirement is unnecessary or cannot be achieved,

(2) A description of an alternative submission that satisfies the purpose of the requirement, or

(3) Other information justifying a waiver.

(b) FDA may grant a waiver if it finds one of the following:

(1) The licensed manufacturer's compliance with the requirement is unnecessary or cannot be achieved,

(2) The licensed manufacturer's alternative submission satisfies the requirement, or

(3) The licensed manufacturer's submission otherwise justifies a waiver.

TITLE 21—FOOD AND DRUGS

**Chapter I: Food and Drug Administration,
Department of Health and Human Services
Subchapter D: Drugs for Human Use**

Part 812

Investigational Device Exemptions

Authority: 21 U.S.C. 331, 351, 352, 353, 355, 360, 360c–360f, 360h–360j, 371, 372, 374, 379e, 381, 382, 383; 42 U.S.C. 216, 241, 262, 263b–263n.

Source: 45 FR 3751, Jan. 18, 1980, unless otherwise noted.

Subpart A—General Provisions

§812.1 Scope.

(a) The purpose of this part is to encourage, to the extent consistent with the protection of public health and safety and with ethical standards, the discovery and development of useful devices intended for human use, and to that end to maintain optimum freedom for scientific investigators in their pursuit of this purpose. This part provides procedures for the conduct of clinical investigations of devices. An approved investigational device exemption (IDE) permits a device that otherwise would be required to comply with a performance standard or to have premarket approval to be shipped lawfully for the purpose of conducting investigations of that device. An IDE approved under §812.30 or considered approved under §812.2(b) exempts a device from the requirements of the following sections of the Federal Food, Drug, and Cosmetic Act (the act) and regulations issued thereunder: Misbranding under section 502 of the act, registration, listing, and premarket notification under section 510, performance standards under section 514, premarket approval under section 515, a banned device regulation under section 516, records and reports under section 519, restricted device requirements under section 520(e), good manufacturing practice requirements under section 520(f) except for the requirements found in §820.30, if applicable (unless the sponsor states an intention to comply with these requirements under §812.20(b)(3) or §812.140(b)(4)(v)) and color additive requirements under section 721.

(b) References in this part to regulatory sections of the Code of Federal Regulations are to chapter I of title 21, unless otherwise noted.

[45 FR 3751, Jan. 18, 1980, as amended at 59 FR 14366, Mar. 28, 1994; 61 FR 52654, Oct. 7, 1996]

§812.2 Applicability.

(a) General. This part applies to all clinical investigations of devices to determine safety and effectiveness, except as provided in paragraph (c) of this section.

(b) Abbreviated requirements. The following categories of investigations are considered to have approved applications for IDE's, unless FDA has notified a sponsor under §812.20(a) that approval of an application is required:

(1) An investigation of a device other than a significant risk device, if the device is not a banned device and the sponsor:

(i) Labels the device in accordance with §812.5;

(ii) Obtains IRB approval of the investigation after presenting the reviewing IRB with a brief explanation of why the device is not a significant risk device, and maintains such approval;

(iii) Ensures that each investigator participating in an investigation of the device obtains from each subject under the investigator's care, informed consent under part 50 and documents it, unless documentation is waived by an IRB under §56.109(c).

(iv) Complies with the requirements of §812.46 with respect to monitoring investigations;

(v) Maintains the records required under §812.140(b) (4) and (5) and makes the reports required under §812.150(b) (1) through (3) and (5) through (10);

(vi) Ensures that participating investigators maintain the records required by §812.140(a)(3)(i) and make the reports required under §812.150(a) (1), (2), (5), and (7); and

(vii) Complies with the prohibitions in §812.7 against promotion and other practices.

(2) An investigation of a device other than one subject to paragraph (e) of this section, if the investigation was begun on or before July 16, 1980, and to be completed, and is completed, on or before January 19, 1981.

(c) *Exempted investigations.* This part, with the exception of §812.119, does not apply to investigations of the following categories of devices:

(1) A device, other than a transitional device, in commercial distribution immediately before May 28, 1976, when used or investigated in accordance with the indications in labeling in effect at that time.

(2) A device, other than a transitional device, introduced into commercial distribution on or after May 28, 1976, that FDA has determined to be substantially equivalent to a device in commercial distribution immediately before May 28, 1976, and that is used or investigated in accordance with the indications in the labeling FDA reviewed under subpart E of part 807 in determining substantial equivalence.

(3) A diagnostic device, if the sponsor complies with applicable requirements in §809.10(c) and if the testing:

(i) Is noninvasive,

(ii) Does not require an invasive sampling procedure that presents significant risk,

(iii) Does not by design or intention introduce energy into a subject, and

(iv) Is not used as a diagnostic procedure without confirmation of the diagnosis by another, medically established diagnostic product or procedure.

(4) A device undergoing consumer preference testing, testing of a modification, or testing of a combination of two or more devices in commercial distribution, if the testing is not for the purpose of determining safety or effectiveness and does not put subjects at risk.

(5) A device intended solely for veterinary use.

(6) A device shipped solely for research on or with laboratory animals and labeled in accordance with §812.5(c).

(7) A custom device as defined in §812.3(b), unless the device is being used to determine safety or effectiveness for commercial distribution.

(d) *Limit on certain exemptions.* In the case of class II or class III device described in paragraph (c)(1) or (2) of this section, this part applies beginning on the date stipulated in an FDA regulation or order that calls for the submission of premarket approval applications for an unapproved class III device, or establishes a performance standard for a class II device.

(e) Investigations subject to IND's. A sponsor that, on July 16, 1980, has an effective investigational new drug application (IND) for an investigation of a device shall continue to comply with the requirements of part 312 until 90 days after that date. To continue the investigation after that date, a sponsor shall comply with paragraph (b)(1) of this section, if the device is not a significant risk device, or shall have obtained FDA approval under §812.30 of an IDE application for the investigation of the device.

[45 FR 3751, Jan. 18, 1980, as amended at 46 FR 8956, Jan. 27, 1981; 46 FR 14340, Feb. 27, 1981; 53 FR 11252, Apr. 6, 1988; 62 FR 4165, Jan, 29, 1997; 62 FR 12096, Mar. 14, 1997]

§812.3 Definitions.

(a) Act means the Federal Food, Drug, and Cosmetic Act (sections 201–901, 52 Stat. 1040 et seq., as amended (21 U.S.C. 301–392)).

(b) Custom device means a device that:

(1) Necessarily deviates from devices generally available or from an applicable performance standard or premarket approval requirement in order to comply with the order of an individual physician or dentist;

(2) Is not generally available to, or generally used by, other physicians or dentists;

(3) Is not generally available in finished form for purchase or for dispensing upon prescription;

(4) Is not offered for commercial distribution through labeling or advertising; and

(5) Is intended for use by an individual patient named in the order of a physician or dentist, and is to be made in a specific form for that patient, or is intended to meet the special needs of the physician or dentist in the course of professional practice.

(c) FDA means the Food and Drug Administration.

(d) Implant means a device that is placed into a surgically or naturally formed cavity of the human body if it is intended to remain there for a period of 30 days or more. FDA may, in order to protect public health, determine that devices placed in subjects for shorter periods are also "implants" for purposes of this part.

(e) Institution means a person, other than an individual, who engages in the conduct of research on subjects or in the delivery of medical services to individuals as a primary activity or as an adjunct to providing residential or custodial care to humans. The term includes, for example, a hospital, retirement home, confinement facility, academic establishment, and device manufacturer. The term has the same meaning as "facility" in section 520(g) of the act.

(f) Institutional review board (IRB) means any board, committee, or other group formally designated by an institution to review biomedical research involving subjects and established, operated, and functioning in conformance with part 56. The term has the same meaning as "institutional review committee" in section 520(g) of the act.

(g) Investigational device means a device, including a transitional device, that is the object of an investigation.

(h) Investigation means a clinical investigation or research involving one or more subjects to determine the safety or effectiveness of a device.

(i) Investigator means an individual who actually conducts a clinical investigation, i.e., under whose immediate direction the test article is administered or dispensed to, or used involving, a subject, or, in the event of an investigation conducted by a team of individuals, is the responsible leader of that team.

(j) Monitor, when used as a noun, means an individual designated by a sponsor or contract research organization to oversee the progress of an investigation. The monitor may be an employee of a sponsor or a consultant to the sponsor, or an employee of or consultant to a contract research organization. Monitor, when used as a verb, means to oversee an investigation.

(k) Noninvasive, when applied to a diagnostic device or procedure, means one that does not by design or intention: (1) Penetrate or pierce the skin or mucous membranes of the body, the ocular cavity, or the urethra, or (2) enter the ear beyond the external auditory canal, the nose beyond the nares, the mouth beyond the pharynx, the anal canal beyond the rectum, or the vagina beyond the cervical os. For purposes of this part, blood sampling that involves simple

venipuncture is considered noninvasive, and the use of surplus samples of body fluids or tissues that are left over from samples taken for noninvestigational purposes is also considered noninvasive.

(l) Person includes any individual, partnership, corporation, association, scientific or academic establishment, Government agency or organizational unit of a Government agency, and any other legal entity.

(m) Significant risk device means an investigational device that:

(1) Is intended as an implant and presents a potential for serious risk to the health, safety, or welfare of a subject;

(2) Is purported or represented to be for a use in supporting or sustaining human life and presents a potential for serious risk to the health, safety, or welfare of a subject;

(3) Is for a use of substantial importance in diagnosing, curing, mitigating, or treating disease, or otherwise preventing impairment of human health and presents a potential for serious risk to the health, safety, or welfare of a subject; or

(4) Otherwise presents a potential for serious risk to the health, safety, or welfare of a subject.

(n) Sponsor means a person who initiates, but who does not actually conduct, the investigation, that is, the investigational device is administered, dispensed, or used under the immediate direction of another individual. A person other than an individual that uses one or more of its own employees to conduct an investigation that it has initiated is a sponsor, not a sponsor-investigator, and the employees are investigators.

(o) Sponsor-investigator means an individual who both initiates and actually conducts, alone or with others, an investigation, that is, under whose immediate direction the investigational device is administered, dispensed, or used. The term does not include any person other than an individual. The obligations of a sponsor-investigator under this part include those of an investigator and those of a sponsor.

(p) Subject means a human who participates in an investigation, either as an individual on whom or on whose specimen an investigational device is used or as a control. A subject may be in normal health or may have a medical condition or disease.

(q) Termination means a discontinuance, by sponsor or by withdrawal of IRB or FDA approval, of an investigation before completion.

(r) Transitional device means a device subject to section 520(l) of the act, that is, a device that FDA considered to be a new drug or an antibiotic drug before May 28, 1976.

(s) Unanticipated adverse device effect means any serious adverse effect on health or safety or any life-threatening problem or death caused by, or associated with, a device, if that effect, problem, or death was not previously identified in nature, severity, or degree of incidence in the investigational plan or application (including a supplementary plan or application), or any other unanticipated serious problem associated with a device that relates to the rights, safety, or welfare of subjects.

[45 FR 3751, Jan. 18, 1980, as amended at 46 FR 8956, Jan. 27, 1981; 48 FR 15622, Apr. 12, 1983]

§812.5 Labeling of investigational devices.

(a) Contents. An investigational device or its immediate package shall bear a label with the following information: the name and place of business of the manufacturer, packer, or distributor (in accordance with §801.1), the quantity of contents, if appropriate, and the following statement: "CAUTION—Investigational device. Limited by Federal (or United States) law to investigational use." The label or other labeling shall describe all relevant contraindications, hazards, adverse effects, interfering substances or devices, warnings, and precautions.

(b) Prohibitions. The labeling of an investigational device shall not bear any statement that is false or misleading in any particular and shall not represent that the device is safe or effective for the purposes for which it is being investigated.

(c) Animal research. An investigational device shipped solely for research on or with laboratory animals shall bear on its label the following statement: "CAUTION—Device for investigational use in laboratory animals or other tests that do not involve human subjects."

[45 FR 3751, Jan. 18, 1980, as amended at 45 FR 58842, Sept. 5, 1980]

§812.7 Prohibition of promotion and

other practices.

A sponsor, investigator, or any person acting for or on behalf of a sponsor or investigator shall not:

(a) Promote or test market an investigational device, until after FDA has approved the device for commercial distribution.

(b) Commercialize an investigational device by charging the subjects or investigators for a device a price larger than that necessary to recover costs of manufacture, research, development, and handling.

(c) Unduly prolong an investigation. If data developed by the investigation indicate in the case of a class III device that premarket approval cannot be justified or in the case of a class II device that it will not comply with an applicable performance standard or an amendment to that standard, the sponsor shall promptly terminate the investigation.

(d) Represent that an investigational device is safe or effective for the purposes for which it is being investigated.

§812.10 Waivers.

(a) Request. A sponsor may request FDA to waive any requirement of this part. A waiver request, with supporting documentation, may be submitted separately or as part of an application to the address in §812.19.

(b) FDA action. FDA may by letter grant a waiver of any requirement that FDA finds is not required by the act and is unnecessary to protect the rights, safety, or welfare of human subjects.

(c) Effect of request. Any requirement shall continue to apply unless and until FDA waives it.

§812.18 Import and export requirements.

(a) Imports. In addition to complying with other requirements of this part, a person who imports or offers for importation an investigational device subject to this part shall be the agent of the foreign exporter with respect to investigations of the device and shall act as the sponsor of the clinical investigation, or ensure that another person acts as the agent of the foreign exporter and the sponsor of the investigation.

(b) Exports. A person exporting an investigational device subject to this part shall obtain FDA's prior approval, as required by section 801(e) of the act or comply with section 802 of the act.

[45 FR 3751, Jan. 18, 1980, as amended at 62 FR 26229, May 13, 1997]

§812.19 Address for IDE correspondence.

If you are sending an application, supplemental application, report, request for waiver, request for import or export approval, or other correspondence relating to matters covered by this part, you must address it to the Center for Devices and Radiological Health, Document Mail Center (HFZ–401), Food and Drug Administration, 9200 Corporate Blvd., Rockville, MD 20850. You must state on the outside wrapper of each submission what the submission is, for example, an "IDE application," a "supplemental IDE application," or a "correspondence concerning an IDE (or an IDE application)."

[65 FR 17137, Mar. 31, 2000]

Subpart B—Application and Administrative Action

§812.20 Application.

(a) Submission. (1) A sponsor shall submit an application to FDA if the sponsor intends to use a significant risk device in an investigation, intends to conduct an investigation that involves an exception from informed consent under §50.24 of this chapter, or if FDA notifies the sponsor that an application is required for an investigation.

(2) A sponsor shall not begin an investigation for which FDA's approval of an application is required until FDA has approved the application.

(3) A sponsor shall submit three copies of a signed "Application for an Investigational Device Exemption" (IDE application), together with accompanying materials, by registered mail or by hand to the address in §812.19. Subsequent correspondence concerning an application or a supplemental application shall be submitted by registered mail or by hand.

(4)(i) A sponsor shall submit a separate IDE for any clinical investigation involving an exception from informed consent under §50.24 of this chapter. Such a clinical investigation is not permitted to pro-

ceed without the prior written authorization of FDA. FDA shall provide a written determination 30 days after FDA receives the IDE or earlier.

(ii) If the investigation involves an exception from informed consent under §50.24 of this chapter, the sponsor shall prominently identify on the cover sheet that the investigation is subject to the requirements in §50.24 of this chapter.

(b) Contents. An IDE application shall include, in the following order:

(1) The name and address of the sponsor.

(2) A complete report of prior investigations of the device and an accurate summary of those sections of the investigational plan described in §812.25(a) through (e) or, in lieu of the summary, the complete plan. The sponsor shall submit to FDA a complete investigational plan and a complete report of prior investigations of the device if no IRB has reviewed them, if FDA has found an IRB's review inadequate, or if FDA requests them.

(3) A description of the methods, facilities, and controls used for the manufacture, processing, packing, storage, and, where appropriate, installation of the device, in sufficient detail so that a person generally familiar with good manufacturing practices can make a knowledgeable judgment about the quality control used in the manufacture of the device.

(4) An example of the agreements to be entered into by all investigators to comply with investigator obligations under this part, and a list of the names and

addresses of all investigators who have signed the agreement.

(5) A certification that all investigators who will participate in the investigation have signed the agreement, that the list of investigators includes all the investigators participating in the investigation, and that no investigators will be added to the investigation until they have signed the agreement.

(6) A list of the name, address, and chairperson of each IRB that has been or will be asked to review the investigation and a certification of the action concerning the investigation taken by each such IRB.

(7) The name and address of any institution at which a part of the investigation may be conducted that has not been identified in accordance with paragraph (b)(6) of this section.

(8) If the device is to be sold, the amount to be charged and an explanation of why sale does not constitute commercialization of the device.

(9) A claim for categorical exclusion under §25.30 or 25.34 or an environmental assessment under §25.40.

(10) Copies of all labeling for the device.

(11) Copies of all forms and informational materials to be provided to subjects to obtain informed consent.

(12) Any other relevant information FDA requests for review of the application.

(c) Additional information. FDA may request additional information concern-

ing an investigation or revision in the investigational plan. The sponsor may treat such a request as a disapproval of the application for purposes of requesting a hearing under part 16.

(d) Information previously submitted. Information previously submitted to the Center for Devices and Radiological Health in accordance with this chapter ordinarily need not be resubmitted, but may be incorporated by reference.

[45 FR 3751, Jan. 18, 1980, as amended at 46 FR 8956, Jan. 27, 1981; 50 FR 16669, Apr. 26, 1985; 53 FR 11252, Apr. 6, 1988; 61 FR 51530, Oct. 2, 1996; 62 FR 40600, July 29, 1997; 64 FR 10942, Mar. 8, 1999]

§812.25 Investigational plan.

The investigational plan shall include, in the following order:

(a) Purpose. The name and intended use of the device and the objectives and duration of the investigation.

(b) Protocol. A written protocol describing the methodology to be used and an analysis of the protocol demonstrating that the investigation is scientifically sound.

(c) Risk analysis. A description and analysis of all increased risks to which subjects will be exposed by the investigation; the manner in which these risks will be minimized; a justification for the investigation; and a description of the patient population, including the number, age, sex, and condition.

(d) Description of device. A description

of each important component, ingredient, property, and principle of operation of the device and of each anticipated change in the device during the course of the investigation.

(e) Monitoring procedures. The sponsor's written procedures for monitoring the investigation and the name and address of any monitor.

(f) Labeling. Copies of all labeling for the device.

(g) Consent materials. Copies of all forms and informational materials to be provided to subjects to obtain informed consent.

(h) IRB information. A list of the names, locations, and chairpersons of all IRB's that have been or will be asked to review the investigation, and a certification of any action taken by any of those IRB's with respect to the investigation.

(i) Other institutions. The name and address of each institution at which a part of the investigation may be conducted that has not been identified in paragraph (h) of this section.

(j) Additional records and reports. A description of records and reports that will be maintained on the investigation in addition to those prescribed in subpart G.

§812.27 Report of prior investigations.

(a) General. The report of prior investigations shall include reports of all prior clinical, animal, and laboratory testing of the device and shall be comprehensive and adequate to justify the proposed investigation.

(b) Specific contents. The report also shall include:

(1) A bibliography of all publications, whether adverse or supportive, that are relevant to an evaluation of the safety or effectiveness of the device, copies of all published and unpublished adverse information, and, if requested by an IRB or FDA, copies of other significant publications.

(2) A summary of all other unpublished information (whether adverse or supportive) in the possession of, or reasonably obtainable by, the sponsor that is relevant to an evaluation of the safety or effectiveness of the device.

(3) If information on nonclinical laboratory studies is provided, a statement that all such studies have been conducted in compliance with applicable requirements in the good laboratory practice regulations in part 58, or if any such study was not conducted in compliance with such regulations, a brief statement of the reason for the noncompliance. Failure or inability to comply with this requirement does not justify failure to provide information on a relevant nonclinical test study.

[45 FR 3751, Jan. 18, 1980, as amended at 50 FR 7518, Feb. 22, 1985]

§812.30 FDA action on applications.

(a) Approval or disapproval. FDA will notify the sponsor in writing of the date it receives an application. FDA may approve an investigation as proposed, approve it with modifications, or disapprove it. An investigation may not begin until:

(1) Thirty days after FDA receives the application at the address in §812.19 for the investigation of a device other than a banned device, unless FDA notifies the sponsor that the investigation may not begin; or

(2) FDA approves, by order, an IDE for the investigation.

(b) *Grounds for disapproval or withdrawal.* FDA may disapprove or withdraw approval of an application if FDA finds that:

(1) There has been a failure to comply with any requirement of this part or the act, any other applicable regulation or statute, or any condition of approval imposed by an IRB or FDA.

(2) The application or a report contains an untrue statement of a material fact, or omits material information required by this part.

(3) The sponsor fails to respond to a request for additional information within the time prescribed by FDA.

(4) There is reason to believe that the risks to the subjects are not outweighed by the anticipated benefits to the subjects and the importance of the knowledge to be gained, or informed consent is inadquate, or the investigation is scientifically unsound, or there is reason to believe that the device as used is ineffective.

(5) It is otherwise unreasonable to begin or to continue the investigation owing to the way in which the device is used or the inadequacy of:

(i) The report of prior investigations or the investigational plan;

(ii) The methods, facilities, and controls used for the manufacturing, processing, packaging, storage, and, where appropriate, installation of the device; or

(iii) Monitoring and review of the investigation.

(c) *Notice of disapproval or withdrawal.* If FDA disapproves an application or proposes to withdraw approval of an application, FDA will notify the sponsor in writing.

(1) A disapproval order will contain a complete statement of the reasons for disapproval and a statement that the sponsor has an opportunity to request a hearing under part 16.

(2) A notice of a proposed withdrawal of approval will contain a complete statement of the reasons for withdrawal and a statement that the sponsor has an opportunity to request a hearing under part 16. FDA will provide the opportunity for hearing before withdrawal of approval, unless FDA determines in the notice that continuation of testing under the exemption will result in an unreasonble risk to the public health and orders withdrawal of approval before any hearing.

[45 FR 3751, Jan. 18, 1980, as amended at 45 FR 58842, Sept. 5, 1980]

§812.35 Supplemental applications.

(a) *Changes in investigational plan*—(1) *Changes requiring prior approval.* Except as described in paragraphs (a)(2) through (a)(4) of this section, a sponsor must obtain approval of a supplemental application under §812.30(a), and IRB approval when appropriate (see §§56.110 and 56.111 of this chapter), prior to implementing a change to an investigational plan. If a sponsor intends to conduct an investigation that involves an exception to informed consent under §50.24 of this chapter, the sponsor shall submit a separate investigational device exemption (IDE) application in accordance with §812.20(a).

(2) Changes effected for emergency use. The requirements of paragraph (a)(1) of this section regarding FDA approval of a supplement do not apply in the case of a deviation from the investigational plan to protect the life or physical well-being of a subject in an emergency. Such deviation shall be reported to FDA within 5-working days after the sponsor learns of it (see §812.150(a)(4)).

(3) Changes effected with notice to FDA within 5 days. A sponsor may make certain changes without prior approval of a supplemental application under paragraph (a)(1) of this section if the sponsor determines that these changes meet the criteria described in paragraphs (a)(3)(i) and (a)(3)(ii) of this section, on the basis of credible information defined in paragraph (a)(3)(iii) of this section, and the sponsor provides notice to FDA within 5-working days of making these changes.

(i) Developmental changes. The requirements in paragraph (a)(1) of this section regarding FDA approval of a supplement do not apply to developmental changes in the device (including manufacturing changes) that do not constitute a signifi-

cant change in design or basic principles of operation and that are made in response to information gathered during the course of an investigation.

(ii) Changes to clinical protocol. The requirements in paragraph (a)(1) of this section regarding FDA approval of a supplement do not apply to changes to clinical protocols that do not affect:

(A) The validity of the data or information resulting from the completion of the approved protocol, or the relationship of likely patient risk to benefit relied upon to approve the protocol;

(B) The scientific soundness of the investigational plan; or

(C) The rights, safety, or welfare of the human subjects involved in the investigation.

(iii) Definition of credible information. (A) Credible information to support developmental changes in the device (including manufacturing changes) includes data generated under the design control procedures of §820.30, preclinical/animal testing, peer reviewed published literature, or other reliable information such as clinical information gathered during a trial or marketing.

(B) Credible information to support changes to clinical protocols is defined as the sponsor's documentation supporting the conclusion that a change does not have a significant impact on the study design or planned statistical analysis, and that the change does not affect the rights, safety, or welfare of the subjects. Documentation shall include information such as peer reviewed published literature, the recommendation of the clinical investigator(s), and/or the data gathered during the clinical trial or marketing.

(iv) Notice of IDE change. Changes meeting the criteria in paragraphs (a)(3)(i) and (a)(3)(ii) of this section that are supported by credible information as defined in paragraph (a)(3)(iii) of this section may be made without prior FDA approval if the sponsor submits a notice of the change to the IDE not later than 5-working days after making the change. Changes to devices are deemed to occur on the date the device, manufactured incorporating the design or manufacturing change, is distributed to the investigator(s). Changes to a clinical protocol are deemed to occur when a clinical investigator is notified by the sponsor that the change should be implemented in the protocol or, for sponsor-investigator studies, when a sponsor-investigator incorporates the change in the protocol. Such notices shall be identified as a "notice of IDE change."

(A) For a developmental or manufacturing change to the device, the notice shall include a summary of the relevant information gathered during the course of the investigation upon which the change was based; a description of the change to the device or manufacturing process (cross-referenced to the appropriate sections of the original device description or manufacturing process); and, if design controls were used to assess the change, a statement that no new risks were identified by appropriate risk analysis and that the verification and validation testing, as appropriate, demonstrated that the design outputs met the design input requirements. If another method of assessment was used, the notice shall include a summary of the information

which served as the credible information supporting the change.

(B) For a protocol change, the notice shall include a description of the change (cross-referenced to the appropriate sections of the original protocol); an assessment supporting the conclusion that the change does not have a significant impact on the study design or planned statistical analysis; and a summary of the information that served as the credible information supporting the sponsor's determination that the change does not affect the rights, safety, or welfare of the subjects.

(4) Changes submitted in annual report. The requirements of paragraph (a)(1) of this section do not apply to minor changes to the purpose of the study, risk analysis, monitoring procedures, labeling, informed consent materials, and IRB information that do not affect:

(i) The validity of the data or information resulting from the completion of the approved protocol, or the relationship of likely patient risk to benefit relied upon to approve the protocol;

(ii) The scientific soundness of the investigational plan; or

(iii) The rights, safety, or welfare of the human subjects involved in the investigation. Such changes shall be reported in the annual progress report for the IDE, under §812.150(b)(5).

(b) IRB approval for new facilities. A sponsor shall submit to FDA a certification of any IRB approval of an investigation or a part of an investigation not included in the IDE application. If the investigation is otherwise unchanged, the supplemental application shall consist of an updating of the information required by §812.20(b) and (c) and a description of any modifications in the investigational plan required by the IRB as a condition of approval. A certification of IRB approval need not be included in the initial submission of the supplemental application, and such certification is not a precondition for agency consideration of the application. Nevertheless, a sponsor may not begin a part of an investigation at a facility until the IRB has approved the investigation, FDA has received the certification of IRB approval, and FDA, under §812.30(a), has approved the supplemental application relating to that part of the investigation (see §56.103(a)).

[50 FR 25909, June 24, 1985; 50 FR 28932, July 17, 1985, as amended at 61 FR 51531, Oct. 2, 1996; 63 FR 64625, Nov. 23, 1998]

§812.36 Treatment use of an investigational device.

(a) General. A device that is not approved for marketing may be under clinical investigation for a serious or immediately life-threatening disease or condition in patients for whom no comparable or satisfactory alternative device or other therapy is available. During the clinical trial or prior to final action on the marketing application, it may be appropriate to use the device in the treatment of patients not in the trial under the provisions of a treatment investigational device exemption (IDE). The purpose of this section is to facilitate the availability of promising new devices to desperately ill patients as early in the device development process as possible,

before general marketing begins, and to obtain additional data on the device's safety and effectiveness. In the case of a serious disease, a device ordinarily may be made available for treatment use under this section after all clinical trials have been completed. In the case of an immediately life-threatening disease, a device may be made available for treatment use under this section prior to the completion of all clinical trials. For the purpose of this section, an "immediately life-threatening" disease means a stage of a disease in which there is a reasonable likelihood that death will occur within a matter of months or in which premature death is likely without early treatment. For purposes of this section, "treatment use"of a device includes the use of a device for diagnostic purposes.

(b) Criteria. FDA shall consider the use of an investigational device under a treatment IDE if:

(1) The device is intended to treat or diagnose a serious or immediately life-threatening disease or condition;

(2) There is no comparable or satisfactory alternative device or other therapy available to treat or diagnose that stage of the disease or condition in the intended patient population;

(3) The device is under investigation in a controlled clinical trial for the same use under an approved IDE, or such clinical trials have been completed; and

(4) The sponsor of the investigation is actively pursuing marketing approval/clearance of the investigational device with due diligence.

(c) Applications for treatment use. (1) A

treatment IDE application shall include, in the following order:

(i) The name, address, and telephone number of the sponsor of the treatment IDE;

(ii) The intended use of the device, the criteria for patient selection, and a written protocol describing the treatment use;

(iii) An explanation of the rationale for use of the device, including, as appropriate, either a list of the available regimens that ordinarily should be tried before using the investigational device or an explanation of why the use of the investigational device is preferable to the use of available marketed treatments;

(iv) A description of clinical procedures, laboratory tests, or other measures that will be used to evaluate the effects of the device and to minimize risk;

(v) Written procedures for monitoring the treatment use and the name and address of the monitor;

(vi) Instructions for use for the device and all other labeling as required under §812.5(a) and (b);

(vii) Information that is relevant to the safety and effectiveness of the device for the intended treatment use. Information from other IDE's may be incorporated by reference to support the treatment use;

(viii) A statement of the sponsor's commitment to meet all applicable responsibilities under this part and part 56 of this chapter and to ensure compliance of all participating investigators with the informed consent requirements of part 50 of this chapter;

(ix) An example of the agreement to be signed by all investigators participating in the treatment IDE and certification that no investigator will be added to the treatment IDE before the agreement is signed; and

(x) If the device is to be sold, the price to be charged and a statement indicating that the price is based on manufacturing and handling costs only.

(2) A licensed practitioner who receives an investigational device for treatment use under a treatment IDE is an "investigator" under the IDE and is responsible for meeting all applicable investigator responsibilities under this part and parts 50 and 56 of this chapter.

(d) *FDA action on treatment IDE applications.* (1) Approval of treatment IDE's. Treatment use may begin 30 days after FDA receives the treatment IDE submission at the address specified in §812.19, unless FDA notifies the sponsor in writing earlier than the 30 days that the treatment use may or may not begin. FDA may approve the treatment use as proposed or approve it with modifications.

(2) Disapproval or withdrawal of approval of treatment IDE's. FDA may disapprove or withdraw approval of a treatment IDE if:

(i) The criteria specified in §812.36(b) are not met or the treatment IDE does not contain the information required in §812.36(c);

(ii) FDA determines that any of the

grounds for disapproval or withdrawal of approval listed in §812.30(b)(1) through (b)(5) apply;

(iii) The device is intended for a serious disease or condition and there is insufficient evidence of safety and effectiveness to support such use;

(iv) The device is intended for an immediately life-threatening disease or condition and the available scientific evidence, taken as a whole, fails to provide a reasonable basis for concluding that the device:

(A) May be effective for its intended use in its intended population; or

(B) Would not expose the patients to whom the device is to be administered to an unreasonable and significant additional risk of illness or injury;

(v) There is reasonable evidence that the treatment use is impeding enrollment in, or otherwise interfering with the conduct or completion of, a controlled investigation of the same or another investigational device;

(vi) The device has received marketing approval/clearance or a comparable device or therapy becomes available to treat or diagnose the same indication in the same patient population for which the investigational device is being used;

(vii) The sponsor of the controlled clinical trial is not pursuing marketing approval/clearance with due diligence;

(viii) Approval of the IDE for the controlled clinical investigation of the device has been withdrawn; or

(ix) The clinical investigator(s) named in the treatment IDE are not qualified by reason of their scientific training and/or experience to use the investigational device for the intended treatment use.

(3) Notice of disapproval or withdrawal. If FDA disapproves or proposes to withdraw approval of a treatment IDE, FDA will follow the procedures set forth in §812.30(c).

(e) Safeguards. Treatment use of an investigational device is conditioned upon the sponsor and investigators complying with the safeguards of the IDE process and the regulations governing informed consent (part 50 of this chapter) and institutional review boards (part 56 of this chapter).

(f) Reporting requirements. The sponsor of a treatment IDE shall submit progress reports on a semi-annual basis to all reviewing IRB's and FDA until the filing of a marketing application. These reports shall be based on the period of time since initial approval of the treatment IDE and shall include the number of patients treated with the device under the treatment IDE, the names of the investigators participating in the treatment IDE, and a brief description of the sponsor's efforts to pursue marketing approval/clearance of the device. Upon filing of a marketing application, progress reports shall be submitted annually in accordance with §812.150(b)(5). The sponsor of a treatment IDE is responsible for submitting all other reports required under §812.150.

[62 FR 48947, Sept. 18, 1997]

§812.38 Confidentiality of data and information.

(a) Existence of IDE. FDA will not disclose the existence of an IDE unless its existence has previously been publicly disclosed or acknowledged, until FDA approves an application for premarket approval of the device subject to the IDE; or a notice of completion of a product development protocol for the device has become effective.

(b) Availability of summaries or data. (1) FDA will make publicly available, upon request, a detailed summary of information concerning the safety and effectiveness of the device that was the basis for an order approving, disapproving, or withdrawing approval of an application for an IDE for a banned device. The summary shall include information on any adverse effect on health caused by the device.

(2) If a device is a banned device or if the existence of an IDE has been publicly disclosed or acknowledged, data or information contained in the file is not available for public disclosure before approval of an application for premarket approval or the effective date of a notice of completion of a product development protocol except as provided in this section. FDA may, in its discretion, disclose a summary of selected portions of the safety and effectiveness data, that is, clinical, animal, or laboratory studies and tests of the device, for public consideration of a specific pending issue.

(3) If the existence of an IDE file has not been publicly disclosed or acknowledged, no data or information in the file are available for public disclosure except as provided in paragraphs (b)(1) and (c) of this section.

(4) Notwithstanding paragraph (b)(2) of this section, FDA will make available to the public, upon request, the information in the IDE that was required to be filed in Docket Number 95S–0158 in the Dockets Management Branch (HFA–305), Food and Drug Administration, 5630 Fishers Lane, rm. 1061, Rockville, MD 20852, for investigations involving an exception from informed consent under §50.24 of this chapter. Persons wishing to request this information shall submit a request under the Freedom of Information Act.

(c) Reports of adverse effects. Upon request or on its own initiative, FDA shall disclose to an individual on whom an investigational device has been used a copy of a report of adverse device effects relating to that use.

(d) Other rules. Except as otherwise provided in this section, the availability for public disclosure of data and information in an IDE file shall be handled in accordance with §814.9.

[45 FR 3751, Jan. 18, 1980, as amended at 53 FR 11253, Apr. 6, 1988; 61 FR 51531, Oct. 2, 1996]

Subpart C—Responsibilities of Sponsors

§812.40 General responsibilities of sponsors.

Sponsors are responsible for selecting qualified investigators and providing them with the information they need to conduct the investigation properly, ensuring proper monitoring of the investigation, ensuring that IRB review and approval are obtained, submitting an IDE application to FDA, and ensuring that any reviewing IRB and FDA are promptly informed of significant new information about an investigation. Additional responsibilities of sponsors are described in subparts B and G.

§812.42 FDA and IRB approval.

A sponsor shall not begin an investigation or part of an investigation until an IRB and FDA have both approved the application or supplemental application relating to the investigation or part of an investigation.

[46 FR 8957, Jan. 27, 1981]

§812.43 Selecting investigators and monitors.

(a) Selecting investigators. A sponsor shall select investigators qualified by training and experience to investigate the device.

(b) Control of device. A sponsor shall ship investigational devices only to qualified investigators participating in the investigation.

(c) Obtaining agreements. A sponsor shall obtain from each participating investigator a signed agreement that includes:

(1) The investigator's curriculum vitae.

(2) Where applicable, a statement of the investigator's relevant experience, including the dates, location, extent, and type of experience.

(3) If the investigator was involved in an investigation or other research that was terminated, an explanation of the circumstances that led to termination.

(4) A statement of the investigator's commitment to:

(i) Conduct the investigation in accordance with the agreement, the investigational plan, this part and other applicable FDA regulations, and conditions of approval imposed by the reviewing IRB or FDA;

(ii) Supervise all testing of the device involving human subjects; and

(iii) Ensure that the requirements for obtaining informed consent are met.

(5) Sufficient accurate financial disclosure information to allow the sponsor to submit a complete and accurate certification or disclosure statement as required under part 54 of this chapter. The sponsor shall obtain a commitment from the clinical investigator to promptly update this information if any relevant changes occur during the course of the investigation and for 1 year following completion of the study. This information shall not be submitted in an investigational device exemption application, but shall be submitted in any marketing application involving the device.

(d) Selecting monitors. A sponsor shall select monitors qualified by training and experience to monitor the investigational study in accordance with this part and other applicable FDA regulations.

[45 FR 3751, Jan. 18, 1980, as amended at 63 FR 5253, Feb. 2, 1998]

§812.45 Informing investigators.

A sponsor shall supply all investigators participating in the investigation with copies of the investigational plan and the report of prior investigations of the device.

§812.46 Monitoring investigations.

(a) Securing compliance. A sponsor who discovers that an investigator is not complying with the signed agreement, the investigational plan, the requirements of this part or other applicable FDA regulations, or any conditions of approval imposed by the reviewing IRB or FDA shall promptly either secure compliance, or discontinue shipments of the device to the investigator and terminate the investigator's participation in the investigation. A sponsor shall also require such an investigator to dispose of or return the device, unless this action would jeopardize the rights, safety, or welfare of a subject.

(b) Unanticipated adverse device effects. (1) A sponsor shall immediately conduct an evaluation of any unanticipated adverse device effect.

(2) A sponsor who determines that an unanticipated adverse device effect presents an unreasonable risk to subjects shall terminate all investigations or parts of investigations presenting that risk as soon as possible. Termination shall occur not later than 5 working days after the sponsor makes this determination and not later than 15 working days after the sponsor first received notice of the effect.

(c) Resumption of terminated studies. If the device is a significant risk device, a sponsor may not resume a terminated investigation without IRB and FDA approval. If the device is not a significant risk device, a sponsor may not resume a terminated investigation without IRB approval and, if the investigation was terminated under paragraph (b)(2) of this section, FDA approval.

§812.47 Emergency research under §50.24 of this chapter.

(a) The sponsor shall monitor the progress of all investigations involving an exception from informed consent under §50.24 of this chapter. When the sponsor receives from the IRB information concerning the public disclosures under §50.24(a)(7)(ii) and (a)(7)(iii) of this chapter, the sponsor shall promptly submit to the IDE file and to Docket Number 95S–0158 in the Dockets Management Branch (HFA–305), Food and Drug Administration, 5630 Fishers Lane, rm. 1061, Rockville, MD 20852, copies of the information that was disclosed, identified by the IDE number.

(b) The sponsor also shall monitor such investigations to determine when an IRB determines that it cannot approve the research because it does not meet the criteria in the exception in §50.24(a) of this chapter or because of other relevant ethical concerns. The sponsor promptly shall provide this information in writing to FDA, investigators who are asked to participate in this or a substantially equivalent clinical investigation, and other IRB's that are asked to review this or a substantially equivalent investigation.

[61 FR 51531, Oct. 2, 1996, as amended at 64 FR 10943, Mar. 8, 1999]

Subpart D—IRB Review and Approval

§812.60 IRB composition, duties, and functions.

An IRB reviewing and approving investigations under this part shall comply with the requirements of part 56 in all respects, including its composition, duties, and functions.

[46 FR 8957, Jan. 27, 1981]

§812.62 IRB approval.

(a) An IRB shall review and have authority to approve, require modifications in (to secure approval), or disapprove all investigations covered by this part.

(b) If no IRB exists or if FDA finds that an IRB's review is inadequate, a sponsor may submit an application to FDA.

[46 FR 8957, Jan. 27, 1981]

§812.64 IRB's continuing review.

The IRB shall conduct its continuing review of an investigation in accordance with part 56.

[46 FR 8957, Jan. 27, 1981]

§812.65 [Reserved]

§812.66 Significant risk device determinations.

If an IRB determines that an investigation, presented for approval under §812.2(b)(1)(ii), involves a significant risk device, it shall so notify the investigator and, where appropriate, the sponsor. A sponsor may not begin the investigation except as provided in §812.30(a).

[46 FR 8957, Jan. 27, 1981]

Subpart E—Responsibilities of Investigators

§812.100 General responsibilities of investigators.

An investigator is responsible for ensuring that an investigation is conducted according to the signed agreement, the investigational plan and applicable FDA regulations, for protecting the rights, safety, and welfare of subjects under the investigator's care, and for the control of devices under investigation. An investigator also is responsible for ensuring that informed consent is obtained in accordance with part 50 of this chapter. Additional responsibilities of investigators are described in subpart G.

[45 FR 3751, Jan. 18, 1980, as amended at 46 FR 8957, Jan. 27, 1981]

§812.110 Specific responsibilities of investigators.

(a) Awaiting approval. An investigator may determine whether potential subjects would be interested in participating in an investigation, but shall not request the written informed consent of any subject to participate, and shall not allow any subject to participate before obtaining IRB and FDA approval.

(b) Compliance. An investigator shall conduct an investigation in accordance with the signed agreement with the sponsor, the investigational plan, this part and other applicable FDA regulations, and any conditions of approval imposed by an IRB or FDA.

(c) Supervising device use. An investigator shall permit an investigational device to be used only with subjects under the investigator's supervision. An investigator shall not supply an investigational device to any person not authorized under this part to receive it.

(d) Financial disclosure. A clinical investigator shall disclose to the sponsor sufficient accurate financial information to allow the applicant to submit complete and accurate certification or disclosure statements required under part 54 of this chapter. The investigator shall promptly update this information if any relevant changes occur during the course of the investigation and for 1 year following completion of the study.

(e) Disposing of device. Upon completion or termination of a clinical investigation or the investigator's part of an investigation, or at the sponsor's request, an investigator shall return to the sponsor any remaining supply of the device or otherwise dispose of the device as the sponsor directs.

[45 FR 3751, Jan. 18, 1980, as amended at 63 FR 5253, Feb. 2, 1998]

§812.119 Disqualification of a clinical investigator.

(a) If FDA has information indicating that an investigator has repeatedly or deliberately failed to comply with the requirements of this part, part 50, or part 56 of this chapter, or has repeatedly or deliberately submitted false information either to the sponsor of the investigation or in any required report, the Center for Devices and Radiological Health will furnish the investigator written notice of the matter under complaint and offer the investigator an opportunity to explain the matter in writing, or, at the option of the investigator, in an informal conference. If an explanation is offered and accepted by the Center for Devices and Radiological Health, the disqualification process will be terminated. If an explanation is offered but not accepted by the Center for Devices and Radiological Health, the investigator will be given an opportunity for a regulatory hearing under part 16 of this chapter on the question of whether the investigator is entitled to receive investigational devices.

(b) After evaluating all available information, including any explanation presented by the investigator, if the Commissioner determines that the investigator has repeatedly or deliberately failed to comply with the requirements of this part, part 50, or part 56 of this chapter, or has deliberately or repeatedly submitted false information either to the sponsor of the investigation or in any required report, the Commissioner will notify the investigator, the sponsor of any investigation in which the investigator has been named as a participant, and the reviewing IRB that the investigator is not entitled to receive investigational devices. The notification will provide a statement of basis for such determination.

(c) Each investigational device exemption (IDE) and each cleared or approved application submitted under this part, subpart E of part 807 of this chapter, or part 814 of this chapter containing data reported by an investigator who has been determined to be ineligible to receive investigational devices will be examined to determine whether the investigator has submitted unreliable data that are essential to the continuation of the investigation or essential to the approval or clearance of any marketing application.

(d) If the Commissioner determines, after the unreliable data submitted by the investigator are eliminated from consideration, that the data remaining are inadequate to support a conclusion that it is reasonably safe to continue the investigation, the Commissioner will notify the sponsor who shall have an opportunity for a regulatory hearing under part 16 of this chapter. If a danger to the public health exists, however, the Commissioner shall terminate the IDE immediately and notify the sponsor and the reviewing IRB of the determination. In such case, the sponsor shall have an opportunity for a regulatory hearing before FDA under part 16 of this chapter on the question of whether the IDE should be reinstated.

(e) If the Commissioner determines, after the unreliable data submitted by the investigator are eliminated from consideration, that the continued clearance or approval of the marketing application for which the data were submitted cannot be justified, the Commissioner will

proceed to withdraw approval or rescind clearance of the medical device in accordance with the applicable provisions of the act.

(f) An investigator who has been determined to be ineligible to receive investigational devices may be reinstated as eligible when the Commissioner determines that the investigator has presented adequate assurances that the investigator will employ investigational devices solely in compliance with the provisions of this part and of parts 50 and 56 of this chapter.

[62 FR 12096, Mar. 14, 1997]

Subpart F [Reserved]

Subpart G—Records and Reports

§812.140 Records.

(a) Investigator records. A participating investigator shall maintain the following accurate, complete, and current records relating to the investigator's participation in an investigation:

(1) All correspondence with another investigator, an IRB, the sponsor, a monitor, or FDA, including required reports.

(2) Records of receipt, use or disposition of a device that relate to:

(i) The type and quantity of the device, the dates of its receipt, and the batch number or code mark.

(ii) The names of all persons who received, used, or disposed of each device.

(iii) Why and how many units of the device have been returned to the sponsor, repaired, or otherwise disposed of.

(3) Records of each subject's case history and exposure to the device. Case histories include the case report forms and supporting data including, for example, signed and dated consent forms and medical records including, for example, progress notes of the physician, the individual's hospital chart(s), and the nurses' notes. Such records shall include:

(i) Documents evidencing informed consent and, for any use of a device by the investigator without informed consent, any written concurrence of a licensed physician and a brief description of the circumstances justifying the failure to obtain informed consent. The case history for each individual shall document that informed consent was obtained prior to participation in the study.

(ii) All relevant observations, including records concerning adverse device effects (whether anticipated or unanticipated), information and data on the condition of each subject upon entering, and during the course of, the investigation, including information about relevant previous medical history and the results of all diagnostic tests.

(iii) A record of the exposure of each subject to the investigational device, including the date and time of each use, and any other therapy.

(4) The protocol, with documents showing the dates of and reasons for each deviation from the protocol.

(5) Any other records that FDA requires to be maintained by regulation or by specific requirement for a category of investigations or a particular investigation.

(b) Sponsor records. A sponsor shall maintain the following accurate, complete, and current records relating to an investigation:

(1) All correspondence with another sponsor, a monitor, an investigator, an IRB, or FDA, including required reports.

(2) Records of shipment and disposition. Records of shipment shall include the name and address of the consignee, type and quantity of device, date of shipment, and batch number or code mark. Records of disposition shall describe the batch number or code marks of any devices returned to the sponsor, repaired, or disposed of in other ways by the investigator or another person, and the reasons for and method of disposal.

(3) Signed investigator agreements including the financial disclosure information required to be collected under §812.43(c)(5) in accordance with part 54 of this chapter.

(4) For each investigation subject to §812.2(b)(1) of a device other than a significant risk device, the records described in paragraph (b)(5) of this section and the following records, consolidated in one location and available for FDA inspection and copying:

(i) The name and intended use of the device and the objectives of the investigation;

(ii) A brief explanation of why the device is not a significant risk device:

(iii) The name and address of each investigator:

(iv) The name and address of each IRB that has reviewed the investigation:

(v) A statement of the extent to which the good manufacturing practice regulation in part 820 will be followed in manufacturing the device; and

(vi) Any other information required by FDA.

(5) Records concerning adverse device effects (whether anticipated or unanticipated) and complaints and

(6) Any other records that FDA requires to be maintained by regulation or by specific requirement for a category of investigation or a particular investigation.

(c) IRB records. An IRB shall maintain records in accordance with part 56 of this chapter.

(d) Retention period. An investigator or sponsor shall maintain the records required by this subpart during the investigation and for a period of 2 years after the latter of the following two dates: The date on which the investigation is terminated or completed, or the date that the records are no longer required for purposes of supporting a premarket approval application or a notice of completion of a product development protocol.

(e) Records custody. An investigator or sponsor may withdraw from the responsibility to maintain records for the period required in paragraph (d) of this section and transfer custody of the records to any other person who will accept responsibility for them under this part, including the requirements of §812.145. Notice of a transfer shall be given to FDA not later than 10 working days after transfer occurs.

[45 FR 3751, Jan. 18, 1980, as amended at 45 FR 58843, Sept. 5, 1980; 46 FR 8957, Jan. 27, 1981; 61 FR 57280, Nov. 5, 1996; 63 FR 5253, Feb. 2, 1998]

§812.145 Inspections.

(a) Entry and inspection. A sponsor or an investigator who has authority to grant access shall permit authorized FDA employees, at reasonable times and in a reasonable manner, to enter and inspect any establishment where devices are held (including any establishment where devices are manufactured, processed, packed, installed, used, or implanted or where records of results from use of devices are kept).

(b) Records inspection. A sponsor, IRB, or investigator, or any other person acting on behalf of such a person with respect to an investigation, shall permit authorized FDA employees, at reasonable times and in a reasonable manner, to inspect and copy all records relating to an investigation.

(c) Records identifying subjects. An investigator shall permit authorized FDA employees to inspect and copy records that identify subjects, upon notice that FDA has reason to suspect that adequate informed consent was not obtained, or that reports required to be submitted by the investigator to the sponsor or IRB have not been submitted or are incomplete, inaccurate, false, or misleading.

§812.150 Reports.

(a) Investigator reports. An investigator shall prepare and submit the following complete, accurate, and timely reports:

(1) Unanticipated adverse device effects. An investigator shall submit to the sponsor and to the reviewing IRB a report of any unanticipated adverse device effect occurring during an investigation as soon as possible, but in no event later than 10 working days after the investigator first learns of the effect.

(2) Withdrawal of IRB approval. An investigator shall report to the sponsor, within 5 working days, a withdrawal of approval by the reviewing IRB of the investigator's part of an investigation.

(3) Progress. An investigator shall submit progress reports on the investigation to the sponsor, the monitor, and the reviewing IRB at regular intervals, but in no event less often than yearly.

(4) Deviations from the investigational plan. An investigator shall notify the sponsor and the reviewing IRB (see §56.108(a) (3) and (4)) of any deviation from the investigational plan to protect the life or physical well-being of a subject in an emergency. Such notice shall be given as soon as possible, but in no event later than 5 working days after the emergency occurred. Except in such an emergency, prior approval by the sponsor is required for changes in or deviations from a plan, and if these changes or deviations may affect the scientific

soundness of the plan or the rights, safety, or welfare of human subjects, FDA and IRB in accordance with §812.35(a) also is required.

(5) Informed consent. If an investigator uses a device without obtaining informed consent, the investigator shall report such use to the sponsor and the reviewing IRB within 5 working days after the use occurs.

(6) Final report. An investigator shall, within 3 months after termination or completion of the investigation or the investigator's part of the investigation, submit a final report to the sponsor and the reviewing IRB.

(7) Other. An investigator shall, upon request by a reviewing IRB or FDA, provide accurate, complete, and current information about any aspect of the investigation.

(b) Sponsor reports. A sponsor shall prepare and submit the following complete, accurate, and timely reports:

(1) Unanticipated adverse device effects. A sponsor who conducts an evaluation of an unanticipated adverse device effect under §812.46(b) shall report the results of such evaluation to FDA and to all reviewing IRB's and participating investigators within 10 working days after the sponsor first receives notice of the effect. Thereafter the sponsor shall submit such additional reports concerning the effect as FDA requests.

(2) Withdrawal of IRB approval. A sponsor shall notify FDA and all reviewing IRB's and participating investigators of any withdrawal of approval of an investigation or a part of an investigation by a

reviewing IRB within 5 working days after receipt of the withdrawal of approval.

(3) *Withdrawal of FDA approval.* A sponsor shall notify all reviewing IRB's and participating investigators of any withdrawal of FDA approval of the investigation, and shall do so within 5 working days after receipt of notice of the withdrawal of approval.

(4) *Current investigator list.* A sponsor shall submit to FDA, at 6-month intervals, a current list of the names and addresses of all investigators participating in the investigation. The sponsor shall submit the first such list 6 months after FDA approval.

(5) *Progress reports.* At regular intervals, and at least yearly, a sponsor shall submit progress reports to all reviewing IRB's. In the case of a significant risk device, a sponsor shall also submit progress reports to FDA. A sponsor of a treatment IDE shall submit semi-annual progress reports to all reviewing IRB's and FDA in accordance with §812.36(f) and annual reports in accordance with this section.

(6) *Recall and device disposition.* A sponsor shall notify FDA and all reviewing IRB's of any request that an investigator return, repair, or otherwise dispose of any units of a device. Such notice shall occur within 30 working days after the request is made and shall state why the request was made.

(7) *Final report.* In the case of a significant risk device, the sponsor shall notify FDA within 30 working days of the completion or termination of the investigation and shall submit a final report to FDA and all reviewing the IRB's and par-

ticipating investigators within 6 months after completion or termination. In the case of a device that is not a significant risk device, the sponsor shall submit a final report to all reviewing IRB's within 6 months after termination or completion.

(8) *Informed consent.* A sponsor shall submit to FDA a copy of any report by an investigator under paragraph (a)(5) of this section of use of a device without obtaining informed consent, within 5 working days of receipt of notice of such use.

(9) *Significant risk device determinations.* If an IRB determines that a device is a significant risk device, and the sponsor had proposed that the IRB consider the device not to be a significant risk device, the sponsor shall submit to FDA a report of the IRB's determination within 5 working days after the sponsor first learns of the IRB's determination.

(10) *Other.* A sponsor shall, upon request by a reviewing IRB or FDA, provide accurate, complete, and current information about any aspect of the investigation.

[45 FR 3751, Jan. 18, 1980, as amended at 45 FR 58843, Sept. 5, 1980; 48 FR 15622, Apr. 12, 1983; 62 FR 48948, Sept. 18, 1997]

TITLE 45—PUBLIC WELFARE

Subtitle A—Department of Health and Human Services,
General Administration
Subchapter A—General Administration

PART 46

Protection of Human Subjects

Subpart C—Additional Protections Pertaining to Biomedical and Behavioral Research Involving Prisoners as Subjects

Subpart D—Additional Protections for Children Involved as Subjects in Research

Authority: 5 U.S.C. 301; 42 U.S.C. 289(a).

Editorial Note: The Department of Health and Human Services issued a notice of waiver regarding the requirements set forth in part 46, relating to protection of human subjects, as they pertain to demonstration projects, approved under section 1115 of the Social Security Act, which test the use of cost—sharing, such as deductibles, copayment and coinsurance, in the Medicaid program. For further information see 47 FR 9208, Mar. 4, 1982.

Subpart A—Basic HHS Policy for Protection of Human Research Subjects

Source: 56 FR 28012, 28022, June 18, 1991, unless otherwise noted.

§46.101 To what does this policy apply?

(a) Except as provided in paragraph (b) of this section, this policy applies to all research involving human subjects conducted, supported or otherwise subject to regulation by any federal department or agency which takes appropriate administrative action to make the policy applicable to such research. This includes research conducted by federal civilian employees or military personnel, except that each department or agency head may adopt such procedural modifications as may be appropriate from an administrative standpoint. It also includes research conducted, supported, or otherwise subject to regulation by the federal government outside the United States.

(1) Research that is conducted or supported by a federal department or agency, whether or not it is regulated as defined in §46.102(e), must comply with all sections of this policy.

(2) Research that is neither conducted nor supported by a federal department or agency but is subject to regulation as defined in §46.102(e) must be reviewed and approved, in compliance with §46.101, §46.102, and §46.107 through §46.117 of this policy, by an institutional review board (IRB) that operates in accordance with the pertinent requirements of this policy.

(b) Unless otherwise required by department or agency heads, research activities in which the only involvement of human subjects will be in one or more of the following categories are exempt from this policy:

(1) Research conducted in established or commonly accepted educational settings, involving normal educational practices, such as (i) research on regular and special education instructional strategies, or (ii) research on the effectiveness of or the comparison among instructional techniques, curricula, or classroom management methods.

(2) Research involving the use of educational tests (cognitive, diagnostic, aptitude, achievement), survey procedures, interview procedures or observation of public behavior, unless:

(i) Information obtained is recorded in such a manner that human subjects can be identified, directly or through identifiers linked to the subjects; and (ii) any disclosure of the human subjects' responses outside the research could reasonably place the subjects at risk of criminal or civil liability or be damaging to the subjects' financial standing, employability, or reputation.

(3) Research involving the use of educational tests (cognitive, diagnostic, aptitude, achievement), survey procedures, interview procedures, or observation of public behavior that is not exempt under paragraph (b)(2) of this section, if:

(i) The human subjects are elected or appointed public officials or candidates for public office; or (ii) federal statute(s) require(s) without exception that the confidentiality of the personally identifiable information will be maintained throughout the research and thereafter.

(4) Research, involving the collection or study of existing data, documents, records, pathological specimens, or diagnostic specimens, if these sources are publicly available or if the information is recorded by the investigator in such a manner that subjects cannot be identified, directly or through identifiers linked to the subjects.

(5) Research and demonstration projects which are conducted by or subject to the approval of department or agency heads, and which are designed to study, evaluate, or otherwise examine:

(i) Public benefit or service programs; (ii) procedures for obtaining benefits or services under those programs; (iii) possible changes in or alternatives to those programs or procedures; or (iv) possible changes in methods or levels of payment for benefits or services under those programs.

(6) Taste and food quality evaluation and consumer acceptance studies, (i) if wholesome foods without additives are consumed or (ii) if a food is consumed that contains a food ingredient at or below the level and for a use found to be safe, or agricultural chemical or environmental contaminant at or below the level found to be safe, by the Food and Drug Administration or approved by the Environmental Protection Agency or the Food Safety and Inspection Service of the U.S. Department of Agriculture.

(c) Department or agency heads retain final judgment as to whether a particular activity is covered by this policy.

(d) Department or agency heads may require that specific research activities or classes of research activities conducted, supported, or otherwise subject to regulation by the department or agency but not otherwise covered by this policy, comply with some or all of the requirements of this policy.

(e) Compliance with this policy requires compliance with pertinent federal laws or regulations which provide additional protections for human subjects.

(f) This policy does not affect any state or local laws or regulations which may otherwise be applicable and which provide additional protections for human subjects.

(g) This policy does not affect any foreign laws or regulations which may otherwise be applicable and which provide additional protections to human subjects of research.

(h) When research covered by this policy takes place in foreign countries, procedures normally followed in the foreign countries to protect human subjects may differ from those set forth in this policy. [An example is a foreign institution which complies with guidelines consistent with the World Medical Assembly Declaration (Declaration of Helsinki amended 1989) issued either by sovereign states or by an organization whose function for the protection of human research subjects is internationally recognized.] In these circumstances, if a department or agency head determines that the procedures prescribed by the institution afford protections that are at least equivalent to those provided in this policy, the department or agency head may approve the substitution of the foreign procedures in lieu of the procedural requirements provided in this policy. Except when otherwise required by statute, Executive Order, or the department or agency head, notices of these actions as they occur will be published in the Federal Register or will be otherwise published as provided in department or agency procedures.

(i) Unless otherwise required by law, department or agency heads may waive the applicability of some or all of the provisions of this policy to specific research activities or classes of research activities otherwise covered by this policy. Except when otherwise required by statute or Executive Order, the department or agency head shall forward advance notices of these actions to the Office for Protection from Research Risks, Department of Health and Human Services (HHS), and shall also publish them in the Federal Register or in such other manner as provided in department or agency procedures. [1]

1. Institutions with HHS-approved assurances on file will abide by provisions of title 45 CFR part 46 subparts A–D. Some of the other Departments and Agencies have incorporated all provisions of title 45 CFR part 46 into their policies and procedures as well. However, the exemptions at 45 CFR 46.101(b) do not apply to research involving prisoners, fetuses, pregnant women, or human in vitro fertilization, subparts B and C. The exemption at 45 CFR 46.101(b)(2), for research involving survey or interview procedures or observation of public behavior, does not apply to research with children, subpart D, except for research involving observations of public behavior when the investigator(s) do not participate in the activities being observed.

[56 FR 28012, 28022, June 18, 1991; 56 FR 29756, June 28, 1991]

§46.102 Definitions.

(a) Department or agency head means the head of any federal department or agency and any other officer or employee of any department or agency to whom authority has been delegated.

(b) Institution means any public or private entity or agency (including federal, state, and other agencies).

(c) Legally authorized representative means an individual or judicial or other body authorized under applicable law to consent on behalf of a prospective subject to the subject's participation in the procedure(s) involved in the research.

(d) Research means a systematic investigation, including research development, testing and evaluation, designed to develop or contribute to generalizable knowledge. Activities which meet this definition constitute research for purposes of this policy, whether or not they are conducted or supported under a program which is considered research for other purposes. For example, some demonstration and service programs may include research activities.

(e) Research subject to regulation, and similar terms are intended to encompass those research activities for which a federal department or agency has specific responsibility for regulating as a research activity, (for example, Investigational New Drug requirements administered by the Food and Drug Administration). It does not include research activities which are incidentally regulated by a federal department or agency solely as part of the department's or agency's broader responsibility to regulate certain types of activities whether research or non-research in nature (for example, Wage and Hour requirements administered by the Department of Labor).

(f) Human subject means a living individual about whom an investigator (whether professional or student) conducting research obtains

(1) Data through intervention or interaction with the individual, or

(2) Identifiable private information.

Intervention includes both physical procedures by which data are gathered (for example, venipuncture) and manipulations of the subject or the subject's environment that are performed for research purposes. Interaction includes communication or interpersonal contact between investigator and subject. Private information includes information about behavior that occurs in a context in which an individual can reasonably expect that no observation or recording is taking place, and information which has been provided for specific purposes by an individual and which the individual can reasonably expect will not be made public (for example, a medical record). Private information must be individually identifiable (i.e., the identity of the subject is or may readily be ascertained by the investigator or associated with the information) in order for obtaining the information to constitute research involving human subjects.

(g) IRB means an institutional review board established in accord with and for the purposes expressed in this policy.

(h) IRB approval means the determination of the IRB that the research has been reviewed and may be conducted at an institution within the constraints set forth by the IRB and by other institutional and federal requirements.

(i) Minimal risk means that the probability and magnitude of harm or discomfort anticipated in the research are not greater in and of themselves than those ordinarily encountered in daily life or during the performance of routine physical or psychological examinations or tests.

(j) Certification means the official notification by the institution to the supporting department or agency, in accordance with the requirements of this policy, that a research project or activity involving human subjects has been reviewed and approved by an IRB in accordance with an approved assurance.

§46.103 Assuring compliance with this policy—research conducted or supported by any Federal Department or Agency.

(a) Each institution engaged in research which is covered by this policy and which is conducted or supported by a federal department or agency shall provide written assurance satisfactory to the department or agency head that it will comply with the requirements set forth in this policy. In lieu of requiring submission of an assurance, individual department or agency heads shall accept the existence of a current assurance, appropriate for the research in question, on file with the Office for Protection from Research Risks, HHS, and approved for federalwide use by that office. When the existence of an HHS-approved assurance is accepted in lieu of requiring submission of an assurance, reports (except certification) required by this policy to be made to department and agency heads shall also be made to the Office for Protection from Research Risks, HHS.

(b) Departments and agencies will conduct or support research covered by this policy only if the institution has an assurance approved as provided in this section, and only if the institution has certified to the department or agency head that the research has been reviewed and approved by an IRB provided for in the assurance, and will be subject to continuing review by the IRB. Assurances applicable to federally supported or conducted research shall at a minimum include:

(1) A statement of principles governing the institution in the discharge of its responsibilities for protecting the rights and welfare of human subjects of research conducted at or sponsored by the institution, regardless of whether the research is subject to federal regulation. This may include an appropriate existing code, declaration, or statement of ethical principles, or a statement formulated by the institution itself. This requirement does not preempt provisions of this policy applicable to department- or agency-supported or regulated research and need not be applicable to any research exempted or waived under §46.101 (b) or (i).

(2) Designation of one or more IRBs established in accordance with the requirements of this policy, and for which provisions are made for meeting space and sufficient staff to support the IRB's review and recordkeeping duties.

(3) A list of IRB members identified by name; earned degrees; representative capacity; indications of experience such as board certifications, licenses, etc., sufficient to describe each member's chief anticipated contributions to IRB deliberations; and any employment or other relationship between each member and the institution; for example: full-time employee, part-time employee, member of governing panel or board, stockholder, paid or unpaid consultant. Changes in IRB membership shall be reported to the department or agency head, unless in accord with §46.103(a) of this policy, the existence of an HHS-approved assurance is accepted. In this case, change in IRB membership shall be reported to the Office for Protection from Research Risks, HHS.

(4) Written procedures which the IRB will follow (i) for conducting its initial and continuing review of research and for reporting its findings and actions to the investigator and the institution; (ii) for determining which projects require review more often than annually and which projects need verification from sources other than the investigators that no material changes have occurred since previous IRB review; and (iii) for ensuring prompt reporting to the IRB of proposed changes in a research activity, and for ensuring that such changes in approved research, during the period for which IRB approval has already been given, may not be initiated without IRB review and approval except when necessary to eliminate apparent immediate hazards to the subject.

(5) Written procedures for ensuring prompt reporting to the IRB, appropriate institutional officials, and the department or agency head of (i) any unantici-

pated problems involving risks to subjects or others or any serious or continuing noncompliance with this policy or the requirements or determinations of the IRB and (ii) any suspension or termination of IRB approval.

(c) The assurance shall be executed by an individual authorized to act for the institution and to assume on behalf of the institution the obligations imposed by this policy and shall be filed in such form and manner as the department or agency head prescribes.

(d) The department or agency head will evaluate all assurances submitted in accordance with this policy through such officers and employees of the department or agency and such experts or consultants engaged for this purpose as the department or agency head determines to be appropriate. The department or agency head's evaluation will take into consideration the adequacy of the proposed IRB in light of the anticipated scope of the institution's research activities and the types of subject populations likely to be involved, the appropriateness of the proposed initial and continuing review procedures in light of the probable risks, and the size and complexity of the institution.

(e) On the basis of this evaluation, the department or agency head may approve or disapprove the assurance, or enter into negotiations to develop an approvable one. The department or agency head may limit the period during which any particular approved assurance or class of approved assurances shall remain effective or otherwise condition or restrict approval.

(f) Certification is required when the research is supported by a federal department or agency and not otherwise exempted or waived under §46.101 (b) or (i). An institution with an approved assurance shall certify that each application or proposal for research covered by the assurance and by §46.103 of this Policy has been reviewed and approved by the IRB. Such certification must be submitted with the application or proposal or by such later date as may be prescribed by the department or agency to which the application or proposal is submitted. Under no condition shall research covered by §46.103 of the Policy be supported prior to receipt of the certification that the research has been reviewed and approved by the IRB. Institutions without an approved assurance covering the research shall certify within 30 days after receipt of a request for such a certification from the department or agency, that the application or proposal has been approved by the IRB. If the certification is not submitted within these time limits, the application or proposal may be returned to the institution.

(Approved by the Office of Management and Budget under control number 9999–0020)

[56 FR 28012, 28022, June 18, 1991; 56 FR 29756, June 28, 1991]

§§46.104–46.106 [Reserved]

§46.107 IRB membership.

(a) Each IRB shall have at least five members, with varying backgrounds to promote complete and adequate review of research activities commonly conducted by the institution. The IRB shall be sufficiently qualified through the experience and expertise of its members, and the diversity of the members, including consideration of race, gender, and cultural backgrounds and sensitivity to such issues as community attitudes, to promote respect for its advice and counsel in safeguarding the rights and welfare of human subjects. In addition to possessing the professional competence necessary to review specific research activities, the IRB shall be able to ascertain the acceptability of proposed research in terms of institutional commitments and regulations, applicable law, and standards of professional conduct and practice. The IRB shall therefore include persons knowledgeable in these areas. If an IRB regularly reviews research that involves a vulnerable category of subjects, such as children, prisoners, pregnant women, or handicapped or mentally disabled persons, consideration shall be given to the inclusion of one or more individuals who are knowledgeable about and experienced in working with these subjects.

(b) Every nondiscriminatory effort will be made to ensure that no IRB consists entirely of men or entirely of women, including the institution's consideration of qualified persons of both sexes, so long as no selection is made to the IRB on the basis of gender. No IRB may consist entirely of members of one profession.

(c) Each IRB shall include at least one member whose primary concerns are in scientific areas and at least one member whose primary concerns are in nonscientific areas.

(d) Each IRB shall include at least one member who is not otherwise affiliated

with the institution and who is not part of the immediate family of a person who is affiliated with the institution.

(e) No IRB may have a member participate in the IRB's initial or continuing review of any project in which the member has a conflicting interest, except to provide information requested by the IRB.

(f) An IRB may, in its discretion, invite individuals with competence in special areas to assist in the review of issues which require expertise beyond or in addition to that available on the IRB. These individuals may not vote with the IRB.

§46.108 IRB functions and operations.

In order to fulfill the requirements of this policy each IRB shall:

(a) Follow written procedures in the same detail as described in §46.103(b)(4) and, to the extent required by, §46.103(b)(5).

(b) Except when an expedited review procedure is used (see §46.110), review proposed research at convened meetings at which a majority of the members of the IRB are present, including at least one member whose primary concerns are in nonscientific areas. In order for the research to be approved, it shall receive the approval of a majority of those members present at the meeting.

§46.109 IRB review of research.

(a) An IRB shall review and have authority to approve, require modifications in (to secure approval), or disapprove all research activities covered by this policy.

(b) An IRB shall require that information given to subjects as part of informed consent is in accordance with §46.116. The IRB may require that information, in addition to that specifically mentioned in §46.116, be given to the subjects when in the IRB's judgment the information would meaningfully add to the protection of the rights and welfare of subjects.

(c) An IRB shall require documentation of informed consent or may waive documentation in accordance with §46.117.

(d) An IRB shall notify investigators and the institution in writing of its decision to approve or disapprove the proposed research activity, or of modifications required to secure IRB approval of the research activity. If the IRB decides to disapprove a research activity, it shall include in its written notification a statement of the reasons for its decision and give the investigator an opportunity to respond in person or in writing.

(e) An IRB shall conduct continuing review of research covered by this policy at intervals appropriate to the degree of risk, but not less than once per year, and shall have authority to observe or have a third party observe the consent process and the research.

(Approved by the Office of Management and Budget under control number 9999–0020)

§46.110 Expedited review procedures for certain kinds of research involving no more than minimal risk, and for minor changes in approved research.

(a) The Secretary, HHS, has established, and published as a Notice in the Federal Register, a list of categories of research that may be reviewed by the IRB through an expedited review procedure. The list will be amended, as appropriate after consultation with other departments and agencies, through periodic republication by the Secretary, HHS, in the Federal Register. A copy of the list is available from the Office for Protection from Research Risks, National Institutes of Health, HHS, Bethesda, Maryland 20892.

(b) An IRB may use the expedited review procedure to review either or both of the following:

(1) Some or all of the research appearing on the list and found by the reviewer(s) to involve no more than minimal risk,

(2) Minor changes in previously approved research during the period (of one year or less) for which approval is authorized.

Under an expedited review procedure, the review may be carried out by the IRB chairperson or by one or more experienced reviewers designated by the chairperson from among members of the IRB. In reviewing the research, the reviewers may exercise all of the authorities of the IRB except that the reviewers may not disapprove the research. A research activity may be disapproved only after review in accordance with the non-expedited procedure set forth in §46.108(b).

(c) Each IRB which uses an expedited review procedure shall adopt a method for keeping all members advised of research proposals which have been approved under the procedure.

(d) The department or agency head may restrict, suspend, terminate, or choose not to authorize an institution's or IRB's use of the expedited review procedure.

§46.111 Criteria for IRB approval of research.

(a) In order to approve research covered by this policy the IRB shall determine that all of the following requirements are satisfied:

(1) Risks to subjects are minimized: (i) By using procedures which are consistent with sound research design and which do not unnecessarily expose subjects to risk, and (ii) whenever appropriate, by using procedures already being performed on the subjects for diagnostic or treatment purposes.

(2) Risks to subjects are reasonable in relation to anticipated benefits, if any, to subjects, and the importance of the knowledge that may reasonably be expected to result. In evaluating risks and benefits, the IRB should consider only those risks and benefits that may result from the research (as distinguished from risks and benefits of therapies subjects would receive even if not participating in the research). The IRB should not consider possible long-range effects of applying knowledge gained in the research (for example, the possible effects of the research on public policy) as among those research risks that fall within the purview of its responsibility.

(3) Selection of subjects is equitable. In making this assessment the IRB should take into account the purposes of the research and the setting in which the research will be conducted and should be particularly cognizant of the special problems of research involving vulnerable populations, such as children, prisoners, pregnant women, mentally disabled persons, or economically or educationally disadvantaged persons.

(4) Informed consent will be sought from each prospective subject or the subject's legally authorized representative, in accordance with, and to the extent required by §46.116.

(5) Informed consent will be appropriately documented, in accordance with, and to the extent required by §46.117.

(6) When appropriate, the research plan makes adequate provision for monitoring the data collected to ensure the safety of subjects.

(7) When appropriate, there are adequate provisions to protect the privacy of subjects and to maintain the confidentiality of data.

(b) When some or all of the subjects are likely to be vulnerable to coercion or undue influence, such as children, prisoners, pregnant women, mentally disabled persons, or economically or educationally disadvantaged persons, additional safeguards have been included in the study to protect the rights and welfare of these subjects.

§46.112 Review by institution.

Research covered by this policy that has been approved by an IRB may be subject to further appropriate review and approval or disapproval by officials of the institution. However, those officials may not approve the research if it has not been approved by an IRB.

§46.113 Suspension or termination of IRB approval of research.

An IRB shall have authority to suspend or terminate approval of research that is not being conducted in accordance with the IRB's requirements or that has been associated with unexpected serious harm to subjects. Any suspension or termination of approval shall include a statement of the reasons for the IRB's action and shall be reported promptly to the investigator, appropriate institutional officials, and the department or agency head.

(Approved by the Office of Management and Budget under control number 9999–0020)

§46.114 Cooperative research.

Cooperative research projects are those projects covered by this policy which involve more than one institution. In the conduct of cooperative research projects, each institution is responsible for safeguarding the rights and welfare of human subjects and for complying with this policy. With the approval of the department or agency head, an institution participating in a cooperative project may enter into a joint review arrangement, rely upon the review of another qualified IRB, or make similar arrangements for avoiding duplication of effort.

§46.115 IRB records.

(a) An institution, or when appropriate an IRB, shall prepare and maintain adequate documentation of IRB activities, including the following:

(1) Copies of all research proposals reviewed, scientific evaluations, if any, that accompany the proposals, approved sample consent documents, progress reports submitted by investigators, and reports of injuries to subjects.

(2) Minutes of IRB meetings which shall be in sufficient detail to show attendance at the meetings; actions taken by the IRB; the vote on these actions including the number of members voting for, against, and abstaining; the basis for requiring changes in or disapproving research; and a written summary of the discussion of controverted issues and their resolution.

(3) Records of continuing review activities.

(4) Copies of all correspondence between the IRB and the investigators.

(5) A list of IRB members in the same detail as described is §46.103(b)(3).

(6) Written procedures for the IRB in the same detail as described in §46.103(b)(4) and §46.103(b)(5).

(7) Statements of significant new findings provided to subjects, as required by §46.116(b)(5).

(b) The records required by this policy shall be retained for at least 3 years, and records relating to research which is conducted shall be retained for at least 3 years after completion of the research. All records shall be accessible for inspection and copying by authorized representatives of the department or agency at reasonable times and in a reasonable manner.

(Approved by the Office of Management and Budget under control number 9999–0020)

§46.116 General requirements for informed consent.

Except as provided elsewhere in this policy, no investigator may involve a human being as a subject in research covered by this policy unless the investigator has obtained the legally effective informed consent of the subject or the subject's legally authorized representative. An investigator shall seek such consent only under circumstances that provide the prospective subject or the representative sufficient opportunity to consider whether or not to participate and that minimize the possibility of coercion or undue influence. The information that is given to the subject or the representative shall be in language understandable to the subject or the representative. No informed consent, whether oral or written, may include any exculpatory language through which the subject or the representative is made to waive or appear to waive any of the subject's legal rights, or releases or appears to release the investigator, the sponsor, the institution or its agents from liability for negligence.

(a) Basic elements of informed consent. Except as provided in paragraph (c) or (d) of this section, in seeking informed consent the following information shall be provided to each subject:

(1) A statement that the study involves research, an explanation of the purposes of the research and the expected duration of the subject's participation, a description of the procedures to be followed, and identification of any procedures which are experimental;

(2) A description of any reasonably foreseeable risks or discomforts to the subject;

(3) A description of any benefits to the subject or to others which may reasonably be expected from the research;

(4) A disclosure of appropriate alternative procedures or courses of treatment, if any, that might be advantageous to the subject;

(5) A statement describing the extent, if any, to which confidentiality of records identifying the subject will be maintained;

(6) For research involving more than minimal risk, an explanation as to whether any compensation and an explanation as to whether any medical treatments are available if injury occurs and, if so, what they consist of, or where further information may be obtained;

(7) An explanation of whom to contact for answers to pertinent questions about the research and research subjects' rights, and whom to contact in the event of a research-related injury to the subject; and

(8) A statement that participation is voluntary, refusal to participate will involve no penalty or loss of benefits to which the subject is otherwise entitled, and the subject may discontinue participation at

any time without penalty or loss of benefits to which the subject is otherwise entitled.

(b) Additional elements of informed consent. When appropriate, one or more of the following elements of information shall also be provided to each subject:

(1) A statement that the particular treatment or procedure may involve risks to the subject (or to the embryo or fetus, if the subject is or may become pregnant) which are currently unforeseeable;

(2) Anticipated circumstances under which the subject's participation may be terminated by the investigator without regard to the subject's consent;

(3) Any additional costs to the subject that may result from participation in the research;

(4) The consequences of a subject's decision to withdraw from the research and procedures for orderly termination of participation by the subject;

(5) A statement that significant new findings developed during the course of the research which may relate to the subject's willingness to continue participation will be provided to the subject; and

(6) The approximate number of subjects involved in the study.

(c) An IRB may approve a consent procedure which does not include, or which alters, some or all of the elements of informed consent set forth above, or waive the requirement to obtain informed consent provided the IRB finds and documents that:

(1) The research or demonstration project is to be conducted by or subject to the approval of state or local government officials and is designed to study, evaluate, or otherwise examine: (i) Public benefit of service programs; (ii) procedures for obtaining benefits or services under those programs; (iii) possible changes in or alternatives to those programs or procedures; or (iv) possible changes in methods or levels of payment for benefits or services under those programs; and

(2) The research could not practicably be carried out without the waiver or alteration.

(d) An IRB may approve a consent procedure which does not include, or which alters, some or all of the elements of informed consent set forth in this section, or waive the requirements to obtain informed consent provided the IRB finds and documents that:

(1) The research involves no more than minimal risk to the subjects;

(2) The waiver or alteration will not adversely affect the rights and welfare of the subjects;

(3) The research could not practicably be carried out without the waiver or alteration; and

(4) Whenever appropriate, the subjects will be provided with additional pertinent information after participation.

(e) The informed consent requirements in this policy are not intended to preempt any applicable federal, state, or local laws which require additional information to be disclosed in order for informed consent to be legally effective.

(f) Nothing in this policy is intended to limit the authority of a physician to provide emergency medical care, to the extent the physician is permitted to do so under applicable federal, state, or local law.

(Approved by the Office of Management and Budget under control number 9999–0020)

§46.117 Documentation of informed consent.

(a) Except as provided in paragraph (c) of this section, informed consent shall be documented by the use of a written consent form approved by the IRB and signed by the subject or the subject's legally authorized representative. A copy shall be given to the person signing the form.

(b) Except as provided in paragraph (c) of this section, the consent form may be either of the following:

(1) A written consent document that embodies the elements of informed consent required by §46.116. This form may be read to the subject or the subject's legally authorized representative, but in any event, the investigator shall give either the subject or the representative adequate opportunity to read it before it is signed; or

(2) A short form written consent document stating that the elements of informed consent required by §46.116 have been presented orally to the subject or the subject's legally authorized repre-

sentative. When this method is used, there shall be a witness to the oral presentation. Also, the IRB shall approve a written summary of what is to be said to the subject or the representative. Only the short form itself is to be signed by the subject or the representative. However, the witness shall sign both the short form and a copy of the summary, and the person actually obtaining consent shall sign a copy of the summary. A copy of the summary shall be given to the subject or the representative, in addition to a copy of the short form.

(c) An IRB may waive the requirement for the investigator to obtain a signed consent form for some or all subjects if it finds either:

(1) That the only record linking the subject and the research would be the consent document and the principal risk would be potential harm resulting from a breach of confidentiality. Each subject will be asked whether the subject wants documentation linking the subject with the research, and the subject's wishes will govern; or

(2) That the research presents no more than minimal risk of harm to subjects and involves no procedures for which written consent is normally required outside of the research context.

In cases in which the documentation requirement is waived, the IRB may require the investigator to provide subjects with a written statement regarding the research.

(Approved by the Office of Management and Budget under control number 9999–0020)

§46.118 Applications and proposals lacking definite plans for involvement of human subjects.

Certain types of applications for grants, cooperative agreements, or contracts are submitted to departments or agencies with the knowledge that subjects may be involved within the period of support, but definite plans would not normally be set forth in the application or proposal. These include activities such as institutional type grants when selection of specific projects is the institution's responsibility; research training grants in which the activities involving subjects remain to be selected; and projects in which human subjects' involvement will depend upon completion of instruments, prior animal studies, or purification of compounds. These applications need not be reviewed by an IRB before an award may be made. However, except for research exempted or waived under §46.101 (b) or (i), no human subjects may be involved in any project supported by these awards until the project has been reviewed and approved by the IRB, as provided in this policy, and certification submitted, by the institution, to the department or agency.

§46.119 Research undertaken without the intention of involving human subjects.

In the event research is undertaken without the intention of involving human subjects, but it is later proposed to involve human subjects in the research, the research shall first be reviewed and approved by an IRB, as provided in this policy, a certification submitted, by the institution, to the department or agency, and final approval given to the proposed change by the department or agency.

§46.120 Evaluation and disposition of applications and proposals for research to be conducted or supported by a Federal Department or Agency.

(a) The department or agency head will evaluate all applications and proposals involving human subjects submitted to the department or agency through such officers and employees of the department or agency and such experts and consultants as the department or agency head determines to be appropriate. This evaluation will take into consideration the risks to the subjects, the adequacy of protection against these risks, the potential benefits of the research to the subjects and others, and the importance of the knowledge gained or to be gained.

(b) On the basis of this evaluation, the department or agency head may approve or disapprove the application or proposal, or enter into negotiations to develop an approvable one.

§46.121 [Reserved]

§46.122 Use of Federal funds.

Federal funds administered by a department or agency may not be expended for research involving human subjects unless the requirements of this policy have been satisfied.

§46.123 Early termination of research support: Evaluation of applications and proposals.

(a) The department or agency head may require that department or agency support for any project be terminated or suspended in the manner prescribed in applicable program requirements, when the department or agency head finds an institution has materially failed to comply with the terms of this policy.

(b) In making decisions about supporting or approving applications or proposals covered by this policy the department or agency head may take into account, in addition to all other eligibility requirements and program criteria, factors such as whether the applicant has been subject to a termination or suspension under paragarph (a) of this section and whether the applicant or the person or persons who would direct or has have directed the scientific and technical aspects of an activity has have, in the judgment of the department or agency head, materially failed to discharge responsibility for the protection of the rights and welfare of human subjects (whether or not the research was subject to federal regulation).

§46.124 Conditions.

With respect to any research project or any class of research projects the department or agency head may impose additional conditions prior to or at the time of approval when in the judgment of the department or agency head additional conditions are necessary for the protection of human subjects.

Subpart B—Additional Protections for Pregnant Women, Human Fetuses and Neonates Involved in Research

Source: 66 FR 56778, Nov. 13, 2001, unless otherwise noted.

§46.201 To what do these regulations apply?

(a) Except as provided in paragraph (b) of this section, this subpart applies to all research involving pregnant women, human fetuses, neonates of uncertain viability, or nonviable neonates conducted or supported by the Department of Health and Human Services (DHHS). This includes all research conducted in DHHS facilities by any person and all research conducted in any facility by DHHS employees.

(b) The exemptions at §46.101(b)(1) through (6) are applicable to this subpart.

(c) The provisions of §46.101(c) through (i) are applicable to this subpart. Reference to State or local laws in this subpart and in §46.101(f) is intended to include the laws of federally recognized American Indian and Alaska Native Tribal Governments.

(d) The requirements of this subpart are in addition to those imposed under the other subparts of this part.

§46.202 Definitions.

The definitions in §46.102 shall be applicable to this subpart as well. In addition, as used in this subpart:

(a) Dead fetus means a fetus that exhibits neither heartbeat, spontaneous respiratory activity, spontaneous movement of voluntary muscles, nor pulsation of the umbilical cord.

(b) Delivery means complete separation of the fetus from the woman by expulsion or extraction or any other means.

(c) Fetus means the product of conception from implantation until delivery.

(d) Neonate means a newborn.

(e) Nonviable neonate means a neonate after delivery that, although living, is not viable.

(f) Pregnancy encompasses the period of time from implantation until delivery. A woman shall be assumed to be pregnant if she exhibits any of the pertinent presumptive signs of pregnancy, such as missed menses, until the results of a pregnancy test are negative or until delivery.

(g) Secretary means the Secretary of Health and Human Services and any other officer or employee of the Department of Health and Human Services to whom authority has been delegated.

(h) Viable, as it pertains to the neonate, means being able, after delivery, to survive (given the benefit of available medical therapy) to the point of independently maintaining heartbeat and respiration. The Secretary may from time to time, taking into account medical advances, publish in the Federal Register guidelines to assist in determining whether a neonate is viable for purposes of this subpart. If a neonate is viable then it may be included in research only to the extent permitted and in accordance with the requirements of subparts A and D of this part.

§46.203 Duties of IRBs in connection with research involving pregnant women, fetuses, and neonates.

In addition to other responsibilities assigned to IRBs under this part, each IRB shall review research covered by this subpart and approve only research which satisfies the conditions of all applicable sections of this subpart and the other subparts of this part.

§46.204 Research involving pregnant women or fetuses.

Pregnant women or fetuses may be involved in research if all of the following conditions are met:

(a) Where scientifically appropriate, preclinical studies, including studies on pregnant animals, and clinical studies, including studies on nonpregnant women, have been conducted and provide data for assessing potential risks to pregnant women and fetuses;

(b) The risk to the fetus is caused solely by interventions or procedures that hold out the prospect of direct benefit for the woman or the fetus; or, if there is no such prospect of benefit, the risk to the fetus is not greater than minimal and the purpose of the research is the development of important biomedical knowledge which cannot be obtained by any other means;

(c) Any risk is the least possible for achieving the objectives of the research;

(d) If the research holds out the prospect of direct benefit to the pregnant woman, the prospect of a direct benefit both to the pregnant woman and the fetus, or no prospect of benefit for the woman nor the fetus when risk to the fetus is not greater than minimal and the purpose of the research is the development of important biomedical knowledge that cannot be obtained by any other means, her consent is obtained in accord with the informed consent provisions of subpart A of this part;

(e) If the research holds out the prospect of direct benefit solely to the fetus then the consent of the pregnant woman and the father is obtained in accord with the informed consent provisions of subpart A of this part, except that the father's consent need not be obtained if he is unable to consent because of unavailability, incompetence, or temporary incapacity or the pregnancy resulted from rape or incest.

(f) Each individual providing consent under paragraph (d) or (e) of this section is fully informed regarding the reasonably foreseeable impact of the research on the fetus or neonate;

(g) For children as defined in §46.402(a) who are pregnant, assent and permission are obtained in accord with the provisions of subpart D of this part;

(h) No inducements, monetary or otherwise, will be offered to terminate a pregnancy;

(i) Individuals engaged in the research will have no part in any decisions as to the timing, method, or procedures used to terminate a pregnancy; and

(j) Individuals engaged in the research will have no part in determining the viability of a neonate.

§46.205 Research involving neonates.

(a) Neonates of uncertain viability and nonviable neonates may be involved in research if all of the following conditions are met:

(1) Where scientifically appropriate, preclinical and clinical studies have been conducted and provide data for assessing potential risks to neonates.

(2) Each individual providing consent under paragraph (b)(2) or (c)(5) of this section is fully informed regarding the reasonably foreseeable impact of the research on the neonate.

(3) Individuals engaged in the research will have no part in determining the viability of a neonate.

(4) The requirements of paragraph (b) or (c) of this section have been met as applicable.

(b) Neonates of uncertain viability. Until it has been ascertained whether or not a neonate is viable, a neonate may not be involved in research covered by this subpart unless the following additional conditions are met:

(1) The IRB determines that:

(i) The research holds out the prospect of enhancing the probability of survival of the neonate to the point of viability,

344

and any risk is the least possible for achieving that objective, or

(ii) The purpose of the research is the development of important biomedical knowledge which cannot be obtained by other means and there will be no added risk to the neonate resulting from the research; and

(2) The legally effective informed consent of either parent of the neonate or, if neither parent is able to consent because of unavailability, incompetence, or temporary incapacity, the legally effective informed consent of either parent's legally authorized representative is obtained in accord with subpart A of this part, except that the consent of the father or his legally authorized representative need not be obtained if the pregnancy resulted from rape or incest.

(c) Nonviable neonates. After delivery nonviable neonate may not be involved in research covered by this subpart unless all of the following additional conditions are met:

(1) Vital functions of the neonate will not be artificially maintained;

(2) The research will not terminate the heartbeat or respiration of the neonate;

(3) There will be no added risk to the neonate resulting from the research;

(4) The purpose of the research is the development of important biomedical knowledge that cannot be obtained by other means; and

(5) The legally effective informed consent of both parents of the neonate is obtained in accord with subpart A of this part, except that the waiver and alteration provisions of §46.116(c) and (d) do not apply. However, if either parent is unable to consent because of unavailability, incompetence, or temporary incapacity, the informed consent of one parent of a nonviable neonate will suffice to meet the requirements of this paragraph (c)(5), except that the consent of the father need not be obtained if the pregnancy resulted from rape or incest. The consent of a legally authorized representative of either or both of the parents of a nonviable neonate will not suffice to meet the requirements of this paragraph (c)(5).

(d) Viable neonates. A neonate, after delivery, that has been determined to be viable may be included in research only to the extent permitted by and in accord with the requirements of subparts A and D of this part.

§46.206 Research involving, after delivery, the placenta, the dead fetus or fetal material.

(a) Research involving, after delivery, the placenta; the dead fetus; macerated fetal material; or cells, tissue, or organs excised from a dead fetus, shall be conducted only in accord with any applicable Federal, State, or local laws and regulations regarding such activities.

(b) If information associated with material described in paragraph (a) of this section is recorded for research purposes in a manner that living individuals can be identified, directly or through identifiers linked to those individuals, those individuals are research subjects and all pertinent subparts of this part are applicable.

§46.207 Research not otherwise approvable which presents an opportunity to understand, prevent, or alleviate a serious problem affecting the health or welfare of pregnant women, fetuses, or neonates.

The Secretary will conduct or fund research that the IRB does not believe meets the requirements of §46.204 or § 46.205 only if:

(a) The IRB finds that the research presents a reasonable opportunity to further the understanding, prevention, or alleviation of a serious problem affecting the health or welfare of pregnant women, fetuses or neonates; and

(b) The Secretary, after consultation with a panel of experts in pertinent disciplines (for example: science, medicine, ethics, law) and following opportunity for public review and comment, including a public meeting announced in the Federal Register, has determined either:

(1) That the research in fact satisfies the conditions of §46.204, as applicable; or

(2) The following:

(i) The research presents a reasonable opportunity to further the understanding, prevention, or alleviation of a serious problem affecting the health or welfare of pregnant women, fetuses or neonates;

(ii) The research will be conducted in accord with sound ethical principles; and

(iii) Informed consent will be obtained in accord with the informed consent provisions of subpart A and other applicable subparts of this part.

Subpart C—Additional Protections Pertaining to Biomedical and Behavioral Research Involving Prisoners as Subjects

Source: 43 FR 53655, Nov. 16, 1978, unless otherwise noted.

§46.301 Applicability.

(a) The regulations in this subpart are applicable to all biomedical and behavioral research conducted or supported by the Department of Health and Human Services involving prisoners as subjects.

(b) Nothing in this subpart shall be construed as indicating that compliance with the procedures set forth herein will authorize research involving prisoners as subjects, to the extent such research is limited or barred by applicable State or local law.

(c) The requirements of this subpart are in addition to those imposed under the other subparts of this part.

§46.302 Purpose.

Inasmuch as prisoners may be under constraints because of their incarceration which could affect their ability to make a truly voluntary and uncoerced decision whether or not to participate as subjects in research, it is the purpose of this subpart to provide additional safeguards for the protection of prisoners involved in activities to which this subpart is applicable.

§46.303 Definitions.

As used in this subpart:

(a) Secretary means the Secretary of Health and Human Services and any other officer or employee of the Department of Health and Human Services to whom authority has been delegated.

(b) DHHS means the Department of Health and Human Services.

(c) Prisoner means any individual involuntarily confined or detained in a penal institution. The term is intended to encompass individuals sentenced to such an institution under a criminal or civil statute, individuals detained in other facilities by virtue of statutes or commitment procedures which provide alternatives to criminal prosecution or incarceration in a penal institution, and individuals detained pending arraignment, trial, or sentencing.

(d) Minimal risk is the probability and magnitude of physical or psychological harm that is normally encountered in the daily lives, or in the routine medical, dental, or psychological examination of healthy persons.

§46.304 Composition of Institutional Review Boards where prisoners are involved.

In addition to satisfying the requirements in §46.107 of this part, an Institutional Review Board, carrying out responsibilities under this part with respect to research covered by this subpart, shall also meet the following specific requirements:

(a) A majority of the Board (exclusive of prisoner members) shall have no association with the prison(s) involved, apart from their membership on the Board.

(b) At least one member of the Board shall be a prisoner, or a prisoner representative with appropriate background and experience to serve in that capacity, except that where a particular research project is reviewed by more than one Board only one Board need satisfy this requirement.

[43 FR 53655, Nov. 16, 1978, as amended at 46 FR 8386, Jan. 26, 1981]

§46.305 Additional duties of the Institutional Review Boards where prisoners are involved.

(a) In addition to all other responsibilities prescribed for Institutional Review Boards under this part, the Board shall review research covered by this subpart and approve such research only if it finds that:

(1) The research under review represents one of the categories of research permissible under §46.306(a)(2);

(2) Any possible advantages accruing to the prisoner through his or her participation in the research, when compared to the general living conditions, medical care, quality of food, amenities and opportunity for earnings in the prison, are not of such a magnitude that his or her ability to weigh the risks of the research against the value of such advantages in the limited choice environment of the prison is impaired;

(3) The risks involved in the research are commensurate with risks that would be accepted by nonprisoner volunteers;

(4) Procedures for the selection of subjects within the prison are fair to all prisoners and immune from arbitrary intervention by prison authorities or prisoners. Unless the principal investigator provides to the Board justification in writing for following some other procedures, control subjects must be selected randomly from the group of available prisoners who meet the characteristics needed for that particular research project;

(5) The information is presented in language which is understandable to the subject population;

(6) Adequate assurance exists that parole boards will not take into account a prisoner's participation in the research in making decisions regarding parole, and each prisoner is clearly informed in advance that participation in the research will have no effect on his or her parole; and

(7) Where the Board finds there may be a need for follow-up examination or care of participants after the end of their participation, adequate provision has been made for such examination or care, taking into account the varying lengths of individual prisoners' sentences, and for informing participants of this fact.

(b) The Board shall carry out such other duties as may be assigned by the Secretary.

(c) The institution shall certify to the Secretary, in such form and manner as the Secretary may require, that the duties of the Board under this section have been fulfilled.

§46.306 Permitted research involving prisoners.

(a) Biomedical or behavioral research conducted or supported by DHHS may involve prisoners as subjects only if:

(1) The institution responsible for the conduct of the research has certified to the Secretary that the Institutional Review Board has approved the research under §46.305 of this subpart; and

(2) In the judgment of the Secretary the proposed research involves solely the following:

(i) Study of the possible causes, effects, and processes of incarceration, and of criminal behavior, provided that the study presents no more than minimal risk and no more than inconvenience to the subjects;

(ii) Study of prisons as institutional structures or of prisoners as incarcerated persons, provided that the study presents no more than minimal risk and no more than inconvenience to the subjects;

(iii) Research on conditions particularly affecting prisoners as a class (for example, vaccine trials and other research on hepatitis which is much more prevalent in prisons than elsewhere; and research on social and psychological problems such as alcoholism, drug addiction and sexual assaults) provided that the study may proceed only after the Secretary has consulted with appropriate experts including experts in penology medicine and ethics, and published notice, in the Federal Register, of his intent to approve such research; or

(iv) Research on practices, both innovative and accepted, which have the intent and reasonable probability of improving the health or well-being of the subject. In cases in which those studies require the assignment of prisoners in a manner consistent with protocols approved by the IRB to control groups which may not benefit from the research, the study may proceed only after the Secretary has consulted with appropriate experts, including experts in penology medicine and ethics, and published notice, in the Federal Register, of his intent to approve such research.

(b) Except as provided in paragraph (a) of this section, biomedical or behavioral research conducted or supported by DHHS shall not involve prisoners as subjects.

Subpart D—Additional Protections for Children Involved as Subjects in Research

Source: 48 FR 9818, Mar. 8, 1983, unless otherwise noted.

§46.401 To what do these regulations apply?

(a) This subpart applies to all research involving children as subjects, conducted or supported by the Department of Health and Human Services.

(1) This includes research conducted by Department employees, except that each head of an Operating Division of the Department may adopt such nonsubstantive, procedural modifications as may be appropriate from an administrative standpoint.

(2) It also includes research conducted or supported by the Department of Health and Human Services outside the United States, but in appropriate circumstances, the Secretary may, under paragraph (e) of §46.101 of Subpart A, waive the applicability of some or all of the requirements of these regulations for research of this type.

(b) Exemptions at §46.101(b)(1) and (b)(3) through (b)(6) are applicable to this subpart. The exemption at §46.101(b)(2) regarding educational tests is also applicable to this subpart. However, the exemption at §46.101(b)(2) for research involving survey or interview procedures or observations of public behavior does not apply to research covered by this subpart, except for research involving observation of public behavior when the investigator(s) do not participate in the activities being observed.

(c) The exceptions, additions, and provisions for waiver as they appear in paragraphs (c) through (i) of §46.101 of Subpart A are applicable to this subpart.

[48 FR 9818, Mar. 8, 1983; 56 FR 28032, June 18, 1991; 56 FR 29757, June 28, 1991]

§46.402 Definitions.

The definitions in §46.102 of Subpart A shall be applicable to this subpart as well. In addition, as used in this subpart:

(a) Children are persons who have not attained the legal age for consent to treatments or procedures involved in the research, under the applicable law of the jurisdiction in which the research will be conducted.

(b) Assent means a child's affirmative agreement to participate in research. Mere failure to object should not, absent affirmative agreement, be construed as assent.

(c) Permission means the agreement of parent(s) or guardian to the participation of their child or ward in research.

(d) Parent means a child's biological or adoptive parent.

(e) Guardian means an individual who is authorized under applicable State or local law to consent on behalf of a child to general medical care.

§46.403 IRB duties.

In addition to other responsibilities assigned to IRBs under this part, each IRB shall review research covered by this subpart and approve only research which satisfies the conditions of all applicable sections of this subpart.

§46.404 Research not involving greater than minimal risk.

HHS will conduct or fund research in which the IRB finds that no greater than minimal risk to children is presented, only if the IRB finds that adequate provisions are made for soliciting the assent of the children and the permission of their parents or guardians, as set forth in §46.408.

§46.405 Research involving greater than minimal risk but presenting the prospect of direct benefit to the individual subjects.

HHS will conduct or fund research in which the IRB finds that more than minimal risk to children is presented by an intervention or procedure that holds out the prospect of direct benefit for the individual subject, or by a monitoring procedure that is likely to contribute to the subject's well-being, only if the IRB finds that:

(a) The risk is justified by the anticipated benefit to the subjects;

(b) The relation of the anticipated benefit to the risk is at least as favorable to the subjects as that presented by available alternative approaches; and

(c) Adequate provisions are made for soliciting the assent of the children and permission of their parents or guardians, as set forth in §46.408.

§46.406 Research involving greater than minimal risk and no prospect of direct benefit to individual subjects, but likely to yield generalizable knowledge about the subject's disorder or condition.

HHS will conduct or fund research in which the IRB finds that more than minimal risk to children is presented by an intervention or procedure that does not hold out the prospect of direct benefit for the individual subject, or by a monitoring procedure which is not likely to contribute to the well-being of the subject, only if the IRB finds that:

(a) The risk represents a minor increase over minimal risk;

(b) The intervention or procedure presents experiences to subjects that are reasonably commensurate with those inherent in their actual or expected medical, dental, psychological, social, or educational situations;

(c) The intervention or procedure is likely to yield generalizable knowledge about the subjects' disorder or condition which is of vital importance for the understanding or amelioration of the subjects' disorder or condition; and

(d) Adequate provisions are made for soliciting assent of the children and permission of their parents or guardians, as set forth in §46.408.

§46.407 Research not otherwise approvable which presents an opportunity to understand, prevent, or alleviate a serious problem affecting the health or welfare of children.

HHS will conduct or fund research that the IRB does not believe meets the requirements of §46.404, §46.405, or §46.406 only if:

(a) The IRB finds that the research presents a reasonable opportunity to further the understanding, prevention, or alleviation of a serious problem affecting the health or welfare of children; and

(b) The Secretary, after consultation with a panel of experts in pertinent disciplines (for example: science, medicine, educa-

tion, ethics, law) and following opportunity for public review and comment, has determined either:

(1) That the research in fact satisfies the conditions of §46.404, §46.405, or §46.406, as applicable, or

(2) The following:

(i) The research presents a reasonable opportunity to further the understanding, prevention, or alleviation of a serious problem affecting the health or welfare of children;

(ii) The research will be conducted in accordance with sound ethical principles;

(iii) Adequate provisions are made for soliciting the assent of children and the permission of their parents or guardians, as set forth in §46.408.

§46.408 Requirements for permission by parents or guardians and for assent by children.

(a) In addition to the determinations required under other applicable sections of this subpart, the IRB shall determine that adequate provisions are made for soliciting the assent of the children, when in the judgment of the IRB the children are capable of providing assent. In determining whether children are capable of assenting, the IRB shall take into account the ages, maturity, and psychological state of the children involved. This judgment may be made for all children to be involved in research under a particular protocol, or for each child, as the IRB deems appropriate. If the IRB determines that the capability of some or all of the children is so limited that they cannot reasonably be consulted or that the intervention or procedure involved in the research holds out a prospect of direct benefit that is important to the health or well-being of the children and is available only in the context of the research, the assent of the children is not a necessary condition for proceeding with the research. Even where the IRB determines that the subjects are capable of assenting, the IRB may still waive the assent requirement under circumstances in which consent may be waived in accord with §46.116 of Subpart A.

(b) In addition to the determinations required under other applicable sections of this subpart, the IRB shall determine, in accordance with and to the extent that consent is required by §46.116 of Subpart A, that adequate provisions are made for soliciting the permission of each child's parents or guardian. Where parental permission is to be obtained, the IRB may find that the permission of one parent is sufficient for research to be conducted under §46.404 or §46.405. Where research is covered by §§46.406 and 46.407 and permission is to be obtained from parents, both parents must give their permission unless one parent is deceased, unknown, incompetent, or not reasonably available, or when only one parent has legal responsibility for the care and custody of the child.

(c) In addition to the provisions for waiver contained in §46.116 of Subpart A, if the IRB determines that a research protocol is designed for conditions or for a subject population for which parental or guardian permission is not a reasonable requirement to protect the subjects (for example, neglected or abused children), it may waive the consent requirements in Subpart A of this part and

paragraph (b) of this section, provided an appropriate mechanism for protecting the children who will participate as subjects in the research is substituted, and provided further that the waiver is not inconsistent with Federal, state or local law. The choice of an appropriate mechanism would depend upon the nature and purpose of the activities described in the protocol, the risk and anticipated benefit to the research subjects, and their age, maturity, status, and condition.

(d) Permission by parents or guardians shall be documented in accordance with and to the extent required by §46.117 of Subpart A.

(e) When the IRB determines that assent is required, it shall also determine whether and how assent must be documented.

§46.409 Wards.

(a) Children who are wards of the state or any other agency, institution, or entity can be included in research approved under §46.406 or §46.407 only if such research is:

(1) Related to their status as wards; or

(2) Conducted in schools, camps, hospitals, institutions, or similar settings in which the majority of children involved as subjects are not wards.

(b) If the research is approved under paragraph (a) of this section, the IRB shall require appointment of an advocate for each child who is a ward, in addition to any other individual acting on behalf of the child as guardian or in loco parentis. One individual may serve as advocate for more than one child. The advocate shall be an individual who has the background and experience to act in, and agrees to act in, the best interests of the child for the duration of the child's participation in the research and who is not associated in any way (except in the role as advocate or member of the IRB) with the research, the investigator(s), or the guardian organization.

APPENDIX

Glossary

Adverse Event—(AE) Any unfavorable or unintended event associated with a research study.

Adverse Event Reports—Investigator reports of all serious and adverse events, injury and deaths given to the sponsor, the IRB and the FDA.

Assurance—Renewable permit granted by a federal department to an institution to conduct research, can be given for individual or multiple projects.

Belmont Report—Ethical Principles and Guidelines for the Protection of Human Subjects of Research. Cornerstone document of ethical principles. Federal regulation of subject protection based on respect for persons, beneficence and justice.

Beneficence—Doing no harm, maximizing benefits while minimizing risks.

Case Report Forms—Study document of all data required by protocol on each subject.

Certified Clinical Research Coordinator—(CCRC) CRC with more than two years experience and with certification earned by passing required program and exam.

Certified IRB Professional—(CIP) IRB administrative personnel with more than two years experience and with certification earned by passing required exam.

Clinical Research—Study of drug, biologic or device in human subjects with the intent to discover potential beneficial effects and/or determine its safety and efficacy. Also called clinical study and clinical investigation. Note that in this manual, this term is used in its narrow sense as used by the FDA. Thus, it does not encompass all the research that is carried out in the clinical setting (e.g., health services research). See also, patient-oriented research.

Clinical Research Associate—(CRA) Person employed by the study sponsor or CRO to monitor a clinical study at all participating sites. See also, monitor.

Clinical Research Coordinator—(CRC) Site administer for the clinical study. Duties are delegated by the investigator. Also called research, study or healthcare coordinator, and data manager, research nurse or protocol nurse.

Clinical Study Materials—Study supplies (i.e., study test article, laboratory supplies case report forms) provided by the study sponsor to the investigator.

Common Rule—1991 agreement to cover all federally-sponsored and federally-conducted research by a common set of regulations.

Consent Form—Contains all relevant study information explained in lay terms and documents voluntary participation of subject. Presented to and signed by subject.

Contract Research Organization—(CRO) A person or an organization (commercial, academic or other) contracted by the sponsor to perform one or more of a sponsor's study-related duties and functions.

Data—Legally defined according to institution. Generally refers to recorded information regardless of form. Most institutions hold title to data while researchers have rights to access data.

Deception—Intentionally misleading or withholding information about nature of experiment.

Declaration of Helsinki—Statement of ethical principles first published by World Medical Association in 1964 to define rules for therapeutic and non-therapeutic research.

Documentation—All forms of records that describe or document study methods, conduct and results, including any adverse events and actions taken.

Drug or Device Accountability Records—(DAR) Required documentation for material accountability, quantity used and left over, and date of disposal.

Ethical Principles and Guidelines for the Protection of Human Subjects of Research—See Belmont Report.

Family Educational Rights and Privacy Act—(FERPA) Covers rights of parents of school children regarding reviewing, amending and disclosing educational records.

Federal-Wide Assurance—(FWA) Permit given to institution for multiple federally funded research grants for a specified period of time. States institution retains responsibility for all research involving humans and that the institution must have an established IRB.

Food and Drug Administration—(FDA) Within DHHS. Enforces Food, Drug and Cosmetics Act and related federal public health laws. Grants IND, IDE, PMA and NDA approvals.

Food Drug and Cosmetic Act—(FD&C Act) States only drugs, biologics and devices proven safe and effective can be marketed.

FDA Form 1572—List of commitments and conduct required by FDA for each investigator performing drug/biologics study. Also referred to as statement of investigator.

Good Clinical Practice—(GCP) International ethical and scientific quality standard for designing, conducting, monitoring, recording, auditing, analyzing and reporting studies. Insures that the data reported is credible and accurate and that subject's rights and confidentiality are protected.

Human Subject—A patient or healthy individual participating in a research study. A living individual about whom an investigator obtains private information or data through intervention or interaction.

Inclusion Criteria—A list of criteria that must be met by all study subjects.

Informed Consent—Information exchange including subject recruitment materials, verbal instructions, written materials, question and answer sessions and signature documenting consent with date. Subjects are given opportunity to choose involvement based on information, comprehension and voluntariness.

International Ethics Guidelines for Biomedical Research Involving Human Subjects—(CIOMS guidelines) Developed by the Council for International Organizations of Medical Sciences in 1982 to guide cross-cultural research.

Institution—Location of research. Retains ultimate responsibility for human subject regulation compliance.

Institutional Review Board—(IRB) Reviews research and consent forms to determine if rights and welfare of subjects are protected.

Investigational Device Exemption—(IDE) Exemption from FD&C Act to study investigational medical devices.

Investigational Materials—Test articles under clinical investigation.

Investigational New Drug Application—(IND) Exemption from FD&C Act to study investigational drug or biologic.

Investigator—Conducts and directs study. Carries ultimate responsibility for research. Is referred to as the principle investigator when acts as a leader for an investigational team. Also referred to as Clinical Investigator by the FDA.

Investigator-Sponsor—Individual with both responsibilities of initiating and conducting a clinical study.

Investigator's Brochure—Relevant clinical and nonclinical data compiled on the investigational drug, biologic or device being studied.

Kefauver-Harris Amendments—Amendment to FD&C Act that requires informed consent for experimental drugs.

Misconduct—Fabrication, falsification, plagiarism or other practices that seriously deviate from those accepted within scientific community for conducting and reporting research.

Monitor—Person employed by the sponsor or CRO who reviews study records to determine that a study is being conducted in accordance with the protocol. A monitor's duties may include, but are not limited to, helping to plan and initiate a study, and assessing the conduct of studies. Monitors work with the clinical research coordinator to check all data and documentation from the study. See also CRA.

Monitoring—Reviewing a clinical study, ensuring conduct, proper records and reports are performed as stated in the clinical protocol, standard operating procedures, GCP and by regulatory requirements.

National Research Act—Act created the National Commission for Protection of Human Subjects of Biomedical and Behavioral research in 1974 and mandated review of studies by institutional review boards and subject protection by informed consent.

New Drug Application—(NDA) An FDA application to market a new drug in the United States.

National Institutes of Health—(NIH) Agency within DHHS that provides funding for research, conducts studies and funds multi-site national studies.

Nuremberg Code—Set of standards proclaimed following trial of Nazi doctors in 1947.

Office for Human Research Protection—(OHRP) Federal government office that issues Assurances and overseas compliance.

Patient—Individual seeking medical care.

Patient Oriented Research—Research conducted with human subjects (or on material of human origin) in which an investigator or colleague directly interacts with human subjects. (NIH definition of clinical research)

Protection of Pupil Rights Amendment—(PPRA) Department of Education regulation that states that surveys, questionnaires and instructional materials for school children must be inspected by parents/guardians.

Protocol—Documentation of study objective, design, methods, statistical methods and organization. The term also includes amendments made to the original document.

Protocol Amendment—Changes or clarifications made in writing to the original protocol.

Recruitment—Act of enrolling subjects with the proper inclusion criteria.

Recruitment Period—Time allowed to recruit all subjects for a study.

Research—Systematic investigation designed to develop or contribute to generalizable knowledge. Includes Clinical Research.

Research Team—Investigator, subinvestigator and clinical research coordinator involved with study.

Risk-Benefit Ratio—Risk to individual subject vs potential benefits. Also called Risk-Benefit Analysis.

Safety Reports—FDA report required by investigator for any serious and unexpected adverse experience.

Serious Adverse Event—(SAE) Any event that results in death, a life threatening situation, hospitalization or prolonged hospitalization, disability, incapacity or a congenital anomaly/birth defect. Also called serious adverse drug reaction (serious ADR).

Source Data—All information contained in original records and certified copies of results, observations or other facets required for the reconstruction and evaluation of the study that is contained in source documents.

Source Documentation—Location that information is first recorded including original documents, data and records.

Sponsor—Individual, company, institution or organization taking responsibility for initiation, management and financing of study.

Standard Operating Procedures—(SOP) Detailed, written procedures for the uniform performance of a function.

Subinvestigator—Helps design and conduct investigation at a study site.

Subject/Study Subject—Participant in a study. See Human Subject.

Telephone Report—Notification via telephone to the FDA of unexpected fatal or life threatening advent associated with clinical study.

Unexpected Adverse Drug Reaction—A reaction that is not consistent in nature or severity with study application.

Unexpected Event—Any incident or reaction that puts subjects or others at risk and is not described in the study plan and/or study application.

Vulnerable Subjects—Group/individual that cannot give informed consent because of limited autonomy (e.g., children, mentally ill and prisoners). Also refers to subjects who may be unduly influenced to participate (e.g., students, subordinates and patients).

Well-being—Subject's physical and mental soundness.

Withdrawal Application—Investigator/sponsor letter to FDA requesting application withdrawal when no additional work is envisioned.

Abbreviations

Abbreviation	Term
ACE	Affiliated Covered Entity
ACHRE	Advisory Committee on Human Radiation Experiments
AE	Adverse Event
AEC	Atomic Energy Commission
AMA	American Medical Association
CBQR	Community-Based Qualitative Research
CCRC	Certified Clinical Research Coordinator
CDC	Centers for Disease Control and Prevention
CE	HIPAA Covered Entity
CFR	Code of Federal Regulations
CE	Clinical Investigator
CIOMS	Council for International Organizations of Medical Sciences
CRC	Clinical Research Coordinator
CRO	Contract Research Organization
DAR	Drug or Device Accountability Record
DHHS	Department of Health and Human Services
DMC	Data Monitoring Committee
FDA	Food and Drug Administration
FERPA	Family Educational Rights and Privacy Act
FWA	Federal-Wide Assurance
GAO	General Accounting Office

GCP	Good Clinical Practice
HGT	Human Gene Transfer
HIPAA	Health Insurance Portability and Accountability Act
Abbreviation	**Term**
IBC	Institutional Biosafety Committee
ICH	International Conference on Harmonization
IDE	Investigational Device Exemption
IIHI	Individually Identifiable Health Information
IND	Investigational New Drug Application
IRB	Institutional Review Board
LAR	Legally Authorized Representative
MPA	Multiple Project Assurance
NBAC	National Bioethics Advisory Commission
NCI	National Cancer Institute
NDA	New Drug Application
NIH	National Institutes of Health
NIOSH	National Institute for Occupational Safety & Health
NPP	Notice of Privacy Practices
OHCA	Organized Health Care Arrangement
OHRP	Office for Human Research Protection
ORI	Office of Research Integrity
PAR	Participatory Action Research
PHI	Protected Health Information
PHS	Public Health Service
PI	Principal Investigator
PMA	Premarket Approval Application
PPRA	Protection of Pupil Rights Amendment
RAC	Recombinant DNA Advisory Committee
TBI	Total Body Irradiation
TPO	Treatment, payment for health care or healthcare operations

INDEX

Protecting Study Volunteers in Research Examination

In an effort to make this manual as useful to as many investigators as possible, it focuses on topics, regulations, and guidelines that are most pertinent to both biomedical and behavioral researchers. The manual does include some information and chapters that are specific to biomedical research and clinical trials in particular. Recognizing that those individuals engaged in behavioral research may not need to be tested on biomedical topics, the following examination was designed to allow individuals and institutions to easily adapt the examination process to meet specific needs.

The examination is presented in two parts. Part 1 is 32 multiple choice questions that cover the general topics that all researchers should be familiar with and should be applied when conducting any research with human subjects. Part 2 consists of 20 true/false case-oriented questions that cover topics in biomedical research. To obtain CME or CE credit, both sections must be completed. Those institutions and individuals who focus exclusively on research in the social and behavioral sciences, however, would be able to complete part 1 without the focus on biomedical research. Institutions may wish to develop their own part 2 examination to cover topics specific to the types of research conducted at the institution.

Part 1: Multiple Choice

Please read the following questions and choose the answer that is the most accurate or best answers the question.

1. The Syphilis Study, the Willowbrook Study and others are frequently cited as examples of research with ethical problems. An important lesson from these studies is that:
   A. researchers may violate ethical norms even though they have good intentions
   B. only biomedical research has been associated with ethical problems
   C. research scandals never result in national legislation or regulations
   D. mistakes of the past can never be repeated

2. In 1981, the FDA and DHHS published federal regulations for the protection of human subjects in biomedical and behavioral research. These regulations were also adopted by other federal agencies in 1991. What two protections do these "Common Rule" regulations mandate?
   A. payment to subjects and compensation for injury
   B. informed consent of subjects and IRB review
   C. confidentiality of research records and privacy guarantees
   D. direct benefit to subjects and elimination of all risks

3. As defined in the Belmont Report, the ethical principle of *respect for persons* relates to the general rule:
   A. obtain consent from subjects
   B. maximize possible benefits and minimize potential risks
   C. the burdens of research should be shared equally
   D. children should not be enrolled in research

4. As defined in the Belmont Report, the ethical principle of *beneficence* relates to the general rule:
   A. obtain consent from subjects
   B. maximize possible benefits and minimize potential risks
   C. the burdens of research should be shared equally
   D. the benefits from research should be applied first to those who cannot afford them

5. As defined in the Belmont Report, the ethical principle of *justice* relates to the general rule:
   A. obtain consent from subjects
   B. maximize possible benefits and minimize potential risks
   C. the burdens of research should be shared equally
   D. local courts have ultimate jurisdiction over research

6. What is included in the official definition of scientific misconduct?
   A. negligence, errors and omissions
   B. fabrication, falsification and plagiarism
   C. incompetence, misbehavior and deviations
   D. differences in interpretations of data

7. Under federal regulations and guidelines, institutions conducting federally funded research are required to:
   A. report all honest errors to the Office of Research Integrity (ORI)
   B. be registered with the OHRP, ORI and FDA
   C. establish a sponsored-programs office that operates the IRB
   D. provide training in research ethics to investigators and investigate reports of scientific misconduct

8. To conduct federally funded research, the regulations require institutions to have which of the following?
   A. a Certificate of Confidentiality
   B. a contract for goods and services
   C. an assurance of compliance with the human subject protection regulations (e.g., Federal-Wide Assurance)
   D. a Business Associate agreement

9. When reviewing research, the IRB has the authority to:
   A. require modifications in consent forms, but not to protocols
   B. disapprove any research with human subject concerns
   C. modify research before it starts, but not afterwards
   D. override an institutional official's disapproval of research

10. What actions must an investigator take to amend/modify the way a study is being conducted?
    A. obtain IRB approval of the change before implementing it
    B. only notify the IRB at the time of study renewal/review
    C. obtain prior IRB approval only if the consent form is to be changed
    D. no action is necessary for already approved studies

11. Investigators must follow the IRB approved protocol. This is:
    A. required even if immediate danger to subjects may result.
    B. only required for federally sponsored research.
    C. a specific requirement for compliance with the regulations.
    D. primarily to prevent sponsors from defaulting on payments for protocol violations.

12. The investigator's professional judgment is essential to maintain the integrity of the research process. Investigators should always:
    A. value human rights and subject welfare more highly than scientific knowledge
    B. value scientific knowledge more highly than human rights and subject welfare
    C. value commercial success over scientific knowledge
    D. value commercial success over human rights and subject welfare

13. The greatest concern for most volunteers in behavioral and social science research is usually:
    A. deception
    B. risk of physical harm
    C. payment for time
    D. privacy and confidentiality

14. In designing and conducting behavioral and social science research, the following is true:
    A. intrusions on privacy are justified by the requirement for absolute confidentiality
    B. deception should never be used
    C. no additional safeguards are needed when studying vulnerable populations
    D. stress, discomfort and other harms should be minimized

15. Certificates of Confidentiality from the Department of Health and Human Services
    A. guarantee absolute confidentiality of research data.
    B. are issued for any research upon request.
    C. do not prevent voluntary disclosures.
    D. prohibit subjects from disclosing research data or involvement.

16. When research is sponsored by a company or agency, a contract should be negotiated that protects the researcher's publication rights. These research contracts are:
    A. not legally enforceable, but provide guidance on study conduct
    B. usually are required to be negotiated and signed by an authorized institutional representative
    C. always signed solely by the investigator as part of the responsibility for conducting the study
    D. illegal if they place limitations on publication rights

17. An example of scientific misconduct in publication is:
    A. changing the results to be reported in a publication for personal gain
    B. accepting financial support to present data or to publish a manuscript
    C. delaying publication of results for two weeks to allow a sponsor to file patent applications
    D. publication of negative results

18. Regarding genetic research,
    A. it is only regulated by federal law, not State law.
    B. it always involves sampling and testing DNA or RNA.
    C. knowledge about the implications for specific genetic mutations is constantly evolving.
    D. the risk associated with genetic testing studies is small.

19. Regarding human gene transfer (HGT) studies carried out at an institution that receives federal support for recombinant DNA research:
    A. By federal regulation, only germline cells can be modified by HGT
    B. Investigators must comply with "Appendix M" of the NIH Guidelines on HGT
    C. Privately funded HGT is not regulated by either NIH or FDA
    D. IBC review is required but it substitutes for IRB review

20. Regarding conflicts of interest in research,
    A. there is only one type of conflict that matters, i.e., financial conflicts.
    B. they indicate a character flaw in the person who has the conflict.
    C. disclosure in consent forms is required by federal regulation.
    D. public concern may lead to additional regulations for investigators to follow.

21. It is important to address conflicts of interest on the part of investigators and institutions because subject safety may be compromised and/or:
    A. journals will not publish research with conflicts, hidden or apparent.
    B. the knowledge produced from the research may be biased.
    C. proper management requires elimination of all conflicts.
    D. they cause obvious bias, and damage the institution's reputation

22. Research with tissues may require informed consent from subjects. When consent will be obtained,
    A. risks of disclosure of the information need not be part of the consent process because they do not cause physical harm
    B. federal regulations for consent always take precedence over State laws
    C. the type of research to be conducted, including whether genetic analysis will be performed should be stated in the consent form.
    D. the consent form should contain a waiver of profits from any commercial products

23. Recruitment advertisements for subjects are considered to be part of the informed consent process. Therefore, ads must
    A. contain all the federal elements of consent
    B. be reviewed and approved by the IRB
    C. only be in written formats
    D. be in both English and expected non-English languages

24. Including representative populations (men, women, minorities and age appropriate participants) in research helps ensure applicability/generalizability of results. Including a representative population is
    A. generally mandatory for NIH-funded and FDA-regulated studies
    B. never to be reviewed by the IRB
    C. only important for adult populations, not for children
    D. only important for human gene transfer studies

25. An example of addressing barriers to minority participation is:
    A. avoiding participation by minority researchers and research staff
    B. providing study materials in languages other than English
    C. being available only during normal business hours
    D. charging for transportation services

26. Community-based qualitative research (CBQR) assumes that:
    A. the community is the authority on its own situation and potential solutions
    B. consent of individual subjects is not necessary
    C. the research team's own cultural values do not differ from those of the study community
    D. unbiased research can only be conducted at sites near the research institution

27. Responsibility for maintaining confidentiality in community-based qualitative research (CBQR) rests with the researcher, however:
    A. masking identities is only permissible for Participatory Action Research (PAR)
    B. gathering and reporting identifying information is required by this research technique
    C. written informed consent may threaten a participant's desire to remain anonymous
    D. Certificates of Confidentiality are required to use this technique

28. According to the Belmont Report, the process of informed consent requires three key components to be adequately addressed to be considered ethically valid. These are:
    A. confidentiality, compassion and comprehension
    B. information, understanding and voluntary agreement
    C. signatures of subject, person obtaining consent and a witness
    D. subject's signature and date plus receipt of a copy of the form

29. When designing the consent process for a study, investigators should consider:
    A. inclusion of required elements of consent
    B. timing of the consent process
    C. who will discuss consent with the potential subject
    D. all of the above

30. When obtaining informed consent, coercion and undue influence should be avoided. Undue influences are harder to control because:
    A. subjects are always in dependent relationships with investigators
    B. research always includes some benefit for subjects
    C. they may be situational/environmental
    D. they are known to the investigator but not to the subject

31. Failure to comply with the HIPAA Privacy Rule can result in:
    A. civil penalties and criminal sanctions against both organizations and investigators
    B. administrative sanctions against the organization only
    C. civil penalties and criminal sanctions, but only against investigators
    D. civil penalties and criminal sanctions, but only against the actual violator, not the investigator

32. According to the HIPAA Privacy Rule, "protected health information" (PHI) includes:
    A. all individually identifiable health information in medical records only
    B. health information that is individually identifiable and created or received by a covered entity
    C. only electronically stored information
    D. de-identified health information held by a covered entity

Part 2: Biomedical Case Studies (True /False)

Please read the following case studies and answer the corresponding questions.

Case Study 1: The drug, "Seizure-stop" is an FDA-approved product marketed in tablet form for treatment of epileptic seizures in patients over 12 years old. Based upon a report in the literature, an investigator wants to conduct an open-label study (i.e., no placebo, no blinding) with this drug for treatment of life-threatening refractory seizures. The study will be conducted with pediatric patients aged 5 to 15.

33. Approved drugs that are used in a research context are governed by the FDA human subject protection regulations.
    A. True
    B. False

34. This study may require an IND because of the change in population from the approved labeling.
    A. True
    B. False

35. If the IRB finds that it is not appropriate to get assent from the children, it may waive the requirement for assent and just require parental permission.
    A. True
    B. False

Case Study 2: A surgeon designs an investigational medical device that is to be used in a study to place sutures in heart valve repairs. The subject population will be adults scheduled for non-emergent surgical repair. Because the "investigator" will also be the patients' surgeon, the protocol calls for an independent physician to obtain consent. Tissue removed from the valves will be provided to another researcher at the institution who is studying why the valves fail. The "tissue" study also involves reviewing the patient records and comparing prior medical histories to the types of defects seen in the valves.

36. If the IRB makes a determination that this is a "significant risk" device, then an IDE is required before the study may start.
    A. True
    B. False

37. The use of another physician to obtain consent will always confuse subjects and will never avoid undue influence.
    A. True
    B. False

38. Because it is "practicable" to obtain consent, a waiver of consent for the specimen study could not be approved by the IRB .
    A. True
    B. False

Case Study 3: The drug, "Snooze-away" is an investigational drug, currently in phase 3 trials as a sedative. The study protocol is a multi-center randomized placebo controlled, double blind design in persons age 21 or over with mild insomnia. The "placebo effect" is expected to be high. Each subject will participate for 2 weeks in this study.

39. The assessment of the risks and benefits of the use of placebo versus the use of available standard sedatives is a required step for investigators and IRBs.
    A. True
    B. False

40. Part of the ethical justification for the acceptable use of placebo in this research study is the IRB's assessment that the use of the placebo will not expose the subject to excessive or unnecessary risks.
    A. True
    B. False

41. A central question that must be answered in this clinical trial is whether the subjects in the placebo control group are being unfairly denied a medical benefit.
    A. True
    B. False

42. The fact that there are standard treatments for insomnia that are available without enrolling in this study must be clearly stated in the consent form.
    A. True
    B. False

43. If a large percentage of potential subjects are known to be non-English speaking, the regulations allow an investigator to enroll them with the English consent form, but require using a translator.
    A. True
    B. False

44. Each principal investigator in this study must have a Form-1572 on file with the FDA.
    A. True
    B. False

45. During a routine site visit, the sponsor's study monitor is permitted to review the accuracy of the case report forms, but cannot review source documents.
    A. True
    B. False

46. After the study has been enrolling for a few weeks, one investigator wants to change the procedure for the initial work-up of subjects. Both the sponsor and the IRB must approve this change.
    A. True
    B. False

Case Study 4: An industry-sponsored clinical trial of an unapproved optical laser system to correct corneal malformations will compare eyes treated with the investigational system to those treated using normal standard of care techniques. A Data Monitoring Committee (DMC) is established to monitor the study. A protocol, a sample consent form and a confidential document listing known risks and background on prior studies are provided to the investigator by the sponsor.

47. The sponsor is permitted to ship the laser device to investigational sites for training before the IDE is filed with FDA.
    A. True
    B. False

48. If the study is put on hold by the sponsor because of "unreasonable risk" to subjects, the sponsor may correct the device and/or protocol procedures and resume the study without further review by the IRB or FDA.
    A. True
    B. False

49. An important role for the DMC in this study is making judgments about early termination of the trial based on the type and extent of reported adverse events, or the efficacy of the laser system.
    A. True
    B. False

50. The investigator should present the consent form and obtain consent from subjects at a pre-operative visit, rather than waiting until the day of the procedure.
    A. True
    B. False

51. Because this is a study conducted under an IDE, only the investigator may obtain consent (i.e., the consent process may not be delegated to other personnel).
    A. True
    B. False

52. If the investigator violates the FDA regulations, fines, debarment, and criminal charges may result
    A. True
    B. False

ABOUT THOMSON CENTERWATCH

Thomson CenterWatch is a Boston-based publishing and information services company that focuses on the clinical trials industry and is a business of the Thomson Corporation. We provide a variety of information services used by pharmaceutical and biotechnology companies, CROs, SMOs and investigative sites involved in the management and conduct of clinical trials. CenterWatch also provides educational materials for clinical research professionals, health professionals and for health consumers. We provide market research and market intelligence services that many major companies have retained to help develop new business strategies, to guide the implementation of new clinical research-related initiatives and to assist in due diligence activities. Some of our top publications and services are described below. For a comprehensive listing with detailed information about our publications and services, please visit our web site at www.centerwatch.com. You can also contact us at (800) 765-9647 for subscription and order information.

22 Thomson Place · Boston, MA 02210
Phone (617) 856-5900 · Fax (617) 856-5901
www.centerwatch.com

CenterWatch Training and Education Manuals

The Investigator's Guide to Clinical Research, 3rd edition

This 250-page step-by-step manual is filled with tips, instructions and insights for health professionals interested in conducting clinical trials. *The Investigator's Guide* is designed to help the novice clinical investigator get involved in conducting clinical trials. The guide is also a valuable resource for experienced investigative sites looking for ways to improve and increase their involvement and success in clinical research. Developed in accordance with ACCME, readers can apply for CME credits. An exam is provided online.

How to Find & Secure Clinical Grants

This 28-page guidebook is an ideal resource for healthcare professionals interested in conducting clinical trials. The guidebook provides tips and insights for new and experienced investigative sites to compete more effectively for clinical study grants.

A Guide to Patient Recruitment and Retention

This 250+ page manual is designed to help clinical research professionals improve the effectiveness of their patient recruitment and retention efforts. Written by Diana Anderson, Ph.D., with contributions from 18 industry experts and thought leaders, this guide offers real world, practical recruitment and retention strategies, tactics and metrics. It is considered an invaluable resource for educating professionals who manage and conduct clinical research about ways to plan and execute effective patient recruitment and retention efforts.

The CRA's Guide to Monitoring Clinical Research

This 400-page CE-accredited book is an ideal resource for novice and experienced CRAs, as well as professionals interested in pursuing a career as study monitors. *The CRA's Guide* covers important topics along with updated regulations, guidelines and worksheets, including resources such as: 21 CFR Parts 50, 54, 56 & 312 Guidelines, various checklists (monitoring visit, site evaluation, informed consent) and a study documentation file verification log. This manual will be routinely referenced throughout the CRA's career. Developed in acccordance with ANCC, readers can apply for CE Credits. An exam is provided online.

eClinical Trials: Planning and Implementation

This invaluable resource is designed to assist biopharmaceutical companies, CROs and investigative sites in understanding, planning and implementing electronic clinical trial (eCT) technology solutions to accelerate and improve their research operations. Written by highly respected thought leaders in the field today, this 180+ page book describes and addresses the concepts and complexities of managing and conducting an optimal eCT, while offering practical guidance, facts and advice on implementing eCT technologies.

Protecting Study Volunteers in Research, Third Edition

The third edition of our top-selling manual addresses current and emerging issues that are critical to our system of human subject protection oversight and now includes an entire chapter on how to implement the HIPAA Privacy Rule in research. The book is designed to help organizations provide the highest standards of safe and ethical treatment of study volunteers. Developed in accordance with the essentials and standards of the ACCME. Readers can apply for up to 7.5 CME credits. Developed in accordance with the essentials and standards of the ANCCC. Readers can apply for up to 9 Nursing Contact Hours. An exam is provided with each manual.

Evaluating the Informed Consent Process

This 12-page booklet reviews the results of a recent survey conducted among more than 1,500 study volunteers. This booklet presents firsthand experiences from study volunteers and offers valuable insights, facts and data on the informed consent process and how this process works.

Online Directories and Sourcebooks

The Drugs in Clinical Trials Database

This database is a comprehensive web-based, searchable resource offering detailed profiles of new investigational treatments in phase I through III clinical trials. Updated daily, this online and searchable directory provides information on more than 2,000 drugs for more than 800 indications worldwide in a well-organized and easy-to-reference format. Search results may be downloaded to Excel for further sorting and analysis. Detailed profile information is provided for each drug along with a separate section on pediatric treatments. *The Drugs in Clinical Trials Database* is an ideal online resource for industry professionals to use for monitoring the performance of drugs in clinical trials; tracking competitors' development activity; identifying development partners; and identifying clinical study grant opportunities.

The eDirectory of the Clinical Trials Industry

Previously available as a printed directory, the new *eDirectory* is a comprehensive, online, searchable and downloadable database featuring detailed contact and profile information on 1,400+ organizations involved in the clinical trials industry. Company profiles can be searched by keyword, company name, city, state, phase focus, therapeutic specialties and services offered. Search results can be downloaded to an Excel spreadsheet for further sorting and analysis.

Profiles of Service Providers on the CenterWatch Clinical Trials Listing Service™

The CenterWatch web site (**www.centerwatch.com**) attracts tens of thousands of sponsor and CRO company representatives every month who are looking for experienced service providers and investigative sites to manage and conduct their clinical trials. No registration is required. Sponsors and CROs use this online directory free of charge. The CenterWatch web site offers all contract service providers—both CROs and investigative sites—the opportunity to present more information than any other Internet-based service available. This service is an ideal way to secure new contracts and clinical study grants.

An Industry in Evolution, 4th edition

This 250-page sourcebook provides extensive qualitative and quantitative information documenting clinical trial industry trends and benchmarked practices. The material—charts, statistics and analytical reports—is presented in an easy-to-reference format. This important and valuable resource is used for developing business strategies and plans, for preparing presentations and for conducting business and market intelligence.

CenterWatch Compilation Reports Series

These topic-specific reports provide comprehensive, in-depth features, original research and analyses and fact-based company/institution business and financial profiles. Reports are available on Site Management Organizations, Academic Medical Centers, Contract Research Organizations, and Investigative Sites. Spanning nearly seven years of in-depth coverage and analyses, these reports provide valuable insights into company strategies, market dynamics and successful business practices. Ideal for business planning and for market intelligence/market research activities.

CenterWatch Shopper!

The *Shopper!* focuses on specific products and services and presents them in a compelling format designed to make it easier for you to compare them and to select the best options for your business needs. Experts and thought leaders contribute tips and pointers to assist you in considering and evaluating various product and service offerings.

CenterWatch Patient Education Resources

As part of ongoing reforms in human subject protection oversight, institutional and independent IRBs and research centers are actively identifying educational programs and assessment mechanisms to use with their study volunteers. These initiatives are of particular interest among those IRBs that are applying for voluntary accreditation with the Association for the Accreditation of Human Research Protection Programs (AAHRPP) and the

National Committee for Quality Assurance (NCQA). CenterWatch offers a variety of educational communications for use by IRB and clinical research professionals.

Informed Consent™: A Guide to the Risks and Benefits of Volunteering for Clinical Trials

This comprehensive 300-page reference resource is designed to assist patients and health consumers in understanding the clinical trial process and their rights and recourse as study volunteers. Based on extensive review and input from bioethicists, regulatory and industry experts, the guide provides facts, insights and case examples designed to assist individuals in making informed decisions about participating in clinical trials. The guide is an ideal educational reference that research and IRB professionals can use to review with their study volunteers, to address volunteer questions and concerns, and to further build relationships with the patient community. Professionals also refer to this guide for assistance in responding to the media.

Volunteering For a Clinical Trial: Your Guide to Participating in Research Studies

This easy-to-read, six-page patient education brochure is designed for research centers to provide consistent, professional and unbiased educational information for their potential clinical study subjects. The brochure is IRB-approved and is used by sponsors, CROs and investigative sites to help set patient expectations about participating in clinical trials. *Volunteering for a Clinical Trial* can be distributed in a variety of ways including direct mailings to patients, displays in waiting rooms, or as handouts to guide discussions. The brochure can be customized with company logos and custom information.

A Word from Study Volunteers: Opinions and Experiences of Clinical Trial Participants

This straightforward and easy-to-read ten-page pamphlet reviews the results of a survey conducted among more than 1,200 clinical research volunteers. This brochure presents first-hand experiences from clinical trial volunteers. It offers valuable insights for individuals interested in participating in a clinical trial. The brochure can be customized with company logos and custom information.

Understanding the Informed Consent Process

Understanding the Informed Consent Process is an easy-to-read, eight-page brochure designed specifically for study volunteers. The brochure provides valuable information and facts about the informed consent process, and reviews the volunteer's "Bill of Rights."

The CenterWatch Clinical Trials Listing Service™

Now in its ninth year of operation, *The CenterWatch Clinical Trials Listing Service*™ provides the largest and most comprehensive listing of industry- and government-sponsored clinical trials on the Internet. In 2003, the CenterWatch web site—along with numerous coordinated online and print affiliations—reached more than 10 million Americans. *The CenterWatch Clinical Trials Listing Service*™ provides an international listing of more than 42,000 ongoing and IRB-approved phase I–IV clinical trials.

CenterWatch Newsletters

The CenterWatch Monthly

Our award-winning monthly newsletter provides pharmaceutical and biotechnology companies, CROs, SMOs, academic institutions, research centers and the investment community with in-depth business news and insights, feature articles on trends and clinical research practices, original market intelligence and analysis, as well as grant lead information for investigative sites.

CWWeekly

This weekly newsletter, available as a fax or in electronic format, reports on the top stories and breaking news in the clinical trials industry. Each week the newsletter includes business headlines, financial information, market intelligence, drug pipeline and clinical trial results.

JobWatch

This web-based resource at www.centerwatch.com, complemented by a print publication, provides comprehensive listings of career and educational opportunities in the clinical trials industry, including a searchable resume database service. Companies use *JobWatch* regularly to identify qualified clinical research professionals and career and educational services.

CenterWatch Content and Information Services

Market Intelligence Reports and Services

With nearly a decade of experience gathering original data and writing about all aspects of the clinical research enterprise, the CenterWatch Market Intelligence Department is uniquely positioned to provide a wide range of market research services designed to assist organizations in making more informed strategic business decisions that impact their clinical research activities. Our clients include major biopharmaceutical companies, CROs and contract service providers, site networks, investment analysts and management consulting firms. CenterWatch brings unprecedented industry knowledge, extensive industry-wide relationships and expertise gathering, analyzing and presenting primary and secondary quantitative and qualitative data. Along with our custom research projects for clients, CenterWatch also facilitates on-site management forums designed to explore critical business trends and their implications. These sessions offer a wealth of data and a unique opportunity for senior professionals to think about business problems in new ways.

TrialWatch Site-Identification Service
Several hundred sponsor and CRO companies use the *TrialWatch* service to identify prospective investigative sites to conduct their upcoming clinical trials. Every month, companies post bulletins of their phase I–IV development programs that are actively seeking clinical investigators. These bulletins are included in CenterWatch—our flagship monthly publication that reaches as many as 25,000 experienced investigators every month. Use of the *TrialWatch* service is FREE.

Content License Services
CenterWatch offers both database content and static text under license. All CenterWatch content can be seamlessly integrated into your company Internet, Intranet or Extranet web site(s) with or without frames. Our database offerings include: *The Clinical Trials Listing Service*™, *Clinical Trial Results, The Drugs in Clinical Trials Database, Newly Approved Drugs, The eDirectory of the Clinical Trials Industry*, and *CW-Mobile* for Wireless OS® Devices. Our static text offerings include: an editorial feature on background information on clinical trials and a glossary of clinical trial terminology.

Continuing Medical Education (CME) Symposia
Continuing medical education (CME) symposia feature a variety of useful and practical topics for clinical research investigators, study coordinators, CRAs, clinical research scientists, physicians and allied health professionals. Thomson CenterWatch has developed flexible, turn-key programs that can be integrated into investigator educational settings in order to promote higher levels of compliance and study conduct performance.

NOTES